HURRICANE

James S. Hirsch graduated from the University of Missouri School of Journalism and he has a master's degree in public policy from the University of Texas. He began his career at the *New York Times*, moving on to the *Wall Street Journal* where he covered some of the most important beats on the paper, including the mutual fund, banking, travel and airline industries. He also contributed numerous essays, profiles, and several stories about race. His pieces have appeared in a *Journal* anthology.

HURRICANE

The Life of
Rubin Carter, Fighter

James S. Hirsch

FOURTH ESTATE • *London*

This paperback edition published in 2000
First published in Great Britain in 2000 by
Fourth Estate
A Division of HarperCollins*Publishers*
77–85 Fulham Palace Road
London w6 8jb
www.4thestate.co.uk

Copyright © by James S. Hirsch 2000

12

The right of James S. Hirsch to be identified as the author of this
work has been asserted by him in accordance with the Copyright,
Designs and Patents Act 1988.

A catalogue record for this book is available from the
British Library.

ISBN 1–84115–130–0

Typeset by Rowland Phototypesetting Limited,
Bury St Edmunds, Suffolk.
Printed in Great Britain by
Clays Ltd, St Ives plc

To Sheryl,
who gave me her love
and never lost the faith

CONTENTS

HURRICANE

1

DEATH HOUSE
RENDEZVOUS

B Y 1980, New Jersey's notorious Death House had been revived as a lovers' alcove, but Rubin "Hurricane" Carter still wanted no part of it.

The Death House was Trenton State Prison's official name for the brick and concrete vault where condemned men lived in tiny cells and an electric chair stood hard against a nearby wall. The first inmate reached the Death House on October 29, 1907. Six weeks later he was dead, his slumped body shaved and sponged down with salt water, the better to conduct the electricity. New Jersey continued to hang capital offenders for two more years. But soon enough the electric chair, with its wooden body, leather straps, and metal-mesh helmet, which discharged three mortal blasts of up to 2,400 volts, was seen as the most felicitous form of execution.

At least one infamous death gave the site a brief aura of celebrity. Richard Bruno Hauptmann, convicted of murdering Charles Lindbergh's baby, was electrocuted in the brightly lit chamber at 8:44 P.M. on April 3, 1936. In later years, sentences were carried out at 10 P.M., after the "general population" prisoners had been placed in total lockup. An outside power line fed the chair to ensure that a deadly jolt did not interfere with the penitentiary's regular lighting. On occasion, "citizen witnesses" crowded into a small green room, with only a rope between them and the chair about ten feet away. The observers watched the executioner turn a large wheel right behind the seated man's ear, thereby activating the lethal current. The body, penitent or obdurate, innocent or guilty, alive or dead, pressed against the restraints until the current was shut off.

The Death House confronted its own demise in 1972, when the U.S. Supreme Court outlawed the death penalty as cruel and unusual punishment. The electric chair, having singed the breath from 160 men, was suddenly obsolete. So prison officials found a new mission for the chamber: it became the Visiting Center.

Despite its macabre history, the VC was a huge hit with most of the prisoners. It marked the first time that Trenton State Prison, a maximum-security facility, had allowed contact visits. Inmates could now touch their spouses, children, or friends. The metal bars were removed from more than two dozen Death Row cells near the archaic chair, its seven electric switches still in place. The rooms were not exactly cozy hideaways, but they became the unsanctioned venue for conjugal meetings. Inmates seeking a bit of privacy tried to reserve cells farthest away from the guards, and the arrangement, as described by some old-timers, gave rise to Death House babies.

But Rubin Carter didn't care a bit. He refused to accept virtually anything the prison offered, and that included visits inside the reincarnated Death House.

He was repulsed by the prospect of sharing an intimate moment among the souls of 160 men, some of whom he knew. Transforming this slaughterhouse into a visiting center, Carter believed, was like turning Auschwitz or Buchenwald into a summer camp for children. It was another way for the state to humiliate prisoners, to express its contempt for the new law that pulled the plug on its chair.

Carter knew well that he could have been one of the chair's immolations. In 1967 he had been found guilty of committing a triple murder in Paterson, New Jersey. He adamantly claimed his innocence. The state sought the death penalty, but the jury returned a triple-life sentence instead. That conviction was overturned in 1976, but Carter was convicted of the same crime again later that year and given the same triple-life sentence.

By the end of 1980, Carter had gone for almost four years without a contact visit. Since his second sentencing in February of 1977, he had not seen his son or daughter, his mother, his four sisters, or his two brothers. Most of his friends were also shut out. He and his wife had divorced. He saw his lawyers in another part of the prison.

But now, on the last Sunday of the year, Carter had a visitor as the result of an unusual letter he'd received three months earlier. As a former high-profile boxer who was known around the country and even the world, he received hundreds of letters each year, but he rarely answered them. In fact, he didn't even open them, allowing them to pile up in his cell. Carter wanted nothing to do with the outside world.

Then came a letter in September, his name and prison address printed on the envelope. Carter could never explain why he opened it except to say that the envelope had *vibrations.* The letter, dated September 20, 1980, was written by a black youth from the ghettos of Brooklyn who, oddly enough, was living in Toronto with a group of Canadians. The seventeen-year-old, Lesra Martin, wrote that he had read Carter's auto-biography, *The Sixteenth Round,* written from prison in 1974, and it helped him better understand his older brother, who had done time in upstate New York. Lesra concluded the letter:

All through your book I was wondering if it would have been easier to die or take the shit you did. But now, when I think of your book, I say if you were dead then you would not have been able to give what you did through your book. To imagine me not being able to write you this letter or thinking that they could beat you into giving up, man, that would be too much. We need more like you to set examples of what courage is all about!

Hey, Brother, I'm going to let it go. Please write back. It will mean a lot.

Your friend,
Lesra Martin

Lesra's words, his efforts to reach out, touched Carter. He responded on October 7. The one-page typewritten note thanked Lesra for his "outpouring of hope, concern and humanness . . . The heartfelt messages literally jumped off the pages."

More letters followed between Lesra, his Canadian guardians — who had essentially adopted the youth to educate him — and Carter in which they discussed politics, philosophy, Carter's own case, and his appeal. But when Lesra asked if he could visit the prison at Christmastime — he was going to be in Brooklyn seeing his family — Carter replied noncommittally. That did not deter Lesra. The bond between the two — and, more important, between Carter and this mysterious Canadian commune that typically shunned friendships with the outside world — had been sealed.

Winter's chill could be felt inside the Trenton State Prison on that

last Sunday of December. Built in 1836 by the famed British architect
John Haviland, the prison is a brooding, monolithic fortress. Haviland
used trapezoidal shapes and austere giganticism to evoke a massive
Egyptian temple. Scarab beetles, which symbolized the soul in ancient
Egypt, were carved into the prison's pink limestone walls. Tributaries
from the Delaware River flowed in front of the prison, in faint mimicry
of the Nile.

But by 1980 the waterways had long since dried up and the pink
limestone had turned brown. Loops of razor-ribbon wire topped
twenty-foot-high concrete walls, and stone-faced guards stood in gun
towers. The prison yard, with a softball field, weight machines, and
handball courts, was said to sit over a cemetery. The yard's red dirt
was so dry that it was regularly sprayed with oil, creating a viscous
sheen that rubbed off on inmates in crimson splotches.

While the prison sought total control of its inmates, Carter defied
the institution at every turn. He did not wear its clothes, eat in its mess
hall, work its jobs, or participate in any organized activity. He refused
to meet with prison psychiatrists, attend parole hearings, or carry his
prison identification card. His rationale was simple: he was an innocent
man; therefore, he would not be treated like a criminal. His defiance
earned him several trips to a subterranean vault known as "the hole,"
where inmates were held in solitary confinement. He was also once
banished to a state psychiatric hospital, where the criminally insane
and other incorrigibles were disciplined.

But Carter had a predatory instinct for survival, and he was eventually
allowed to live quietly in his fourth-tier cell. He continued to fight for
his freedom in the courts, but by now he had immersed himself in
books on philosophy, history, metaphysics, and religion. Searching for
meaning in his own life, he turned his cell into "an unnatural laboratory
of the human spirit." He studied, wrote, and tutored other inmates
about the need to look within themselves to find answers to the world
outside.

Carter had been on this personal journey for more than two years
by the time a guard came to his cell and told him he had a contact
visitor. Suspecting it was the letter-writing youth, Carter walked down
his tier, through the center hub of the prison, and past the infirmary,
which was conveniently next to the Death House. (The infirmary used
to receive the electrocuted bodies.) Before entering the Death House,

he gritted his teeth and disrobed for a strip search — standard procedure for every prisoner before and after a contact visit. Searching for contraband, a guard ran his hand through Carter's hair and looked inside his mouth, under his arms, beneath his feet, and up his rectum. This degrading invasion was another reason Carter avoided contact visits.

Once inside the chamber, Carter reserved a cell on the lower tier, placing his plastic identification tag and a pack of Pall Malls on two chairs. The prison visitors soon filed in and quickly joined their friend or loved one. Finally, only two people were left — Carter and a slip of a youth. The young man was trembling.

Growing up in the slums of Brooklyn, Lesra Martin knew plenty of people who had gone to prison, but this was his first time inside a pen. The high stone walls, metal gates, and claustrophobic corridors were imposing enough, but the brusque security checks were even more unnerving. He emptied his pockets, was frisked, was scanned by a hand-held metal detector, and had his right hand stamped with invisible ink. He had brought a package of Christmas cards, socks, and a hat from his Canadian guardians but was not allowed to deliver it because all packages have to come through the mailroom, where they are opened and inspected. Lesra registered and was given a number, but as he passed through the prison in single file, he was jarred by the guards' shrill orders.

"Get back in line!"

"Don't speak to the person in front of you!"

"Have your ID ready!"

"Put your things in your locker!"

As Lesra stood in the waiting room, he finally heard "four-five-four-seven-two, up!"

That was Carter's prison number. Lesra waited before a dim holding bay. As the steel doors opened and visitors began walking in, several women took deep breaths while others held hands. A guard checked the right hand of each visitor with a blue fluorescent light. After about twenty people filed in, the guard yelled, "Bay secure!" The doors shut, and there was a long moment of helplessness, of captivity. Then doors on the other side opened, and everyone moved out. The experience dazed Lesra, who had arrived wanting to cheer up a prisoner but was made to feel as if he had done something wrong himself.

Rubin Carter understood the feeling.

"You must be Lesra," Carter said. He saw a frightened but good-looking young man about six inches shorter than he. (Carter was only five foot eight.) The prisoner's appearance stunned the teenager. Every picture Lesra had seen of Carter showed him with a clean-shaven head, a thick goatee, and a menacing stare. Now he had a full Afro, a mustache, and a smile. The two embraced, then walked to the cell Carter had reserved. They sat facing each other and leaned forward so passing guards could not hear their conversation.

Lesra recounted his harrowing experience getting to the Visiting Center. "How do you survive in here?" he asked.

"I don't acknowledge the existence of the prison," Carter said. "It doesn't exist for me."

Lesra noticed that the guards patrolling the corridor did not walk as closely to their cell as to other cells, giving them a bit more privacy as a sign of respect. Lesra also heard inmates as well as guards refer to Rubin as "Mr. Carter." When Lesra called him "Mr. Carter," he laughed. "You can call me Rubin, or better yet, Rube." As the inmate explained his refusal to participate in prison activities, Lesra remembered the words of Bob Dylan's song "Hurricane," which had been released in 1975 amid an outpouring of celebrity support:

> But then they took him to a jailhouse
> Where they tried to turn a man into a mouse.

The jailhouse, Lesra realized, had failed.

He described how he left his home in Bedford-Stuyvesant and moved to Toronto, where his new Canadian family was educating him. The arrangement puzzled Carter, and he told Lesra he need not worry about being alone. "I know they're treating you well because of your smile, but if you're ever not happy there, you let me know," he said. The young man gave him the phone number to his home in Canada.

About an hour passed. As the visit was about to end, a prisoner who had a Polaroid camera approached them.

"You like me to take a picture of you and your son, Mr. Carter?"

"Absolutely!" he responded.

Lesra turned and began walking toward a wall that he believed would make a fine backdrop. Carter yanked him back.

"We don't go that way," he said. "That's where the chair was."

The electric chair had been removed a year or so earlier and was now in the Corrections Department Museum in Trenton. But the bolts were still in the ground, and the imprint of the chair was visible. The picture was taken against a different wall, with the two standing next to each other, smiles creasing their faces, Carter's arm draped across Lesra's shoulders.

As the two walked toward the holding bay, Lesra said, "I wish I could just walk you right on out."

"Don't worry," Carter said. "I'm with you."

This encounter marked the beginning of Carter's reemergence from his self-imposed shell. He would always have a special bond with Lesra, but he would develop far more important ties with the Canadian commune, and its members would provide vital support on Carter's journey through the federal courts. At the same time, the group's strong-willed leader, Lisa Peters, and Carter would become intense but doomed soulmates in an unlikely prison love affair. But all that was in the future. After his visit to the Death House, Carter returned to his cell, lay down on his cot, and stared at the picture of Lesra and himself.

2

WILD WEST ON THE PASSAIC

AT THE TIME of Rubin Carter's arrest in 1966, his hometown of Paterson, New Jersey, was dominated by Mayor Frank X. Graves. A smallish man with heavy jowls and thinning hair, he was one of the last of the old city bosses. He controlled every department in his bureaucracy, personally answered phone calls from irate citizens, and referred to anything in Paterson as "mine," as in "my City Hall" or "my police force." He had no hobbies and read few books. He did have a wife and three daughters, but Paterson was his life, and he took any infraction inside its boundaries as a personal wound. Faced with white flight and fears of rising crime rates, he launched a law-and-order crusade with a hard-edged moralism.

No one doubted his audacity. Graves had won two Purple Hearts in World War II for injuries suffered during the invasion of Italy. As mayor, he usually carried a pistol. Driving around Paterson in his black sedan, he monitored the police and fire radio scanners, his ears perked for any signs of disorder. He personally led several raids on what he called "hotbeds of prostitution," and he denounced white suburbanites who came to Paterson to pursue ladies of the night. He donned a firefighter's suit and busted up a bookmaking operation. He ordered the police to issue a warrant to the poet and Paterson native son Allen Ginsberg for smoking pot. Ginsberg, in town for a poetry reading, escaped to New York.

Nothing flustered Graves more than Paterson's surplus of taverns.

There were too damn many of them, about three hundred and fifty, give or take a stray moonshiner with a back porch brew strong enough to rip your gut out. The mayor attacked the jazz bars and gin joints, sometimes twenty on a block, as carriers of moral decay, seedy venues of gambling, brawling, and whoring. The very names of the bars — Cabin of Joy, Blue Danube, Polynesian Club, Bobaloo — evoked exotic, bacchanalian pleasures, which he felt threatened Paterson's social equilibrium.

Graves was particularly concerned about the so-called ghetto bars and personally led raids on them to break up fights or ferret out other wrongdoing. Indeed, "checking" these bars, which entailed cops pushing, shoving, and threatening patrons, was a favorite method for maintaining the balance of terror between blacks and the authorities, however much observers decried these tactics as Gestapo-like.

Blacks took considerable pride in their rollicking circuit of jazz clubs and playhouses, burlesque shows and barrooms. They clustered at the bottom of Governor Avenue, known as "down the hill," abutting the Passaic River and just outside Paterson's cheerless Central Business District. Frank Sinatra and Nat "King" Cole had played in black Paterson. So had Lou Costello, the fleshy wit who was a native son. But for the black machine operators and silk dye workers, the seamstresses and secretaries, Paterson's nightlife was not about glamour or celebrities. It was about loud music, hard drinking, and dirty dancing. They cashed their checks on Friday and had money to spend on the weekend. Young men on the make, dressed in dark suits and narrow black ties, some with razor blades in their pockets, danced the slop, the boogaloo, or the grind. Well-dressed young women, many of them domestics, flirted with their suitors. The revelers, sometimes en masse, sometimes in a trickle, strolled through the neon-lit, one-way streets long into the night, circulating through the Kit Kat Club, the Do Drop Inn, or the Ali Baba. When these clubs closed at 3 A.M., the party moved to after-hours clubs tucked behind darkened grocery stores or to "basement socials," where entrants paid a quarter to the house, slipped downstairs with their bottle in a brown bag, and swayed with a partner beneath an undulating red light.

The most popular black club, the Nite Spot, stood on the corner of Governor and East Eighteenth Streets. Female impersonators gave it a racy edge, while a black tile floor with drizzles of gray, a cover charge, and a kitchen grill conferred a veneer of sophistication. The crowd grooved on the wooden dance floor to Alvin Valentine's jazzy, sweet-tempered organ and sipped Dewar's White Label Scotch and Johnnie Walker Red (which was smoother than Black). Managers allowed in "young blood," or bucks under the age of twenty-one, while bartenders sneaked bottles of wine to youngsters at the back door, charging them double. Paterson's most famous resident, the boxer Rubin Carter, gave the Nite Spot added cachet. He had his own table, Hurricane's Corner.

Drinking holes for white Patersonians, if not exactly respectable, were more . . . decorous. They had less colorful names — Bruno's, Kearney's, Question Mark — and were typically called taverns. They were scattered through the Polish and Lithuanian neighborhoods of the city's Riverside section, through Little Italy in the center of town, and through the Irish enclaves of South Paterson. They served cream ale, a flat brew made locally with a thick foamy top and a potent kick. Many of these taverns had sawdust on the floor, pool tables in the back, and grills in the kitchen. Patrons ate burgers, watched Friday-night boxing matches on black-and-white televisions, and threw darts. They cursed with Old World epithets.

The beery dens were in all neighborhoods and welcomed all comers. Gangsters and millworkers, politicians and merchants, nurses and hookers, blacks and whites, rich and poor — they all had their hangouts, they were out there somewhere, and Frank Graves could not stop them.

It was not as if he had nothing else to worry about. The exodus of industry, commerce, and the middle class had sent his city into a long downward spiral. Paterson, only 8.36 square miles, sits in the lowland loop of the Passaic River, its southern banks lined by abandoned red-brick cotton mills, empty factories, and rusting warehouses. At night, Main Street was deserted as street lamps cast islands of light on discount stores: John's Bargain Store, ANY SHOE for $3.33, the five-and-ten. Displays of plastic shoes and acetate dresses were fragile remnants of a once-pulsating business district. Across Main Street stood Garrett Mountain, a camel's hump of a hill that offered a view of the world beyond Paterson. When the smog cleared and the sun was out, residents could discern Manhattan's metallic skyline, 15 miles southeast.

Graves's campaign against the bars was, in fact, a battle against the city's raucous history. Since its founding, Paterson had been the Wild West on the Passaic, where bare-knuckled industrialists converged with brawny immigrants and infamous scoundrels. Alexander Hamilton, smitten by the Great Falls of the Passaic River, founded Paterson in 1791 with the belief that water-powered mills would turn the city into a laboratory for industrial development. Initially, Paterson was not a city at all but a corporation, called the Society for the Establishment of Useful Manufacturers, or SUM. The Panic of 1792 almost sank SUM, but it survived, and Paterson flourished as a freewheeling outpost of frontier industrialism.

Fueled by iron ore from nearby mines, charcoal from abundant forests, and coal from Pennsylvania, Paterson in the nineteenth century attracted inventors, romantics, and robber barons who made goods used across the country and beyond. In 1836 Sam Colt, unable to raise money for a factory by roaming the East Coast with a portable magic show, found backers in Paterson, where he manufactured his first revolver. John Holland, an Irish nationalist, built the first practical submarine in Paterson in 1878, his goal being "to blow the English Navy to hell." (The Brits turned out to be principal buyers of the new weapon.)

It seemed that Patersonians believed anything was possible, reckless or otherwise. In the 1830s "Leaping" Sam Patch, a cotton mill foreman, became the only man to jump off the Niagara Falls successfully without a protective device. (He was less successful jumping off the Genesee Falls; his body turned up in a block of ice on Lake Ontario.) Wright Aeronautical Corporation undertook a more constructive if no less daring mission in 1927: it built a nine-cylinder, air-cooled radial engine that propelled Charles Lindbergh to Paris on the first solo Atlantic flight. Paterson's most famous product was silk — enough to adorn all the aristocrats in Europe, if not the Victorian homes and furtive mistresses of the silk barons themselves. Silk lured thousands of European immigrants to Paterson. By 1900 they filled three hundred and fifty hot, clamorous mills, weaving 30 percent of all the silk produced in the United States.

Between 1840 and 1900, Paterson's population increased by 1,348 percent, to 110,000 residents, making it the fastest-growing city on the East Coast. Newly arrived Germans, Irish, Poles, Italians, Russians, and Jews carved out sections of the city, and ethnic taverns followed. By 1900 Paterson had more than four hundred bars, where tipplers bought cheap, locally brewed beer and reminisced about the old country. Even in the 1950s, long after the immigrant waves had been assimilated, the Emil DeMyer Saloon, in the oldest part of the city, north of the river, hung out a sign that read: "French, Dutch, German, and Belgian Spoken Here."

The bars, of course, were also seen as contributing to alcoholism, broken marriages, and lost weekends. Wives complained to the priest of Saint John the Baptist Cathedral, William McNulty, that their husbands were quaffing down their wages. Dean McNulty, who led the church for fifty-nine years until he died in 1922, would patrol the bars on Friday nights and swat the guzzlers home with his wooden walking stick.

Booze was hardly enough to calm the tensions that stirred in the crowded three-family frame tenements. The factory laborers, with their dye-stained fingers and arthritic backs, chafed at the excesses of the rich. In 1894 Paterson's largest silk manufacturer, Catholina Lambert, built a hulking medieval castle near the top of Garrett Mountain, hiring special trains to bring four hundred guests to its opening reception. But in the streets below, vandalism was rampant, strikes common, and political passions high. In 1900, when Angelo Bresci, a Paterson anarchist, returned to his homeland of Italy and murdered King Humbert I, a thousand anarchists in Paterson gathered to celebrate. Between 1850 and 1914, Paterson was the most strike-ridden city in the nation. The strife reached its brutal climax in 1913, when a five-month strike left gangs of workers and police roaming the streets and attacking one another. Paterson's silk industry, and the town itself, never recovered.

While World War II spurred a brief economic revival, mechanization threw weavers out of work, and textile factories needing skilled labor moved to the South. Wright Aeronautical went from a wartime peak of sixty thousand employees to five thousand, then moved to the suburbs. The Society for the Establishment of Useful Manufacturers dissolved in 1946. The Great Falls became a favorite spot for suicides and murder.

Lacking leadership and vision, Paterson continued its long economic slide in the 1960s, and like other cities in New Jersey, it became a wide-open rackets town. Bookies ran the wirerooms in a club on lower Market Street, placing bets on horse races and football games. The most popular form of gambling, the grease that lubricated the Paterson economy, was the "numbers." It cost as little as a quarter or even a dime, and everyone played, including the cops. Bettors dropped off their money at a storefront, typically a bar but perhaps a bakery or grocery. Bets were made on the closing number of the Dow Jones Industrial Average, the winning numbers from a horse race, or the *New York Daily News*'s circulation number, which was published on the back page in each edition. The following day, the two-bit gamblers either griped about their bad luck or picked up their winnings, typically six hundred times their bet, meaning $60 on a ten-cent wager or $150 on a quarter. Win or lose, they put down another bet. Numbers runners ferried the cash to the mobsters, who controlled the game, and the small business owners who collected the cash got a cut. It was another way for the bustling taverns to stay in business, but it did little to help Paterson regain its glory.

In *On Paterson,* Christopher Norwood wrote this elegy for the city in the middle 1960s: "The mills, the redbrick buildings where people produced commodities and became commodities themselves, still stand in Paterson, but most are abandoned now. The looms are no more, their noisy, awkward machinery long vandalized or sold for scrap. Vines, weeds and sometimes whole trees have grown through their stark walls, the walls unadorned except for small slits, outlined in a contrasting brick pattern, left for windows."

This was the city Frank Graves ran from 1960 to 1966. Despite the deteriorating economy, the mayor wanted the police force to be his legacy. Graves himself was a policeman manqué. He had ridden in police cars as a kid and relished the crisp blue uniforms, the recondite radio codes, and the peremptory wail of a car siren. But his father, Frank X. Graves, Sr., would not allow his son to work on the force. Frank Sr. was a city power broker who owned a lucrative cigarette vending-machine company. He also covered the police for the *Paterson Evening News* for fifty years, and no son of his was going to chase petty thieves on the street. So, as mayor, Frank Jr. gloried in turning the police into his fiefdom. He spent time at the police station and person-ally answered incoming calls. He approved all hires, assignments, and promotions. He interrogated suspects. He chastised traffic cops who failed to direct cars with sufficient authoritarian snap. He required patrolmen to salute him, and offenders were summoned to the captain's office the next day for a reprimand. Graves decreed that all police calls receive a response within ninety seconds, resulting in siren-blaring patrol cars careening through Paterson's narrow streets. "The police force," Graves said, "is the city." And no task was too trivial. He once sent a phalanx of patrol cars to a nearby suburb to search for Tiger, a dog who'd strayed from Paterson.

But Graves came under fire for turning the city into a police state; there were charges of brutality and even torture. In 1964 the state ordered Passaic County to convene a grand jury to investigate reports that Paterson police had burned a prisoner's body with matches and poured alcohol into his nose. The grand jury made no indictments but recommended that the department photograph prisoners both before and after questioning. The barroom raids were seen as grandstanding ploys, sacrificing basic patrol work. Although drug-related crimes were the city's worst problem, there was only one man in the Narcotics Bureau.

Paterson's swelling black population especially feared the mostly white police force and resented Graves's apparent indifference to their grievances. During the Depression, blacks made up less than 2 percent of the city's population. By the middle 1960s, they were about 20 percent. Between 1950 and 1964, 18,000 blacks and Hispanics moved into Paterson as 13,000 whites moved out. At the same time, good factory jobs were disappearing quickly, creating tensions between whites and blacks for a piece of the shrinking economic pie. Many black immigrants settled in the Fourth Ward and established taverns and nightclubs. Housing there was a shambles. Old wooden structures slouched beneath the weight of their new occupants; many of the units lacked plumbing, central heating, or private baths. A citywide survey showed that when a black family moved into a tenement, the rent was increased. There were long waiting lists for low-income municipal housing, and when blacks tried to move out of the Fourth Ward, they were refused or stalled by white real estate agents. Health conditions were horrid. A protest group offered a bounty of ten cents for each rat found in a home and delivered to City Hall. A court injunction snuffed out the rodent rebellion.

The anger in the black community was finally unleashed in August 1964, when a three-day riot broke out, primarily in the Fourth Ward. No one was killed, but the cataract of violence unnerved white Patersonians, who still made up 75 percent of the city's 140,000 residents. Black youths shattered more than a dozen store windows at the intersection of Godwin and Graham Streets while a black youngster battling sixteen policemen was pushed through a plate glass window. Factory fires, Molotov cocktails, and errant shotgun blasts sent panic through the city. A marked law enforcement car from Maryland appeared with two German shepherd police dogs, although the authorities said they were never loosed on the rioters. Black leaders blamed the uprising on police harassment and overcrowded housing conditions, saying it was simply too hot to stay indoors, and they demanded rent control in blighted areas and a new police review board.

The riot was part of a summer of uprisings that broke out in Harlem, in Jersey City and Elizabeth, New Jersey, in Rochester, New York, and in small black enclaves in Oregon and New Hampshire. In each case, a street arrest triggered escalating hostilities, but only Paterson had Frank Graves.

The mayor tried to keep control. At a luncheon in Paterson on August 12 for Miss New Jersey, he promised, "Paterson will be completely safe for you tonight." By nightfall, Graves probably hoped, Miss New Jersey was smiling in some other part of the state, because violence erupted once again in Paterson. Graves personally led the police through a ravaged ten-block area and narrowly missed serious injury when a bottle was thrown at him as he stepped from his car. Confronted by the overturned vehicles, shattered storefronts, and broken streetlights, Graves blamed the riot on "the worst hooligans that man has ever conceived." His rhetoric, combined with his hard-nosed police, left little doubt among blacks that Graves was less interested in civil rights than civil repression.

Thoughts of race and crime were probably not on the mind of seventeen-year-old William Metzler when he arrived at work on Thursday, June 16, 1966. Metzler was an attendant for his father's ambulance company in Paterson, working a midnight–8 A.M. shift. Employees stayed awake for two-hour stretches, sipping coffee, eating doughnuts, and monitoring the police radio. Some time after 2 A.M. on June 17, Metzler began hearing a series of police calls amid escalating panic. One call said, "Holdup." Another: "Shooting." And yet another, "Code one for ambulances," which meant emergency.

Metzler and his older brother, Walt, raced their ambulance twelve blocks to the scene of the crime: the Lafayette Grill at 128 East Eighteenth

Street, a nondescript neighborhood bar on the first floor of a tired three-story apartment building. When the ambulance arrived, a police car and two officers were on the site. William Metzler opened the bar's side door, on Lafayette Street, walked inside, and literally slid across the bloody tile floor, almost falling into the red stream. Amid the cigarette and nut machines, a pool rack and jukebox and black-and-white television above the L-shaped bar, a scene of mayhem emerged: there were four bullet-ridden bodies — two dead, two alive, all white. It was, Metzler said years later, "a Wild West scene."

While the shooting itself would be subject to one of the longest, most bitterly contested criminal proceedings in American history, no one would ever dispute the distinctively sadistic nature of the rampage. These basic facts were known within days.

Two black men entered the bar through the side door, one carrying a 12-gauge shotgun, the other a .32-caliber handgun. The bartender, James Oliver, age fifty-one, flung an empty beer bottle at the assailants, then turned to run. As the bottle shattered futilely against the wall, a single shotgun blast from seven feet away ripped through Oliver's lower back, opening a two-by-one-inch hole. The bullet severed his spinal column, literally breaking the man in half. Oliver fell behind the bar, dead, two bottles of liquor lying near his tangled feet and cash strewn on the floor.

At about the same time the second assailant, holding the handgun, fired a single bullet at Fred Nauyoks, a sixty-year-old regular sitting on a barstool. The bullet ripped past Nauyoks's right earlobe and struck the base of his brain, killing him instantly. He slumped over as if asleep, his head lying in a pool of blood, a lit cigarette between his fingers, his shot glass full, and cash on the bar ready to pay for the fresh drink. His foot remained on the stool's footrest.

The pistol-carrying gunman then fired a bullet at William Marins, a forty-three-year-old machinist who had been at the bar for many hours, sitting two stools down from Nauyoks. The bullet entered his head near the left temple, caromed through the skull, and exited from the forehead by the left eye. He survived his wound and was able to describe the assailants to the police.

Seated in a different section of the bar was fifty-one-year-old Hazel Tanis, who had just arrived from her waitressing job at the Westmount Country Club. The assailant with the shotgun fired a single blast into her upper right arm. Then the second shooter turned and emptied his remaining five bullets, the muzzle of the gun as close as ten inches from the victim. Four bullets struck their mark: the right breast, the lower abdomen, the vagina, and the genital area. Tanis survived and was able to describe the gunmen to the police, but she developed an embolism four weeks later and died.

From the outset, the Lafayette bar murders became intertwined with another brutal homicide in Paterson. About six and a half hours earlier, a white man named Frank Conforti walked into the Waltz Inn, about four blocks from the Lafayette. Conforti had sold the bar to a black man, Roy Holloway, who was paying him in weekly installments. On this night, Conforti came to collect his last payment, but a heated argument broke out over the amount owed. Conforti stormed out of the tavern and returned moments later with a double-barreled shotgun. He blasted Holloway in the upper right arm; when Holloway tried to flee, he fired again, this time striking him in the head. Conforti was arrested for murder.

The police immediately suspected that the Lafayette bar shooting was in retaliation for the Waltz Inn murder. At the Waltz Inn, a white man with a shotgun killed a black bartender. At the Lafayette bar, a black man with a shotgun killed a white bartender. An eye for an eye. The Lafayette bar slaying chilled the white establishment. Black vigilantism, of course, was unacceptable. What's more, the bar itself had long been a tiny neighborhood hangout for the Italians, Lithuanians, Poles, and other Eastern European immigrants who lived on the southern boundary of the working-class Riverside section.

But by the summer of 1966, the neighborhood was changing quickly. Blacks, moving north along Carroll and Graham Streets, were now living near and around the Lafayette bar. But the bar was still a watering hole for its traditional base of white workers, not blacks. Indeed, rumors circulated that the bartender refused to serve blacks. In time the bar, under different owners and different names, would be a black gathering spot for a black neighborhood. But on June 17, 1966, it was seen as a white redoubt against a coming black wave.

For a city the size of Paterson, the Lafayette bar shootings — four innocent victims, including one woman, three ultimately dead — would have been jarring under any circumstance. There had been only six murders in Paterson since the beginning of the year. But the overlay of race, of black invaders and white flight and a hapless neighborhood bar with a neon Schlitz sign and threadbare pool table, elevated the tragedy further.

Frank Graves assigned 130 police officers (out of a force of 341) to the investigation, promising promotions and three-month vacations to the arresting officers. He initially offered a $1,000 reward for information that led to an arrest, then raised it to $10,000. The Paterson Tavern Owners Association chipped in another $500. That the crime occurred in a bar confirmed the mayor's conviction that taprooms were whirlpools of disorder. "We have three hundred and fifty" taverns, Graves thundered. "We should only have a hundred."

He repeatedly referred to the Lafayette bar murders as "the most heinous crimes" and "the most dastardly crimes in the city's history." Two days after the shooting, Graves told the *Paterson Evening News,* "We will stay on this investigation until it is solved. There will be no such thing as a dead end in this case. If we hit a roadblock, we'll back up and get on the main road until it is solved. These are by far the most brutal slayings in the city's history."

The pressure to solve the worst crime in Paterson's long history would soon lead to the most feared man in the town.

3

DANGER ON THE STREETS

AT THE TIME of the Lafayette bar murders, Rubin Carter was a twenty-nine-year-old prizefighter and one of the great character actors of boxing's golden era. The middleweight stalked opponents across the ring with a menacing left hook, a glowering stare, and a black bullet of a head — clean-shaven, with a sinister-looking mustache and goatee. Outside the ring, Carter cultivated a parallel reputation of a dashing but defiant night crawler. He settled grudges with his fists and was not cowed by the police. His intimidating style sent chills through boxing foes and cops alike, making him a target for both.

Regardless of where he walked, Carter always turned heads. At five feet eight inches and 160 pounds, he had an oversize neck, broad shoulders, and trapezoidal chest, with contoured biceps, thick hands, a tapering waist, and sinuous legs. A broadcaster once said of Carter, "He has muscles that he hasn't even rippled yet."

He was obsessed with fine clothing and personal hygiene, passions he inherited from his father. Lloyd Carter, Sr., believed that immaculate apparel showed a black man's success in a white man's world. A Georgia sharecropper's son with a seventh-grade education, Lloyd earned a good living as a resourceful and indefatigable entrepreneur. He owned an icehouse, a window-washing concern, and a bike rental shop, and he wore his success proudly. He had his double-breasted suits custom-made in Philadelphia, favored French cuffs, and wore Stacy Adams two-tone alligator shoes. He bought his children shoes for school and for church; but if the school shoes had a hole, church shoes could not be worn to classes. No child of his would enter a house of worship with scuffed footwear.

Rubin Carter was just as meticulous as his father, if somewhat flashier. He instructed a Jersey City tailor to design his clothes to fit his top-heavy body. He placed $400 suit orders on the phone — "Do you have any new fabrics? ... Good. Put it together and I'll pick it up" — and he favored sharkskin suits, or cotton, silk, all pure fabrics, an occasional vest, and iridescent colors. His pants were pressed like a razor blade. He wore violet and blue berets pulled rakishly over his right ear, polished Italian shoes, and loud ties.

Carter trimmed his goatee with precision and clipped his fingernails to the cuticle. He collected fruit-scented colognes while traveling around the United States, Europe, and South Africa, then poured entire bottles into his bath water, soaked in the redolent tub, and emerged with a pleasing hint of nectar. Every three days Carter mixed Magic Shave powder with cold water and slathered it on his crown and face. He scraped it off with a butter knife, then rubbed a little Vaseline on top for a shine. His wife, Tee, complained that the pasty concoction smelled like rotten eggs, so she made him shave on their porch, but the result was Carter's riveting signature: a smooth, shiny dome.

Nighttime was always Carter's temptress, a lure of sybaritic pleasures and occasional danger. On his nights out, he left his wife at home and cruised through the streets of Paterson in a black Eldorado convertible with "Rubin 'Hurricane' Carter" emblazoned in silver letters on each of the headlights. He strolled into nightclubs with a wad of cash in his pocket and a neon chip on his shoulder. He bought everyone a round or two of drinks and mixed easily with women, both white and black. An incorrigible flirt, he danced, drank, and cruised with different women most every night.

But club confrontations often got Carter in trouble. He faced assault charges at least twice for barroom clashes, including once from the owner of the Kit Kat Club. Carter, contending he was unfairly singled out because of his swaggering profile, was cleared. But stories swirled about his hair-trigger temper. In an oft-repeated tale, Carter once found a man sitting at his table at the Nite Spot. When the man was slow to leave Hurricane's Corner, Carter knocked him out with a punch, then took his girl.

Carter pooh-poohs such tales, although he says he would have told the man to sit elsewhere if other tables had been available. His dictum was that he never punched anyone unless first provoked, but he acknowledges that he was easily antagonized and, once aroused, showed little mercy on his tormentor. Adversaries came in all stripes. He once knocked a horse over with a right cross. The horse had had it coming: it tried to take a bite out of Carter's side. The knockdown, publicized in local and national publications, added to Carter's street-fighter reputation and legendary punching prowess.

Hedonistic excess was hardly uncommon in the boxing world; nonetheless, it was not widely known that Carter was an alcoholic during his career. Some thought Carter drank to make up for his dry years in prison: between 1957 and 1961, Carter had been sentenced to Trenton State Prison for assault and robbery. The inmates surreptitiously made a sugary wine concoction, "hooch," but good liquor was hard to come by.

Outside prison, vodka was Carter's drink of choice. Straight up, on the rocks, in a plastic cup, in a glass, from a bottle, it didn't matter; it just had to be vodka. He was not a binge drinker but a slow, relentless sipper, and he could drink a fifth of vodka in a single night. Carter stayed clear of the bottle, mostly, when in training, but when he was out of camp, he kept at least one bottle of 100-proof Smirnoff's in his car; friends hitching a ride got free drinks.

Carter concealed his drinking as much as possible. It was a sign of weakness and undermined his image as an athletic demigod. To avoid drinking in clubs, he picked up liquor in stores and drank in his car, sometimes with drinking buddies, sometimes alone. He tried not to order more than one drink at any one club on a given night. His wife rarely saw him imbibe and had no idea of the scope of his addiction. He carried Certs and peppermint candies to mask the alcohol on his breath, and he never got staggering drunk.

While Carter was a dedicated night owl, he was also a celebrity loner whose ready scowl stirred fear in bystanders, and he shunned close personal ties. He was often silent and moody, and many blacks in Paterson viewed him with a mixture of respect, envy, and fear. "Everybody loved Rubin, but no one was his friend," said Tariq Darby, a heavyweight boxer from New Jersey in the 1960s. "I remember seeing him once in that black and silver Cadillac. He just turned and gave me that nasty look."

Tensions were more overt between Carter and Paterson's white majority as he flaunted his success in ways that he knew would tweak the establishment. He owned a twenty-six-foot fishing boat with a double Chrysler engine, which was docked at a marina in central New Jersey. He owned a horse, a once-wild mare he named Bitch, and rode in flamboyant style on Garrett Mountain. Dressed in a fringed jean jacket, a ten-gallon hat, and spur-tipped boots, Carter was hard to miss passing the white families picnicking on the hillside, and he didn't mind when his riding partner was a white woman.

Carter's shaved head, at least twenty-five years before bald pates became a common fashion statement among African Americans, had its own political edge. In the early 1960s, many blacks used lye-based chemical processors to straighten their curls and make their hair look "white." White was cool. But Carter's coal-black cupola sent a message: he had no interest in emulating white people. In fact, he shaved his head in part to mimic another glabrous black boxer, Jack Johnson, who won the heavyweight title in 1908 but was reviled as an insolent parvenu who drove fancy cars, drank expensive wines through straws, consorted with white women, and defied the establishment.

Carter's showy displays jarred white Patersonians, who had a very different model for how a black professional athlete should act. They cherished Larry Doby, a hometown hero and baseball pioneer. On July 5, 1947, Doby joined the Cleveland Indians, breaking the color barrier in the American League. He was the second black major league player, following Jackie Robinson by eleven weeks. This feat spoke well of Doby's hometown, Paterson, and Doby seemed to always speak well of the city. Never mind that Doby, who grew up literally on the wrong side of the Susquehanna Railroad tracks, knew well the racism of Paterson. As a kid going to a movie or vaudeville show at the Majestic Theater, he had to sit in the third balcony, known as "nigger heaven," and he could not walk through white sections of Paterson at night without being stopped by police. Even after he became a baseball star, Doby was thwarted by real estate brokers from buying a home in the fashionable East Side of Paterson. He eventually moved his family to an integrated neighborhood in the more enlightened New Jersey city of Montclair.

But in public Doby was always a paragon of humility and deference. After he helped the Indians win the World Series in 1948, he was feted in Paterson with a motorcade. A crowd of three thousand gathered at Bauerle Field in front of Eastside High School, his alma mater, and city dignitaries gave effusive speeches about a black man whose deeds brought glory to their town. Then Doby took the microphone: he thanked the mayor and his teachers and coaches, concluding with these words: "I know I'm not a perfect gentleman, but I always try to be one."

No white authority figure in Paterson ever called Rubin Carter a gentleman, perfect or otherwise. He was viewed not simply as brash and disrespectful but as a threat. Bad enough that he could knock down a horse with a single punch. Carter also owned guns, lots of them — shotguns, rifles, and pistols. He learned to shoot as a boy, practicing on a south New Jersey farm owned by his grandfather, and he honed his skills as a paratrooper for the 11th Airborne in the U.S. Army. He used his guns mostly for target practice but also for hunting, roaming the New Jersey woodlands with his father's coon dogs. Carter could nail a treebound raccoon right between the eyes. He also owned guns for protection, and he had some of his suits tailored wide around the breast to accommodate a holster and pistol, which he would wear when he feared for his safety.

Like Malcolm X, Carter advocated that blacks use whatever means necessary, including violence, to protect themselves. He participated in the March on Washington in 1963, but two years later he rebuffed Martin Luther King, Jr.'s request to join a demonstration in Selma, Alabama. Carter knew he would not, could not, sit idly in the face of brutal attacks from law enforcement officials, white supremacists, or snarling dogs. "No, I can't go down there," he told King. "That would be foolishness at the risk of suicide. Those people would kill me dead."

Carter did not accept the mainstream civil rights approach of passive resistance. He believed the sacrifices that blacks were making, whether on the riot-torn streets of Harlem or in the bombed-out churches of Birmingham, were unacceptable. Malcolm X had been killed. So too had James Chaney, Andrew Goodman, and Michael Schwerner, three young civil rights workers, Medgar Evers, a black civil rights leader, and others unknown. *Nonviolence is Gandhi's principle, but Gandhi does not know the enemy,* Carter thought.

When under attack, Rubin Carter believed in fighting back; in his view it was the police who were usually doing the attacking. But his many scrapes with the cops, plus some intemperate comments to a reporter, gave the authorities reason to believe that he was able, even likely, to commit a heinous crime.

In addition to the assault and robbery conviction in 1957, Carter, at fourteen, and three other boys attacked a Paterson man at a swimming hole called Tubbs near Passaic Falls. The man was cut with a soda water bottle and his $55 watch was stolen. Carter was sentenced to the Jamesburg State Home for Boys, but he escaped two years later. In the 1960s, his fracases with the police were common. In one incident, on January 16, 1964, a white officer picked him up after his Eldorado had broken down on a highway next to a meatpacking factory near Hackensack, New Jersey. He was driven to the town's police headquarters, then accused of burglarizing the factory during the night. He had been locked in a holding cell for four hours when a black officer arrived and recognized him. "Is that you in there, Carter? What the hell did you get busted for, man?" Carter let out a stream of invective about the cops' oppressive behavior. He was finally released after the black officer demanded to know the grounds on which he was being held. According to the official record, Carter had been arrested as a "disorderly person" for his "failure to give good account," and the charge against him was dismissed.

Hostilities between Carter and the police, in New Jersey and elsewhere, escalated to a whole other level after a *Saturday Evening Post* article was published in October 1964. The story was a curtain raiser for the upcoming middleweight championship fight between the challenger, Carter, and Joey Giardello, the champ. The article, which introduced Carter to many nonboxing fans, was headlined "A Match Made in the Jungle." Actually, the bout was to take place in Las Vegas, but "Jungle" referred to Carter's feral nature. He was described as sporting a "Mongol-style mustache" and appearing like a "combination of bop musician and Genghis Khan." With Carter fighting for the crown, "once again the sick sport of boxing seems to have taken a turn for the worse," the article intoned. Giardello, photographed playfully holding his two young children, was the consummate family man. Carter sat alone, staring pitilessly into the camera.

In his interview with the sportswriter Milton Gross, Carter raged against white cops' occupying black neighborhoods in a summer of unrest, and he exhorted blacks to defend themselves, even if it meant fighting to their death. He told the reporter that blacks were living in a dream world if they thought equality was around the corner, that reality was trigger-happy cops and redneck judges.

That part of the interview, however, was left out of the article. Instead, Gross printed his reckless tirade so that it was Carter, not the police, who looked liked the terrorist. Describing his life before he became a prizefighter, Carter told the writer: "We used to get up and put our guns in our pockets like you put your wallet in your pocket. Then we go out in the streets and start shooting — anybody, everybody. We used to shoot folks."

"Shoot at folks?" Carter was asked, because this seemed too much to believe and too much for Carter to confess even years later.

"Just what I said," he repeated. "Shoot at people. Sometimes just to shoot at 'em, sometimes to hit 'em, sometimes to kill 'em. My family was saying I'm still a bum. If I got the name, I play the game."

This was sheer bluster on Carter's part — no one had ever accused him of shooting anyone — but it was how he tried to rattle his boxing opponents and shake up white journalists. He invented a childhood knifing attack — "I stabbed him everywhere but the bottom of his feet" — and the story quoted a friend of Carter's who recounted a conversation with the boxer following a riot in Harlem that summer. The uprising occurred after an off-duty police lieutenant, responding to a confrontation between a sharp-tongued building superintendent and black youths carrying a bottle, shot to death a fifteen-year-old boy. Carter, according to his friend, said: "Let's get guns and go up there and get us some of those police. I know I can get four or five before they get me. How many can you get?"

This fulsome remark sealed his image for the police and now for a much larger public. On the Friday-night fights, the showcase for boxing in America, Carter stalked across television screens throughout the country as the ruthless face of black militancy. He was seen as an ignoble savage, a stylized brute, an "uppity nigger." He was out of control and, more than ever, he was a targeted man. (He was also not to be the champion. The Giardello fight, rescheduled for December in Philadelphia, went fifteen rounds; Carter lost a controversial split decision.)

After the *Saturday Evening Post* article appeared, authorities in Los

Angeles, Pittsburgh, Akron, and elsewhere approached Carter when he was in town for a fight. On the grounds that he was a former convict, they demanded that he be fingerprinted and photographed for their files. At the time, the Federal Bureau of Investigation's clandestine political arm, COINTELPRO (for "counter intelligence program"), was spying on Martin Luther King, Jr., Malcolm X, and other civil rights leaders. Carter believed that by 1965, the FBI had begun tracking him, which simply made him more defiant.* In the summer of 1965, for example, Carter arrived in Los Angeles several weeks early for a fight against Luis Rodriguez. The city's police chief, William Parker, soon called Carter in his motel on Olympia Boulevard and told him to get down to headquarters.

"So, you thought you were sneaking into town on me, huh?" Parker said. "But we knew you were coming, boy. The FBI had you pegged every step of the way."

"No, I wasn't trying to sneak into your town. I just got here a little bit early," Carter said. A woman whom Carter had seen tailing him at the airport and his motel was standing in the office. He motioned her way, then looked back at the police chief. "My God," he said. "She's got a beautiful ass on her, ain't she?"

By June 1966, Carter's last prizefight had been more than three months earlier in Toledo, against the Olympic gold medalist Wilbert "Skeeter" McClure. The match ended in a draw. He feared he faced increased police surveillance and harassment as black militancy became a greater force across America. Instead of young people marching together arm-in-arm and singing "We Shall Overcome," new images emerged of combative black men and women wearing black berets and carrying guns, their fists raised in defiance. Social justice was not enough. Black separatism and empowerment were part of the new agenda. Malcolm X's legacy was being carried on by charismatic leaders like Stokely Carmichael and Bobby Seale, whose cries for "black power" galvanized growing numbers of disaffected black youths while igniting a backlash from frightened whites. Paterson swirled with rumors that

---

* FBI files released through the Freedom of Information Act indicate that Carter was under investigation at least by 1967. The report could not be read in full because the FBI had blacked out many sections, evidently to protect its informants.

black organizers had come from Chicago to reignite the protests that had ripped the city apart two summers earlier.

Rubin Carter knew he needed to get off the streets.

Carter had a match coming up in Argentina in August, and he was moving to his training camp on Monday, June 20. Camp itself was a small sheep farm in Chatham, New Jersey, run by a man from India named Eshan. On Thursday the sixteenth, beneath a warm afternoon sun, Carter filled the trunk of his white 1966 Dodge Polara with boxing equipment. He could almost feel the canvas under his feet, and he was grateful.

In the evening his wife made dinner for her husband and their two-year-old daughter, Theodora. Mae Thelma, known as Tee, looked like a starlet, with dark chocolate skin, a radiant smile, and arched eyebrows. She sometimes tinted her hair with a bewitching silver streak. She was also quiet and self-conscious. As a young girl in Saluda, South Carolina, Tee had crawled into an open fireplace, disfiguring several fingers on her left hand. Thereafter she often wore long white gloves to conceal her scars, or she kept her hand in her coat pocket and slipped it under tables, sometimes awkwardly, at clubs or restaurants. Rubin had dated her for months before he finally caught a glimpse of the injury. On their next date, he pulled off to the side of the road, took her left hand, and pulled off her glove. "Is this what you've been hiding from me all this time?" he asked. "Do you think I would love you any less?"

When Tee told him she was pregnant, she feared he would abandon her; she herself had grown up in a fatherless home. Instead, Rubin promptly proposed, and they were wed on June 15, 1963. Carter families, Rubin knew, did not go without fathers, and their children did not go on welfare. Theodora was born seven months later. Rubin and Tee had an unspoken agreement: Rubin took care of his business, and Tee took care of Rubin. They each had their own friends and socialized separately. Tee never watched any of Rubin's fights. Some nights, when they ended up at the same club, the people around them often didn't know they were married.

This deception gave rise to some pranks. One night, sitting at the opposite end of the bar from his wife, Carter asked a bartender, "Would you please send down a drink to that young lady and tell her I said she sure looks pretty."

The unsuspecting bartender walked down to Tee. "This drink comes from that gentleman up there, and he says you sure look pretty."

She wrinkled her nose at Rubin. "Tell him I think he looks good too."

The flirtation ended with Tee's accepting Rubin's offer to go home with him, leaving the bartender in awe of this Lothario's good luck.

The couple's three-story home, in a racially mixed neighborhood in Paterson, was comfortably decorated with a blondish wood dining room table, blue sofas with gold trim, African artifacts hanging on the walls, and an oil painting of the family. On the night of June 16, Carter watched a James Brown concert on television, doing a few jigs in the living room with Theodora. During the commercials, he repaired to the bedroom to dress for the night and returned to the living room with a new ensemble in place. Black slacks. White dress shirt. Black tie. Black vest. A cream sport jacket with thin green and brown stripes. Black socks. Black shoes. A splash of cologne, and a dab of Vaseline on his cleanly shaven head.

That night Carter decided to drive the white Polara, which was blocking the Eldorado in the garage. (He leased the Polara as a business car for the tax writeoff.) It was a warm evening, and Carter, at the outset, had business on his mind. He had a midnight meeting with his personal adviser, Nathan Sermond, at Club LaPetite to discuss the Argentina fight; the promoters were balking at giving Carter a sparring partner in Buenos Aires. Carter was also to meet, at the Nite Spot, one of his sparring partners, "Wild Bill" Hardney, who would be joining him in camp the following week. But by 11 P.M., the night was taking some unusual twists.

Sipping vodka outside the Nite Spot with a group of people, Carter bumped into a former sparring partner, Neil Morrison, known as Mobile for his Alabama roots. Carter had been looking for him for months because he suspected him of stealing three of his guns from his Chatham training camp. The theft — of a .22 Winchester, a bolt-action .22 rifle, and a 12-gauge pump shotgun — had occurred the previous fall when Morrison was staying in the camp. Morrison, dressed in dungarees and a white T-shirt, had just been released from prison, and Carter confronted him, accusing him of stealing the guns.

"Man, you know I would never do that," Morrison said.

"I know a person who's seen you with my guns," Carter said. A childhood friend, Annabelle Chandler, had told Carter she saw Morrison with the weapons.

"The hell you do!" Morrison said.

Carter, Morrison, and two other Nite Spot regulars agreed to drive over to Chandler's apartment, in the nearby Christopher Columbus Projects. There they found Chandler in the bathroom, sick. She had recently returned from the hospital and was suffering from cancer. Carter entered the bathroom and told her he had brought Morrison with him so she could repeat how she saw him with Carter's guns.

"If I had known you were going to tell him, I wouldn't have told you," she told Carter.

"Well, forget about it," he said in deference to her illness. Carter dropped the matter; his guns had been stolen and sold and lost forever. The group returned to the Nite Spot. Little did Carter know that in years to come, this chance encounter with Neil Morrison and quick jaunt to a run-down housing project to visit a dying woman would be used against him in a devastating way.

The night was unusual for another reason. Word had spread that Roy Holloway, the black owner of the Waltz Inn, had been slain by a white man, Frank Conforti. When the police arrested Conforti, a crowd of people, mostly blacks but not including Carter, angrily yelled at the white assailant. Holloway's stepson, Eddie Rawls, was the bartender at the Nite Spot, and he pulled up to the club when Carter was in the midst of his dispute with Morrison. Carter expressed his condolences to Rawls, who was coming from the hospital. The group chatted for several minutes before Rawls went inside the club.

There was a buzz at the Nite Spot and other black clubs about a "shaking," or retaliation of some sort, for the Holloway murder. Carter, however, had never met Holloway and was never heard to express any anger over the murder. He had other things on his mind. Thursdays were known as "potwashers night." Domestics were given the night off, and the women got into the Nite Spot for free through the back door. By 2 A.M., as the crowd began to thin out at the Nite Spot, Carter was still looking for a date. When last call was announced, he approached the bar and asked for the usual, a vodka. He took out his wallet, but when he discovered it was empty, he told the bartender he'd have to pay up later.

Carter had planned to go to an after-hours social club, so he had to head home to get some money. He spotted his sparring partner, "Wild Bill" Hardney, and asked if he would go with him so Tee would not complain about his going out again. But Hardney, preoccupied with his girlfriend, begged off.

Then Carter noticed John Artis on the dance floor. The former high school football and track star was a sleek, high-spirited dancer who practiced his steps at home, following the advice of one of his uncles: "When you dance, be original and be different from the others. Take a step and change it, and always be smooth."

Nineteen-year-old Artis loved fast cars and pretty girls, and that night, dressed in a sky-blue mohair sweater with a JAA monogram, matching light blue sharkskin pants, and gold loafers, he was certainly on the prowl. But it had been a long boozy evening — he had been sick earlier — and he was winding down. He had just performed a dazzling boogaloo when Carter called out to him. "Nice moves, buddy," he said. "Wanna take a ride?" Overhearing the conversation was John "Bucks" Royster, a balding alcoholic drifter who was friendly with Carter. Royster, figuring drinks would be available in the car, asked if he could join them. Outside, Carter flipped Artis the keys and asked him to drive. Then Carter climbed in the back seat, slumped down, and called out directions to his house, about three miles southeast of the Nite Spot.

Artis had only met Carter a couple of times. He rambled on about how boxing was not his favorite sport, but his friends would be impressed when they heard he'd been driving Hurricane's car, even if it wasn't the Eldorado. There was talk about women they knew, who was looking fine and who wasn't, and other idle conversation. Their chatter came to a quick end at 2:40 A.M. when the Polara crossed Broadway and a police car, lights flashing, pulled up next to it. A policeman motioned Artis to stop about six blocks north of Carter's house.

Artis pulled out his license as Sergeant Theodore Capter, flashlight in hand, approached the car. A second officer, Angelo DeChellis, walked behind the car and wrote down the license number, New York 5Z4 741. Artis handed over his driver's license but couldn't find the registration. "It's on the steering post, John," Carter said as he sat up in the back. Carter was relieved when he saw Capter, a short, graying officer who had been on the force for eighteen years and had always gotten along

with him. "Hey, how you doing, Hurricane?" Capter asked, flashing
his light in the back. "When's your next fight?"

"Soon," Carter said. "But what's wrong? Why did you stop us?"

"Oh, nothing, really. We're just looking for a white car with two
Negroes in it. But you're okay. Take care of yourself."

Carter shrugged off the incident. Unknown to him, a police radio
call had gone out a short while earlier indicating that a white car with
"two colored males" had left a shooting scene at the Lafayette Grill.
Capter and DeChellis had spotted a white car followed by a black car
speeding out of Paterson. The officers gave chase, jumping on Route
4 heading toward New York, but they never saw the cars again. So they
had returned to Paterson when they saw and stopped Carter's car.

Artis drove on to Carter's house, where Carter went inside, collected
about $100, and told Tee he was going back out. The trio returned to
the Nite Spot, which was closing down, so Carter instructed Artis to
drive to Club LaPetite, on Bridge Street, to look for Hardney. But they
discovered that that club too had closed; after sitting in the car for a
few minutes, Artis and Royster decided to call it a night.

Artis, who was still driving, dropped off Royster on Hamilton Street
sometime after 3 A.M. With Carter now in the front seat, he continued
down Hamilton, then turned right at East Eighteenth Street. At the
intersection of East Eighteenth and Broadway, Artis put on his right
blinker and waited for the signal to change. Suddenly, a patrol car came
screeching behind them. The cop hurriedly said something into his car
radio, opened his car door, and hustled over to the bewildered Artis
and Carter. Then they recognized Sergeant Capter again.

"Awww, shit, Hurricane, I didn't realize it was —" But before he
could finish, four other squealing police cars arrived at the intersection.
Someone else took charge and as Capter stepped away, Carter made
eye contact with him and said, "Aw, fuck!" Other officers, their guns
pulled, circled the Dodge. "Get out of that car," barked one cop. "No,
stay in the car," another yelled. After a few more moments of confusion,
an officer looked at Artis and pointed in the opposite direction on East
Eighteenth Street. "Follow that car," he yelled.

"What car?" Artis asked. But there was no time to talk. The sirens
went off and the police cars began to peel away. Artis turned the car
around and the cavalcade began racing up East Eighteenth. Artis had
never been arrested and had never had any trouble with the police.

Now he looked into his rearview mirror and saw a cop leaning out the window of the car behind them, pointing a shotgun at him. Artis felt his testicles tighten. "Damn, Rubin, damn! What's going on?" he yelled.

Carter was also petrified. He had no idea where they were heading, only that they had turned East Eighteenth Street into the crazy backstretch of a stock car race. He saw landmarks fly by. There was a cousin's home on the corner of East Eighteenth and Twelfth Avenue. There was the Nite Spot on the corner of East Eighteenth and Governor. But then the juggernaut sped beyond the black neighborhoods into unknown territory. Finally, the lead police car slowed down and made a sharp left turn at Lafayette Street, five blocks north of the Nite Spot. A crowd of people in the brightly lit intersection scattered as the pacer car screeched to a halt. The other vehicles followed suit.

Everything seemed to be in miniature. The streets were so narrow, the intersection so compressed, that any car whipping around a corner could easily crash into an apartment building or a warehouse. "What the fuck are we doing here?" Carter blurted. Neither he nor Artis had ever been inside the Lafayette bar; Carter had never even heard of the place. *These are not my digs, but whatever went down, it had to be bad.*

A scene of chaos lay before them. An ambulance had pulled up next to the bar, where a bloodstained body was being hauled out on a stretcher beneath the neon tavern sign. The throng of mostly white bystanders, many in pajamas, robes, or housecoats, milled about the Dodge, parked on Lafayette Street and hemmed in by police cars. There was panicked crying and breathless cursing, the slap of slamming car doors, and the errant static of police radios. Whirling police lights gave the neighborhood's old brick buildings a garish red light as about twenty white cops, wearing stiff-brimmed caps, shields on their left breast, and bullet-lined belts, whispered urgently among one another.

The neighbors, some weeping, began to converge on the Dodge. Peering into the open windows, they looked at the two black men with anger and suspicion. Carter and Artis both sat frozen, unclear why they had been brought there but fearing for their lives. *This is how a black man in the South must feel when a white mob is about to lynch him,* Carter thought, *and the law is going to turn its head.* Finally, a grim police officer approached Artis.

"Get out of the car."

"Do you want me to take the keys out?"

"Leave the keys."

Then another officer intervened. "Bring the keys and open the trunk!"

"No problem," Artis said.

As Artis headed to the rear of the car, Carter hesitated. *If I get out of this car, it could be the worst mistake I've ever made.* Artis opened the trunk, and a cop rummaged through Carter's boxing gloves, shoes, headgear, and gym bag.

Another officer motioned to Carter to step out. Carter opened the door, but he had held his tongue long enough. "What the hell did you bring us here for, man?"

"Shut up," the officer shouted as he cocked the pistol. "Just get up against the wall and shut up, and don't move until I tell you to."

As Carter and Artis walked toward the bar at the corner of Lafayette and East Eighteenth, a hush settled over the crowd. With bystanders forming a semicircle around the two men, Carter and Artis stood facing a yellow wall bathed in the glare from headlights. Artis turned his right shoulder and searched for a familiar face, maybe someone from racially mixed Central High School, his alma mater, but he saw only white strangers. The police frisked them brusquely but found nothing on them or in Carter's car or trunk. Another ambulance arrived, and Artis felt the hair on his neck rise when he saw another body, draped in a white sheet, roll past him on a stretcher.

Finally, a paddy wagon pulled up and someone shouted, "Get in!" Carter and Artis stepped inside and were whisked away. Sitting by themselves, the two men were once again speeding through Paterson, heading to the police headquarters downtown. No one had asked them any questions or accused them of anything. They could see the driver through a screen divider but were otherwise isolated. "Something terrible is going on, but what's it got to do with us?" Artis asked.

Carter, disgusted, told him to stay calm. "Don't volunteer anything, but if someone asks you any questions, tell them the truth. The cops are just playing with me, as usual. It'll all be cleared up soon."

The paddy wagon stopped downtown, and the doors swung open at police headquarters. Built in 1902 after a devastating fire wiped out much of Paterson, the building is a hulking Victorian structure with dark oak desks and wide stairways. But Carter and Artis had barely gotten inside when there was another commotion. "Get back in!" someone shouted, and the two men returned to the wagon, which peeled off again. Now they headed on a beeline south on Main Street, eventually stopping at St. Joseph's Hospital, Paterson's oldest, where plainclothes detectives were waiting. Carter and Artis were hustled out of the truck and into the emergency room. Everything seemed white, the walls and curtains, the patients' gowns and nurses' uniforms, the floor tile and bedsheets. The room had that doomy hospital smell of ether and bedpans and disinfectant. The only patient was a balding white man lying on a gurney, a bloody bandage around his head, an intravenous tube rising from his arm, and a doctor working at his side.

"Can he talk?" asked one of the detectives, Sergeant Robert Callahan.

The doctor, annoyed at the intrusion, shot a disapproving glance at the detective, then at Carter and Artis. "He can talk, but only for a moment." The doctor lifted the lacerated head of William Marins, shot in the Lafayette bar. The bullet had exited near his left eye, which was now an open, serrated cut. He was pallid and weak.

"Can you see clearly?" Callahan asked the one-eyed man. "Can you make out these two men's faces?"

Marins nodded his head feebly. Callahan pointed to Artis. "Go over and stand next to the bed." Artis walked over.

"Is this the man who shot you?" Callahan asked.

Marins paused, then slowly shook his head from side to side. Callahan then motioned for Carter to step forward. "What about him?"

Again, Marins shook his head.

"But, sir, are you *sure* these are not the men?" Callahan asked in a harder voice. "Look carefully now."

Carter had been relieved when the injured man seemed to clear him and Artis. But now he concluded the police were going to do whatever they could to pin this shooting on them. Previous assault charges against Carter had been dismissed. Police surveillance had yielded little. Now, this: pell-mell excursions through the night, an angry mob outside a strange bar, a one-eyed man lying in agony, and Carter an inexplicable suspect. He had had enough. As Marins continued to shake his head, Carter closed his eyes, clenched his fists, and spilled his boiling rage. "Dirty sonofabitch!" he yelled. "Dirty motherfucker!"

Back at police headquarters, in the detective bureau, Carter found himself in a windowless interrogation room. It was familiar ground.

He had been questioned in the same room twenty years earlier for stealing clothing at an outdoor market. (His father had turned him in.) Two battered metal chairs and a table sat beneath a cracked, dirty ceiling. Artis was left to stew in a separate room, which had green walls, a naked light bulb, and a one-way mirror in the door. Artis could see, between the door and the floor, the black rubber soles of the officers outside his door. He knew they were watching him.

Both men lingered in their separate rooms for several hours, their alcoholic buzz long worn off. They simply felt exhaustion. At around 11 A.M., the door to Carter's room opened and Lieutenant Vincent DeSimone, Jr., walked in. The two men had a history. DeSimone joined the Paterson Police Department in 1947 and had been one of the officers who questioned the teenage Carter after he assaulted the man at the swimming hole. DeSimone was a coarse and intimidating old-school cop, who would quip about suspects, "He's so crooked, they'll have to bury him standing up." A relentless interrogator, he was known for his ability to elicit confessions through threats and promises. He would do anything for a confession, including pulling out a string of rosary beads to bestir a guilty conscience. He hated the 1966 *Miranda* decision, in which the U.S. Supreme Court ruled that no confession can be used against a criminal defendant who was not advised of his rights. The ruling, DeSimone feared, gave confessed criminals a loophole.*

In the 1950s he joined the Passaic County Prosecutor's Office as a detective specializing in homicides, and he was known for keeping index cards in his pocket so he wouldn't have to carry a notebook. His bosses viewed him as the finest law enforcement official in the state, their own Javert, and his power and reputation were unquestioned.

But on the streets of Paterson's black community, DeSimone had a different reputation entirely, for he embodied the racist, bullying tactics of an overbearing police force. His confessions had less to do with gumshoe police work than with intimidation, and he was feared. Frankly, he looked scary. In World War II he had taken a grenade blast in the face, and despite several surgeries, his jowly visage was disfigured. A scar inched across his upper lip, which was pulled tightly back, and

* The *Miranda* decision had been issued only days before the Lafayette bar murders. DeSimone testified that he gave Carter his *Miranda* warning, which Carter denies.

drool sometimes gathered at the side of his mouth. He had thick eyeglasses, spoke in a gravelly voice, and wore an open sport jacket across his thick, hard gut, revealing his low-slung holster.

DeSimone was tense when he entered Carter's holding room. He had been awakened at 6 A.M. with news of the shooting, and he stopped off at the crime scene before going to the police station. Despite his many years in police work, this was his first interrogation for a multiple homicide.

"I'm Lieutenant DeSimone, Rubin. You know me." He sat down heavily and pulled out his pen and paper.

"You can answer these questions or not," he continued. "That's strictly up to you. But I'm going to record whatever you say. Just remember this. There's a dark cloud hanging over your head, and I think it would be wise for you to clear it up."

"You're the only dark cloud hanging over my head," Carter said.

DeSimone was joined by two or three other officers. Over the next couple of hours, Carter recounted his whereabouts on the previous night, from the time he left his home after watching the James Brown special to his two encounters with Sergeant Capter. He mentioned his trip to Annabelle Chandler's and various club stops. When DeSimone finally told Carter that four people had been shot, Carter waved off the suspicion: "I don't use guns, I use my fists. How many times have you arrested me around here for using my fists? I don't use guns."

Carter was certain the interrogation was just another example of police harassment for his bellicose reputation. He felt his position on fighting was well known to DeSimone and the other officers: he would fight only if provoked. He did not imagine that even an old antagonist like DeSimone would consider him a suspect for killing people inside a bar he had never entered.

During the questioning, DeSimone shuttled back and forth between Carter and Artis in parallel interrogations. It was more difficult to write down the answers from Artis, who spoke faster. DeSimone also told Artis that "there was a dark cloud hanging over you," but he said the young man had a way out. "When two people commit a murder, you know who gets the short end of the stick? The guy who doesn't have a record, and you don't have a record. That's the guy they really stick it to. Tell us what you know."

"I don't know anything," Artis said.

By midday Carter's wife heard he had been picked up, and she came to the station.

"Do you want me to call a lawyer?" Tee asked.

"What do I need a lawyer for?" Carter responded. "I didn't do anything, so I'll be out of here shortly."

Later, while Carter was heading to the bathroom, he was taken past several witnesses who supposedly saw the assailants fleeing the crime scene. One was Alfred Bello, a squat, chunky former convict who was outside the bar when the police arrived. He told police at the crime scene that he had seen two gunmen, "one colored male . . . thin build, five foot eleven inches. Second colored male, thin build, five foot eleven inches." Another was Patricia Graham, a thin, angular brunette who lived on the second floor above the bar and said she saw two black men in sport coats run from the bar after the shooting and drive off in a white car. Both Bello and Graham would later provide critical testimony in the state's case against Carter, giving different accounts from those in their initial statements.

A police officer asked the group of witnesses if they recognized Carter. "Yeah, he's the prizefighter," someone said. Asked if he had been spotted fleeing the crime scene, the witness shook his head.

After DeSimone completed his questioning of Carter, he gathered up his papers. "That's good enough for the time being, but there's one thing more that I'd like to ask. Would you be willing to submit to a lie detector test?"

"And a paraffin test, too," Carter said without hesitation. "But not if any of these cops down here are going to give it to me. You get somebody else who knows what he's doing."

At 2:30 P.M., Sergeant John J. McGuire, a polygraph examiner from the Elizabeth Police Department, met Carter in a separate room. A barrel-chested man with short hair, McGuire had just been told about the shootings, and he was in no mood for small talk. "Carter, let me tell you something before you sit down and take this test," he said in a tight voice. "If you have anything to hide that you don't want me to know, then don't take it, because this machine is going to tell me about it. And if I find anything indicating that you had *anything* to do with the killing of those people, I'm going to make sure your ass burns to a bacon rind."

"Fuck you, man, and give me the goddamn thing."

McGuire wrapped a wired strap around Carter's chest, and Carter put his fingers in tiny suction cups. He answered a series of yes-or-no questions and returned to his holding room. After another delay, McGuire showed up and laid out a series of charts tracking his responses. DeSimone and several other officers were there as well. Pointing to the lines on the chart, McGuire declared, "He didn't participate in these crimes, but he may know who was involved."

"Is that so?" DeSimone asked.

"No, but I can find out for you," Carter said.

Sixteen hours after they had been stopped by the police, Carter and Artis were released from the police station. Carter was given his car keys and went to the police garage, only to find that the car's paneling, dashboard, and seats had been ripped out. The following day, June 18, Assistant County Prosecutor Vincent E. Hull told the *Paterson Morning Call* that Carter had never been a suspect. Eleven days later Carter, as well as Artis, testified before a Passaic County grand jury about the Lafayette bar murders. DeSimone testified that both men passed their lie detector tests and that neither man fit the description of the gunmen. Notwithstanding the adage that a prosecutor can indict a ham sandwich — prosecutors are given a wide berth to introduce evidence to show probable cause — the prosecutor in the Lafayette bar murders failed to indict anyone. Carter traveled to Argentina and lost his fight against Rocky Rivero. The promoter never did give him a sparring partner. The thought flashed through Carter's head that he should just stay in Argentina, which had no extradition treaty with the United States. That way, the Paterson police would no longer be able to hassle him. Instead he returned home.

On October 14, 1966, Carter was picked up by the police and charged with the Lafayette bar murders.

4

MYSTERY WITNESS

IT WAS THE BREAK everyone had been waiting for. On October 14, 1966, the front page of the *Paterson Evening News* screamed the headline: "Mystery Witness in Triple Slaying Under Heavy Guard." A three-column photograph, titled "Early Morning Sentinels," showed tense police officers in front of the Alexander Hamilton Hotel on Church Street guarding the "mystery witness." An unnamed hotel employee said he saw the police hustle a "short man" into an elevator the day before at 6 P.M. The elevator stopped on the fifth floor, where a red-haired woman was seen peering out from behind a raised shade.

The newspaper story raised as many questions as it answered, but the high drama indicated that a breakthrough had occurred in the notorious Lafayette bar murders, now four months old. Excitement swirled around the Hamilton, where a patrol car was parked in front with two officers inside, shotguns at the ready. Roaming behind the hotel were seven more officers, guarding the rear entrance. A police spotlight held a bright beam on an adjoining building's fire escape, lest an intruder use it to gain access to the Hamilton. Two more shotgun-toting cops stood inside the rear entrance, and detectives roamed the lobby. Overseeing the security measures, according to the newspaper, was Mayor Frank Graves.

John Artis saw the headline and thought nothing of it. He assumed he had been cleared of any suspicion of the Lafayette bar shooting after he testified before the grand jury in June and no indictments had been issued. At the time, Artis was at a crossroads in his own life. His mother had died from a kidney ailment a month after he graduated from

Central High School in 1964. Mary Eleanor Artis was only forty-four years old, and her death had devastated John, an only child. He knocked around Paterson for several years, working as a truck driver and living with his father on Tyler Street. In high school, he had been a solid student and a star in two sports, track and football, and he sang in the choir at the New Christian Missionary Baptist Church. He had giddy dreams of playing wide receiver for the New York Titans (later known as the New York Jets). He also had a bad habit of driving fast and reckless — he banged up no fewer than eight cars — but he had no criminal record and never had any problems with the police. Neither of his parents had gone to college, and they desperately wanted their only child to go. By the fall of 1966, Artis had been notified by the Army that he had been drafted to serve in Vietnam, but he was trying to avoid service by winning a track scholarship to Adams State College in Alamosa, Colorado, where his high school track coach had connections.

On October 14, dusk had settled by the time Artis finished work. It was Friday, the night before his twentieth birthday, and an evening of dancing and partying lay ahead. He stopped at a dry cleaner's to pick up some shirts, then went into Laramie's liquor store on Tyler Street to buy an orange soda and a bag of chips. He and his father lived above the store. As he was paying for the soda, the door of the liquor store swung open. "Freeze, Artis!" a cop yelled. "You're under arrest!"

Artis saw two shotguns and a handgun pointed at him. "For what?" he demanded.

"For the Lafayette bar murders!"

"Get outta here!"

Police bullying of blacks in Paterson was so common that Artis thought this was more of the same, an ugly prank. But then two officers began patting him down around his stomach and back pockets. Artis handed his clean shirts to the liquor store clerk and told him to take them to his father. His wrists were then cuffed behind his back. *Damn,* Artis thought, *these guys are serious!* On his way out of Laramie's, Artis yelled his father's name: "JOHHHHN ARTIS!" As he was shoved into a police car, Artis saw his father's stricken face appear in the second-story window.

Rubin Carter was at Club LaPetite when one of Artis's girlfriends approached him with the news: John had been arrested.

"For what?" Carter asked.

"I don't know, they just arrested him."

Like Artis, Carter had seen the "Mystery Witness" headline in the newspaper but hadn't given it a second thought, and he didn't connect the headline to Artis's arrest. Carter, distrustful of the police, feared for Artis's safety, so he got into his Eldorado and drove to police headquarters to check up on the young man. As he neared the station, he put his foot on the brake; then, out of nowhere, detectives on foot and in unmarked cars swarmed around his car.

"Don't move! Put your hands on the wheel! Don't move!"

Here we go again, was all Carter could think. But this police encounter proved to be much more harrowing than his June confrontation. His hands were quickly cuffed behind his back, and he was shoved into the back seat of an unmarked detective's car. According to Carter, the officers did not tell him why they had stopped him or what he was being charged with. Instead, with detectives on either side of him, the car doors slammed shut and the vehicle sped away, followed by several other unmarked cars. Carter had no idea where they were going, or why. Soon the caravan headed up Garrett Mountain, cruising past the evergreens and maple trees. Even at night Carter knew the winding roads because he often rode his horse on the mountain. The motorcade finally came to a stop along a dark road, and there they sat. Detectives holding their shotguns milled around, and Carter heard the crackling of the car radios and officers speaking in code. They did not ask him any questions. *Damn! They're going to kill me.* They sat for at least an hour, then Carter heard on the car radio: "Okay, bring him in." He always assumed that someone had talked the detectives out of shooting him.

At headquarters, Carter was met by Lieutenant DeSimone and by Assistant County Prosecutor Vincent E. Hull. It was Hull who spoke: "We are arresting you for the murders of the Lafayette bar shooting. You have the right to remain silent . . ." The time was 2:45 A.M. Unknown to Carter, Artis had also been taken to Garrett Mountain, held for more than an hour, then returned to headquarters and arrested for the murders. The *Evening News* said the arrests "capped a cloak-and-dagger maneuver masterminded by Mayor Graves," who grandly praised his police department: "Our young, aggressive, hard-working department brought [the case] to its present conclusion."

Some nettlesome questions remained. Though the police searched the city's gutters and fields and dragged the Passaic River, they never found the murder weapons. The authorities were also not divulging *why* Carter and Artis killed three people. Robbery had already been ruled out, and the *Evening News* reported on October 16 that the police had determined there was no connection between the Roy Holloway murder and the Lafayette bar shooting. Such details were unimportant. The *Morning News* rejoiced at the arrest, trumpeting on the same day that the newspaper "exclusively broke the news that the four-month-old tavern murders were solved."

Carter figured his arrest was tied to the November elections. Mayor Graves, prohibited by law from running for a fourth consecutive term, was hoping to hand the job over to his chosen successor, John Wegner. What better way to show that the city was under control than by solving the most heinous crime in its history? After the election, Carter reckoned he'd be set free.*

But sitting in the Passaic County Jail, where each day he was served jelly sandwiches, Carter learned through the jailhouse grapevine that two hostile witnesses had emerged. Alfred Bello, the former con who had been at headquarters following the crime, and Arthur Dexter Bradley, another career criminal, were near the Lafayette bar trying to rob a warehouse on the night of the murders. Questioned by the police that night, Bello said he could not identify the assailants. But suddenly his memory had improved. Both Bello and Bradley now told police that they had witnessed Carter and Artis fleeing the crime scene.

The Passaic County Prosecutor's Office took the case to a special grand jury empaneled in the basement of the YMCA, convened to investigate the sensational killing of a young housewife named Judy Kavanaugh. On November 30, Carter heard a radio report on the loudspeakers in jail that the grand jury had indicted Kavanaugh's husband for the murder. Paul Kavanaugh was in a cell near Carter's. Then, almost as an afterthought, the announcer said: "Rubin 'Hurricane' Carter and John Artis were also indicted for the Lafayette bar slayings."

The twining of the Kavanaugh and the Lafayette bar murders fueled rumors for many years to come. Speculation centered on the role that

---

* Even with Carter in jail, Wegner lost to the reform candidate, Lawrence Kramer.

the mob may have played in persuading the prosecutor's office to pursue enemies of the underworld. The Mafia connection was more direct in the Kavanaugh case. Eight months after the killing, a small-time hood named Johnny "the Walk" DeFranco died from a slit throat, the victim of a gangland-style murder. Prosecutors put forth a theory that Judy Kavanaugh had been involved in a counterfeiting and pornography ring and was silenced when she panicked, while DeFranco was later killed to keep him silent about her death. Five people were ultimately indicted for one or both crimes, including Harold Matzner, the young publisher of a suburban newspaper company in New Jersey. He had backed a series of articles that tried to link the Passaic County Prosecutor's Office to the underworld. All the defendants in both crimes, including Matzner, were ultimately acquitted amid allegations of witness tampering and gross misconduct inside the prosecutor's office.*

Carter's indictment also generated discussion about the underworld in Paterson. Mobsters had approached Carter about throwing fights, but he had always refused. In theory, this would give the mob an incentive to turn against him — just as the mob had an incentive to turn against Harold Matzner. Rumors circulated that mobsters, seeking vengeance against Carter, gave the prosecutor's office conclusive evidence of his guilt, but the evidence could never be introduced because of its origins. The rumor is fantastic, but it gained some currency over the years as prosecutors, seemingly armed with little direct proof of guilt against Carter or Matzner, pursed each man with zeal. Other unsettling parallels between the Kavanaugh and Lafayette bar murders would surface in time.

When Carter heard about his indictment on the radio, he was shocked. Even though he had hired a lawyer, he still believed that the authorities planned to release him. But after being jailed for about six weeks, he guessed that prosecutors sought the indictment against him because they feared a possible lawsuit against Passaic County for false arrest. (Carter had no such intention.) If a jury returned a verdict of not guilty, prosecutors could say they had done their best with the

---

* In a letter to Governor Richard Hughes in 1968, F. Lee Bailey, who represented Matzner, wrote: "I have never, in any state or federal court, seen abuses of justice, legal ethics, and constitutional rights such as this case has involved."

evidence they had. Carter's shock soon gave way to fury and fear. He was now trapped in jail until his trial. With little to do, he began writing letters to people who had seen him on the night of June 16 and who could serve as his alibi witnesses.

To those who knew Carter, the accusation didn't make sense. His friends and family believed he *was* capable of killing three people, but not in the fashion of the Lafayette bar murders. Despite his inflammatory comments in the *Saturday Evening Post,* Carter was known for advocating self-defense, specifically against police harassment. Violence was justified, indeed necessary, against aggressors, he argued, but not against innocent bystanders. Why would he walk into an inoffensive bar and shoot a room full of strangers? It never made sense, and the authorities offered no explanation.

Moreover, when Carter did exact revenge and lash out, he used only his fists. The rules of the streets were clear. Punks and sissies used guns or knives; warriors used their fists. If Carter wanted to punish or even kill someone, he would consider it an insult to his manhood if he did not use his bare hands. He would want the victim to *know* that it was "Hurricane" Carter meting out his punishment. Carter owned and occasionally carried guns, but that was because of his own fears — perhaps exaggerated, perhaps not — that he would be shot at. What is clear is that until the Lafayette bar murders, no one had ever accused Carter of pointing a gun at another person.

The Lafayette bar shooting "wasn't Rubin's style," said Martin Barnes, an acquaintance of Carter's who was elected mayor of Paterson in the 1990s. "If you were bad, you did it with your hands, and Rubin did it strictly with his hands."

Carter initially wanted F. Lee Bailey to represent him, but the famed defense lawyer was already embroiled in the Kavanaugh case, so instead he hired Raymond Brown from Newark. Brown was known for being the only black lawyer in the state to take on whites. He did not, at first glance, look like a dragon slayer in his rumpled brown and gray suits, Ben Franklin-type bifocals, and a plaid hat. He smoked a pipe and ambled around in a kind of slouch, as if he were getting ready to sit down after every step. But he was an expansive orator whose voice filled a courtroom, a firebrand with a rapier wit. In his fifties, he had short, dust-colored hair and a high yellow complexion; in fact, he was light enough to pass for white. When he was in the Army, an officer candidate once told him, "Be careful, some people will think you're a nigger." "I am!" Brown shot back.

The trial against Carter and Artis took place at the Passaic County Court on Hamilton Street, where grandeur and tradition welcomed every visitor. Completed just after the turn of the century, the building featured large white Corinthian columns and a ribbed dome with a columned cupola; on it stood a blindfolded woman holding the scales of justice. In the courtroom where Carter was tried, the judge's large dark wood desk stood on a platform in dignified splendor. On the desk lay a black Bible with its red-edged pages facing the gallery. An American flag stood to the side.

Paterson was a tinderbox as jury selection began on April 7, 1967. The establishment was terrified that blacks would riot if the defendants were found guilty. Black youths had rioted three summers before, and a conviction of Paterson's most celebrated, most feared, most hated black man could trigger another firestorm. To quell any possible disturbance, the courthouse was transformed into a fortress, with extra uniformed and plainclothes police perched in the building's halls and stairwells, on the streets outside, and on neighborhood rooftops. The roads around the building were blocked off. The authorities questioned known troublemakers and even rummaged through garbage cans in search of contraband. According to an internal FBI report dated May 27, 1967, an informant told the agency that in the "Negro district, five large garbage cans were filled with empty wine and beer bottles and some beer cans ... and these might be a source of Molotov cocktails ... and this condition could be caused by the feeling of people regarding the Carter-Artis trial."

Presiding was Samuel Larner, an experienced New Jersey lawyer who had recently been appointed to the Superior Court in Essex County and had already developed a reputation as a no-nonsense judge. Larner gained widespread acclaim in the 1950s when he spearheaded an investigation of government corruption in Jersey City. The inquest triggered more than fifty indictments, culminating in the suicide of one employee and the resignation of several others. Sam Larner knew Ray Brown well. The two men were co-counsel for John William Butenko, an American engineer, and Igor Ivanov, a Soviet national, who just a few years earlier had been convicted of conspiracy to commit espionage.

Judge Larner had been reassigned from Essex to Passaic County, evidently because Passaic was either experiencing a shortage of judges or a backlog of cases. Carter always suspected he had been reassigned to keep Ray Brown under control. Larner intervened often when Brown was pressing witnesses, and their jousting was a running sideshow during the trial.

Each day during the voir dire, for example, the proceedings lasted into the early evening. Then one afternoon Judge Larner abruptly rose at 4 P.M. and declared, "The court is adjourned." The stunned courtroom silently watched the judge walk toward his chamber. Suddenly, Ray Brown stood up.

"Judge Larner!"

"What is it now, Mr. Brown?"

"Tell me, Judge Larner, why is this night different from all other nights?"

It was the first night of the Jewish holiday of Passover, and the judge needed to get home. He first glared at Brown for his effrontery in questioning a judge's decision to end the day prematurely. Then he realized Brown's clever invocation of a line from the Passover Seder. Larner smiled at his former colleague and continued out the door.

Carter, however, found little to smile about. He had never been on trial before. When he did something wrong, he owned up to it, as he had ten years earlier when he pled guilty to robbery and assault. Carter figured he was in trouble during jury selection, a three-week ordeal that saw one potential juror dismissed for being a member of Hitler's youth movement in Germany and another for believing that blacks who grew up in ghettos were more prone to violence. Despite such efforts, the jury that was selected comprised four white women, nine white men, and one black man — a West Indian. Fourteen jurors in all, two of whom would be selected as alternates at the end of the trial. *This was a jury of my peers?* Carter thought. *Aside from being a different color than all but one of them, I probably had more education than any person sitting on the jury, and even I didn't understand a damn thing that was going on.*

The prosecuting attorney was Vincent Hull, the son of a state legislator, whose precise, low-key manner contrasted sharply with Brown's showmanship. Hull was young, slim, and conservatively dressed with prematurely gray hair. In his opening statement, he described how the

two defendants, after circling the bar in Carter's 1966 Dodge, parked
the car, walked into the Lafayette bar, and without uttering a word
"premeditatedly, deliberately, and willfully" shot four people, killing
three of them. Hull meticulously described the victims and their wounds
and asserted that Detective Emil DeRobbio found an unspent 12-gauge
shotgun shell and an unspent .32 S&W long bullet in Carter's car. Those
were the same kinds of bullets, Hull said, used in the bar shooting.
When Hull completed his opening, he thanked the jury and sat down.

Judge Larner turned to the defense table. "Mr. Brown," he said.

Ray Brown rose from the table, his glasses perched on his nose and
a legal document in his hand. While the prosecutor had not mentioned
race except as it related to the identification of the suspects, Brown
argued that Carter stood accused because the police were looking for
a Negro on the night in question, and therefore every Negro was suspect.
Brown told the jury that Carter didn't know what happened in the
bar and refuted Hull's assertions point by point, including the alleged
discovery of bullets in the Dodge. If the police actually found the bullets
on the night of the crime, Brown asked, why wasn't Carter arrested
then instead of four months later?

To convict, the state needed a unanimous vote of guilt from the jurors,
so Brown's strategy was to direct his entire defense to the West Indian
juror, hoping to persuade him that the state was victimizing his client.
"Any man can be accused," Brown thundered, "but no man should have
his nerves shredded and his guts torn out without a direct charge."

"Mr. Brown!" Judge Larner exploded. "I don't want to interrupt
you, but I think it is time you limited yourself to the facts to be shown,
and let's get beyond the speeches on philosophy."

"This is not philosophy, Your Honor. This is a fact."

The state's first witness, William Marins, who lost his left eye in the
shooting, set the tone for the trial. Carter had hoped that Marins, a
balding, stocky man in his forties who was the lone survivor of the
tragedy, would convince the jurors that he and Artis were not the
gunmen in the same way he had convinced the police at St. Joseph's
Hospital after the shooting. Marins was now an unemployed machinist
— and an unsympathetic witness. He told the court that on the night
of the crime, he had been shooting pool and drinking beer with another
patron, Fred Nauyoks. Also in the bar were Jim Oliver, the bartender,
and Hazel Tanis. Suddenly, two colored men entered the place between

two-thirty and three o'clock in the morning, shooting everyone inside. One gunman, with a mustache, swung a shotgun. The other, standing directly behind him, had a pistol. Marins said he felt a sharp pain in the left side of his head, noticed smoke curling out of the shotgun barrel, and passed out. When he awoke, "I was bleeding and bleeding and bleeding. I waited for the police to come."

Throughout the questioning, Marins emphasized that he was in a state of shock after the shooting and was in no condition to identify the gunmen. By the time Brown began his cross-examination, it was clear Marins was not about to exonerate Rubin Carter and John Artis.

"Do you feel like testifying some more, Mr. Marins," Brown asked, "or would you like a glass of water?"

"No," Marins snapped.

"You gave a statement to the police about what happened in this place, did you not?"

"Yes, but I was in a state of —"

"I didn't ask you, sir —" Brown said.

Judge Larner interrupted. "Just answer the particular question, Mr. Marins."

Brown produced numerous official statements that Marins had given about the shooting, one as late as October 20, 1966. "Now, you repeatedly told these officers, did you not, that [the gunmen] were thin, tall, light-skinned Negroes, didn't you?"

"I said they were colored," Marins protested.

Carter, of course, was short, thickly built and black as soot, so Brown homed in on Marins's previous descriptions, which seemed to have ruled Carter out as a suspect. Shuffling between the witness stand and the defense table, Brown noted that his description matched that of Hazel Tanis, who told police before she died that the gunmen were about six feet tall, slimly built, light-complexioned and had pencil-thin mustaches. Isn't that the same description you gave? Brown asked Marins.

"No!" Marins insisted. "I told [the police] the man had a dark mustache, or well, it was a mustache. I didn't look at him that long . . . I was in a state of shock."

Brown had one more card to play. "Your Honor, please. At this time I would like to ask that Your Honor unseal depositions given by this man in a civil suit brought by him in January of 1967."

Carter had no idea what was going on.

"Mr. Marins," Brown said, "do you know that you are the plaintiff in an action against Elizabeth Paraglia owner of the Lafayette Grill?"

"True."

"Do you recall having testified in depositions taken before a notary public . . . on December 16, 1966?"

"True."

"Do you recall signing these depositions and stating under oath they were true?"

"True."

"You were out of the hospital?"

"True."

"You had been discharged?"

"True."

"Your health then permitted you to go to a lawyer's office and give depositions, is that correct?"

"True."

"Your lawyer was present?"

"True."

Brown bored in. "You were asked, 'Did you recognize the men who shot you?' Your answer: 'I know they were colored, light-colored, and one in particular, the first one with a shotgun, had a mustache that I just happened to see, and the man in back of him was about the same height.' Did you give him that answer?"

"True," Marins replied meekly.

"You were asked, 'How tall are they?' You said, 'Six feet, maybe five eleven, six feet.' Is that correct?"

"Well, I said six feet. Maybe."

"Isn't it a fact that you told Detective Callahan six feet, slim build, sir?"

"When was this?"

"June 17, 1966, in the emergency room."

"I don't remember because I was in a state of shock."

"Were you in a state of shock in December 1966?"

The judge had seen enough. "He said no, and he doesn't remember what he told Detective Callahan, whether it is the same or not."

Brown had cut Marins to shreds, but there was no joy at the defense table. The lone survivor had inexplicably changed the very statements that had once helped clear Carter and Artis of suspicion, and Carter quietly seethed.

Despite his renowned temper, Carter remained calm during the proceedings. Hundreds of times he had to stand up before prospective jurors to be identified, but he never balked or showed any annoyance. The *Evening News* said he acquired the stance of a "mild-mannered student." His wife brought him a clean suit and dress shirt every night at the jail, and throughout the trial he took copious notes on a yellow legal pad. Only once did Carter vent his rage in the courtroom. His nemesis, Vincent DeSimone, sat next to Hull at the prosecutor's table. During one recess, Carter's daughter wandered over to the table and began playing and laughing with the lieutenant. Carter bolted out of his seat and grabbed the three-year-old.

"Come here," he said. "You don't talk to this punk. He's trying to put your father in jail."

DeSimone leaned back and smiled.

"Fuck you, you fat pig," Carter said. "You leave my daughter alone."

The state had little evidence linking Carter and Artis to the shooting. The police had neglected to brush the Lafayette bar for fingerprints or conduct paraffin tests on the defendants' hands after they were picked up. There were no footprints, no bloodstains, no murder weapons, no motive. There was conflicting testimony about Carter's car. One witness, Patricia Graham Valentine (Patricia Graham at the time of the shooting), lived in an apartment above the bar. She said Carter's white Dodge "looked like" the getaway car; both cars had triangular, butterfly-type taillights. But another witness, Ronnie Ruggiero, also saw the getaway car and testified that he thought it was a white Chevy, not a white Dodge. Ruggiero, a white boxer, had driven in Carter's Dodge Polara before. Then there were the bullets. Detective DeRobbio testified that he found a .32-caliber S&W lead bullet and a Super X Wesson 12-gauge shotgun shell in Carter's car. But ballistics experts testified that the bullets found at the crime scene were .32 S&W long *copper-coated* bullets and Remington Express *plastic* shells. The bullets in Carter's car were indisputably different from those used in the crime, but Judge Larner allowed the lead bullet into evidence because it *could* have been fired from a .32-caliber pistol. The same could have been said for the 12-gauge shell, but Larner still excluded that as evidence. His logic confounded the defense team.

The state's case rested on the shoulders of its two eyewitnesses, Alfred Bello and Arthur Dexter Bradley. As a thief, Bello was more pathetic than petty. By the age of twenty-three, he had already been convicted five times on various charges of burglary and robbery. In one instance, he robbed a woman of a makeup case valued at one dollar, a cigarette case valued at two dollars, and a pocketbook valued at twenty dollars. Carter assumed that the reward for his conviction, now up to $12,500, looked mighty tempting compared to such nickel-and-dime thieving. A heavy drinker who had threatened his classmates with a penknife in grade school, Bello had spent so much time in Paterson's police headquarters that DeSimone's secretary referred to him as the lieutenant's adopted son. Bello was short and fat with greased-back hair. He talked too loud and he wore high-heeled shoes. He had a tattoo on his right arm that read: "Born to Raise Hell." He had been discharged from the Army for fraudulent enlistment. He had also been in state reformatories off and on for several years, and he was out on parole when the Lafayette bar shooting occurred. At the time of the murders, he was serving as "chickie," or lookout, for Bradley's break-in at the Ace Sheet Metal Company.

He was the state's "mystery witness."

Bello took the stand with an air of insouciant invincibility, basking in the spotlight of his sudden fame. In his answers to Hull's questions, he gave his account of the night in question. While waiting for Bradley to break into the warehouse with a tire iron, Bello said he saw a white Dodge driving around the block with three colored men inside. He thought he saw something sticking up between one of their legs that looked like a rifle barrel. Then he decided he wanted a cigarette, so he walked to the Lafayette bar to buy a pack. As he walked toward the tavern, he heard two shots, then two shots more, then he saw two colored fellows walking around the corner, talking loud and laughing. One had a shotgun, the other a pistol. They were fourteen feet away and saw Bello, but Bello ran to safety. So the gunmen drove away in their white car. The two men, Bello said, were Rubin Carter and John Artis.

Bello then walked to the bar and saw the bodies on the floor. He went to the cash register to get a dime to call the police; instead, he stole money from the register. He left the bar, gave the pilfered cash to Bradley, and then returned to the tavern because he feared a witness had seen him leaving the crime scene. He saw Carter and Artis when the police brought them to the bar and later at the police station, but under questioning by police, he did not identify them. Then in October, Bello gave another statement to police, claiming he saw the two defendants fleeing the crime scene. He said he did not identify them on the night of the murders because he feared that doing so would endanger him.

The lies, at least to Carter, were transparent. Why would a man engaged in a surreptitious criminal activity decide to walk to a bar and buy a pack of cigarettes? How could an overweight, high-heeled Bello elude a world-class professional athlete and a former high school track star? Why would testifying now put him in less danger than on the night of the murders? Why would Carter have let the police take him to the bar if he knew somebody had seen him? *Shit!* Carter thought. *I wouldn't have lost anything by killing the police too — if I had been the killer!*

Ray Brown's cross-examination entangled Bello in a thicket of half-truths and inconsistencies. Even the most innocuous inquiries caught Bello in lies.

"Where were you living in June of 1966?" Brown asked.

"One-thirty-eight Redwood Avenue," Bello answered.

"Did you tell the police on June 17, 1966, where you lived?" Brown asked.

"Yes."

"Where did you tell them you lived?"

"It had to be Redwood Avenue," he said.

"Would you look at this please." Brown showed him a written statement. "I show you S-40 for identification. Is there a date in the upper left-hand corner?" he asked.

"June 17, 1966," Bello said.

"Is that your signature?"

"Yes."

"What does it say with respect to your full name, age, and address?"

"Maple Avenue," Bello conceded.

"Where did you live in June of 1966?" Brown asked again.

"On Maple Avenue."

"You lived in Clifton?" Brown asked.

"Yes."

"You have difficulty recalling where you lived less than a year ago?"

"I'm not very good on dates," Bello said.

"You're not very good on memory either, are you," Brown snapped.

Bello conceded that he had lied to the police on the night of the murders when he said the assailants had chased him up the street; now he claimed the gunmen did not chase him at all — and he also tried to backpedal from his initial description of the men.

"You told, at the very scene, other police officers . . . that these men were of slim build, five eleven or so, is that correct?" Brown asked.

"I meant to say one was a little taller than the other," Bello said.

The witness said he could not recall exactly what he had told the police. Brown pulled out Bello's original police statement on the description of the two gunmen.

"Do you deny telling Officer Unger and Officer Greenough on the morning of the seventeenth of June, 1966, that one man was five eleven and the other was five eleven and that both were slim built? You deny that?"

"I don't deny anything. If it is there, it must be true."

Bello then tried to explain more fully what he did after he entered the bar. He did not have a dime to make a telephone call, he said, so he stepped over the bleeding dead body of Jim Oliver to reach the cash register. "I went in there to try to help, and when I went to the cash register to get that dime, basically I am a thief. I will admit that." With the courtroom in titters, he continued. "I did go to the cash register to get a dime, but when I seen this money, knowing myself, knowing that I am a thief, I did take some money. But I am not an assassin. Remember that."

With $62 of stolen cash in hand, Bello stepped back over Oliver's corpse and left the bar.

Bello was grilled on the witness stand for two days, and Ray Brown ended his interrogation with a flourish of indignation.

"When you stole that money from the cash register sitting behind the bar, did you have to pass by Hazel Tanis lying there on the floor begging for help?"

"Yes," Bello answered.

"And Mr. William Marins slumped on the barstool shot in the head?"

"Yes."

"And Fred Nauyoks lying dead at the bar?"

"Yes, Mr. Brown."

"Then you stepped over Jim Oliver lying dead behind the bar to get to the cash register. When did you do all of this, mister?"

"Do what?" Judge Larner intervened.

Brown whipped around and looked at the judge. "Slay the bartender," he said.

"What!" Judge Larner screamed.

"When did he slay the bartender?" Brown repeated. "That is addressed to him," pointing to Bello.

"Objection!" shouted the prosecutor.

"Answer that," the judge told Bello.

"It is not to my knowledge," the witness said defiantly.

"No further questions, *Your Honor,*" Brown snarled, stalking away. "Not to his knowledge," he said derisively as he passed the jury.

Arthur Dexter Bradley, a lanky, red-haired twenty-three-year-old, already had six convictions under his belt by the time of the trial. But unlike Bello, he was locked away in the Morris County Jail, and he had additional charges pending on four armed robberies. He was a poor thief and a worse prisoner: he had tried to escape from jail and failed. He testified that he recognized Carter running down Lafayette Street after the shooting, even though he had only seen Carter once before, two years earlier. Asked by Hull to point out the man he saw running down the street, Bradley pointed to Carter.

"Pointing where," Judge Larner asked. "Tell us again."

This time Bradley spoke. "That Negro right there."

That Negro, indeed. The dividing line of this trial had been clearly drawn, and it cut along race. The prosecutor and his staff were white. The investigators and police officers were white. The judge was white. The victims were white. Their family and friends in the courtroom were white. The state's witnesses were white. The jury, save one man, was white. The courtroom clerk was white. The courthouse guards were white, and the courthouse attendees were white. Rubin Carter was black, bald, and bearded. His co-defendant was black. His lawyer was black. His alibi witnesses were black. His family and friends who crowded the courtroom were black. Could a white juror look at that contrasting tableau and not be affected? Carter feared not. He believed that once a juror is called to serve the government, he takes on the mantle of the government. The juror is now part of a famous case. He is now part of the system, and he is going to do what the system wants. In Carter's mind, the juror thinks: Maybe the government didn't prove it, but they must know something. Otherwise, we wouldn't be here.

Carter kept his feelings about race to himself. In fact, he surprised both Brown and John Artis's lawyer, Arnold Stein, by not complaining of racial prejudice. "With Bello and Bradley, I'd say, 'Fuck these white sons-of-bitches,'" Brown recalled many years later. "Carter would say, 'They're sons of bitches,' but he wouldn't say they were white. To this day, I've never heard him say a racial epithet."

Carter and Artis both testified. Carter gave the same account of his whereabouts on the night of the murder that he had already given the police and grand jury. He took the stand wearing the same clothing he had worn that night, including his cream sport coat. Patricia Graham Valentine had testified that she saw two well-dressed Negroes in dark clothes fleeing the bar.

After two and a half weeks of testimony, Ray Brown, in his closing argument, shambled over to the jury box and made clear what he thought this trial was all about: race. He started slowly, noting that the jurors needed to be guided by reason, "not passion, not prejudice, not bias. Reason. Reason. Reason." He ticked off Carter's alibi witnesses, who said they were around him between two and two-thirty on the night of the crime, then he reared back and lit into Bello and Bradley. He reminded the jury of the witnesses' criminal records and that Bello in particular offered testimony that contradicted his previous statements. Is it not reasonable, Brown said, to assume that Bello "is testifying for hope, for favor?" He called Bello and Bradley "jackals" and "ghouls," said the judge had prevented him from implying that they were responsible for the murders, but "I will imply with all my might" that they were somehow involved.

"Remember what [Bradley] said. It will remain with me forever for a special reason. I remember . . . he said, 'That Negro over there.' What is that, an animal? Well, I will tell you, in his voice it was there, and everything around this case revolves around that simple fact. They were Negro . . ."

Brown told the jury that his client had lived since 1957 "without a blemish" and that he "is now a human being standing in fear of his life . . . Can you believe that this man who did not run, who did not hide, did this, did these things? How can you believe this . . . ?" Almost three hours into his summation, Brown reiterated that Carter did not fit the description of the killers; then, exhausted and with tears in his eyes, he closed by denouncing the courtroom proceeding and the city of Paterson.

"This is probably the last place in the entire world where a trial like this could go on," he said. "Where else would they tolerate three weeks of picking a jury? Where else would they tolerate lawyers sometimes bumbling, sometimes stumbling? ... Where else would they tolerate this in the world, where else but here? Why then must this man suffer because he rode the streets of Paterson, minding his own business, a black man driving a white car? I know you won't stand for it. Thank you."

The courtroom was stirred by Brown's stem-winding broadside — muffled sniffles, angry voices — although the jurors sat with stone faces. After the lunch recess, Vince Hull made his methodical summation in a monotone, shoring up maligned witnesses and reconciling contradictions in testimony. Marins could not be held accountable for failing to identify the defendants at the hospital, Hull said, because he was under sedation. The prosecutor acknowledged that financial rewards were offered in June of 1966 to anyone who helped the police solve the crime, but if Bello and Bradley were testifying for money, why did they wait until October? While Hull lacked the drama of Ray Brown, he was able to turn the weaknesses of his case into apparent strengths. For example, the testimony of Bello and Bradley revealed numerous contradictions in their accounts of what happened that night. Bello said he saw three people driving by in a white car. Bradley said he saw four people. Bradley said he saw the car going west on Lafayette Street. Bello saw the car on Sixteenth Street. These and other inconsistencies only proved one thing, Hull said, that these witnesses had to be telling the truth! Lying witnesses would have been more coordinated. "If they were so interested in the reward," Hull asked, "why didn't they get their stories straight?"

Hull proved himself a master rhetorician. For example, several character witnesses for John Artis, including Robert Douglas, his pastor, testified that the defendant was a nonviolent, honest young man. Given that no motive was adduced, the jurors might very well doubt that a peaceful, law-abiding kid would brutally kill three people without any provocation. Hull's response: The character witnesses did not know their man. "What weight can their testimony have as to [Artis] being law-abiding and nonviolent after hearing all of the testimony as to what transpired in and around the Lafayette Grill on the morning of June 17, 1966." This sophistry bewildered Artis. Hull discredited his character witnesses by citing the very crime that his character witnesses said he was incapable of committing.

Hull finished his summation with a bit of high theater.

"Ladies and gentlemen of the jury, when you retire to the jury room, all of the exhibits in this case that have been admitted in evidence will be in there with you, including this bullet, this .32 S&W long Remington Peters. That will be one of the items that goes into the jury room with you, and after you deliberate upon the facts in this case, and weigh all of them carefully, that bullet, small in size, will get larger and larger and larger, and that bullet will call out to you and say to you, Bello and Bradley told the truth. That bullet will call out to you and say to you that Carter and Artis lied, and that bullet will get louder and larger and it will cry out to you like three voices from the dead, and it will say to you Rubin Carter and John Artis are guilty of murder in the first degree . . ."

Hull then emptied out three bags of bloody clothes on a table in front of the jury, each bag's contents in a separate pile. Beside each heap he placed a picture of the decedent whose clothes they were, the photos showing each person laid out on slabs in the morgue.

"There once was a man," the prosecutor continued, "a human being by the name of James Oliver, a bartender at the Lafayette Grill, and he wore this shirt, and he looked like this when he was placed into eternity by a 12-gauge shotgun shell. There once was a man, a fellow human being by the name of Fred Nauyoks who lived in Cedar Grove, and he had the misfortune of going to the Lafayette Grill on June 16–17, 1966, and this is how his life ended when he was murdered in cold blood with a .32-caliber bullet through his brain. And there once was a human being, a woman by the name of Hazel Tanis, and she wore these clothes, these bullet-riddled clothes, when she was shot, not once, not twice, not three times — four times; two of the bullets passed through her and two remained in her body, and she clung on to life for nearly a month, and on July 14 of 1966 she passed away, and this is what became of this fellow human being.

"Ladies and gentlemen, on the question of punishment, the facts of this case clearly indicate that on the morning of June the seventeenth of 1966, the defendants, Rubin Carter and John Artis, forfeited their rights to live, and the State asks that you extend to them the same measure of mercy that they extended to James Oliver, Fred Nauyoks, and Hazel Tanis, and that you return verdicts of murder in the first degree on all the charges without a recommendation. Thank you."

The following day, May 26, 1967, Judge Larner gave the jurors lengthy instructions, advising them that they had to return with a unanimous verdict. He also pointed out that "the race of the defendants is of no significance in this case except as it may be pertinent to the problem of identification." Finally, he turned to a woman who had been seated at a desk beside him throughout the trial. "All right. You may proceed, Miss Clerk." The woman got up and started to spin the wooden lottery box that held the names of the fourteen jurors. Carter frantically tugged Ray Brown's coat sleeve.

"What the hell is she doing?" Carter hissed into his ear. "Get her away from that damn box."

"Shh, Rubin," Brown whispered back. "She's only picking the twelve jurors who will decide the verdict. Two of the fourteen will have to go."

With a sweep of her hand, the clerk pulled the West Indian's name out of the box, leaving an all-white jury to decide the defendants' fate. It did not take long. The jurors deliberated for less than two hours, then returned to the courtroom, which quickly filled with spectators and reporters. Court officers searched the purses of entering women to guard against smuggled weapons. There were wild rumors that Carter's allies, in the event of a guilty verdict, would try to break him out. City detectives, plainclothes policemen, and uniformed officers from the county Sheriff's Department circled the room and lined the building's corridors. Outside, patrolmen were on alert that a guilty verdict could trigger riots in the street.

In the courtroom, the four women jurors had tears in their eyes. The others took their seats with bowed heads. Rubin Carter, John Artis, and their lawyers rose from their seats. A hush fell over the room as the jury foreman, Cornelius Sullivan, announced the verdict: "Guilty on all three counts." After a long pause he continued: "And recommend life imprisonment."

Carter's head dropped, but he showed no emotion. Artis's legs buckled, and he clenched a fist. The stunned silence of the courtroom was suddenly pierced by a scream from Carter's wife, her prolonged wails sending a dagger into Rubin's heart and alarming seasoned court observers. "She let out a scream the likes of which I've never heard before or since," said Paul Alberta, a local reporter, many years later. "It was the kind of scream of someone being physically tortured."

Tee thought the trial would have a Perry Mason ending: a defense attorney would spin around, point to a member of the gallery, and identify the true killer. Now she collapsed to the floor, unconscious; a friend and three attendees carried her limp body out of the room. Judge Larner asked that the jurors be polled to be sure that they agreed with the verdict. Each one announced: "I agree." One juror, a short, elderly woman with gray hair and glasses, looked at Carter on her way out. "I feel nothing for him," she said, then pointed to Artis, "but I feel so sorry for him."

The summer of 1967 was the worst of the decade's "red hot summers." From April through August, violence raged in 128 cities from Jersey City to Omaha, from Nashville to Phoenix. The most destructive conflagrations erupted in Newark, where 26 people were killed, and Detroit, where 43 perished. In all, 164 disorders resulted in 83 deaths, 1,900 injuries, and property damage totaling hundreds of millions of dollars.

But Paterson remained calm. The convictions of Rubin Carter and John Artis brought to a close the worst crime in the city's history. Judge Larner, noting Carter's "antisocial behavior in past years," sentenced him to three life sentences, two consecutive and one concurrent. Artis, as a first-time offender, received three concurrent life sentences. The only thing that surprised Carter was that the jury did not recommend the electric chair. Why would a white jury spare the life of two black men found guilty of such a barbaric act? *Mercy? Shit! They've fried niggers for less.* Maybe the jury felt pity for Artis and thus spared them both from the chair. Maybe the jury had doubts about their guilt. It didn't matter — not now, not ever. *One lie covers the world*, Carter thought, *before truth can get its boots on.*

5

FORCE OF NATURE

TRENTON STATE PRISON did not tolerate dissidents. The gray maximum-security monolith ran according to an intractable set of rules that completely controlled its captives' lives. Prison guards often said: "The state always wins," meaning, rebellious prisoners ultimately comply. Rubin Carter would test that motto unlike any other inmate in New Jersey's history. But opposition to authority was nothing new for him. It was, in fact, his nature.

Born on May 6, 1937, in the Passaic County town of Delawanna, Carter learned early on that the men in his family are not intimidated by threats. His father was one of thirteen brothers who all grew up on a cotton farm in Georgia. According to family lore, one brother, Marshall, was once seen fraternizing with a white woman. Panic surged through the house as word arrived that the Ku Klux Klan planned to crash the Carter home. The boys' father, Thomas Carter, sent several of his sons to Philadelphia, instructing them to return with fifteen guns — one for each member of the family. The Klan arrived, but the Carters, fortified with weapons, stood their ground, and the hooded riders retreated. Shortly thereafter, the family packed up and moved to New Jersey — although each brother would return to Georgia to select a bride.

The Klan story, no doubt embellished over the years, impressed on Rubin the importance of family pride and unity. His father, Lloyd, also regaled his seven children with stories of tobacco-chewing crackers in the South hunting down black men, then tarring or hanging them. On cold nights at home, Lloyd Carter told these stories around a coal-stoked burner as his children ate roasted peanuts sent by relatives in the South. Rubin, in stocking feet, would stretch his legs toward the crackling stove and let his mind race through the Georgia swamps, chased by whooping rednecks and howling dogs. The specter scared him, but he felt protected by the closeness of his family.

When Rubin was six, the Carters moved to Paterson, to a stable, racially mixed neighborhood known as "up the hill" — a few blocks away from poorer residents, who were literally "down the hill." Lloyd Carter made good money with his various business enterprises. He traded in for a new car every two or three years, and the Carters were the first black family in the neighborhood to own a television. But working two jobs six days a week — Sundays were for praying — wore him down, and his wife, Bertha, worried about his health. A lean, strong, bespectacled man just under six feet tall, Lloyd defended himself by quoting the Holy Scriptures. "Bert," he said, "'whatsoever thy hand findeth to do, do it with thy might; for there is no work, nor device, nor knowledge, nor wisdom, in the grave, whither thou goest.'"

Lloyd Carter also disciplined his children with a religious zeal. A deacon in his Baptist church, he forbade the children from playing records or cards at home. Listening to the radio or dancing in the house was also prohibited. While he spoke softly, he carried a hard switch, and Rubin gave his father ample reason to use it.

The boy's penchant for fighting often earned him swift punishment, but Rubin felt he had good reason to fight. He stuttered severely, stomping his foot on the ground to push the words out, and bitterly fought any kid who teased him for this impediment. His father had stammered as a youth, and *his* father had struck him with a calf's kidney to try to cure him. Somehow Lloyd did overcome his speech problem, but he didn't give his son much help. On the contrary, Rubin's parents believed an old wives' tale that severe stuttering indicated that the speaker was lying, which meant Rubin seemed unable to tell the truth. His response was to avoid talking, but that fueled the perception that he was stupid. To compensate for his stumbling tongue, the boy excelled in physical activities. He was muscular, fast, and fearless, and he saw himself as a protector of other people, particularly his siblings.

His brother Jimmy, for example, was two years older than Rubin, but he was studious, quiet, and prone to illness. When the Carters lived in Delawanna, Jimmy was sent to the basement to fetch coal from the family bin, but a neighborhood bully who was stealing the coal beat him up in the process. With his parents off at work, Rubin went to the basement himself to avenge the Carter name. It was his first fight. As he later wrote:

> A shiver of fierce pleasure ran through me. It was not spiritual, this thing that I felt, but a physical sensation in the pit of my stomach that kept shooting upward through every nerve until I could clamp my teeth on it. Every time Bully made a wrong turn, I was right there to plant my fist in his mouth. After a few minutes of this treatment, the cellar became too hot for Bully to handle, and he made it out the door, smoking.

Bullies were not the only victims of Rubin's wrath. In a Paterson grammar school, he once looked out his classroom door and saw a male teacher chasing his younger sister Rosalie down the hall. He raced out the door, tackled the teacher, and began swinging. The school expelled Rubin, prompting his father to beat him with a belt. But the beatings at home did not deter the boy, who continued to lash out at most anyone, even a black preacher who lived in the neighborhood. He owned a two-family home, and when he saw Rubin, at the age of ten, flirting with a girl who also lived in the house, he shooed him off the porch. But Rubin punched back with all his strength. The dazed preacher reported the incident to Rubin's father, who stripped his son, tied him up, and whipped him.

Lloyd Carter feared that his son's pugnacity would cost him his life one day, specifically at the hands of whites, and that fear led to a searing childhood incident. Each summer, Lloyd and his brothers drove their families in a caravan from New Jersey to Georgia, where they stayed with relatives, worked on farms, told stories, and sang and prayed together. On one occasion after church, some cotton farmers gathered in a grove to sing and picnic. A white man selling ice cream bars stopped nearby, and children carrying dimes raced to get a treat. Rubin had barely torn his wrapper when his father landed a heavy blow on his face, sending Rubin and the ice cream in opposite directions. Lloyd Carter never said why he struck his son; years later Rubin realized that his father feared white men, and he wanted his son to feel that same fright as well. Instead, the nine-year-old, his face puffed and bruised, came away with a very different lesson. He had taken his father's best shot, and now he no longer feared the man. Moreover, Rubin determined that he was never going to let another person hurt him again. Not his father, not a police officer, not a prison guard, not a mayor, not a bum. Nobody.

Young Rubin welcomed any physical challenge — the more dangerous, the better. He swam in the swift waters of the Passaic River, jumped off half-built structures at construction sites, ran down mountains, and rode surly mules on his grandfather's farm. On a swing set in the Newman playground, he swung so high that he flipped completely around in full circles. On one occasion, he and a friend, Ernest Hutchinson, were cutting through a backyard when a big bulldog ran at them. "I was going nuts, but Rubin told me to stand behind him," Hutchinson recalled. "All of the sudden, the dog leaps and — *bam!* — Rubin hits him right in the chest. The dog rolled over and couldn't catch his breath. I'll never forget that. We were ten years old."

Rubin continued to rebel against his father's rules. Even on a simple walk to P.S. 6 on Carroll and Hamilton Streets in Paterson, he had to make his own way. Lloyd Carter stood on the porch of their Twelfth Avenue home and made sure all his children took the safest, most direct route. When the brood was out of his sight, Rubin ducked into an alley, hopped a fence, and took a different, longer way. He was literally incapable of following the crowd.

But misdeeds landed him in more serious trouble — with both his father and ultimately the police. Rubin stole vegetables from a garden owned by one of his father's co-workers, ransacked parking meters, and led a neighborhood gang called the Apaches. When he was nine, the Apaches crashed a downtown marketplace, stealing shirts and sweaters from open racks, then fleeing to the hills. Rubin gave his stolen goods to his siblings. When his father saw the new clothes, price tags still attached, and was told that Rubin was responsible, he beat his son with a leather strap, then called the police. The boy was taken to headquarters — his first encounter with the police. He would always resent that his father had initiated what would become a lifelong battle with law enforcement officials. The following day, the Child Guidance Bureau placed him on two years' probation for petty larceny.

For all the confrontations between father and son, Rubin noticed that he liked to do many of the same things as his father. While his two brothers and four sisters often begged off, Rubin hunted with his father and accompanied him on trips to the family farm in Monroeville, New Jersey. His mother told him that his father was hard on him because Lloyd himself had also been a rebel in his younger days. Now, the father saw himself in his youngest son.

That did not become clear to Rubin until he was in his twenties, when he and his father went to a bar in Paterson where the city's best pool shooters played. As they walked in, the elder Carter quipped, "You can't shoot pool."

A challenge had been issued. Rubin considered himself an expert player, and he had never seen his father with a cue stick. Indeed, Lloyd hadn't been on a table in twenty years. They played, betting a dollar a game, and Lloyd cleaned out his son's wallet.

Rubin, shocked, simply watched. "Where did you learn to play?" he asked.

"How do you think I supported our family during the Depression?" his father replied. "I had to hustle."

Unknown to his children, Lloyd Carter had been a pool shark, and his disclosure seemed to clear the air between him and Rubin. "Why do you think I always beat on you?" Lloyd said later that night. "You wouldn't believe how many times your mother said, 'Stop beating that boy, stop beating that boy.' But I saw me in you." Lloyd Carter had also rebelled against authority, and he knew that was a dangerous trait for a black man in America. "I was trying to get that out of you," he told his son, "before it got hardened inside."

It was too late, however. Rubin's defiant core had already stiffened and solidified.

For all the turmoil in his youth, Carter actually fulfilled one of his boyhood dreams: he wanted to join the Army and become a paratrooper. In World War II the Airborne had pioneered the use of paratroopers in battle. It was not, however, the division's legendary assaults behind enemy lines that captivated Carter. Nor was it the Airborne's famed esprit de corps or its reputation for having the most daring men in the armed forces. Carter liked the uniforms. Even as a boy he had a keen eye for sharp clothing, and he admired the young men from Paterson who returned home wearing their snappy Airborne outfits: the regimental ropes, the jauntily creased cap, the sterling silver parachutist wings on the chest, the pant legs buoyantly fluffed out over spit-shined boots.

By the time Carter enlisted, however, the uniform was not his incentive. At seventeen, Carter escaped from Jamesburg State Home for Boys, where he had been serving a sentence for cutting a man with a bottle and stealing his watch. On the night of July 1, 1954, Carter and two confederates fled by breaking a window. They ran through dense woods, along dusty roads, and on hard pavement, evading farm dogs, briar patches, and highway patrol cars. Carter's destination was Paterson, more than forty miles away. When he reached home, the soles on his shoes had worn off. His father retrofitted a fruit truck he owned with blankets, and Rubin hunkered down in the pulpy hideaway while detectives vainly searched the house for him. Soon Carter was shipped off to relatives in Philadelphia. He decided, ironically, that the best way for him to hide from the New Jersey law enforcement authorities was by joining the federal government — the armed forces. With his birth certificate in hand, he told a recruiting officer that he was born in New Jersey but had lived his whole life in Philly. No one ever checked, and Rubin Carter, teenage fugitive, was sent to Fort Jackson, South Carolina, to learn to fight for his country.

Carter was no patriot, but soldiering allowed him to do what he did best: wield raw physical power. The Army, in some ways, was similar to Jamesburg, the youth reformatory. Carter lived in close quarters with a group of young men, and he was told what to do and when to do it. Individual opinions were forbidden; and just as a reformatory was supposed to correct a wayward youth, the Army was supposed to turn a civilian into a soldier. Carter spent eight grinding weeks in basic training, followed by eight more weeks to join the Airborne. He was then sent to Jump School in Fort Campbell, Kentucky. Recruits were known as "legs," because graduates received their paratrooper boots. Each class began with about 500 would-be troopers; as few as 150 would graduate. The school's relentless physical demands thinned the ranks, as recruits were eliminated by the early morning five-mile runs, the pushups on demand, the pullups, the situps, the expectation to run everywhere while on the base, even to the latrine.

Most difficult of all, however, trainees had to learn to leap twelve hundred feet from a C-119 Flying Boxcar. To prepare, they hung from the "nutcracker," a leather harness suspended ten or fifteen feet above-ground. They lay on their backs strapped to an open parachute while huge fans blew them through piles of sharp gravel until they were able to deflate the chute and gain their footing. There was also the "rock pit." Soldiers stood on an eight-foot platform, jumped into the air, and did a parachute-landing fall onto the jagged bed of rocks. They then got up and did it over and over again until ordered to stop. To quit was tempting, but the Army sergeants and corporals who ran the Jump School gave those who faltered a final dose of humiliation. They were forced to walk around the base with a sign on their shirt that read: "I am a quitter."

To Carter, Jump School was "three torturous weeks of twenty-four-hour days of corrosive annoyance." But when he executed his first jump, he excitedly wrote home about it, flush with pride, and later described the sensation.

> There was no time for thought or hesitation. I could only hear the dragging gait of many feet as man after man shuffled up to the door and jumped, was pushed, or just plain fell out of the airplane. The icy winds ripped at my clothing, spinning me as I hit the cold back-blast from the engines, and then I was falling through a soft silky void of emptiness, counting as I fell: "Hup thousand — two thousand — three thousand — four thousand!" A sharp tug between my legs jerked me to a halt, stopping the count, and I found myself soaring upwards — caught in an air pocket, instead of falling. I looked up above me and saw that big, beautiful silk canopy in full blossom and I knew that everything was all right. The sensation that flooded my body was out of sight! I didn't feel like I was falling at all; rather, the ground seemed to be rushing up to meet me.

The ground, however, gave Carter a jolt of reality. Even though the armed forces had officially been desegregated under President Truman, racial segregation and inequality still prevailed. Riding a train from Philadelphia to Columbia, South Carolina, black soldiers were shoe-horned into the last two cars while whites rode in relative comfort in the first twenty-odd vehicles. When paratrooper trainees were bused from South Carolina to Fort Campbell, Kentucky, passing through Georgia, Alabama, and Tennessee, blacks sat in the back of the bus. At dinnertime, whites ate at steakhouses while blacks had to stay outside and eat cold baloney sandwiches and lukewarm coffee.

This experience pricked Carter's racial consciousness for the first time. Whites and blacks had mixed easily in his old neighborhood in

Paterson, and while Jamesburg State Home segregated the inmates, Carter assumed that whites slept in their own quarters because they were weaker than blacks and therefore vulnerable in fights. But as his bus rolled through mountainsides of quaking aspens, he saw white farmers guzzling beer at resting stops, their drunken rebel shrieks grating his nerves. Their pickup trucks carried mounted gun racks, and they eyed the black soldiers suspiciously. Carter suddenly realized why his father and uncles drove their families through the Deep South in caravan style. He had thought it reflected the family's solidarity, but he now understood that it was to provide safety in numbers. He felt angry that his parents had not told him about the true dangers that lay across the land — in the South and throughout the country. This discovery came at the very moment Carter was training to fight for America. He decided from here on he would defend himself in the same fashion that he was defending his country — with guns. If his adversaries, be they communists or crackers, had weapons, so too would he. Carter kept these thoughts to himself, however. Speaking out was not his style. But his silence, about race and all other matters, would soon end.

By the time the winter winds blew through Fort Campbell in 1954, the 11th Airborne was preparing to transfer to Europe. Carter was one of three hundred paratroopers recruited from the States to be part of the advance party. Their destination: Augsburg, Germany. Founded almost two thousand years ago, Augsburg is one of those languorous Bavarian towns that lolls in the shadows of its history. Grand fountains and tree-shaded mansions with mosaic floors evoke a golden age of Renaissance splendor. In the Lower Town, among a network of canals and dim courtyards, small medieval buildings once housed weavers, goldsmiths, and other artisans. Nearby is Augsburg's picturesque Fuggerei, the world's oldest social housing project that still serves the needy. Built in 1519, it consists of gabled cottages along straight roads and preaches the maxim of self-help, human dignity, and thrift.

But Augsburg's patrician munificence and cobblestone alleys were far removed from the fervid world of Private Rubin Carter. He spent most of his time on the Army base, a member of Dog Company in the 502nd Parachute Infantry Regiment. Each day began at 6 A.M. with an hour's run on the cement roads surrounding the compound. Even on the coldest winter mornings, Dog Company ran in short-sleeve shirts, their frozen breath from shouted cadences hanging in the Augsburg air.

"Hup-Ho-o-Ladeeoooo!" the sergeant yelled.

"Hup-Ho-o-Ladeeoooo!" the Dog Company echoed.

"Some people say that a preacher don't steal!"

"Hon-eee! Hon-eee!"

"Some people say that a preacher don't steal — but I caught three in my cornfield!"

"Hon-eee-o Ba-aa-by Mine!"

Military maneuvers on the steep hills around Augsburg were a weekly exercise. The soldiers clambered up and down the slopes in leg-burning labors, firing blank bullets to secure a hill or to push back an imaginary enemy. But Carter learned what the real nemesis was on his first maneuver.

"Oh shit!" someone yelled. "It's comrades' 'honey wagons.'"

A fetid smell swept across the hills. On nearby cropland, farmers took human excrement from outhouses, slopped it in honey wagons, and spread it across their potato and cabbage fields. There was no defense against this invasion, but Carter never complained. *Shit, the stench inside prison is worse.*

Carter attended daily military classes in the "war room," where maps of the European terrain hung on the wall and the platoon's weapons were stored. He studied heavy weapons, rifles, and mortars, memorizing their firepower. Carter trained as a machine gunner; his job would be to back up the front line.

He liked the rigors and responsibilities of Army life, but his early days in Augsburg were marked by isolation and loneliness. His stutter, as always, deterred him from reaching out to others. He was also afraid that the Army would discover the deceptive circumstances of his enlistment and that he was a wanted man in New Jersey. Best to keep a low profile, he figured. So he never spoke up in class, he ate alone in the mess hall, and he rarely socialized at the service club, where friendships were forged over watered-down beer and folds of cigarette smoke. On weekends, he took the military bus to Augsburg. The town had an aromatic blend of fresh bread, spicy bratwurst, and heavy beer, a piquant scent that would hang on the soldiers' leather jackets long after they returned to the States. Augsburg's horse-drawn wagons and pockmarked buildings from a 1944 air raid added to the town's quaint and battered charm; but for most soldiers, its attractions were the liquor and the women. At one restaurant, each table was equipped with a telephone so that male patrons could ring nearby ladies of the evening and request a date.

Carter, however, rarely socialized and did not stray far from Augsburg's Rathausplatz, the town square. He had no special interest in its statue of Caesar on an elaborate sixteenth-century fountain. He simply was afraid he would be stranded if he missed the bus home.

The Airborne troops conducted weekly practice jumps in a nearby drop zone. One morning, after falling from the sky, Carter was folding his parachute when he heard a strange voice from over his shoulder.

"How you doin', little brother?"

Carter looked up but said nothing. A man he had never seen before had landed within twenty yards of him, but the close touchdown did not appear to be accidental.

"I've been watching you," the strange man said, "and I think you've got a problem."

"W-w-what's that?" Carter demanded, stunned by the stranger's effrontery.

"We'll talk about that later," the stranger said. "Let's go back to the base."

Ali Hasson Muhammad was unlike anyone Carter had ever met. A Sudanese Muslim, Hasson had immigrated to America and was now trying to earn early citizenship by serving in the Army. He wanted to give Carter guidance as much as friendship. With braided hair that wrapped around his head and a shaggy beard, he was like a sepia oracle. While other authority figures in Carter's life — his father, reformatory wardens, Army sergeants — had lectured him, Hasson spoke in parables designed to redefine Carter as a black man.

Walking back to their barracks one night, Hasson told Carter how a fat countryman from Sudan fell asleep while shelling peas in the attic of his cramped hovel. "The hut mysteriously caught on fire, and the village people rushed in to save the farmer," he said. "But they couldn't do it, because the man was too fat and the attic too small to maneuver him over to the stairs. The townsmen worked desperately, but without success, to save the man before it was too late. Then the village wise man came upon the scene and said, 'Wake him up! Wake him up and he'll save himself!'"

Black Americans were also asleep, Hasson told Carter, and they would have to wake up to save themselves. Hasson was a slender man who spoke softly and worked as a clerk because he refused to carry a weapon. But his dark, glaring eyes conveyed the passion of his beliefs. "Nobody can beat the black man in fighting, or dancing, or singing," he told Carter. "Nobody can outrun him or outwork him — as long as the black man puts his mind and soul to it." Tears of frustration welled in Hasson's eyes. "What on God's earth ever gave the black man in America the stupid, insidious idea that white men could out-think him?"

Carter heard Hasson's ardent pleas but never really absorbed them. *What does this have to do with me?* He didn't understand some of Hasson's more opaque sermons and euphemisms, and he had trouble believing Hasson's thesis of black superiority. What evidence was there in his own life to prove such a claim?

The evidence soon surfaced a half mile from Carter's barracks. The Army's Augsburg fieldhouse, with a sloped quarter-mile track, a basketball court, and weight machines, was the social and athletic epicenter of the base. Even on nights when frost covered the ground, the creaking gym retained a muggy, pungent atmosphere from the men's concentrated exertions.

Carter rarely entered the fieldhouse. But after pouring down a few too many beers at the service club one night, he and Hasson took a shortcut through the gym. There, they were stopped cold by what they saw — prizefighting. The 502nd regimental boxing team was in training, and the drills seemed to produce their own wonderful soundtrack: the staccato beat of speed bags, the plangent thuds of fists against heavy bags, the testosterone snorts of determined fighters. Carter and Hasson watched for a good while.

"Shit!" Carter said suddenly. "I-I-I can beat all these niggers." Hasson looked at him in disdain. "I can see why you don't open your mouth too much," he said. "Every time you open it, you stick your foot right in it. So why don't you just finish the job and tell that gentleman over there what you've just told me. Maybe he can straighten you out."

Hasson motioned to a young, ruddy-faced coach named Robert Mullick, whose blond hair was sheared so short you could see the pink of his skull. His blue eyes sparkled as he reviewed the boxers working out.

The boxing ring was the Army's surrogate battlefield, where champions were wreathed in glory, and the boxing coach trained his men to show no mercy. "Lieutenant?" Hasson said, grinning. "My little buddy thinks he can fight. In fact, he honestly feels that he can take most of your boys right now. So he's asked me to ask you if you could somehow give him a chance to try out for the team."

Mullick looked over Hasson's shoulder at Carter, who suddenly felt his silver parachutist wings hanging heavily on his shirt. Paratroopers were known as a cocky crew, often boasting that one of them could do the work of ten regular soldiers. They were also disliked for another reason: they received higher pay than the GIs, driving up the price of prostitutes.

Now Carter thought his parachutist wings were like a bull's-eye, signaling to the grim lieutenant that this was his chance to teach at least one saucy trooper a lesson. "So, you really think you can fight, huh?" Mullick asked. "Or are you just drunk and you want to get your stupid brains knocked out? Is that what you want to have happen, soldier?"

Carter's first reaction was to do what he always did when someone challenged him: knock him down, teach him some respect, show him he wasn't to be meddled with. But he held back his fists if not his lip.

"I-I-I can fight — I can fight," Carter stammered. "I'll betcha on that."

"You will?" Mullick said, a grin creasing his face. "Well, I'm going to give you a chance to do just that, but not tonight. You've been drinking, and I don't want any of my boys to hurt you unnecessarily. Just leave your name and I'll call you down tomorrow. Maybe by then you won't think you're so goddamn tough." He turned his back to Carter; the conversation was over.

The next day Carter lay in bed, petrified. He had always been a streetfighter, and a good one at that. His gladiator skills had earned him the position of "war counselor," or chief, of his childhood gang. War counselors negotiated the time and place of rumbles between gangs, but sometimes they agreed to fight it out between themselves. Carter always relied on "cocking a Sunday," or slipping in a wrecking ball of a punch when his opponent wasn't expecting it. He didn't know how to move around a boxing ring, to counterpunch or to tie up, and his chances of cocking a Sunday on a skilled fighter seemed impossible.

But Mullick was not about to let Carter off the hook. His drunken challenge was a slur against Army boxers, and now he would pay for it. Through a company clerk, Mullick ordered Carter to report to the fieldhouse. When he arrived, the arena was abuzz. Prizefighting was a big sport in Germany, and the impending fight had attracted droves of Army personnel, including sportswriters from *Stars and Stripes*, the Army newspaper. It seemed that the dismantling of a brassy parachute jumper would liven up an otherwise slow day in the Cold War.

Carter stood unnoticed in the doorway, watching two fighters in the ring hammer each other. The short dark fighter was bleeding from a gash over his eye. The other fighter seemed to be suffocating from his smashed nose, spitting out gobs of blood from his mutilated mouth. The crowd stood, cheered, roared for more mayhem, indifferent to who was winning or losing as long as someone toppled over. Carter knew he was out of his class.

When the bout was over, Mullick jumped down from the apron — he had officiated the fight — pushed through the crowd, and found Carter. "Are you ready for that workout now, mister?" Mullick asked. "Or do you have a hangover from boozing it up too much last night and want to call it off?" Carter shook his head.

The lieutenant nodded, wheeled around, and strode back toward the ring, where his fighters were clustered. Carter admired the sweaty black faces. They were scarred and ring-battered, but they seemed to have a closeness about them that transcended their ebony surface. *They were men of great courage,* Carter thought. *You'd have to shoot them to stop them, for their pride and integrity couldn't be broken.*

Finally, breaking away from the squad and climbing into the ring was a large boxer with a sculpted chest and stanchions for legs. He shook out his arms, flexed his ropy muscles, and shadowboxed in a glistening ritual. *I have to admit, the nigger looks good,* Carter thought.

The mob of spectators jumped to their feet and shouted their conqueror's name. He was Nelson Glenn, six feet one inch of animal power, the All-Army heavyweight champ for the previous two years. Mullick climbed through the ropes and began lacing on his fighter's gloves. At the same time, he motioned Carter to enter the ring. It was too late to back out, so he climbed in, Hasson on his heels.

Carter felt the adrenaline pump through his stout body and he showed no fear. He felt light on his feet but also strong, resolute. He was not going to flinch, to back down, to quit. He felt a sharp, electrifying twinge of self-respect. *Nelson Glenn will have to bring ass to get ass.* But he also felt the loneliness, the vulnerability, of the boxing ring. There was no escape.

Hasson tied on Carter's liver-colored gloves and offered some counsel. "Stay down low, and watch out for his right hand," he whispered softly. "And try to protect yourself at all times." Carter nodded.

Mullick called both fighters to the center of the ring to explain the ground rules, but he spotted a problem with Carter. Like Glenn, Carter wore his standard green Army fatigues (long pants, shortsleeve shirt) and tight Army cap, but Mullick pointed to Carter's shoes. "What are those?" he asked.

"My boots," Carter said.

Mullick rolled his eyes. "What size shoe do you wear?" he asked.

"Eight and a half," Carter responded.

"You need boxing shoes," Mullick said, more in pity than disgust. He fetched a pair from one of his own boxers and Carter sheepishly made the switch. Now he was ready.

The bell rang.

Glenn came out dancing, jabbing, grunting, contemptuous of this no-brain, no-brand opponent who presumed to step into the ring with the champion. Carter tried to stay beneath his crisp left hand, pursuing his adversary like a cat in an alley fight. Carter bobbed, feinted, ducked, then lashed out with his first punch of the fight — a whizzing left hook that caught Glenn flush on his chin, spilling him to the canvas. The blow may have startled Carter as much as Glenn.

Glenn bounced up quickly but was now groggy. He was surprised by the power of a mere welterweight. Carter returned to the attack and bored in with a quick, crunching left hook, then another, then a third, the last shot sending Glenn's mouthpiece flying out of the ring. Nelson's eyes turned glassy, his arms fell limp, and he started sinking softly to the canvas. Carter realized he could hear himself panting; the crowd was stunned into silence. Then pandemonium erupted. Spectators stood on their seats, whooping, gaping in disbelief at the knocked-out champion, cheering long and hard for Carter. The former hoodlum was now a hero. He had cocked a Sunday.

The triumph did more for Carter than prove he could slay a Goliath. It gave his life purpose and legitimacy. The boxing ring became his new universe, a place where his splenetic spirit and brawling soul were not only accepted but celebrated. His enemy couldn't hide behind a warden's desk or a police badge. He now stood face-to-face with his rival, and each bout had a moral clarity: the best man won, and if you fight Rubin Carter, *you better bring ass to get ass.*

After the Nelson Glenn fight, Carter never held an Army weapon again. Mullick cut through the Army's red tape and transferred Carter to a Special Service detachment for boxers for the 502nd. They lived in their own building, three glorious floors for twenty-five men. The first floor held a vast recreational area, with ping-pong tables and pool tables, as well as a kitchen. The second floor was sectioned off with bathtubs and shower stalls, whirlpools and rubbing tables, while the top floor had secluded sleeping quarters. This was nirvana in the Army.

Carter was accepted immediately by the other boxers, including Glenn. For one who always preferred isolation, he felt strangely comfortable with these men. Some were black, some were Hispanic, some were white, but they were all fellow warriors. They felt no need to engage in the braggadocio common among the other soldiers. The only vocabulary that mattered was boxing. Past fights, future fights, championship fights. Carter spoke the same language as everyone else, and winners had the final say.

Soldiers who saw Carter's matches have vivid memories of them more than forty years later. William Mielko, an Army sergeant, remembered Carter's entering the ring in Munich to fight a member of the 503rd regiment. When the announcer declared the names of the boxers, two bugles blared, and a six-foot six-inch, 250-pound heavyweight entered the ring wearing a black hood over his head with two slits for his eyes. His body was wrapped in shackles. It was a frightening spectacle, but when the heavyweight rid himself of the hood and chains, he faced Carter. "Carter looked over at his trainer," Mielko recalled, "and the trainer said, 'First round.'" And that was the round in which Carter knocked him out with a furious combination of punches.

In one year Carter won fifty-one bouts — thirty-five by knockouts — and lost only five, and he won the European Light Welterweight Championship. But he was even more proud of a very different accomplishment.

Again, it was Hasson who tackled the matter of Carter's speech impediment. No one had ever spoken to Carter about his stuttering except his parents, who said that the problem would disappear if he stopped lying. Rubin was at a loss. All he knew was that if anyone laughed at his clumsy tongue, he would flatten him. Hasson, however, saw Carter's speech problem as a barrier not only to communication but to knowledge. Wrapped in a coat of silence, Carter came to believe what others said about him: he didn't talk because he was dumb, and education was useless for someone with such low intelligence.

When they first met in the drop zone, Hasson's comment — "I think you've got a problem" — was an oblique reference to Carter's stammer. Later, on one of their walks across the base, Hasson spoke bluntly: "Your stuttering is a permanent troublemaker, and if you're too embarrassed to go back to school, then I'll go with you."

The two men enrolled in a Dale Carnegie speech course at the Institute of Mannheim, where they were briefly stationed. The institute breathed prestige, with tall white marble columns and long, winding staircases. Carter thought it looked like something the Third Reich would have built. Many of the German students spoke more English than Carter did. The classes themselves were taught by kind, middle-age German men who imparted sage advice.

"Just think about what you're going to say first, then say it," one teacher said. Carter learned that he could sing songs without stammering, and he was able to replicate the relaxed fluidity of music in his own speech. He practiced by chanting Army cadences *("Hup-Ho-o-Ladeeoooo!")* as well as gospels from his church in Paterson. Words soon flew out of his mouth like doves released from a cage. *Freedom!* Powerful oratory was no stranger to Carter. He had five uncles and a grandfather who were all Baptist preachers, and his father's voice was so resonant that churchgoers sat near him just to hear him pray. Rubin too proved to be a persuasive, even gifted, speaker who used ministerial cadences in stem-winding speeches. He also felt free to expand his own mind. His formal education had ended in eighth grade, and the only books he ever read were cowboy novels. Now he attended classes on Islam four nights a week and embraced Allah, renaming himself Saladin Abdullah Muhammad. "Allah is in us all, and man himself is God," Hasson told Carter.

While Carter's new religious faith would wane over the years, his discovery of books and passion for knowledge sustained him through his darkest hours. He never forgot what Hasson once told him: "Knowledge, especially knowledge of oneself, has in it the potential power to overcome all barriers. Wisdom is the godfather of it all."

Discharged from the Army on May 29, 1956, Carter returned to Paterson with the intention of becoming a professional prizefighter. But he quickly discovered that he could not elude his past. He was arrested on July 23 for escaping from Jamesburg and sent to Annandale Reformatory, where inmates' short-short pants evoked the image of incarcerated Little Bo Peeps. Carter was released from Annandale on May 29, 1957, but embittered about his reincarceration, he shelved his boxing ambitions, got a job at a plastics factory, and began drinking heavily. He liked to spend time at Hogan's, a club that attracted pimps and hustlers, pool sharks, and virtually every would-be gangster in the black community. Carter was enthralled by the diamonds they wore, the bills they flashed, and the luster of their shoes.

Less than five weeks after he was released from Annandale, Carter left Hogan's one day after a good deal of drinking. Walking through Paterson, he went on a brief, reckless crime spree. He ripped a purse from a woman, a block later struck a man with his fist, then robbed another man of his wallet. All the victims were black. When Carter reported to work the next day, the police arrested him. He pled guilty to the charges of robbery and assault but could never explain or excuse why he committed the crimes. He served time in both Rahway and Trenton state prisons, where he received various disciplinary citations for refusing to obey orders and fighting with other inmates. He did not make a particularly good impression on prison psychologists. In a report dated August 30, 1960, one psychologist, Henri Yaker, commented on Carter:

> He continues to be an assaultive, aggressive, hostile, negativistic, hedonistic, sadistic, unproductive and useless member of society who will live from society by mugging and who thinks he is superior. He has grandiose paranoid delusions about himself. This individual is as dangerous to society now as the day he was incarcerated and he will not be in the streets long before he will be back in this or some other institution.

Carter was released from prison in September 1961, but that description — assaultive, sadistic, useless — would be used against him long into the future.

In the sixties, the center of the boxing universe was the old Madison Square Garden, with dingy, gray locker rooms and a balcony where rowdy fans threw whiskey bottles at the well-dressed patrons below. During bouts, a haze of smoke from unfiltered cigarettes hovered in the air. Men in sport shirts sipped from tin flasks in between rounds, while other fans sat with cigars, lit or unlit, that never left their lips. The Friday-night fights, televised across the country and sponsored by the Gillette Company, were an institution, and a marquee boxer could earn tens of thousands of dollars. But before reaching the big time, the pugs had to fight in satellite arenas in Pittsburgh, Philadelphia, Boston, Chicago, Akron, and elsewhere. In later years, cable television would put any hot boxing prospect on the air after only a few fights. But at this time fighters typically had to learn their craft and pay their dues over several years before receiving that sort of publicity.

Rubin Carter felt he had paid his dues — in prison. While incarcerated, he concluded that prizefighting was his best hope of making a living and avoiding trouble. He trained in prison yards for four years, lifting weights, pounding the heavy bag, and accepting bouts with all comers. Once he left prison and entered the ring as a professional, it was soon evident that few could match his blend of intimidation, theatrics, and might. This crowd-pleasing style resulted in his first televised fight only thirteen months after he turned pro, when he knocked out Florentino Fernandez in the first round with a right cross to the chin. A black-and-white photograph of Fernandez falling out of the ring, his body bending like a willow over the middle rope as Carter glared down at him, sent an unmistakable message: the "Hurricane" had arrived.

Carter never really liked his boxing nickname. It was given to him by a New Jersey fight promoter, Jimmy Colotto, who saw the marketing potential of depicting a former con as an unbridled force of nature. Carter's preferred symbol was a panther. In the ring, Carter's trainers wore the image of a panther's black head, its mouth open wide, on the back of their white cotton jackets. The image had nothing to do with race or politics (the Black Panther organization was not formed until

1966). Carter simply admired the panther's speed and stealth, its predatory logic.

But Hurricane stuck, and for good reason. When Carter entered the ring, he *was* a force of nature. His head and face were already glistening from a layer of Vaseline. He wore a long black velvet robe and a black hood knotted with a belt of gold braid. There was something ominous, even alien, about him. When the Pennsylvania State Athletic Commission ordered Carter to shave his goatee for a fight in Philadelphia, some sportswriters opined that the goatee was the seat of Carter's power. The boxer looked foreshortened and brutally compact. The lustrous pate, the piercing eyes, the bristling beard, the sneering lips — and the violent criminal record — sent frissons of fear and delight through the crowd. Before a match, the announcer would introduce other boxing champions, past and present, in the crowd, and the conquerors would hop up in the ring, wave to the fans, and shake hands with the opposing fighters. Carter, however, refused to shake hands or even acknowledge their presence. Prowling around the canvas, he kept his eyes down and, in the words of one opponent, looked like "death walking." When the battle began, he attacked straight on, punches whistling. No dancing, no weaving, no finesse. He rarely jabbed. Just heavy leather. Carter liked the violence.

While Carter often found trouble on the streets, his training camp in Chatham provided sanctuary. He and several sparring partners escaped to camp six weeks before a bout. They awoke at 5 A.M. and ran up to twenty miles through steep, wooded hills. Carter liked the dark frigid mornings best, when icicles formed in his goatee and the only sounds were the pounding of shoes on pavement and the stirrings of a sleepy cow.

After an eggs and bacon breakfast and rest time, Carter resumed his training in the small gym. He jumped rope for forty minutes, pumped out five hundred pushups, lifted neck weights, pounded the heavy bag and speed bag, pushed against a concrete wall to build muscle mass, and did chinups until he dropped.

A sparring session was no different from a televised fight: in each, Carter locked out the rest of the world and tried to destroy his opponent. At the beginning of his career, he lived in Trenton and trained in the same Philadelphia gym as Sonny Liston, the feared heavyweight who reigned as champion from 1962 to 1964. Liston's heavy blows made it difficult for him to find sparring partners. One day Carter volunteered to go a few rounds, despite giving up five inches and fifty pounds. While most boxers spar to improve their footwork, punching combinations, or defensive maneuvers, neither Liston nor Carter had the patience for such artistic subtleties. Both were former convicts — Liston for armed robbery — and they rarely exchanged more than a few words. Theirs was an unspoken code of respect through pugilistic mayhem, and they sparred fiercely and repeatedly. But after one three-round session, Carter removed his battered headgear and found it soaked with blood. He was bleeding from both ears. He fled from Trenton that night and moved to Newark. He knew if he returned to the Philadelphia gym the next day and Liston needed a partner, he would do it again. He could never turn down a challenge, even if it meant risking serious injury.

Like Liston, Carter beat his sparring partners unmercifully. To soften the blows, Carter used oversize gloves and his partners wore a foam rubber protective strap around their ribs. In training camp, he sparred against three or four boxers a day, always punching against a fresh body. These sessions were followed by more calisthenics, then by a few rounds of shadowboxing, then by a shower and a rubdown. After a dinner of steak, fish, or chicken, Carter took a walk in the clean country air and thought about the next day's workout.

Only two years after he became a professional fighter, Carter wanted a shot at the middleweight title. He had won eighteen and lost three, with thirteen knockouts. But in October 1963, he lost a close ten-round decision to Joey Archer, and he needed a victory to put him back on track for a shot at the championship. That put him on a collision course with Emile Griffith.

Griffith was a native of the Virgin Islands who moved to New York when he was nineteen. His boss encouraged him to try his hand at boxing, and he was an instant success, winning the New York Golden Gloves. He turned professional at twenty. Griffith liked to crouch in the ring, stick his head in the other guy's chest, and pound the midsection. He could also dance and jab, backpedal and attack; he never tired. And he was deadly. In a bout at Madison Square Garden on March 24, 1962, Griffith took on Benny "Kid" Paret for the third time in less than twelve months, the decisive match in a bitter war between the two men. Paret provoked Griffith at their weigh-in by calling him *maricon*, "faggot." That night, Griffith was knocked down early, but he pinned Paret in the corner in the twelfth round and felled him with a torrent of angry punches, prompting Norman Mailer to write later: "He went down more slowly than any fighter had ever gone down, he went down like a large ship which turns on end and slides second by second into its grave. As he went down, the sound of Griffith's punches echoed in the mind like a heavy ax in the distance chopping into a wet log."

Paret was removed from the ring on a stretcher, lapsed into a coma, and died ten days later; he was twenty-five.

At the end of 1963, Griffith was the champion of the welterweight division (for boxers 147 pounds and under) and had been named *Ring* magazine's Fighter of the Year with a record of thirty-eight wins and four losses. Now he wanted a shot at the middleweight crown (for boxers 160 pounds and under), and that led to his match with Carter.

Their bout was to take place in Pittsburgh's Civic Arena on December 20. The two men were sparring partners and friends, but in the days leading up to the match, Carter launched a clever campaign to strike Griffith at his point of vulnerability: his pride. The idea was to provoke him before the fight so that he would abandon his strongest assets — his speed and stamina — and go for a quick knockout. Carter began planting newspaper stories that Griffith was going to run and hide in the ring and hope that Carter tired. In a joint television interview the day before the fight, the host asked Griffith if he dared to stand toe-to-toe with the Hurricane.

"I'm the welterweight champion of the world," Griffith snapped. "I've never run from anyone before, and I'm not about to start with Mr. Hurricane Carter now!"

"Then I'm going to beat your brains in," Carter shot back.

Griffith laughed in the face of Carter's hard glare. "I've never been knocked out either," Griffith said. "But if you don't stop running off at the mouth, Mister Bad Rubin Hurricane Carter, I'm going to turn you into a gentle breeze and then knock you out besides." Griffith was now seething, so Carter raised the temperature a little more.

"Knock me out!" Carter said, turning to the live audience. "If you even show up at the arena tomorrow night, that'll be enough to knock me out! I oughta cloud up and rain all over you right here. You talk like a champ, but you fight like a woman who deep down wants to be raped!"

The audience, knowing what happened to Benny Paret, gasped. Griffith clenched his jaw. Carter had laid his trap.

The following night, the city's steel plants and foundries spewed smoke into the frozen air. Inside the Civic Arena, Griffith's mother was in the crowd, and the champion entered the ring as a confident 11–5 favorite. Griffith started out methodically, firing jabs, standing toe-to-toe, swapping punch for punch. He wanted to prove that he could take Carter's best shots and win a slugfest. This was exactly what Carter had hoped for.

Carter popped him in the mouth with a stiff jab; Griffith responded with an equal jolt to Carter's mouth. Carter pumped a jab to his forehead; Griffith fired one back on him. Carter backed up, looked at him, snorted, then raced in with a jab followed by a powerful left hook to the gut.

The air came out of Griffith, who tried to grab Carter, but Carter slipped away. "Naw-naw, sucker," Carter mumbled through his mouthpiece. He drilled home another salvo of lefts and rights — "You gotta pay the Hurricane!" Carter yelled — then dropped Griffith with a left hook.

"One! . . . Two! . . . Three."

The crowd was stunned into silence, then stood and cheered. Griffith staggered to his feet to beat the count, but he was now an easy target. Carter smashed left hooks to the body and devastating rights to the head. Griffith dropped to the canvas, badly hurt. He tried to stand but stumbled instead. The referee, Buck McTiernan, stepped in and stopped the fight. The time was two minutes and thirteen seconds into the first round. "A left hook sent Griffith on his way to dreamland!" the television announcer yelled.

Carter's upset cemented his reputation as one of the most feared men in boxing. It also earned Carter a shot at the title the following year. But the Griffith fight marked the pinnacle of his boxing career. Carter lost his championship bout on December 16, 1964, to Joey Giardello, a rugged veteran whose first professional fight had been in 1948, in a controversial fifteen-round decision. Giardello's face was puffed into a mask while Carter was unmarked, and a number of sportswriters who saw the fight thought Carter won. But challengers typically have to beat a champ decisively to win a decision, and Carter didn't.

The bout occurred on December 16, 1964. The following year, Carter received another jolt — this time, political. He was invited to fight in Johannesburg, South Africa, a country about which he knew virtually nothing. He had never heard of Nelson Mandela or the African National Congress or even apartheid. But just as the Army exposed him to bigotry in the Deep South, boxing now put him in the midst of a more virulent racism. Arriving in Johannesburg a couple of weeks before his September 18 bout, he was guided around the city by Stephen Biko. In years to come, Biko would become the leader of the Black Consciousness movement, advocating black pride and empowerment, and would found the South African Students Organization. But in 1965, he was an eighteen-year-old student and fledgling political activist, and he gave Carter a quick education in black oppression. Walking through Johannesburg, the American's roving eye glimpsed a tight-skirted white woman. "Whoa, man!" he said. Biko grabbed Carter's arm. "You can't say that. They'll kill us! They'll kill us!"

Racial strife was indeed high. The previous year, Nelson Mandela and other black leaders were handed life sentences for conspiring to overthrow the government. The ANC had been banned in 1961; but clandestine meetings were still being held, and Biko took Carter to some of these nocturnal gatherings. There he learned about black South Africans' bloody struggle, dating almost two hundred years, for political independence. He also had his own encounter with the South African police. He was almost arrested one night for walking outside without a street pass.

The boxing match was against a cocky black fighter named Joe "Ax Killer" Ngidi who had a potent right hand. More than 30,000 fans packed into Wemberley Stadium on a sunny afternoon, and as Ngidi danced about the ring in a pre-bout warm up, Carter noticed that some of the fans were carrying spears.

"I don't know what that means," his advisor Elwood Tuck told him, "but get that sucker out of there quick."

Carter was confident. South African boxers, he believed, viewed the sport as dignified and noble but lacked savagery. That shortcoming could not be applied to Carter, and even though he was a foreigner, his ferocity made him a crowd favorite in South Africa. When he KO'd "Ax Killer" Ngidi in the second round, fans stood on their feet, raised their spears and yelled, "*KAH-ter! KAH-ter!*" But after Carter reached his dressing room, he was pinned in by a mob of supporters, and the scene turned ugly. To leave the stadium, a battalion of gun-carrying Afrikaner cops formed a wedge and told Carter and his entourage to follow its lead. As they pushed through the crowd, a white officer pummeled several black fans. Carter, outraged, moved to strike the cop, but was blocked by one of his handlers and was once again reminded that such a move would ensure his own demise.

In the following days, Carter was named a Zulu chief outside Soweto and given the name "Nigi" — the man with the beautiful beard. He was now an African warrior, and he wanted to apply the same principles in his second homeland that he always applied in the U.S.: blacks must use whatever means necessary, including violence, to defend themselves. From what he could tell, South African blacks were defenseless, armed with rocks and spears against the Afrikaners' guns and rifles. Before Carter left Johannesburg, he pledged to Stephen Biko that he would return.

Carter had committed crimes before, but now he was going to do something far more dangerous. He was going to smuggle guns to the ANC. First, he prowled bars in New Jersey and New York, where hardluck customers traded their guns for drinks and tavern owners ran a second business in arms sales. Carter accumulated four duffel bags for their weapons, then persuaded Johannesburg promoters to set up another fight. This time, his opponent would be an American, Ernie Burford, against whom Carter had split two previous matches. That Carter would travel all the way to South Africa to fight another American made no sense to outsiders, and he told few people about his true motivation, not even Burford. If the South African authorities caught him running guns to the ANC, he would probably never have left the country alive. But the trip turned out to be a great success. He delivered the guns to a grateful Biko, and he knocked out Burford in the eighth round on February 27, 1966.

Eight months later, Carter was arrested for the Lafayette bar murders, and he never heard from Stephen Biko again.

In a few short years, Biko founded the Black Consciousness movement, advocating black pride and empowerment, and he would become one of the most celebrated leaders of black South Africans' fight against a murderous regime. His activism, however, frequently placed him under police detention, and in 1977 he died from head injuries while under custody, provoking international outrage. He was thirty years old.*

After Carter's loss to Giardello, his boxing career lasted for twenty-two more months. During that period he won 7, lost 7, and had 1 draw. (He ended his career with 28 wins, 11 losses, and 1 draw.) He blamed the losses on increased police and FBI harassment, in New Jersey and elsewhere, and there is credibility to that excuse. The *Saturday Evening Post* article, which included Carter's intemperate remarks about the police and his own ruffian past, was published in October 1964. Carter, according to Paterson police records, was arrested twice in the next six months on "disorderly person" charges. (He was found not guilty on one charge and paid a $25 fine on another.) In a sport that requires complete focus, Carter's concentration was no doubt disturbed by these rising tensions with the law.

But Carter's own stubbornness hurt him. He worked out with intensity but resisted his trainers. One, Tommy Parks, devised an ingenious double-cross. He began giving Carter "opposite commands." If he wanted Carter to do roadwork the next morning, he would instruct his fighter to sleep late. Five A.M. would roll around and, sure enough, Carter was ready for roadwork. His footwork needed sharpening? Parks told him to concentrate on his punching. Invariably, Carter followed the "opposite command," thereby doing exactly what Parks desired.

Carter also lacked discipline. During training, he would get bored at night, sneak out of camp, and go to Trenton or another town to meet women and carouse. He never drank in front of his trainers, but Parks thought he knew when Carter had been tipping the bottle. His skin seemed to grow yellow and his eyes were in soft focus. Carter once had a sparring match in Newark with a tough but unaccomplished fighter named Joe Louis Adair. Carter had been drinking the previous night, and he was sluggish in the ring. Adair knocked him down in the first round, and a newspaper published a story about the Hurricane's improbable pummeling. "Rubin was a Mike Tyson with heart," Parks said in an interview years later. "But drinking was the bane of his career." Carter, asked about that assessment, agreed.

* Coincidentally, Denzel Washington played both Stephen Biko in *Cry Freedom* in 1987 and Rubin Carter in *The Hurricane* twelve years later.

Parks specialized in working with troubled kids, but he was removed as Carter's trainer in 1963 because the boxer's manager wanted a white trainer to improve Carter's marketability on television. But the change hurt in the ring. Carter preferred black trainers like Parks and said his subsequent white trainers varied in effectiveness. His own effectiveness may also have been diminished because he stopped scaring opponents. His invincible armor, once cracked, gave his competitors more confidence. Carter's image and tenacity still made him a crowd favorite, though, and at the end of 1965 he was ranked fifth among middleweights by *Ring* magazine. Carter believed that, had he not been arrested for the Lafayette bar murders, he would have fought again for the championship. But his imprisonment ended those dreams forever.

Also spoiling the concentration Carter needed to thrive as a boxer was the betrayal of his manager, Carmen Tedeschi. Short and rotund, Tedeschi wore shiny silk suits, kept a cigar in his mouth, and talked a good game. He lived in Saddlebrook, New Jersey, and raised pigeons for a hobby and profit. Carter met Tedeschi in 1962 through one of his uncles, and he befriended Tedeschi's wife and three children, chaperoning the oldest daughter to a high school dance. But Carter had misplaced his trust. Like many boxers, he allowed his manager to hold his winnings, then the manager doled out cash as the fighter needed it. Tedeschi drummed up fights for Carter, paid the trainers, cut men, and sparring partners, and gave the boxer plenty of money to lavish perks on his family and himself. But Carter didn't keep track of how the winnings were being spent and saved. After he had been with Tedeschi for more than a year, the manager wrote Tommy Parks a $25 check — which bounced. Parks knew his fighter was in trouble.

"Rubin, you better watch your money, man," Parks told him. "What do you have in the bank?"

"I've got $70,000," Carter replied.

"You don't got a dime," Parks said.

And he didn't, but Carter kept Tedeschi around as long as he was getting him fights and giving him spending money. The ruse came to an end in 1964. An agent from the Internal Revenue Service told him he owed the government $95,000 in back taxes. That was impossible, Carter said, because his manager paid his taxes after every fight. But Tedeschi had kept the money for himself. Carter finally fired him a few months before the Giardello fight. The chicanery deepened his distrust of others and taught him that he could not let anyone else control his fate. The squandered earnings cost Carter dearly when his legal fees depleted his savings, and his wife and daughter were forced to live off welfare checks. In the end, the back taxes were never paid. Short of cash and then incarcerated, Carter left the ring owing money — a fitting coda to a promising boxing career that fell painfully short.

6

BOXER REBELLION

B Y THE TIME Rubin Carter arrived in 1967, Trenton State Prison
was an anachronism, a fortress frozen in time. Guards began
their eight-hour shifts at twenty minutes after the hour — 6:20
A.M., 2:20 and 10:20 P.M. — because those times coincided with the
arrival of the trolley. But the last trolley ran in 1934. It didn't matter.
The trolley schedule still dictated the prison schedule. Built in 1836, the
prison originally lay beyond Trenton, surrounded by open fields. But
the city literally grew around the prison. By the sixties, the thirteen-and-
a-half-acre institution was wedged in a working-class neighborhood of
Poles, Slavs, and Czechs who toiled in steel mills and factories of their
own grim design. To outsiders, the prison was an ominous and inscrutable stronghold, where the roar of an inmates' softball game conjured
up a neighborhood park while tower guards with shotguns, pistols, and
gas grenades evoked the power of a police state to crush the criminal
spirit.

No one doubted that Trenton State Prison crushed spirits, eighteen
hundred at a time, criminal or otherwise, amid the brooding atmosphere of naked electric light bulbs, echoing corridors, walls encrusted
with the paint of decades, and the stale air of rooms shut up too long.
In this surreal and violent world, prisoners raised rats as pets and hid
knives in wooden crucifixes over their cots. Fights among prisoners
were common, but there was no handshaking, no touching of gloves,
no wishing each other well when the bout was over. Just who was dead
and who was alive, and dying in prison carried its own gruesome risks.

Some inmates exacted posthumous revenge by mutilating an enemy's corpse in the prison morgue.

The prison's decaying innards pushed inmates to the edge of survival, or beyond. In 1973 a radiator pipe erupted in a cell, melting the flesh off a young prisoner named Daniel Hogan.* Summers were a scourge. The stone and brick buildings, with no air conditioning or proper ventilation, heated up like a pizza oven, and the steam pipes glistened with sweat. "Ninety-ninety days" were the worst: ninety-degree temperature, ninety percent humidity. The smallest cells were seven and a half feet long, four and a half feet wide, and seven feet high. The largest cells were less than twice that size; with up to four occupants, a bit of flatulence could set off a melee.

The sounds of the prison — the shrill bells, the cell counts, the wheezing radiators — had their own predictable, hopeless rhythms. So thin were the walls that a prisoner could not brush his teeth without being heard throughout the tier. The ceilings, the floors, the doors, the walls, the toilets, the sinks, the beds — everything was made of steel, including the "breaks," the noisy contraptions that ran the locking system. Every hour of every day, prisoners heard corrugated steel rasping against corrugated steel, the constant clanging of steel doors opening and shutting in a deafening march to infinity.

An inmate at San Quentin once defined prison as "a metropolis of men without women, a beehive without honey, caged loneliness without privacy, a ranch where all the sheep are black, a cement park with barbed wire shrubbery, and an enormous microscope, under which psychiatrists study the smear from civilization's ulcers."

Trenton State Prison was to be different. Its original goal, inspired by reform-minded Quakers, was to keep inmates isolated in relatively large cells, where they could be rehabilitated through solitary meditation, Bible reading, and piecework. The oldest cells, now part of 4 Wing, have oak doors set low so that each time a prisoner enters or leaves he must bend his head in penance. But those fine goals had long since given way to an environment of en masse domination, where multi-tiered cellblocks enabled a few passing guards to monitor hundreds of men in their cages; inmates were subject to up to twenty counts a day.

---

* The death resulted in the dismissal of two guards for neglect of duty.

An invisible web of rules and timetables dictated the prisoner's every move. According to the *Handbook for Inmates,* issued to each new arrival, prisoners were to step promptly out of their cell when the prison bell sounded and report to the dining hall, to an industrial shop, or to another assignment. They were to walk in line, two abreast, and maintain good posture with their face held forward, their hands out of their pockets. They could not leave their place in line unless so ordered. Any violation of these rules would result in disciplinary action. An inmate could not spend more than $25 a month at the commissary for cigarettes, soap, toothpaste, and other items, and he could not receive or send more than five letters a month unrelated to his legal case. Each letter was screened by a prison employee.

Rubin Carter knew the rules of Trenton State Prison well. He had spent four years there, beginning in 1957, for robbing three people in Paterson and assaulting one of them. Carter called his crime the most despicable thing he'd ever done, and he served his time. Now, at the age of thirty, he was returning for a crime he said he did not commit. Wrists handcuffed, legs shackled, he was driven in an unmarked police car from Paterson to Trenton, with a different state trooper escorting the car through each county. John Artis rode in a separate car. Carter felt as if he were on public display. Instead of taking the New Jersey Turnpike, the fastest route, the caravan traveled through the small towns along Route 1, which allowed pedestrians to view the quarry.

When Carter reached the prison, he was still in the clothes he wore for his sentencing: an expensive gray suit with a light blue shirt, a gray-blue tie, and black patent leather shoes. He also wore a diamond ring, appraised at $5,000, and a gold watch, and he sported a thick goatee. His hands and feet freed, he walked through the main entrance, a small steel door with a slot of bulletproof glass, and was led down a hall lined with administrative offices, an area known as the Front House. Before him lay two more steel doors, the second of which would put him in the prison proper. But before he left this outer hall, he was taken to a different room. There, the prison began the process of sanding away an inmate's identity.

Ahead of Carter was an elderly black man with a carefully coiffed shock of silver-tipped hair. He gave his name, age, crime, and sentence to a guard behind a table. Then he disrobed, piled his clothes in a heap, and removed his jewelry. As another guard carted off his civilian belongings, the man submitted to a strip search. Still naked, he received a drinking cup, a spoon, blankets, and a khaki prison uniform with NJSP stenciled on the back and thick black stripes, about the width of a cell bar, along the sides. He also exchanged his name for a five-digit number, 45471. He was now a ward of the state, and his very self seemed to evaporate like a drop of water on a hot stove.

"Next!" roared the guard processing the new inmates. It was now Carter's turn. "Where do you want your clothes sent? Here, fill out this form." He threw a pair of striped prison pants on the table in front of Carter. "Take 'em off and put 'em in the box," the guard said, motioning to Carter's gray suit.

Carter looked at the guard, looked at the striped pants, then looked again at the guard. He suddenly realized what he had to do. If he was going to maintain his self-respect, if he was going to live with dignity, he had to treat the system as if it did not exist. Of course! He would ignore the prison. *Why should I be a good prisoner when I haven't been a bad civilian? That's the depth of insanity.*

"No," Carter told the guard. He pushed back the uniform. "I would like to speak to someone in charge."

The guard became livid. "Oh would ya? Well, people in hell would like a glass of ice water too. C'mon, get those duds off. Move it along. I ain't got all day to fuck around with fish."

"Fish," in prison jargon, were newcomers, but this fish was not moving. The guard called out to his superior, a sergeant, a so-called white hat. (Prison guards at sergeant or above wore white hats; the rest, blue caps.)

"What's the holdup here?" the sergeant asked.

"This guy's not getting undressed."

"What do you mean, not getting undressed?" The sergeant, outraged, looked at Carter. "Get undressed!"

Carter shook his head. "No, I won't." The inmates in line began to rustle, guards moved about, and the standoff escalated to a higher officer. The chief deputy keeper, his white hat adorned with a gold braid, walked into the room. He knew Carter from his previous stay.

"Carter, you've been here before," the chief deputy said. "You know what the rules are."

Carter wanted to reason with him. "Look, I realize you had nothing to do with my being here, and I'm willing to stay here until I can get out. But I'm not doing anything for you. I'm not working for you, I'm not eating your food, I'm not wearing your clothes, and I'm not shaving my goatee. You just tell me where to go, and I'll go."

The room was silent as Carter raised the stakes even further. "The one thing I will not tolerate at all is for anybody to ever put their hands on me. Because if anyone does, you're going to have to kill me. Because if you don't, I'm going to kill *you*. So that's that. We're straight now."

Few things in prison were more foolish than disobeying a guard, but threatening to kill the chief deputy was certainly one of them. The chief deputy stared at Carter, face flushed, then barked, "Take him to the warden!" Surrounded by guards, Carter walked through two more sets of steel doors and into the Center, a large rotunda from which the cellblocks radiate out. Moving from one cellblock, or wing, to another required passing through the Center. A guard known as the traffic cop stood on a star and directed these mass movements, as inmates migrated from cellblock to industrial shop to the dining hall to the prison yard. The Center was also the prison's administrative and communications hub, and now Carter, his bald head glistening, was the focus of attention. He felt the indignant, incredulous eyes of guards, administrators, secretaries, visitors, and inmates. The warden appeared, and the encounter was brief. "Carter, we heard you were coming," he said. "Are you gonna put these clothes on?"

"No," Carter replied.

"Take him to the 'hole'!" Carter walked toward 1 Wing, but nobody touched him.

Trenton State Prison had different levels of solitary confinement, but the "hole" was the most punitive. At the far end of a dim corridor, a hole was literally cut into the wall. Three iron-barred gates guarded the entrance, with steps descending between each gate. About thirty-five cells lined the narrow concrete tier. The "hole" was deeper than a grave.

Solitary confinement was to be the rehabilitative cornerstone of Trenton State Prison, sealing inmates from the "vicious association" of congregate living. But the ravages of isolation were soon apparent. Two years after the prison opened, the "keeper," or warden, concluded that the hermitic life seemed to have little effect on criminal behavior. In fact, it caused deteriorating physical and mental health, "leading to solitary vices and mental degeneration." This understanding caused Trenton State, among other institutions, to abandon solitary confinement for the general inmate population, using it instead strictly as punishment. It is, aside from capital punishment, the most severe form of legal retribution inside a prison. Nelson Mandela said he found solitary confinement the most forbidding aspect of prison life, where the human mind played tricks and the pain of loneliness was palpable. After a time in solitary, he said, he relished the company of insects in his cell and found himself on the verge of initiating conversations with a cockroach.

Rubin Carter, still dressed for dinner at the Ritz, walked into the lurid "hole." There were no showers. No faucet. No toothbrush. No toilet; only a bucket. There were no lights, no books, no contact with guards or inmates. Quiet was the rule, rancid the air. The door's steel bars were so tightly aligned that Carter could not squeeze his fingers through them. He was fed through an opening at the bottom of the door: one cup of water three times a day, four slices of bread. His bed was a concrete slab.

It was always dark in the "hole," but there were layers of darkness. Along the corridor hung a wire mesh net; behind it guards sat at desks. The desks had individual lights, so yellowish rays eked through the mesh and fell hazily on the tier. This created an inner and outer darkness in the cell or on the tier, shadows within shadows, silhouettes of stale bread and urinous buckets and shades of passing humanity. Eyes adjusted, Carter could soon see nothingness.

Day after day, he silently fumed but never voiced his anger: a scream signaled that a prisoner was about to break, that the institution had won. Instead, Carter paced. His cell was barely wider than his armspan, but the length accommodated four strides. So Carter paced — *one, two, three, four; one, two, three, four* — and he seethed. He was furious at everyone: at Bello and Bradley, at DeSimone, at the prosecutor, at the judge, at the jury, at his own lawyer. Teeth grinding, fists clenched, he wanted to destroy everyone who had put him there. *One, two, three, four; one, two, three, four.* Carter could adjust to the isolation. He had always been a loner, spending countless hours by himself in youth reformatories, in prison, and in training. The near-starvation diet also didn't bother him; he cared little about food. What he could not tolerate was that the authorities *knew* his incarceration was unjust. That knowledge — call it conspiracy among the powerful or acquiescence among yes-men — really got him mad. *One, two, three, four; one, two, three, four.*

Every fifteen days Carter was allowed to take a shower, and every thirty days he received a medical inspection. His suit was rotting off his emaciated body, but he still wore his diamond ring and gold watch. This deprivation did not dull his thinking, and he had a lot on his mind. From now on he only had one goal: to get out of prison. All his time, all his energy, would be dedicated to that objective. He decided he needed to do two things. First, he was going to study the law so that he would be able to direct his lawyers and guide his appeal. Second, he was going to write a book that would tell his life story and his side of the Lafayette bar shootings. He even had a working title: *Kill, Baby, Kill.* These goals were tall orders. He had never read a law book, let alone a legal brief, and he had never written more than five or six pages for a school assignment. But somehow Carter would learn the law and write his autobiography. He just had to figure out how.

To begin with, however, he had to get out of the "hole" on his terms — without wearing prison garb or giving up his ring, his watch, or his goatee.

One, two, three, four; one, two, three, four.

During one of Carter's checkups at the prison hospital, the doctor discovered a serious problem. Slumped in a chair, weak, unshaven, his clothes dripping off, Carter was told a detached retina was forming in his right eye. It was probably an injury from his boxing days, and without surgery, vision would be lost in that eye. An operation sounded like science fiction to Carter, but going blind in one eye would end his boxing career, which he fully intended to pursue once he was released. The ophthalmologist wanted to operate in his own clinic, which had better equipment, but prison officials would not permit Carter to leave the institution. Like the authorities who feared he would try to escape after the verdict, the prison administrators feared that he would flee if he were allowed to seek medical care beyond the prison walls. So Carter was admitted to the prison hospital.

After the surgery, he stayed in the hospital for three or four weeks with a patch over his eye. Life was good there. He was able to shower, shave, and wear clean white hospital pajamas. The nurses and other prisoners brought him food and cigarettes — and no convalescence would be complete without some hooch.

Hooch was a sweet wine that prison "brewmeisters" concocted with water, juice, sugar, and yeast. The inmates rustled up the ingredients from kitchen confederates, stirred the potion together, and let it ferment for several days. Hooch emitted a nostril-searing aroma, and anyone caught with it was subject to disciplinary action. But the inmates found creative ways to conceal the smell, such as burying hooch jugs in the prison yard, sprinkling talcum powder on the top of containers, or even storing the wine in an empty fire extinguisher. Now Carter, dying for a drink, created his own hospital still.

He filled some extra water cooler jugs with the water, orange juice, sugar, and yeast. He sealed the top with layers of foil, then punctured it with a long, narrow hospital tube. He put the jug in a cupboard under his bathroom sink and pointed the tube out a small hole in the back wall of the cupboard so the vapors would disappear into the prison's rotting entrails. Three days later, it was ready to drink. Best damn hooch Carter ever had.

Ingenuity would be Carter's byword for years to come as he tried to survive prison without complying with its rules. While he was in the hospital, he figured out how he could dress like a free man without violating prison policy. Patients wore white cotton pajamas, and inmates who worked in the kitchen, the barber shop, or the hospital could walk about the prison in their white uniforms. When Carter left the hospital, he asked a prison tailor to turn his white hospital PJs into a respectable-looking uniform. The tailor sewed buttons on the open fly, flared out the legs with extra white material, and stitched on belt loops for a ropy waistband. He turned the pajama top into a tunic, with a high collar, layered front, and buttons. This combination blended in with the other white outfits, and no one demanded that he discard it. He also had to improvise to maintain his shaved head. He could still get Magic Shave in the commissary, but he normally shaved with a butter knife. So he traded some cigarettes for a kitchen spatula, spoons being the only utensils available to inmates, and shaved his head with an implement otherwise used to spread icing on cake.

Carter's hospital sojourn, however, ended in disaster. When his eye-patch was removed, he saw only blurred images, then blackness. The operation that was supposed to save his right eye had, in fact, taken the eye. Although the doctor claimed he was handicapped by the prison facilities, Carter always believed that the original diagnosis was phony and that the prison intentionally took his right eye to make him vulnerable to attack. Inmate hierarchies are determined by toughness, and Carter had become the equivalent of a legendary but handicapped gunslinger — an easy target for some new quick-draw artist. No prisoner ever did challenge Carter, but the loss of the eye was still devastating. It took years for him to regain his equilibrium fully. And it meant, if freed, he would not be able to resume his boxing career, his only means of making a living.

When Carter was released from the hospital, he was sent not to the "hole" but to 7 Wing, the cellblock designated for "incorrigibles." He walked down the corridor with one eye and his first pair of glasses, wearing pajamas and slippers. He was #45472, but he still had his ring, his watch, and his goatee, and no one touched him. Indeed, Carter tried to stick to the edicts he'd issued on his first day. He rarely ate in the dining room. Other inmates, particularly the younger ones who called him "Mr. Carter," respected his celebrity and his warrior reputation, and they helped him maintain his independence by bringing him food. They brought mostly canned goods, beans, and soup, which Carter warmed up with a wire coil. When Carter's family sent him a birthday cake, a guard crushed it in a search for weapons and handed Carter the crumbs.

He refused to see parole officers, and he rarely worked in any prison shop, even though an inmate's sentence was reduced one day for each five days he worked. This calculation was meaningless to Carter. He could die in prison, and he would still owe the State of New Jersey two lives. Moreover, he rejected the traditional relationship between prisoner and prison, in which a mix of good behavior and contrition could be used to gain freedom. In his view, any type of parole or reduced sentence simply validated the court's verdict. It was not freedom that Carter demanded. It was exoneration.

He did submit to four psychological exams, but to him, talking to prison shrinks was aiding and abetting the enemy. In one report, the consulting psychologist Jack Milgram wrote: "During the present interview, Carter was belligerent, held himself aloof from the interview and refused to discuss himself . . . By his total non-verbal manner, it is assumed that he will be manipulative and violent."

Carter also loathed meeting with any prison representative because he had more important things to do. He was reading the transcripts of his trial and studying law books in the prison library. He even bought a few through mail catalogues, including a used copy of *Black's Law Dictionary*, which opened up a strange and forbidding world. *Sua sponte. Inter alia. Nolo contendere. Coram nobis. Writ of mandamus. Writ of error.* Carter sequestered himself like a monk in the library, a small rectangular room with old school desks equipped with a writing arm. He tried to read everything that related to his case: about evidence, search and seizure, perjury. Law students who wanted to help prisoners brought Carter copies of legal material from the state library. He learned that an appellate court could overturn his conviction not on the grounds of innocence or guilt but only if the authorities violated any law in securing the conviction.

So he spent months studying the *Miranda* case, which had been decided by the Supreme Court just four days before the Lafayette bar murders. In *Miranda v. Arizona,* the high court ruled that a suspect in police custody must be warned that he has the right to remain silent and that he has the right to an attorney. Carter claimed he had never received his *Miranda* warning; no one even *knew* about *Miranda,* he said. He read not only the Supreme Court's 5–4 decision but also its pedigree: the four cases and their appeals on which *Miranda* was based. He took notes on a legal pad and compared them with notes he had taken during his trial and with the actual transcripts.

Carter approached his appeal like a prizefight. He had to learn the rules, understand his enemy, overcome his own weaknesses, and execute a strategy. "He spent an incredible amount of time in the library," said Robert Hatrack, the prison's director of education. "He minded his own business and pursued his case, every detail." Cell lights were automatically turned off at 9:30 P.M., but light from the tier fell through the window bars of Carter's cell door. He sat with his back against the door and caught the pale rays on his books and court documents, and he typed out legal briefs that were used by his lawyer, Raymond Brown, in appealing his conviction to the New Jersey Supreme Court. Said Tariq Darby, the heavyweight boxer from New Jersey who served time with Carter: "He'd be typing his case all night long, and I would tell him, 'You either innocent or you possessed.'"

On July 15, 1969, the New Jersey Supreme Court affirmed the convictions of Rubin Carter and John Artis with a unanimous vote, 7–0. The appeal failed because Lieutenant DeSimone asserted that he gave Carter the proper warning; the defendant had no way of proving otherwise. Also failing on appeal was the assertion that Alfred Bello and Arthur Dexter Bradley perjured themselves in exchange for reward money and leniency from prosecutors. Chief Justice Joseph Weintraub said little about the credibility of the state's two key witnesses. He did write that the ability of the lone survivor, William Marins, to tell what happened on the night of the murders was "obviously impaired" because he had been shot in the head, and "he could contribute little more than that the armed men were Negroes." Evidently, Marins's original statements exonerating the defendants didn't count because he was "impaired," but his impairment did not preclude him from identifying the race of the killers.

Carter was devastated. Whenever his wife and daughter visited him in prison, he always told them he would be getting out shortly. On one occasion, an inmate was taking pictures of prisoners and their guests; when Tee asked Rubin if they could be photographed, he said absolutely not. "I am a free man." But on the Saturday after the state supreme court decision, Carter's family visited, and he felt nothing but shame and humiliation. His legal fees had burned through his savings, and now Tee and Theodora were living on public assistance. Looking at them through the bulletproof glass, Carter wept. As he later wrote in a prison journal about his family's going on welfare:

> They were the first Carters . . . to accept such a disgraceful position in life . . . I have never talked about this because, first, it might well embarrass my wife and daughter; and, secondly, I know without a doubt that I am certainly capable of snatching the breath from a person who would make some kind of wrong remark about this situation.

Carter became more intemperate than ever, and his anger spilled over one day in 1970 when he pummeled a mentally disturbed inmate named Wallace. Carter said the man had been about to throw a pot of hot coffee on him in the dining hall and castigated the administration for allowing Wallace to circulate in the general population. But a prison psychiatrist, in a report dated April 24, 1970, said Carter was showing "paranoid symptomatology" and placed him on Thorazine, an anti-psychotic drug. It was the last examination he ever submitted to by a prison shrink, for he viewed the head doctors as prison bureaucrats who rubber-stamped the warden's opinions. The next time a guard came to his cell with a pass for him to see a psychiatrist, Carter said, without looking up, "I don't have time. I'm busy."

Trenton State officials had had enough of their obstinate inmate. For reasons never explained to Carter, in 1971 he was transferred about sixty miles north to Rahway State Prison, in Rahway, New Jersey. Built in 1896, Rahway looked like a starfish on steroids, with four wings of mustard brick radiating from a round building with a yellowish dome. It had originally been used as a youth reformatory and was more spacious and less oppressive than Trenton State. The inmates watched movies, shot pool, and had contact visits.

Despite the better atmosphere, a riot broke out on Thanksgiving eve of 1971. An inmate named Clay Thomas, drunk from hooch, walked into an auditorium where other inmates were watching a porno movie and threw a folding chair through the screen. Carter was in the audience, and he tried to convince Thomas, also a former boxer from Paterson, to stop. "Clay, why are you doing this shit, man?" he asked. "If the state police come in here, we're all grass, and I'm on the top of the list."

Carter feared a repeat of Attica, the maximum-security prison near Buffalo, New York, which had erupted in a riot less than three months before; forty-three people had been killed. Tensions in the Rahway auditorium rose when the warden, Sam Vukcevich, entered. "Let's break this shit up, men!" he said. "You can't win!" Thomas and some of the other inmates — there were six hundred in the auditorium — thought otherwise, and they began threatening the warden and more than twenty guards.

Carter told the boozy crowd that he would have nothing to do with their shenanigans and walked out, with many following him. But a rumble ensued in the auditorium, and Vukcevich was struck from behind with a fire extinguisher and a chair, repeatedly kicked, and stabbed five times with a switchblade. Seven guards were also beaten and taken hostage. About two hundred inmates took control of two prison wings, burning mattresses, looting cells, setting off tear gas, and raping other inmates; they hung a bedsheet from a window declaring, "Remember Attica." Prison administrators turned off the water and heat. State troopers carrying shotguns circled the institution as massive lights were brought to the scene, lighting Rahway like Yankee Stadium.

The riot ended after twenty-seven hours when the insurgents, hung over, cold, and hungry, released the hostages. Governor William T. Cahill sent in Raymond Brown, Carter's former lawyer, as part of the negotiation team. Vukcevich's life was saved when an inmate, once an Army medic, used a safety pin and thread to close his wounds. Remarkably, no one was killed in the worst prison riot in New Jersey's history. Prison officials credited Carter, who had retreated to 3 Wing with other inmates and secured the safety of one guard, with preventing the riot from spreading further.

Carter felt contempt for the "big-time Mao Tse-tungs" who rioted with no purpose in mind and could have gotten everyone killed. But there turned out to be a silver lining for him inside the tear gas cloud. The riot drew the attention of Richard Solomon, a recent film school graduate in New York, who envisioned a movie or documentary about Carter's life. He visited Carter frequently over the next four years and ultimately played a major role in his becoming a cause célèbre. He was also the rainmaker for Carter's book. At the time, Carter had completed about a hundred pages, but he had not written a word in several years. Solomon recognized that a book could raise awareness about the case, rallying supporters to Carter's cause and advancing his own film aspirations. He made a cold call to a twenty-three-year-old editor at Viking Press. Linda Yablonsky read the pages and was impressed by the energy and power of Carter's writing. She persuaded the publisher to give Carter an advance of $10,000 to complete the manuscript.

Carter was stunned but euphoric. Viking's commitment gave him some precious dollars to continue his legal appeals. It also meant he had the opportunity to tell his story unfiltered by prosecutors, witnesses, or anyone else. In addition, Carter and Yablonsky developed a close friendship, in which Carter tried to explain himself and his surroundings to his young editor, and she tried to help her author channel his rage into a cohesive narrative. Yablonsky often drove to Rahway for all-day meetings with Carter. At the time, she was having problems in her personal life, but Carter invariably cheered her up with funny stories about his own life or the offbeat characters in a prison. She liked visiting him, then one day realized the oddity of going to prison to feel better about herself. This pattern — Carter's lifting the spirits of his supporters, even playing the role of counselor or father figure — occurred several times during his incarceration. The prisoner knew that before these supporters could help him, he had to help them.

Much of the work between Carter and Yablonsky was conducted through the mail. Over a three-year period, his letters took her into his confidence and gave the clearest indication on record of his thoughts. For one thing, they revealed his disdain of the other prisoners. On June 22, 1972, Carter wrote:

> I hate their half-ass revolutionary attitudes; their useless, empty rhetoric of would be Cleavers, Newtons and Bobby Seales ... They want to be jailhouse-revolutionaries without having to suffer the consequences of being in jail; and then they want to be <u>men</u> instead of the insignificant <u>males</u> that they are — but they don't know how to go about doing this either. Because they know that they are exactly what they appear to be: a bunch of fuck-up misfits just waiting for the next batch of dope to arrive so they can go back to their cells and continue their dreams about being revolutionaries.

But what emerges most often in these letters are the conflicting waves of Carter's fury, the desire for destructive vengeance juxtaposed with his loneliness and despair, his righteous anger leavened with touches of pragmatism, vulnerability, and irrepressible flirtations toward his pretty brunette editor. On her visits to Rahway, Yablonsky wore short skirts, which made the guards nervous but also caught Rubin's eye. On November 7, 1972, Carter wrote:

> Dear Little Buddy:
> ... How are you baby? I hope to "somebody" — somewhere that you're feeling better than I am; because this place is killing me! I've been down in the dumps the past few weeks or so, and can't seem to pull myself up and out of it, either ... There seems to be an ominous undercurrent of something terrible lurking in the deep bowels of this nasty cesspool. It's intangible — but I can feel it; it is not something that I can put my hands on directly ... yet its there everywhere ...
> The undeniable truth is that most of these jiveassed play-cops really think that every blackman in this joint is basically made up of the same synthetic material. They refuse to differentiate between different people, to recognize and respect a man's individuality when they come across it, and I'm afraid that shiftless proclivity is going to be their downfall.
> Because Rubin is struggling for his life and breath with every ounce of savvy at my command, trying hard to maintain my cool, fighting to stay out from under the ground; but if one of these fools — inmate or cop — fuck up and jeopardize these six long years that I've put in here and maybe

my eventual freedom, too ... I got to kill him! I <u>got</u> to take his life, and once started, I got to wipe-out everything around until I've been wasted myself ... and that worries me. Because it can happen so easily.

I have no control over my own life, here ... I only wish I could build me a hut far out in the fields by myself, and live there alone for the remaining time before going back to court. Because, if I get turned down there, this institution won't have to come look for me ... I'll come looking for them. Because I'm afraid that my time ain't long if this nonsense keeps building up the way it is. Morbid, huh? It's even worse than that, Baby!

... While these stinking jiveassed motherfuckers are still walking around here drinking hooch, fucking fags and getting fucked — talking sideways out of their nasty faces. I hate these bastards! If I had a big bomb, I'd drop it in here — even killing my own self; just to rid the world of these useless scum.

So, Linda, I haven't been writing lately ... haven't even retyped the chapters we worked on yet. But I will. Have no fear. I'll get myself together pretty soon. Your letter ought to do it. (smile) You know what? This may come as a surprise to you, but then again it may not ... but I've actually thought about you a thousand times if I thought about you once. I wanted to write ... really I did, I wanted to pour out how I felt; I needed somebody to talk. But again, I was under the impression that you were busy and didn't wish to be disturbed. But even more than that, the way I was feeling, I might have insulted you. I might have overstepped my bounds, so to speak, because I'm not sure that I would have been able to separate State from Self; keeping this thing strictly on a business basis and not making a damn fool of myself. You know what I mean?

Sometimes a place like this makes insane thoughts for real strange companions. Maybe it's only because you are the only woman that I come in physical contact with here. Oh well, marks-o-miss, its neither here nor there, but I have been rather concerned about you lately. What? No, don't laugh ... it ain't funny worth a damn. I'm not the granite rock you make me out to be after all, you see ... I like to be warm and cuddly too, sometimes (smile).

Take care of yourself, Baby. Let me hear from you more often, and let me know whenever you think that you'll be coming out here ... I wouldn't miss that pleasure for nothing in the world. Be good now, you hear? And if you can't be good ... at least be careful. May whoever you worship — bless and keep you,

Always with Love
Rubin

P.S. I'm not trying to "pimp" but I could use some stamps about now. What you say? Well all right, then. (smile) Rubin

Years later, Yablonsky described the letter as "the most fantastic correspondence" she had ever received. And while she considered Carter a very special friend, the two did keep separate "state and self" and maintained a platonic relationship.

Carter's fears about losing control, about trying to wipe out everything around him, almost came true in one very close call. Unlike his years at Trenton State, where he remained aloof from the general population, Carter became active in inmate politics at Rahway. In the aftermath of riots there, in Attica, and in other prisons, a jailhouse reform movement emerged. It typically featured the organization of inmate committees charged with airing grievances to prison administrators or outside officials. Carter initially ignored the Rahway Inmate Committee, but he then got involved amid the growing concerns of prisoners' medical conditions, including his own. Problems with his wasted right eye returned. When he began to feel pain, he was sent to a hospital in Newark, where doctors removed the stitches left in the eye from the previous surgery. This deepened Carter's anger at his medical mistreatment in prison. At the same time, Carter learned that another Rahway inmate had died, apparently from lack of medical attention. Faced with these concerns, he decided to plunge into prison politics.

Like most prisons, Rahway had conflicting factions — Muslims, Italians, Hispanics, urban blacks, and others. Carter sought the support from the toughest man in each group, who collectively made up the leaders in the prison. Promising to expand prisoners' rights and improve conditions, Carter was elected chairman of the Rahway Inmate Committee. He changed the name to the Rahway People's Council and pushed for humanitarian changes, such as replacing the long, impersonal dining tables with smaller tables for four. Carter, who was still wearing his own clothes, typically dungarees, prodded the administration to allow all prisoners to wear civilian clothes, mustaches, and beards, to permit televisions in cells, and to install two pay phones on each wing. There were plans to increase the medical staff. Carter demanded that prisoners be treated with respect and that they take pride in themselves. "Don't leave your manhood at the front gates and expect to pick it up on your way out," he would say.

The changes reflected the reform spirit of the time, and some would have taken place without Carter's prodding. He remained the consummate rebel — he wore a black turban because he knew it was forbidden

— and his growing power base was seen as a threat to the administration. He and the warden, Robert Hatrack, the former education director at Trenton State, clashed over such issues as Carter's desire to turn Rahway's administrative segregation area — its version of the "hole" — into a holding center for refugees. Carter, according to prison reports, talked openly about "getting rid of Hatrack" and allowing the inmates to run the prison. Hatrack believed that he was out of control. When Carter signed a consent form on March 7, 1974, allowing a photographer to shoot his picture, Carter scratched out "inmate" at Rahway Prison and wrote "God." Was he delusional or simply tweaking his captors? The administration wasn't taking any chances.

On April 30, tensions in the prison were high with rumors of a "lockdown," in which all inmates were confined indefinitely to their cells. Carter called a meeting in the prison's Drill Hall at 7 P.M. Standing on a table and using a microphone, he gave a speech before two hundred inmates. According to prison records, Carter criticized the administration for being untruthful and disparaged the medical and education departments and the prison food. But he also urged restraint, pleading with the inmates to channel their grievances through the council. "We don't want revolution but evolution," Carter declared. "We have won the battle [in prison improvements], but we're losing the war because we're not working as one. Your committee knows what to do with the victory . . . Rioting," he said, was not necessary, but he exhorted the inmates "to make the state serve you and not you serve the state." He concluded: "If there is going to be a fight around here or if there is going to be any killing, I will be the first to die." Carter stepped down to cheers.

Later that night, Carter lay on his cot reading the galleys of his autobiography, *The Sixteenth Round: From Number 1 Contender to Number 45472*. These pages were the climax of an arduous two-year struggle for Carter, who could not read without moving his lips. Often sitting shirtless in his cell, he would run his index finger down the pages of a pocket dictionary. When he found the right word, he voiced each letter and searched his antiquated Underwood typewriter for the corresponding key. He struck each one with the focus and intensity of a left jab. To a prisoner in a nearby cell, L. J. Cochran, the pecking sounds all night long — *tap, pause; tap, pause* — were the equivalent of Chinese water torture.

Carter spent many nights scrubbing the typewriter's metal hammers with steel wool so that the letters printed cleanly. He bristled at Yablonsky's cuts and objected to Viking's title, believing that the reference to #45472 was dehumanizing. Still, he was proud of his achievement, confident that his story — a rending mix of impassioned grievances and operatic violence (in Paterson, in youth reformatories, in the Army, in the boxing ring) — would pierce the conscience of readers and generate support for his cause.

Carter's joy that evening, however, was tempered by a growing unease. Nighttime was hazardous for inmates who ran afoul of the administration. Guards rarely beat inmates during the day, lest other prisoners intervene and set off a full-scale riot. But at night, when inmates were locked in their cells, guards could deliver their punishment discreetly.

The tier lights were supposed to be dimmed at 10 P.M., but tonight the lights stayed on. Any deviation from the clockwork schedule was ominous. Carter knew that the Drill Hall meeting had not been sanctioned by the administration, that his day of reckoning had finally come. And he knew exactly what he was going to do. He was going to fight. He had spent fifteen of his thirty-six years behind bars, and now he would take out as many guards as he could before they took him out. Carter put away his glasses and peeled off his dungarees and T-shirt. He pushed his footlocker and his desk in front of his door. He put on a black hooded sweatshirt and matching black sweatpants, then smeared Vaseline across his face as a protective layer against Mace and pulled up the black cowl, the better to slip the guards' heavy clubs. He sat, waited, and watched. Finally he heard the rumblings of heavy boots, first softly, then louder, echoing up the metal stairs and along the concrete corridor. His door was solid except for a rectangular opening at eye level, and Carter watched as a battalion of guards, at least twenty, surrounded his door. They wore riot helmets with plastic shields over their eyes, bulletproof vests, and combat boots; they carried riot sticks and Mace. One held a video camera to film the impending furor. If they killed Carter, they could show it was self-defense. The Hurricane, sweating as in the old days, his eyes narrowed, was ready to rumble.

There was a knock on his door and Bobby Martin, a squat, rugged North Carolinian with blond hair, peered inside. Martin commonly took his beefs with prisoners out in the yard, where he and his foe took their shirts off and settled the matter in a straight-up fight. Martin usually won. Carter admired his toughness, and a friendship had blossomed. A few years earlier, two Muslim prisoners cornered Martin on 4 Wing, and the guard had no escape. Carter suddenly appeared and told the inmates, "If you want him, you're going to have to take me first." The Muslims left; Martin didn't forget.

The guard was off duty when he heard that Carter was in trouble, and he was still in civilian clothes when he reached Carter's door.

"Hey, Rube, what's going on?"

"I don't know," Carter said. "But they're coming to get me."

"I don't know where you're going, but I just know you've got to go. What are you going to do?"

"Whatever's necessary."

"Rube, they told me you're going to kill the first four people who go in there."

"Yeah?"

"Who do you think is going to be the first one in there, Rube?" After a long pause, Martin answered his own question: "Me."

"Aw, shit; this is supposed to be your night off!" Carter said.

"You can knock out the first twenty that come in, but it makes no difference. There will be twenty more."

"Bobby, I've got my galley proofs here. This is my way out. I can't let them take this because I know that's what they're going to do."

"Rube, if you put the manuscript in your pants, I'll cuff you and go wherever they send you. I'll make sure the manuscript stays safe and gets sent wherever it needs to go."

Carter pondered the offer. "You would do that?"

"Yeah."

"Okay, let's go."

Carter was immediately brought before a prison tribunal called the Adjustment Committee, three people who conveniently enough all worked for the prison. Neither Carter nor any other prisoner could be transferred from Rahway unless he was found guilty of violating prison rules. The committee promptly found Carter and four other council leaders guilty of "inciting and holding an illegal meeting." Prisons often crack down on ringleaders and make examples of them to the rest of the inmates. In this case, Carter and Tommy Trantino were singled out. Trantino, like Carter, was a charismatic prison rebel who had been convicted in 1964 for slaying two police officers. Nicknamed "the rabbi" — he was half Jewish, half Italian — Trantino became New Jersey's first long-haired inmate when he refused to cut his hair on Death Row in Trenton, and he published a book about prison life just a few months before the Drill Hall incident. While the other three inmates found guilty of inciting were transferred to Trenton or Leesburg State Prison, Carter and Trantino were ordered to the "Vroom building."

Carter had been inside the New Jersey corrections system since he was fourteen, and he thought he knew of every holding cell, every assignment center, every death trap, in the statewide complex. But he had never heard of the Vroom building; he just knew the name had a wicked ring. With Martin at his side and a restraining belt around his waist, Carter was hauled down to Trenton. But instead of going to the state prison, he was driven along a winding country road. The car stopped at a huge, Gothic-looking structure set back from the road on desolate grounds. Carter later learned that this was the Trenton Psychiatric Hospital, and behind it was a small brick building officially known as the Vroom Readjustment Unit, or VRU, which held the criminally insane and other incorrigibles.* Sending prisoners to a mental hospital recalled the Soviet treatment of dissidents, and Carter was not prepared for the experience. He gave the galley proofs to Martin; then, still shackled, he entered the VRU in the dead of night. A guard walked him down a long gray corridor to a set of sliding doors that opened automatically. After they walked through, the doors closed — but the next set of doors stayed sealed. For a long moment they were trapped, interred in the stomach of a century-old building . . . until the other doors opened. Carter stepped through quickly. He was led down another corridor lined with human cages, from which soft cries and occasional screams escaped. The front of the cells was lined with steel mesh, which prevented the prisoners from throwing feces at passersby.

The Vroom building was defined by the isolation it imposed. The inmates rarely left their cells except for brief trips every few days to a prison yard. Meals were served in the cells. The units had cement extrusions that prevented communication with adjacent inmates, and the guards refused to talk to or even acknowledge the existence of their

---

* The building was named after New Jersey's former governor Peter D. Vroom, Jr., who advocated prison reform in the 1830s.

captives — except at night, when Carter saw and heard guards beating and brutalizing prisoners.

Carter, fortunately, had help on the outside. His transfer was publicized in newspaper stories, and lawyers who specialized in prisoners' rights filed a suit in federal court alleging that the State of New Jersey illegally transferred Carter and Trantino to the VRU. In the meantime, Dave Anderson, a sports columnist for the *New York Times* who had written previous stories about Carter in Rahway, visited him at the VRU. It was a blistering June day, and as Anderson was escorted down a hallway, he heard an odd hiss. He looked around and noticed old radiators chugging out heat. *Heat!* Anderson met Carter in a small windowless room, and as the interview progressed, the temperature rose and the room became a sauna. Both men were sweating and, after twenty minutes, Anderson had had enough.

"Rubin, this has nothing to do with you," he said, "but coming in here I heard this hissing, and I heard the radiator was on, and it's ninety-five degrees out!"

"In the winter," Carter replied, "they turn the motherfucker off."

He would not be in the Vroom building much longer. After a hearing, U.S. District Court Judge Clarkson S. Fisher ordered that Carter and Trantino be released from the VRU, ruling that their due process rights had been violated and that "inciting" was not a recognizable offense under the prison's disciplinary rules. Carter's suit for damages was not resolved for nine more years, but after ninety-two days he was freed from the clammy purgatory of the New Jersey corrections system. Carter was returned not to Rahway, however, but to the more restrictive Trenton State Prison. Little did he know that the biggest surprise in his legal battle was about to occur.

7

RADICAL CHIC REDUX

FRED HOGAN DID NOT believe it. He read the newspaper clips over and over again, the ones his father had just sent him. It was the summer of 1967, and the clips showed Rubin Carter leaving the courthouse in handcuffs and triumphant headlines announcing his conviction. "Holy shit," Hogan kept muttering. Sitting on his Army cot in Augsburg, Germany, where he served in the 24th Infantry Division, Hogan was thousands of miles from his home in Jersey City. He had boxed as a teenager, and he had met Carter a few times at his training camp in Chatham. (Hogan's father, a jailhouse guard, knew Carter's manager.) Hogan had been mesmerized by Carter's left hook and by his rhetorical jabs urging youngsters to stand up for themselves and act like men. Carter had given Hogan an autographed red and yellow poster promoting one of his Madison Square Garden fights, and Hogan hung the memento in his Army barrack. After Carter was charged with the Lafayette bar murders, Hogan's father began sending him newspaper articles about the unfolding drama. The whole thing — the arrest, the trial, the conviction — smelled rotten. If the jurors really believed that two black men shot down three white people, they would have fried the killers. There was no mercy for blacks in Paterson, not in the sixties. And Hogan never believed that Carter would have wasted three people with a shotgun. He would have used his hands.

Discharged from the Army in 1968, Hogan returned to New Jersey and landed a patrolman's job on the Atlantic Highlands police force. His Irish-Catholic, blue-collar upbringing gave him an affinity for the underdog; he only issued about ten tickets in two years and was more inclined to buy a bum a cup of coffee than to shoo him off the streets. That way he also made a friend. When he noticed a newspaper ad for job openings in the New Jersey Public Defender's Office, he figured that would be a better way to help people in need. The job paid more as well, $8,600 a year. He was hired as an investigator in the department's Monmouth County bureau.

Hogan had not contacted Carter since returning to the States. But his new job often took him to New Jersey's prisons. On one visit to Rahway in late 1970, he decided to see Carter. They met in a visiting room, and Hogan immediately noticed that Carter was not wearing a standard brown prison uniform but some kind of modified white doctor's outfit.

"Rubin Carter, my name is Fred Hogan, and you probably don't remember me," he began, explaining that he had visited Carter at his training camp.

Carter indeed had no memory of Hogan, who was now heavyset, had a thick handlebar mustache, and wore leisure suits.

Hogan got to the point: "I think you got fucked."

Carter nodded but said little. He didn't trust strangers under any circumstance, and when they visited him in prison, he felt he was on display in a cage, like a tiger in a zoo. "How do you know?" Carter asked.

"Based on what I've read, and I'd like to find out more."

"You can do what you want." Carter shrugged. The meeting ended quickly and edgily.

Hogan's blunt, street-smart style made him popular among the inmates. After the Thanksgiving Day riot at Rahway, prisoners asked that he represent them on a negotiating committee with the administration. Hogan had another important attribute, tenacity, and it slowly won Carter over. He was willing to investigate Carter's case on his own time, initially outside the auspices of the Public Defender's Office. He got his own copy of the trial transcripts plus other court exhibits not available to Carter, and on weekends he drove the hundred-mile round-trip to Rahway. While sipping black coffee and piling up cigarette butts, Hogan and Carter pored over the record from the two-and-a-half-week trial.

"I believe you didn't do it, but the truth has nothing to do with this," Hogan told Carter during one meeting. "You can be antisystem if you want, but the only way you're going to get out of here is through the system. You have to show me where you were wrongfully convicted."

"Bello and Bradley," Carter said, stressing the same points that Ray Brown had made in the trial: Alfred Bello and Arthur Dexter Bradley committed perjury in exchange for reward money and leniency from the prosecutors for their own crimes.

Bello, as it happened, was back in jail for burglary by 1973, and Hogan heard through the prison grapevine that he was saying he was "troubled" by his Lafayette bar testimony. Hogan knew that the five-year statute of limitations for perjury had expired, so it was clear what had to be done. "If Bello and Bradley lied," he told Carter, "then the key is getting them to recant." Such statements, he assumed, would force the authorities to give Carter a new trial.

Hogan's decision to investigate Carter's case — on his own time — befit his maverick style, but he could also be irresponsible. He drank too much scotch and vodka, once rolling a state car while intoxicated.* His solo style in the Carter case irritated his superiors. They eventually assigned the case to him officially, but they feared his friendship with Carter and his willingness to devote so much of his own time could compromise the investigation. Hogan, in fact, did use poor judgment. He held Carter's advance money for *The Sixteenth Round,* assuming a fiduciary responsibility for a client of the Public Defender's Office. He thought he was doing Carter a favor, but Passaic County prosecutors later depicted Hogan as less Carter's advocate than his business partner. Hogan's chumminess with Carter also did not sit well with certain colleagues, and the investigator received anonymous letters at work branding him a "nigger lover."

But Hogan was also the first true believer, someone outside Carter's circle of friends and family who believed in his innocence. Unlike many later supporters, who saw Carter as a symbol of racial injustice in America, Hogan studied the details of his case and saw it as the fight for one man's freedom. In the years ahead, Carter often said that he would have died in prison if not for Fred Hogan.

While Hogan prowled New Jersey for Bello and Bradley, Richard Solomon had much bigger ambitions. The young film graduate from New

---

* Hogan became an alcoholic in the late seventies, but he kicked the bottle in 1982.

York University wanted to make the Hurricane's fight for freedom part of the cultural zeitgeist. Solomon originally approached Carter strictly for his own reasons. He believed the convict's life would make a compelling screenplay or documentary. Solomon had no film credits to his name, but he had watched Carter box on television and was captivated by his black-hat image. He was not particularly interested in the truth about the Lafayette bar murders or even in Carter's innocence or guilt. Young, ambitious, and desperate for a break, he simply wanted a good story.

Solomon sent letters to Rahway after the Thanksgiving riot but never received a response. He finally went to the prison himself and saw Carter under the guise that he represented an attorney. (His father was a prominent labor lawyer.) Carter's hard stares and stiff body language intimidated Solomon — he's no Sidney Poitier, he thought — but he made his pitch: he wanted to make a film about Carter's life, and if he made money on the project, Carter would make money. All he needed was Carter's cooperation.

Carter initially resisted the offer. He thought this affluent but sheltered, skinny Jewish kid from Manhattan, sitting in this New Jersey prison, was from Mars. But Solomon kept returning to Rahway. Early sessions between the two were rocky, as Carter, scowling, rebuffed any questions. But he soon recognized that Solomon could help him. He did not really care about making money, but he hoped Solomon, through a film or other connections, could drum up support for him. Carter had nothing to lose, so he opened up and talked freely about his childhood in Paterson and his Army and boxing days. At the same time, Solomon shared his own fears about trying to make something of his own life, of the months he spent holed up in his parents' apartment, of living up to family expectations, of his relationship with his girlfriend. Carter spoke to Solomon's parents on the phone about their son. A close bond formed, and Carter became a surrogate father for the young man.

During this process, Solomon became convinced of Carter's innocence. He had no doubt that Carter was capable of violence, even brutality, but he also concluded that Carter was thoughtful, calculating. The prosecutors' theory — that Carter shot a room full of people, then picked up a neighborhood alcoholic, John "Bucks" Royster, then casually drove around the streets of Paterson until the police picked him up — didn't make sense. Carter would have had to be both brutal and stupid, and he wasn't stupid. Solomon still wanted to make a film, but now he decided he would directly help Carter's fight for freedom.

While Hogan searched for new evidence, Solomon plotted ways to give Rubin's plight "an aura of Greek tragedy." With the civil rights era ebbing, he believed he could tap into pools of white guilt over continued racial inequities in the criminal justice system. While the publication of *The Sixteenth Round,* expected in the fall of 1974, might help, Solomon needed a respected journalist to investigate the case and legitimate Carter's claims of innocence. He found Selwyn Raab.

In the fall of 1973, Solomon read a profile about Raab's investigative work concerning the murders of two young career women in Manhattan ten years earlier. A young black man, George Whitmore, had allegedly confessed to the crime, but Raab pursued the story for eight years, initially for the *New York World-Telegram and Sun,* and uncovered exonerating evidence. Whitmore was eventually freed. Raab wrote a book about the case, and CBS bought the screen rights for a movie, transforming the rumpled reporter into a bald detective named Kojak. The success of the movie led to the *Kojak* series on television.

Living on Manhattan's Lower East Side, Raab had boxed as a youngster, had a soft spot for underdogs, and was aware of the commercial value of breaking a big story. He was working at WNET, New York City's public television station, when he got a call from Solomon. The journalist agreed to look into the matter but told Solomon — and later Carter — that if his investigation proved Carter guilty, he would report exactly that. He read the trial transcripts, visited Paterson, and conducted interviews and quickly became skeptical of the state's case. In Paterson he retraced the steps of Bello and Bradley and concluded that Bradley had lied when he testified that he was standing outside the Ace Sheet Metal Company when he saw Carter driving down the street. The metal company was in a depressed lot, and Raab thought a clear view of a passing car was impossible.

Raab, who was no stranger to jailhouse interviews, spoke at length to Carter and found him convincing. He also interviewed John Artis and found nothing in his background or character that would explain the savagery for which he had been convicted. Finally, Raab found the defendants' behavior on the night of the crime — specifically, picking up Royster like a limousine service after allegedly shooting four people in cold blood — ridiculously inconsistent with guilt.

Like Hogan, Raab believed the key to raising doubts about Carter's guilt was finding Bradley and Bello. If Bradley was lying, maybe Bello was too. So Raab and Hogan worked together, tracking down Bello in Bergen County Jail in November 1973. Bello hinted that he hadn't told the truth, but he wouldn't talk in specifics; he then made bail and disappeared. Shortly thereafter, Raab was promoted to executive editor at WNET and had to give up his reporting. He handed his files over to a balding, bespectacled reporter named Harold Levinson, who continued the hunt with Hogan. When they found Bradley in May 1974 at his home in Wayne, New Jersey, he initially greeted them with a baseball bat in hand.

Like Bello, Bradley had also told fellow prisoners over the years that he had lied in the Carter case to save his own skin. Hogan and Levinson told him that now the five-year statute of limitations for perjury had expired, and they wanted his help. In a four-hour conversation in a parking lot behind his home, Bradley walked off a few times, but he was also angry with the police for not coming to his defense after his most recent arrest. He finally acknowledged that he had not seen anyone the night of the crime and that he had been pressured into testifying by police. He signed a statement of recantation.

That left Bello to seal the story. But by June Raab was back in the hunt. He had taken a job as a reporter with the *New York Times*, and he renewed his investigation. He found Bradley, who repeated his recantation. Then, in September, Bello resurfaced in Bergen County Jail, serving a nine-month sentence for burglary. This time he was ill, despondent, battling alcoholism — and angry with Lieutenant DeSimone, who had not kept him out of jail. So Bello talked, separately, to Raab, Hogan, and Levinson. And Bello too signed a statement of recantation.

Before Raab wrote his story, he drove to Paterson to interview DeSimone. Sitting in the lieutenant's small office, Raab told him about the recantations. "These guys are liars," DeSimone said. "We don't manufacture witnesses." When Raab persisted, DeSimone, who was coatless, leaned back in his chair, allowing a clear view of his sidearm holster. "I have a bad heart," he told Raab. "If I go out, maybe you'll be going with me." He patted his gun.

"Who's going to believe a scrawny reporter like me took you on?" Raab replied. "I have a job to do."

DeSimone then brusquely kicked him out of the office. As Raab recalled years later, "DeSimone screamed invectives that would make a piano player in a whorehouse blush."

For Rubin Carter, Raab's arrival at the *Times* was a godsend: now the story that eviscerated the state's case against him had the imprimatur of the country's most powerful newspaper. Raab's lengthy front-page article on September 27, 1974, did more than describe the recantations. It also depicted Passaic County investigators, particularly DeSimone, as bullying racists who were willing to do whatever necessary to convict Carter and Artis. "There's no doubt Carter was framed," Bradley said in the article. Both Bello and Bradley said that in return for false testimony, they were promised favorable treatment on criminal charges that each man faced. After Carter's murder trial, for example, Bradley pleaded guilty to robbery and other charges in five different New Jersey counties. He could have received prison terms totaling more than eighty years. Instead, he served only three years. "There's only one reason I testified," Bradley said. "That was all the time" he could serve in prison. "They never would have got me to talk otherwise. I saw a way out of my own mess." Bello also said he had committed perjury in hopes of receiving the reward money.

Both Bello and Bradley told Raab they were recanting out of remorse. Bradley said his conscience troubled him, and "sooner or later, I knew the truth would come out." In addition, Bello said his recent arrest for burglary showed "the cops are out to get me anyway, and there's no reason for me to protect them anymore." Bello repeated his accusations in a press conference that day, although the handcuffed prisoner would not allow news cameras to shoot him head-on.

The most incendiary part of the *Times*'s article was the racist comments attributed to law enforcement officials in Paterson or Passaic County. According to Bello, detectives referred to Carter and Artis as "niggers, Muslims, animals, and murderers." They told him he would be performing a "public service" by "getting them off the streets," thereby protecting whites. "They told me, 'Help your own people,'" Bello said, "and I went for it." Raab, describing his brief but fiery encounter with DeSimone, wrote that the lieutenant said these comments were "nonsense," then "ordered this reporter to leave his office."

The timing of the article could not have been more propitious for

Carter. It came one month after Richard Nixon had resigned from the presidency, when government cover-ups and official corruption dominated the news. The analogy between Watergate and Carter's case was promptly established in an October 3 editorial in the *Times,* "New Jersey Justice." Calling for the case to be reconsidered by the New Jersey courts, the editorial concluded, "[If] Watergate taught nothing else, it did teach there is no greater threat to society than illegal abuse of power by those sworn to uphold the law."

The Sixteenth Round had also just been released. Even critics who faulted the book's excessive finger pointing — at duplicitous boxing promoters, perfidious prosecutors, and white America in general — had to acknowledge that the recantations bolstered Carter's claim that he had been framed.* But Carter knew that his autobiography and the *Times* article were not enough to broaden his support. He needed to reach the masses. He needed public outcry. He needed an advertising man, and he found one in George Lois.

The son of a Greek florist, Lois became Madison Avenue's wunderkind in the 1960s by designing outlandish, arresting covers for *Esquire* magazine. There was Richard Nixon, in 1968, receiving a makeover with lipstick, nose powder, and hair spray; a smiling Lieutenant Calley, on trial for the My Lai massacre, photographed with four Vietnamese children; and Muhammad Ali, posing as the martyr Saint Sebastian — head tilted in anguish, arms behind his back, and bloody arrows affixed to his body. Lois, screaming, scheming, coaxing, persuaded Jack Nicholson to pose nude, cigar in hand, for a cover, but it was killed before publication. Fiery resolve was the lanky adman's trademark. He once got kicked out of his YMCA in Manhattan for fighting during pickup basketball games, but he was readmitted after he got testimonial letters from Bobby Kennedy, Mickey Mantle, and other luminaries he rubbed shoulders with in the overlapping worlds of politics, sports, and advertising.

Lois, like many boxing fans, had followed Carter's case in the news-

* The *New York Times*, while disclosing racism in the Carter case, was not without its own blinders. In its October 15, 1974, review of the book, the *Times* ran the headline "Even the Inarticulate Testify." Nothing in the article suggested that Carter was inarticulate; in fact, he is well-spoken, but the newspaper evidently assumed that a black prisoner could not be articulate.

papers and figured Carter was guilty, that the murders were a doomed extension of the hostility he showed in the ring. Then Lois got a call from Solomon, who asked if he wanted to help drum up publicity for Carter. Lois was already reading *The Sixteenth Round*. When he finished, he called Solomon back and expressed interest. Solomon, who had been rebuffed by other advertising executives, cautioned Lois that if he took up Carter's cause, he could lose clients. "Hey, schmuck, you working for or against this nigger?" Lois said. "I'll do it."*

Lois visited Carter in Trenton State and mapped out a full campaign that included a large celebrity drive, fund-raising activities, bumper stickers, videotapes of Rubin speaking, brochures invoking Watergate, and a T-shirt that read: "The Only Innocent Hurricane." In March 1975, Lois bought a one-column, three-inch ad on page 2 of the *New York Times*. Signed by Rubin "Hurricane" Carter, No. 45472, it began: "Counting today, I have sat in prison 3,135 days for a crime I did not commit. If I don't get a retrial, I have 289 years to go."

Lois understood the nexus of celebrity, media, and public opinion, and he knew he needed to repackage Carter for the masses — or at least the white masses. Carter was not simply an angry black man fighting for his freedom but a victim of racial bias whose plight defined America. In one publicity brochure, Carter was photographed behind bars with the tag line: "All who love America would love to see this man free." Lois believed that Carter was innocent, but he also recognized that the former boxer could fill a political void. At the time, the civil rights movement, Vietnam, and Watergate had run their course. The political left was complacent. Rubin Carter, charismatic, persuasive, betrayed, could change all that.

By the spring of 1975, Lois and Solomon had launched the Hurricane Trust Fund to raise money for legal expenses. They sought out power brokers and business leaders, the gorgeous and the glamorous, attaching them to the masthead like amulets. Lois worked his connections in the worlds of sports, entertainment, business, and politics. The pitch was straightforward. The only witnesses who placed Carter at the scene of the crime now admit they lied. There were no fingerprints, no murder

---

* According to Lois, Ed Horrigan at Cutty Sark pulled an $8-million-a-year account from Lois's agency, Lois Holland Callaway Inc. Horrigan told Lois to "stop working for the nigger."

weapons, no motive; just a bunch of redneck cops off the Jersey turn-pike. There was already talk about an executive pardon from New Jersey's governor.

"Of course Carter's innocent!" Lois would yell at a prospective supporter. "But all he's asking for is a new trial!"

Solomon courted celebrities differently. Viewing them as jaded stars desperate for a new thrill, he said he had something to offer that was better than money or drugs or fancy cars or pricey furs. "Hey, you want to go to a maximum-security prison?" he would tell a potential backer. "You can meet a black guy they say has killed three people."

The entreaties worked. A slew of celebrities, white and black, put their names on the Hurricane Fund or spoke out on Carter's behalf. From Hollywood came Dyan Cannon, Ellen Burstyn, William Friedkin, and Burt Reynolds. Entertainers included Roberta Flack, Harry Belafonte, Stevie Wonder, Ben Vereen, and Johnny Cash. The presidents of Bristol Myers Products and Gulf & Western Industries wrote to the governor of New Jersey. There were politicians: Congressman Ed Koch, Manhattan Borough President Percy Sutton, Mayor Lee Alexander of Syracuse, and Mayor Kenneth Gibson of Newark. Also signing on were Claude Brown, Coretta Scott King, the Reverend Jesse Jackson, Geraldo Rivera, Norman Mailer, Jimmy Breslin, Henry Aaron, Walt Frazier, and Don King.

Carter held court for these big-name entertainers. The talk show host Mike Douglas interviewed Carter from prison, with Dyan Cannon, a flower in her hair, sitting nearby. Tom Snyder arrived for an appearance on the *Tomorrow* show. "I have not been rehabilitated because I have not committed a crime," Carter told the silver-haired host. "I was making $100,000 a year at the time. Why should I stick up a bar for pennies?"

Lois and the others visited Carter in rented Rolls-Royces and Ferraris. The adman wanted to create the impression that financial heavyweights were backing Carter, a tactic that might convince New Jersey's governor to grant Carter a pardon. Lois also figured that blue-collar guards would associate wealthy supporters with political power and therefore not mistreat Carter lest the entire prison bureaucracy suffer. These supporters were soon promoting the idea of Carter's running for public office while Solomon wrote his screenplay and sold it to two independent movie producers. (It was never made.)

Muhammad Ali was Carter's most high-profile advocate. The heavy-weight boxing champion, who was friendly with both Lois and Carter, admired those who bucked the system and refused to compromise with the powers-that-be. His world title had been stripped from him in 1967 after Ali, a Muslim, refused to serve in the armed forces on religious grounds. Ali now saw Carter as a kindred spirit, a black man who had been unfairly punished because of his race. As Ali promoted his October 1, 1975, fight with Joe Frazier, the "thrilla in Manila," he pleaded Carter's case in television appearances, to newspaper reporters, and even in the Ali–Frazier fight program. Ali handwrote, in a sloppy blue scrawl, that he and Frazier didn't like each other but they agreed on one thing: "We dedicate ourselves to doing all we can in helping free Rubin Hurricane Carter, a Great Man who was unjustly imprisoned." In a rare show of amity, both Ali and Frazier signed the note.

Public backing for Carter slowly grew. The NAACP compared Carter's case to the Scottsboro trial. A group based in Newark, the New Jersey Defense Committee, collected fifteen thousand signatures demanding that Brendan Byrne, the state's low-key governor, free Carter. More than a dozen elected officials from New Jersey and New York appealed to Byrne to order an investigation into the handling of the case. Mayor Gibson of Newark declared September 6 "Rubin Carter Day" in his predominantly black city. That same day, the nearby city of East Orange renamed one of its main thoroughfares "Justice for Rubin Carter Avenue." Nelson Algren, the radical novelist known for bestsellers like *The Man with the Golden Arm,* moved to Paterson in December 1974 to research Carter's case.*

Lois's strategy paid off as Carter's cause took on the accouterments of an antiwar protest or a civil rights demonstration. On October 17, 1975, Ali led a one-mile march through Trenton on Carter's behalf, culminating in a rally of sixteen hundred shouting, shoving demonstrators outside the state capitol. Using a microphone on the State House steps, surrounded by Muslim bodyguards carrying walkie-talkies,

---

* Algren wrote a magazine piece about Carter before the *Times* published the recantation story. Algren suggested that Carter was innocent, but both *Esquire* and *Playboy,* apparently uncomfortable with this thesis, rejected the piece. Algren then tried to write a book about Carter's case, but he ultimately settled for a fictitious account in *The Devil's Stocking.*

Ali called Carter's case "New Jersey's Watergate," blithely predicted that Carter would be freed in a few days, and extended his hand to an unlikely comrade. "I'd like to thank my number one friend, Joe Frazier," who joined the protest march less than three weeks after Ali had beaten him in their brutal fight.

Protesters hoped to pressure Governor Byrne to grant Carter and Artis executive pardons, which would end the case with their release, or clemency, which would release them from prison temporarily, until the judicial proceedings were completed. One protest sign wryly noted: "Gov. Byrne: Release Carter & Artis, win two sure votes." Another said: "My God, they pardoned Nixon." The governor, an Ivy League product whose blond hair and good breeding gave him a golden-boy image, sent out ambiguous signals about the case.* On the day of the protest, Byrne met with a small group of celebrity supporters, but he was less impressed with Ali and Frazier than with Ellen Burstyn, whom he admired. But Burstyn did not leave much of an impression regarding the Carter case. At a news conference after the meeting, the governor had little to say about Carter except that he would consider a clemency petition, if filed, on its merits.

The Carter bandwagon proved to be a mixed blessing. It deepened the hostility toward Carter among his adversaries, particularly New Jersey law enforcement officials. In addition, boosters who saw Carter as a trendy cause did not know the background of his case, and they later bailed out at the first whiff of trouble. Just as liberal support of the Black Panthers in the late sixties gave rise to "radical chic," Rubin Carter's cause acquired a certain opportunistic sympathy.

Ultimately, neither the politicians nor the protesters were going to free Carter. As Fred Hogan had told him, his passage to freedom would come by working through the judicial system. Unfortunately, that passage seemed forever clogged. By 1974, both Carter and John Artis were indigent, and they were represented by lawyers from the state's Public Defender's Office. The lawyers asked for a new trial following disclosure

---

* Governor Byrne had indirectly been involved with the original case. As the Essex County prosecutor in 1967, he made a leniency plea on behalf of Arthur Dexter Bradley. Byrne and four other county prosecutors were asked to do so by the Passaic County Prosecutor's Office as consideration for Bradley's testimony. Byrne's intervention later fueled conspiracists' claims that Carter's jailing implicated even the governor of the state.

of the recantations in September. The following month, a hearing was held by the original trial judge, Samuel Larner of the New Jersey Superior Court. It was a peculiar arrangement. For Judge Larner, accepting the veracity of the recantations would be admitting that two petty thieves — and the state's two key witnesses — had made a mockery of him and his courtroom. But under New Jersey law, the presiding trial judge was required to hear the first stage of an appeal, on the theory that the judge was already familiar with the case. In this particular case, Judge Larner decreed on December 11 that the recantations "lacked the ring of truth." In a stinging, forty-six-page ruling, he seemed offended by the demand for a new trial, writing:

> Does the mere fact that state's witnesses give recanting post-trial testimony necessarily entitle the defendants to a new trial? Absolutely not! If mere recantation in itself dictates a new trial, the entire judicial process could be frustrated by the mere whim of a witness recanting his testimony.

Carter then fired his public defender lawyers, saying they had failed to consult him properly on legal strategy. He convinced an experienced criminal lawyer in New York, Myron Beldock, to take his case. Lewis Steel, another New York attorney, agreed to represent Artis. The change in counsel meant that Carter desperately needed to raise money, even if it meant paying only a fraction of his legal expenses. The Hurricane Fund brought in sympathy checks from outraged liberals, but that was not enough. He needed to spread the word beyond the liberal elite and blacks. It would take the man who made "blowin' in the wind" a catchphrase for mournful dissent to turn the Hurricane into a pop icon of social injustice in the seventies.

Carter was not a Bob Dylan fan, but the ever-present Solomon was. The aide-de-camp felt he had grown up with Dylan's social protest songs in the sixties, and he believed the songwriter could use Carter's travails to express similar themes in the seventies. He wrote an impassioned letter to Dylan's office in the spring of 1975. He did not ask Dylan to write a song about Carter; he simply explained the injustice that had been committed. Some weeks later, the phone rang in Solomon's apartment.

"What do you want from me?" Dylan asked.

"I've followed your music for a long time," Solomon said, "and based upon that, I thought this might interest you. Do you want to meet him?"

"Yeah, maybe."

"He's in a maximum-security prison," Solomon said.

"Is it dangerous?"

"No."

"Let me give it some thought."

When they hung up, Solomon turned to his girlfriend. "You watch and see. He'll get involved in this case and write a song."

"Why?" she asked.

"Because that's what he does for a living."

Solomon sent Dylan a copy of *The Sixteenth Round*. Impressed, Dylan agreed to visit Carter that summer. Carter prepared for the meeting by reading a book of Dylan's lyrics and listening to his songs. Dylan, for his part, knew little of Carter beyond Solomon's letter and the book. But the two men, sitting across from each other in the morning hours at the prison library, quickly found common ground.

Both men were performers and crowd pleasers. But they were also reclusive, shy, and restless. Carter, the black middleweight with a vicious left hook whose parents were raised in the Jim Crow South, could appreciate Dylan, the Jewish troubadour with a harp rack whose ancestors escaped the tyrannies of the Russian czar. They both felt an affinity for the powerless and thought they had a responsibility to speak out on their behalf. These connections emerged in their first conversation. Carter did most of the talking — about his case, about prison, about religion, about society, and about how this country seemed to be promoting nothing but concrete. He had brought a poem with him about a bird in search of flight and freedom, and he told Dylan that his songs would have much more power if his music reached a multiracial audience.

"You're a sixteen-cylinder man operating on four cylinders," Carter said.

Dylan laughed, but he saw the toll of prison life. He was taken aback when he heard about Carter's looted right eye, and he feared that Carter's anger was giving way to exhaustion and apathy. He tried to empathize with Carter, telling him he had been in France because "people just suck my soul, just suck me dry." But Dylan was mostly taciturn — which reminded Carter of himself, who hadn't spoken much as a youth because of his stuttering. Dylan listened, asked questions, took notes. He was different from the many others who had questioned Carter. Over the years, most people who met Carter — reporters, lawyers, law clerks, prisoners — believed in his innocence. But Dylan was not simply probing his innocence or guilt. To Carter, the folksinger was searching for something else entirely, as if he were asking, "Who are you, man? What are you? Are you what I see?"

Dylan felt as if it was the first time he had really *talked* to someone in ages, and he had no doubt that Carter would be vindicated. Carter's commanding presence also made Dylan believe that he was a natural leader. "I want to come back," Dylan said as he left. At dusk, as he drove away from the prison, he saw a billboard that read: "Wallace and Carter." He chuckled and said to himself, "That might be the next [presidential] ticket."

Dylan did not attach his name to the Hurricane Fund. He did not want to be part of the crowd; that wasn't his style. He wanted to make his own statement. Dylan had strayed from his protest music of the early sixties. But in those songs he had used the plight of a single victim to amplify broader social struggles. Class conflict and racial inequity lay at the heart of "The Lonesome Death of Hattie Carroll," about the 1963 death of a hard-working domestic whose attacker, a wealthy social-ite, received a light sentence because of his politically prominent father. (The victim's race was never mentioned but was assumed to be black.) Carter's plight gave Dylan a similar opportunity. Initially, he struggled with the lyrics, but he drew on his passion for movies for guidance, structuring "Hurricane" as if he were writing stage directions on a film script. Thus, the first stanza read:

> Pistol shots ring out in the barroom night
> Enter Patty Valentine from the upper hall
> She sees the bartender in a pool of blood
> Cries out, "My God, they killed them all!"

> Here comes the story of the Hurricane . . .

Dylan, who wrote the song with Jacques Levy, was to record it on October 24 at Columbia Studio 1 in Manhattan. But that afternoon George Lois, who had been consulted on the lyrics, discovered a factual error. The writers had confused Bello and Bradley, placing Bradley at the scene of the crime. Lois, pacing in his Fifth Avenue office in a surplus safari jacket, made a series of phone calls to Dylan at the Gramercy Park Hotel. "Yeah, yeah, they say it's potentially libelous the way it stands now. It was Bello in the bar, not Bradley." Several minutes later Levy called Lois, who grabbed a pen and scribbled the corrections. "And another man named Bello, right, moving kinda mysteriously — that's great, that's a great image, you can just see him prowling around, great correction, yeah, yeah."

Lyrics in hand, Dylan went to the studio with a clutch of musicians, including Scarlett Rivera, whose Gypsy violin would provide a haunting interplay with Dylan's harmonica. The group arrived at 10:30 P.M., but nothing seemed to go right. Technical problems pushed off the recording time until midnight. Dylan's harmonica slipped from his harp rack during the first take. Dylan botched a take when he blew a line about Bello. In a previous version Bello robbed "bodies." In the new version it was "registers." Dylan was told that "bodies" was libelous; "registers" was not. After five hours, Dylan and his entourage departed, leaving his producer with eleven takes from which to construct the story of the Hurricane.

At eight minutes and thirty-three seconds, "Hurricane" was an ode to Rubin Carter's innocence, pitting him against "criminals in their coats and ties [who] are free to drink martinis and watch the sun rise." Carter thought it was a great piece of music, even though he couldn't dance to it. The song used simple street language, was accessible to the masses, and, in the words of Allen Ginsberg, "was the kind of song that the last rebels of the sixties were demanding [Dylan] write."

In fact, "Hurricane" became the centerpiece of a Dylan tour that tried to recapture the spirit of the sixties, a traveling hippie musical revue whose changing cast of characters included Joan Baez, Joni Mitchell, Ginsberg, several film crews, a writer, and relatives of the entourage. Conceived in a Greenwich Village bar in the summer of 1975, the tour began in October and was called the Rolling Thunder Revue. It traveled through small New England towns, played primarily in more intimate venues, and charged as little as $8 a ticket. Publicity about Carter and fund-raising on his behalf gave the tour a mission beyond its music. This served Carter's purpose as well as Dylan's. At a time when political apathy was more prominent than activism, Carter was the perfect choice to reestablish the links between artists and social issues.

Dylan agreed to end the tour on December 8 with a benefit concert for Carter, called "Night of the Hurricane," at Madison Square Garden. But he also wanted to perform before Carter himself. So the night before, the Rolling Thunder Revue, accompanied by George Lois, rolled into the Clinton Correction Institution for Women in Clinton, New Jersey. The previous month, Carter had been transferred there amid concerns that the Trenton prison could not handle the crush of journalists, supporters, and others suddenly interested in his case. Clinton was a far cry from Trenton State. It used to be exclusively for women; now a third of the three hundred inmates were men. The prison looked more like a modern farm, with low-lying buildings, rolling hills, and green grass. This relatively comfortable setting, however, wreaked havoc with Lois's hopes for a heart-wrenching publicity photo of Dylan providing succor to a tormented prisoner.

"I can't believe this place," Lois said, walking through the prison. "I didn't know it was this open. I can't find any fucking bars. Where are the bars, Rubin?"

"There ain't none," Carter said.

This was a PR man's nightmare, a prison without bars. "What a fucking image. This joint looks like a country club."

Lois was in despair as he walked through the prison lobby. Then he stopped short and pointed to a grille hanging down from the ceiling. "What's that?"

"It's a gate, sir," a guard said.

Lois's eyes lit up. "What does it look like when it's down? Does it look like bars?"

"I suppose."

"Pull it down, pull it down," Lois screamed. The steel grille descended from the ceiling. "We got our bars!" He was exuberant. "Get Dylan. Tell him Rubin wants to talk to him." Dylan arrived with Ken Regan, a photographer for the tour.

"Hey, Rube, how you doing, man?" asked Dylan, dressed in a feathered hat and multiple scarves. He poked his fingers through the steel latticework to meet Carter's as Regan clicked away with his Nikon. A few weeks later, a two-page photo of the celebrities would appear in *People* magazine with the caption: "Bridging a prison gate in New Jersey, Rubin 'Hurricane' Carter, inside, and Bob Dylan, out, rap before showtime." Never mind the deception. It was one of Lois's niftiest publicity coups.

The three major networks taped Dylan's prison performance of "Hurricane," with Carter nodding to the beat. Afterward, Carter held a press conference. Even though he had filed a pardon application with Governor Byrne, he made no effort to extend an olive branch. Carter was still fuming, and neither an eponymous ballad nor a country club prison would slake his anger. He referred to "the powers-that-be" as "criminals who have covered this up, who are now cringing in their wormy corners, they know that if people stay together, that means power."

When a reporter said, "We know that a new trial is coming up —" Carter cut him off. "There is no such thing as 'we know there is almost a new trial.' There is no such thing. We're talking about right and wrong here. Two men in prison illegally for nine years for being framed for committing a crime, and there's no evidence anywhere that suggests they did anything. So we're talking about right and wrong, talking about in jail or out of jail. We're not talking about almost out of jail. So I am in jail, so until I am out of jail, then we can start talking about a new trial. But until that time there's no such thing, because the very people who created this monster in 1966 are still in power today."

While the recantations raised public support for Carter, they never persuaded any court to overturn his conviction. Rather, it was a remarkable blunder by the Passaic County Prosecutor's Office that opened the door to Carter's freedom. As the office prepared for the recantation hearings before Judge Larner in October 1974, Assistant Prosecutor John Goceljak learned that Lieutenant DeSimone and Sergeant Robert Mohl had secretly taped one of their interrogations of Alfred Bello on October 11, 1966, and Goceljak listened to the interview on the scratchy tape. Early in the questioning, which took place in Wayne, New Jersey, DeSimone told Bello, "Now, I understand you have some information for us . . . I'm interested in one thing, Al, and that's the truth."

Goceljak thought he had hit the jackpot. The tape, he believed, would counter Bello's claim that the police had coerced his testimony. Goceljak entered the transcript into the recantation hearing. "This is a great tape," he told DeSimone.

The tape, however, included far more than DeSimone's appeal for the truth. It revealed promises that DeSimone made to Bello in exchange for his testimony. This disclosure contradicted Bello's claim on the witness stand that he did not receive any promises from the police for his testimony. Moreover, the tape was a raw display of the character and style of these two men, and it wasn't pretty. DeSimone swooped around his prey like a hawk, mixing racial appeals, subtle threats, leading questions, and religious zeal to produce the statement he wanted. And Bello proved he was an execrable thief, indifferent to human suffering, and capable of bending even the most trivial truths. In one priceless exchange, DeSimone asked Bello his age.

"Twenty-three," Bello said.

"And your date of birth?"

"Twenty-six November, 1943."

DeSimone did the math and realized that Bello was wrong. "That means this November, this year, this November you'll be twenty-three. You're really twenty-two now."

"No," Bello insisted. "Twenty-four this November."

Confused, DeSimone persisted. "This November you'd be twenty-four? Forty-three is your date of birth? Nineteen forty-three?"

"The twenty-sixth day, November," Bello replied confidently.

"Yeah, that's right," Mohl chimed in. "He'll be twenty-four this November."

DeSimone, defeated, moved on to other subjects. Alfred Bello, age twenty-two, was twenty-three years old for the interview.

DeSimone's views on race were cast in sharp relief. He repeatedly referred to Carter as "boy," even though Carter was twenty-nine at the time. That may have been the harmless old-school vernacular of a gruff cop, but DeSimone clearly played on Bello's racial fears to win his confidence. Bello, who was on parole at the time, was asked his parole officer's name.

"Mr. Bailey," Bello replied.

"Uh, is this a white man?" DeSimone asked.

"Colored," Bello said.

"You see why I ask you this, Al, I'm interested in your welfare," DeSimone said. "Now let me say this is one of the main reasons we're at Wayne today and not in Paterson. You follow me?"

"Yes."

"You can understand that we coulda talked to you at Paterson, but we're not talking to you at Paterson for a specific reason. Now, I understand you have some information for us." The shift — from the race of the parole officer to the need for information — was seamless. Then DeSimone explained to Bello why he raised the matter of the parole officer's race. "I understand that you have fear. You understand what I mean? Of the colored people and their supposed movements where they are strictly for the colored. You understand what I mean?" The message was clear: the colored parole officer would not follow Bello to the city of Wayne. There, a couple of white guys could talk in peace.

DeSimone, however, offered Bello more than a buffer from colored people. In exchange for his testimony, the lieutenant vowed that he would try to transfer Bello's parole to another state. When Bello asked if DeSimone could get his parole dropped, he said, "I assure you I will go to the top people in the State of New Jersey. I promise you this." And Bello could trust him, DeSimone said. Even prisoners knew the lieutenant was a man of his word. "You ask them about DeSimone," he told Bello. "You know what the word that comes out of there is? Rough but right. I don't bullshit. If I tell them I'm gonna do something, I do it. I'm not an easy guy. You understand what I mean?"

"Yeah."

"But I'm right because I live by the good book."

Bello was shown a photograph of John Artis and asked if he was one of the gunmen. "It's possible, but I'm not actually sure," Bello said. He was then shown a photograph of Carter and asked if he had ever seen him before the night of the shootings. "Uh, no," Bello said. After prodding from Sergeant Mohl, Bello agreed that he did know Carter.

"Well, I mean," Mohl continued, "can you tell the lieutenant whether that was Rubin Carter or wasn't Rubin Carter fleeing the bar?"

"Well, it was Rubin Carter as far as I know, or his brother," Bello said.

But after repeated questioning, Bello concluded that the two men he saw were undoubtedly Carter and Artis. DeSimone also made a blatant attempt to coax Bello into identifying the getaway car as Carter's. Initially Bello said that he saw a "white Pontiac or a white Chevy." Moments later he again referred to the white car. DeSimone saw an opening.

"It was parked near there," he said, "in that vicinity, a white Dodge, right?"

"Well, I don't know if it was a Dodge," Bello said.

"Oh well, a white car. All right."

Bello later described how he walked into the bar to see four bleeding bodies. He heard the cries of the two survivors, but, he told DeSimone, he said to himself, "I should clean this fucking place out . . . I'll take a little bit of . . . pin money." He estimated he stole about twenty-five singles. But it soon occurred to him that people were dying, and maybe he should help.

"So I figure if I leave the bar and there's this woman and she's bleedin', and the other guy, he's fucked up. So I figure, you know how people are, they're not going to walk down to that bar [and help]. So I figure if I call the police, maybe they'll get there, maybe they'll save somebody's life. You know what I mean?"

Toward the end of the interrogation, DeSimone invoked the Ten Commandments in a thunderclap of indignation: "Look, let me say this to you, let me say this to you, Al. There are laws of man and there are laws of God."

"Yes."

"If these guys did it, they not only violated the law of man, they violated the law of God, which says, 'Thou shalt not kill' . . . You understand what I mean?"

Carter's lawyers understood that they now had grounds for another appeal. They petitioned the New Jersey Supreme Court in November 1975, arguing, among other things, that the prosecutor suppressed evidence by failing to disclose to the defense the contents of the tape — specifically, the promises of help DeSimone made to Bello.

But by now the case had taken another bizarre twist. Governor Byrne needed guidance or at least political cover on what to do. In September he asked a black state assemblyman, Eldridge Hawkins, to investigate the matter. Hawkins, a Democrat from Essex County, was one of the most prominent black politicians in New Jersey, and he studied the Carter case with Prentiss Thompson, an investigator with the Essex County Prosecutor's Office who was a former karate champion from Canada. Hawkins's investigative style was not entirely conventional. He used a hypnotist to try to elicit truthful testimony from one witness, a black woman named Annie Ruth Haggins who said she was at the Lafayette bar right before the shooting. Hawkins also told John Artis that he should answer questions about the murders while under hypnosis or after taking truth serum. Evidence of Artis's truthfulness, Hawkins said, would be weighed heavily by the governor.

According to Artis, Hawkins offered him more than truth serum advice. At the time, Artis was considered a model prisoner at minimum-security Leesburg State Prison and was participating in an inmate college program at Glassboro State College. As he was preparing for school one morning, Artis was told he had a one-day furlough to visit his father in Paterson. He had not been home in nine years. When he arrived, he was met by his father and Hawkins.

"I know you didn't kill anybody," Hawkins said, "but you were there or you knew about it. If you sign a statement saying that, I can guarantee you'll be home by Christmas" — three weeks away. Artis refused to sign the statement because it would have implicated Carter. He told Hawkins that even a Christmas homecoming would not prompt him to admit to a crime that neither he nor Carter committed. "If you know I didn't kill anybody, why don't you go back and tell the governor that?"

Hawkins, in so many words, did just that. His report, submitted in December, posited that Carter and Artis were not the gunmen but were in or around the tavern at the time of the shooting, making them an accessory to the murders. Hawkins concluded that two other black men, Elwood Tuck, the manager of the Nite Spot, and Eddie Rawls, whose stepfather had been murdered earlier in the evening, were the likely killers. This report, however, was ignored by the governor and the Passaic County Prosecutor's Office, leaving the impression that Byrne had ordered the investigation to buy time until the courts settled the case.

"The Night of the Hurricane" at Madison Square Garden began with a drink flung into the face of a U.S. congressman and almost ended with the announcement of a gubernatorial pardon. On one level, the December 8 event represented the peak of Carter's transformation into a cultural icon. The Garden had sold out the day the event was announced. The tickets, priced at $12.50, were going for $75 outside the Garden. On the guest list, among many others, were Ed Koch, Coretta Scott King, Bill Bradley, and Candice Bergen. Rumored appearances by John Lennon, George Harrison, Ray Charles, and Marvin Gaye did not materialize, but Roberta Flack, whose soulful ballads were hardly associated with Bob Dylan, was added to the bill, and Joni Mitchell was still on the tour.

The concert, however, also marked the beginning of the end of the Carter coalition. Specifically, it laid bare a racial schism among supporters. While George Lois and a handful of whites ran the Hurricane Trust Fund (rechristened Freedom For All Forever), a black activist named Carolyn Kelley, a bail bondswoman in Newark, was recommended to Carter to start up the New Jersey Defense Committee. Carter had been concerned about the dearth of black supporters. Kelley remedied that through a New Jersey petition drive, demonstrations in Trenton and Newark, and other publicity efforts. But hostilities emerged between Carter's white and black supporters over money, publicity, and control. Lois was accused of turning Carter into the ultimate advertising campaign and receiving an excessively high reimbursement — $43,000 — for his agency's promotion of the Garden concert. Kelley, a Muslim, was said to be leveraging her position as Carter's spokeswoman in a self-serving bid for leadership in the New Jersey black community. She was also accused of squandering money on limousine rides and expensive hotel suites.

The dissension literally spilled out into the open before the Garden concert at a nearby hotel, where Muhammad Ali and his entourage were staying (and running up a $3,000 bill, paid for by the concert's proceeds). Lois and Paul Sapounakis, who ran the Blue Angel restaurant, strolled through Ali's floor and encountered John Conyers, the black congressman from Detroit who had taken up Carter's cause. According to Lois, Sapounakis and Conyers had gotten into an argument when Lois came to his friend's aid.

Conyers was sitting at a table. "Are you part of that group?" he asked Lois.

"Yeah," Lois said.

"You white guys think you're pretty hot stuff," Conyers said.

Lois was happy to return the salvo: "Fuck you, and your mother and sister too!"

"You're slimy bastards," Conyers shot back.

With that, Sapounakis flung his highball into the congressman's face, ice cubes and all, then he and Lois spun around and made a quick exit.

The concert itself had some zany moments. During a song by Jack Elliot, the sweet-voiced country singer from Brooklyn, Joan Baez ran onto the stage with a blond wig and white go-go boots. She was hauled off by security after thirty seconds of dancing the hustle. Then there was Dylan himself, weaving about onstage, resplendent in a white Wallace Beery shirt, black vest, white makeup, and a lavishly flowered, feathered Pat Garrett hat. Ali took the stage, telling the predominantly white crowd that it had "the connections and the complexion to get the protection" for Carter. Carter himself listened to the event on the telephone and, through a loudspeaker, thanked Dylan and the audience for their support.

Meanwhile, chaos reigned behind the scenes. During the concert, Channel 5 News in New York reported that Governor Byrne was preparing to pardon Carter. According to Larry Sloman, whose book *On the Road with Bob Dylan* recounted the Dylan tour, Carter urged Dylan to announce his imminent freedom to the crowd. "Okay," Dylan said. "You're going to hear a roar like you never heard before." But then Lois and Sapounakis stepped in and said the report should be confirmed. They raced through the Garden's musty corridors before finally locating a phone. When a security guard blocked them from using it, Lois yelled, "Look, man, Dylan's about to announce something to twenty thousand people and we've got to confirm it first and we got to use these phones." Tempers rose, and Lois, out of control, threw a wild punch; only the intervention of a Garden official defused the confrontation. Lois finally called the governor's office to learn that there was no truth to the pardon report. Just as Dylan walked onstage to announce it, Lois barreled out and yelled: "Don't announce anything!" Dylan, barely, was saved from prematurely releasing Carter and making one of the most embarrassing gaffes of his career.

The concert capped the minuet between Dylan and Carter, a relationship that was founded on good faith and respect but that also served each man's interests. "Hurricane," released the following month on Dylan's *Desire* album, shot up the charts. It created an indelible impression of justice gone awry on a generation of music fans, who would never forget its plaintive line: "And an all-white jury AGREEEED!" The ballad also showed that fame had not diluted Dylan's own social conscience. As the *New York Times* wrote in its review of the concert: "Mr. Dylan has reinvigorated the flagging folkrock scene, and he may well have reinvigorated the fashion of political commitment among artists. Most important of all, however, he has reinvigorated himself."

For Carter, the song became an anthem, bringing him national and even international recognition. Long after he himself left the spotlight, "Hurricane" still lamented the "hot New Jersey night" that put "an innocent man in a living hell." The association between boxer and songwriter waned in the coming years, when their individual interests were no longer aligned, but Carter would always be grateful to "the sixteen-cylinder man" for amplifying his cause and immortalizing his name.

While Governor Byrne would probably not have issued a pardon to Carter and Artis under any circumstance, the issue became moot when the two men withdrew their pardon application on December 16. Carter said a pardon could be interpreted as an acknowledgment of guilt. Only complete exoneration — or a new trial, in which he was acquitted — would satisfy him. And he soon got his chance. On March 17, 1976, the New Jersey Supreme Court, in a 7–0 decision, overturned the convictions of Carter and Artis. The court ruled that the prosecutors, in failing to disclose the Bello tape to the defense, withheld material evidence favorable to the defendants, thereby violating the defendants' right to a fair trial. The 1974 recantation hearing also revealed for the first time that DeSimone had made similar promises to Bradley, saying that he would appeal for lenient treatment with every prosecutor's office in the state where charges against Bradley were pending. This promise, too, was never disclosed to the defense, which could have used these promises to impeach the testimony of Bello and Bradley and further undermine their credibility.

The opinion was written in dry, bloodless prose, but it represented a rout for many people: for DeSimone and former Assistant Prosecutor Hull, who suppressed the evidence; for Judge Larner, who on appeal upheld the conviction; and for the new Passaic County prosecutor, Burrell Ives Humphreys, who argued the case before the state's highest court. At the time, Dylan's "Hurricane," mocking the New Jersey authorities as criminals, triumphantly blared across the airwaves. The singer was right. Muhammad Ali was right. The Madison Avenue spinmeisters and the Hollywood jet-setters and the political blowhards were all right.

But worst of all, at least to the losing side, Rubin Carter was right.

Wearing an orange print dashiki over an orange turtleneck sweater, Carter entered a room full of reporters at the state prison in Clinton the day the state supreme court's decision was announced. His arms were linked with those of Carolyn Kelley and the Reverend Ralph David Abernathy, the civil rights leader and president of the Southern Christian Leadership Conference. Carter sat at a long table draped with a white cloth. A sign on the table read: "Rubin Hurricane Carter, Victim."

"What you are seeing is a person who has been raped of his freedom for nine and a half years," Carter told reporters. "What you're seeing is a person who has become blind in this penitentiary for lack of proper medical attention. What you're seeing is a person who has been without his wife and daughter for nine and a half years for crimes he did not, would not, and could not commit."

Carter spewed inflamed but hollow rhetoric. Asked if he was bitter, he said, "I think you say I sound rather bitter because I am bitter, that I have a right to be bitter. But I think that you are saying that I sound bitter because you are only looking at what you want to see and don't recognize what you see."

Three days later, Ali posted much of the cash bail for Carter ($20,000) and Artis ($15,000). He also gave Carter a roll of hundred-dollar bills. Now thirty-eight, Carter was free, but he was not celebrating. The Passaic County prosecutor had already announced that he was personally going to retry the case. "I'm home, but I'm not free," Carter told friends on the night of his release. "You don't know the enemy."

8

REVENGE OF PASSAIC COUNTY

BURRELL IVES HUMPHREYS, the Passaic County Prosecutor, did not fit the bill of a hard-nosed officer of the court. A pale, plumpish man with a round face, he was a self-described liberal and anti-Vietnam activist, although he gave up his membership in the American Civil Liberties Union when he was appointed prosecutor in 1975. He had been active in civic affairs in northern New Jersey for two decades, and civil rights was a particular interest. Like other white lawyers in the vanguard of the movement, Humphreys believed the law could be used to remedy racial injustices. As a young lawyer in the early 1950s, he joined the National Association for the Advancement of Colored People and, for more than ten years, served on the panel of hearing examiners for the state's Division of Civil Rights. Humphreys referred to Martin Luther King, Jr., as his "idol," and he represented black clients pro bono several times. He had once filed complaints against the Paterson Police Department on behalf of New Jersey's Council of Churches, and he successfully sued the Packanack Lake Country Club, a resort community in Wayne, for prohibiting blacks from buying property in the community.

Although a Democrat, Humphreys was an outsider to the political establishment, and his appointment by Governor Brendan Byrne was opposed by top state Democrats, including the head of the Passaic County Democratic Party. A number of police departments in New Jersey also protested the appointment. Nevertheless, Humphreys, at the age of forty-eight, took office as prosecutor in June 1975 and promptly shook up a department known for patronage. He fired six investigators, two assistant prosecutors, and other assorted hacks, including members of his own party. "I found a butcher, a baker, and now I'm looking for a candlestick maker," Humphreys said at the time.

But there was one old-timer Humphreys did not throw overboard: Vincent DeSimone. In fact, Humphreys promoted him to "acting" chief of county detectives, a position that led one reporter to call DeSimone "the most influential and powerful police officer in Passaic County." Humphreys himself wanted to be a judge, but assailed from all sides in his new position, he would need DeSimone, a forceful veteran, to help him administer the office.

Humphreys knew little of the Rubin Carter case when he became prosecutor, but he was told that a crisis loomed and that he needed to read up on the matter immediately. Carter's new lawyers from New York were appealing the 1967 conviction to the state supreme court, and public support, notably among New Jersey blacks and various white celebrities, was rallying behind the former boxer. With the state's two key witnesses now saying that their testimony had been coerced by racist officers in Paterson, editorials in both New Jersey and New York urged that Carter be granted a pardon or given a new trial.

If any prosecutor in New Jersey might have been sympathetic to Carter's case, presumably it would have been Humphreys, for he knew that Paterson's police department had plenty of rogues. But when he read the Carter file, he concluded that the conviction was clean. When the state supreme court took up the case in January 1976, Humphreys delivered the oral argument for the state. He promptly lost his first high-profile case in a 7–0 ruling, so he had to decide whether to retry the matter. Carter had become — thanks to Bob Dylan and others — an internationally recognized symbol of injustice, but he was still seen by many in Passaic County and elsewhere as the quick-tempered thug who collected guns and threatened police.

For guidance, Humphreys relied heavily on DeSimone, who had overseen the murder investigation and who had been depicted by Carter as the architect of an effort to frame him. Wounded by rhetorical salvos, furious at the overturned conviction, and victimized by the "motherfucking media," DeSimone could not abide to see Carter vindicated. Only a second trial would redeem the "acting" chief and the whole New Jersey law enforcement establishment.

The chance for redemption would come. Humphreys, convinced of Carter's guilt and unwilling to overturn the work of his own office, decided to retry the case, thus pitting a civil rights leader against a civil rights cause célèbre. In an unusual move, Humphreys announced that he would personally handle the case, his first as a prosecutor. He formed the Carter-Artis task force, with about a dozen investigators, to look into the murders yet again, and he received an additional $70,000 to his $1.9 million budget to finance the effort. He seemed to approach the matter with an open mind. He wrote to the lawyers of the two defendants, asking that Carter and Artis submit to lie detector tests. If the tests indicated they were innocent, Humphreys said he would drop the charges.

Carter and Artis refused the offer. They had already taken, and passed, polygraph exams on the day of the murders, and they had still been convicted. They didn't trust anyone associated with the Passaic County Prosecutor's Office, and they were confident that a second trial would acquit them. Indeed, chances for a second conviction seemed remote. Ten years had passed since the murders. The only witnesses placing the defendants at the scene of the crime had reversed their testimony. The murder weapons had not been found. And Rubin Carter was on a roll.

Carter always liked the spotlight, and his newfound celebrity opened the door to speaking engagements at universities, including Princeton and Fairleigh Dickinson. Before he began a talk, a songwriter friend, Thom Kidrin, sang a ballad he wrote about Carter. As he crooned his last line, "his life fades away in a Trenton pen," Carter strode onstage dressed in a conservative dark suit. Kidrin videotaped the speeches and helped Carter refine his presentation, instructing him on how to tilt his head, jut his jaw, or use his hands. To create a more commanding look, Carter occasionally put aside his wire-rim glasses in favor of top-half black-framed glasses reminiscent of Malcolm X. He talked not only about racial injustice but poverty and homelessness. He still denounced New Jersey law enforcement officials and the Passaic County media for stirring up hostility against him, but he tried to show a softer, lighter side as well. "Prison is a vicious place," he would tell audiences. "As a matter of fact, one night I heard a rustling under my steel bunk that was supposed to be my bed, and I looked under and there I saw a cockroach pull out a switchblade on a mouse that was stealing his cheese. Now, if that ain't vicious . . ."

Meanwhile, some of his supporters were urging him to consider running for Congress; others talked about a movie of his life and national speaking tours. Invitations of all kinds began to come in. He went to a Passover Seder. He attended weddings. He vacationed in Florida. He granted television interviews. His forbidding glare would still draw gasps, but that only added to his appeal. He had the name, the look, and the message.

But Carter could hardly enjoy his freedom. At times he felt like the "house nigger," whose presence among whites soothed their racial consciousness. His descriptions of courtroom lynchings and prison purgatories seemed out of place at weekend lawn parties. There was also stress at home. Tee thought she would have her husband again, but he was frequently away, attending to efforts to bring in money through speaking engagements, movie proposals, or other business deals. But the money wasn't enough, and his family remained on welfare. The pressures also affected his relationship with his daughter. Theodora, now twelve, had seen her father in prison once a month for ten years, but now there was little communication between them. Rubin felt like a stranger in his home; traveling was safer. "You have an exaggerated opinion of your own self-importance," Tee said. Then she told him something that raised his anxieties further: she was pregnant with their second child.

The news shocked Carter, who was not earning enough to feed one child. The pressures, however, had just begun to mount.

Ed Carter, Rubin's cousin, was a member of the old guard in the civil rights movement. Believing in political equality and racial justice through nonviolent means, he belonged to the Student Nonviolent Coordinating Committee in the sixties, the nation's first civil rights organization to put "Nonviolent" in its name. He went to the South on freedom rides and participated in sit-ins. In Passaic County, he ran a government antipoverty program, recruiting Rubin, in his prizefighting days, to give speeches to youth groups. After Rubin was convicted, Ed remained an unwavering supporter. So when the publicity guru George Lois complained to Rubin that he had few black supporters, Rubin approached Ed for help. His cousin found Carolyn Kelley.

The bail bondswoman from Newark became Carter's most resolute supporter. A slender, sharp-tongued, forty-ish woman, she visited Carter in prison and left certain of his innocence and determined to help. She created the New Jersey Defense Committee for Rubin Carter, organized rallies, and collected fifteen thousand signatures demanding that Carter and Artis be given new trials. She told reporters that prison officials were "liars" and accused them of "blackmail." According to Carter, she fancied herself the Winnie Mandela of New Jersey, the principal voice of her wrongfully imprisoned partner. After Carter was released from prison, she was frequently seen by his side at press conferences.

But on the morning of June 7, 1976, Kelley held a different sort of press conference from a bed in Crippled Children's Hospital in Newark. There she tearfully told reporters that Carter had tried to kill her with his bare hands. The alleged attack occurred on April 29 in Landover, Maryland, where they were to attend a Muhammad Ali–Jimmy Young fight. Kelley said Carter assaulted her in Room 223 of a Sheraton hotel. Her tale of giddy, unprovoked violence seemed like a scene out of *A Clockwork Orange*. According to Kelley, she went to Carter's room when she had a problem with the hotel bill. When he opened the door, Carter simply started laughing and then went into the bathroom, Kelley said.

> At that point, he was gargling with a bottle of Charlie cologne. He spit the cologne out, he came out of the bathroom and I was by the edge of the bed and he just burst out laughing again. The next thing I knew he had hit me in my face and spun me around, I felt myself turning and spinning, and I felt myself going down and fighting to hold on to consciousness . . . And then he raised his foot to kick me, still laughing all this time, and I managed to turn over, and he started kicking me in the back . . . I guess I must have turned back over, and he wasn't laughing then, but he was in a stooped position with his hands around my throat telling me he was going to kill me.

Kelley said she was unconscious after the beating. A wire photo showed her lying in bed, her head propped on pillows and a hospital identification band around her wrist. A front-page headline above the picture in the *Paterson Evening News* read: "Rubin Delivers Knock Out Punch?"

In fact, Kelley's press conference raised more questions than it answered. Despite the putative attack, Kelley had not filed any criminal or civil complaints against Carter. She said she had head and back pains but was otherwise vague about her injuries and medical treatment. She looked remarkably fit for a woman who claimed to have been brutally assaulted by a muscular man who could knock a horse over with a single punch. At her side was her son, Michael, who had played a role in the incident. Michael told reporters that after the supposed beating, he put his unconscious mother on an airplane for Newark. Asked why he did not admit her to a Maryland hospital, he said it was hard to act "rational," given the circumstances. At what point Kelley regained consciousness on her flight home was unclear.

Carter, through his lawyers, vehemently denied the incident, saying that an "irreconcilable dispute arose" in April over Kelley's financial demands. But money was only part of the problem. Kelley and Carter had become romantically involved when Carter was still in prison. According to Carter, Kelley, who was divorced, wanted to continue the affair after he was released, but he refused. He also said she demanded $100,000 as compensation for her efforts in raising money on his behalf; otherwise she would go to the Passaic County prosecutors and allege he had beaten her. A bitter quarrel ensued, but Carter denied he made any physical contact.

Kelley's accusations prompted Humphreys to try to revoke Carter's $20,000 bail, and a nine-day hearing was held in July. Kelley, attending the hearing with a walking cane, was represented by William Kunstler, the ringmaster-lawyer in search of a courtroom circus. The hearing revealed that Kelley had gone to three different hospital emergency rooms in the first two days after her return to Newark, but three doctors, two nurses, and an ambulance attendant testified there was no evidence of swelling or bruises. On the other hand, three women who saw Kelley when she got off the plane, as well as a doctor who saw her at home, testified that she had had bruises and swelling on the left side of her face. Ultimately, Judge William Marchese issued a mixed ruling. He concluded that Carter had struck Kelley but could not determine if the incident caused her the injuries she alleged. The judge also acknowledged that Kelley and her son gave inconsistent and contradictory testimony. He declined to revoke Carter's bail but limited his travel to New Jersey. He also declined the state's request for a psychiatric examination of Carter. More than two months after the alleged attack — and right before the hearing — Kelley did file a complaint in Maryland with the State's Attorney for Prince George's County. After investigating the matter, the State's Attorney declined to charge Carter, citing insufficient evidence.

While Carter won a narrow legal victory, he lost big in the court of public opinion. Kelley was not a redneck cop or ambitious white prosecutor. She was a black woman who had dedicated the past year to Carter, and her incendiary if unsupported charges ratified the raving, psychopathic image that Carter's enemies claimed was his true nature. That the details of her story did not add up or could not be corroborated was immaterial. Carter's public support evaporated. The incident also energized the Passaic County prosecutors and investigators. Public opinion had returned to their favor, and they would be rewarded by returning this heathen to his cage. "Mrs. Kelley's charges," Humphreys told the *New York Times,* "have removed the halo of martyrdom that the defense was trying to create for Mr. Carter."

Carter quietly seethed. He had spent the past two years positioning himself as an innocent man who only fought back when he was under attack, and now he watched the unraveling of his public image. He didn't understand how anyone could find Kelley's accusation credible — if he had hit her, he would have killed her — but he was also furious with himself. His relationship with his supporters had always been strictly business. If they could help him win his freedom, he would help them achieve their goals, be it boosting their careers or building their self-esteem. But his relationship with Kelley had become personal, and her betrayal deepened his distrust of others. Mixing whimsy and anger, he later wrote in a prison journal:

> What happened to me with that Kelley woman has shown me that the next female I become involved with for whatever reason will be a cow! Because a cow won't deceive you; won't argue with you, and won't double-cross you either . . . and it doesn't cost anything to feed because all it needs is some grass — and if a cow makes you mad for any reason whatsoever, you can kill and <u>eat</u> it! So a cow is really the way to go.

Meanwhile, Carter was losing other key allies. He had a bitter falling out with George Lois, accusing Lois of looting his defense fund for personal gain. Lois accused Carter of ingratitude, squeezing him and other white supporters out and aligning himself with black activists instead. Even Richard Solomon fell by the wayside. He said Carter forced him out after he expressed concerns over the handling of fund-raising money. Carter said he dismissed Solomon from his defense team after Solomon refused to carry out an order regarding negotiations with Bob Dylan's Garden appearance. Ironically, Solomon had approached Carter with a strict business proposition — a movie about his life — but he came to revere the prisoner as a father figure. He realized too late that his idol's sole objective was freedom, not paternal guidance. The two men never spoke again.

By the fall of 1976 there were no more celebrity testimonials for Carter. There were no more rallies or financial contributions, and the fund-raising money evaporated thanks to poor financial controls. While the Madison Square Garden concert generated $217,000 in revenue and the performers donated their time, only $104,000 remained after paying for hotel bills, a cast party, and promotions. A month later, a second fund-raising concert at the Astrodome in Houston generated $397,787 in ticket sales — but lost money due to unaccounted-for expenses.

Expectations that Muhammad Ali or Bob Dylan or Candice Bergen would attend Carter's second trial never panned out. By the time it began on November 11, a relatively small contingent of supporters appeared in court. Older relatives wearing conservative white shirts and skinny ties mingled with husky bodyguards who favored sunglasses and fezzes. Missing from the courtroom was Carter's wife. Tee, in the final months of her pregnancy, stayed home.

The trial took place not in Paterson's ornate old courthouse but in an attached concrete annex built in the late sixties. The sixth-floor courtroom had modern paneled walls, soft leather seats for the jury, and a red tweed rug. Bright lights put a brilliant shine on Carter's bald head, while a balky radiator frequently overheated the room, forcing at least one witness — DeSimone — to constantly wipe his face with a paper towel during his testimony.

Unlike the first trial, when Carter was represented by Raymond Brown from Newark, now he wanted an attorney from outside New Jersey, someone whose livelihood did not depend on practicing law in the Garden State. In 1974 Richard Solomon had asked Selwyn Raab for the names of good lawyers. On the list was Myron Beldock, a short, scholarly, white New Yorker who spoke softly in the courtroom. Beldock, who billed at $250 an hour, had just completed years of pro bono work representing George Whitmore, the wrongfully convicted black man whose case Raab had investigated. Still exhausted from that experience, he initially refused Carter's request to see him. But in December 1974, after Judge Larner denied a new trial based on the recantations, Carter called Beldock again.

This time, the lawyer went to Rahway State Prison. In the course of two hours, the men smoked several packs of cigarettes as Carter laid out the long history of his case. Beldock was an old-fashioned liberal, a graduate of Harvard Law School who had represented conscientious objectors during the Vietnam War, an amateur photographer who still wore berets from his year at the Sorbonne in Paris. He left his meeting with Carter feeling that the prisoner was smart, believable, passionate, articulate — and innocent. And he took the case. He figured that, given the flimsy evidence, Carter's conviction would be overturned and the charges would be dropped in less than one year.

John Artis also had a new lawyer, Lewis Steel. Like Beldock, Steel was a white New York liberal, a former staff lawyer for the NAACP who had represented civil rights protesters in Connecticut and Massachusetts and black students in Texas, West Virginia, and Tennessee. But unlike the relatively sedate Beldock, Steel was a flamethrower. The NAACP fired him in 1968 for writing a scathing article in the *New York Times* about the Warren Court, "Nine Men in Black Who Think White." Steel was a bit pudgy, with an expressive face framed by dark, unruly hair and thick sideburns. He also had a sharp tongue, and during the Carter-Artis murder trial, he clashed often with Judge Bruno Leopizzi. The two men flaunted their contempt for each other — which surely did not help Steel, the outsider from New York, in the eyes of the jury.

Steel believed Leopizzi had become an advocate for the prosecution, while the judge thought Steel was grandstanding for the press. The burly, white-haired judge had been one of New Jersey's finest criminal lawyers, and he chafed at anyone who did not follow his edicts. About a month into the trial, he complained to Steel that he was arriving late in the courtroom. "If I say nine o'clock, you're here at quarter after," the judge muttered. "If I say quarter of nine, you're here at nine o'clock. I don't understand. You are like babies, very frankly."

Before the trial opened, the assignments division of the Superior Court, noting biased coverage against the defense from the Passaic County press, ruled that the jury would be drawn from neighboring

Hudson County. Unlike the all-white jury in the first trial, the second trial's twelve-person panel included two blacks. However, during jury selection, the prosecutors removed every prospective black juror with a college education, according to the defense attorneys, and the two blacks selected were both elderly. As James Lieber, a lawyer who covered the trial for a Philadelphia radio station, later wrote for *The Nation,* the composition of the jury — four clerks, a telephone operator, a keypunch operator, two retired men, a housewife, an unemployed man, and a utility man — bespoke working-class lives, family responsibility, and moderation, if not conservatism. A lawyer who saw the jury early in the trial told Lieber, "It's all Kmart. The case is over." Maybe not, but Carter himself was all Saks Fifth Avenue, his well-tailored suits and tinted shades standing in sharp contrast to the jurors' workday attire.

Shortly before the trial, the defense team learned that Alfred Bello had renounced his recantation and would once again testify that he saw Carter and Artis fleeing the crime scene. Bello's flip was bewildering. He had denied his 1967 testimony in an affidavit to Fred Hogan of the New Jersey Public Defender's Office, in interviews with two journalists, in testimony before Judge Larner at the recantation hearing in 1974, and in two separate affidavits in 1975 to state Assemblyman Eldridge Hawkins, who had investigated the case for Governor Byrne. Bello also denied his original testimony in December 1975 before a special grand jury sitting in Essex County, which heard evidence unearthed by Hawkins. The grand jury did not return an indictment against Carter, Artis, or anyone else.

Initially Bello's recanted version was that he simply could not identify the gunmen fleeing the bar. Then, in his statements to Hawkins and the grand jury, he said he was actually *in the bar* when the shootings occurred, but used Hazel Tanis's body as a shield against the bullets. Bello said he saw Carter and Artis outside the bar, but they were not the gunmen. Bello stuck to what became known as the "in the bar" account as late as June 1976, when he was questioned by Passaic County investigators.

Carter was livid that a perjurer with an admitted drinking problem and multiple felonies would be allowed to return as the state's star witness. If the same witness were black and the defendants white, would he be permitted to testify again? Carter thought not, and Bello's reappearance was evidence to him that America had not progressed one step since he had been arrested. Speaking in front of television cameras on the courthouse steps, he said, "If this witness can come back in this courtroom today ten years later and have at his hands, or on his tongue, the lives of two people, then, brother, justice ain't nowhere."

But Bello was indeed back, more outlandish than ever. Dressed in a tight suit and red cowboy boots, he chewed gum or candy, belched, and spoke the patter of radio crime drama. "I'm here just to state the facts," he said on his first day of testimony, leaning back in his chair, his blue jacket stretched tight across his chest. He looked, in Lieber's words, like a "fattish ringer for Lou Costello," a pompadoured buffoon who played to the crowd. Asked to draw a diagram of a gymnasium where he saw Carter at a boxing exhibition, Bello stood up, quickly scribbled a crude rectangle, then sat down, ready for the next question. When Beldock asked why he gave Hawkins a false testimony, Bello responded, "At that time I didn't care about anyone except me."

"I know you never care about anyone except you, do you, brother?"

"Priority first," Bello proudly replied.

On another occasion, a frustrated Beldock tried to elicit from Bello a detailed description of Carter's face.

"I'm not asking whether he's Clark Gable," Beldock said. "I want to know what you saw."

"Well," Bello deadpanned, "he definitely wasn't Clark Gable."

Bello not only returned to his 1967 testimony — that he was *outside the bar* and that he saw Carter and Artis running from the crime scene carrying weapons — but now he had a new detail. He testified that when the police returned Carter and Artis to the bar that night, he told the cops *at that time* that they were the men he saw running from the tavern. (No police witness corroborated that testimony.) Bello also had an explanation of why he recanted his original testimony: it was all about money. He accused Fred Hogan of offering him a percentage of royalties on *The Sixteenth Round* in exchange for his statement exonerating Carter, a claim Hogan denied in his own testimony. (The book never produced royalties anyway.) Bello said that Selwyn Raab promised him a job at the *New York Times* in exchange for his statement, and that Raab gave him $10 for cigarettes on two occasions when he was in jail. Raab, on the stand, denied he ever made such a promise and said he frequently left a little spending money for prisoners he interviewed. Bello also spun an elaborate story of his own literary ambitions. He said he met a furniture salesman, Melvin Ziem, and a real estate agent, Joseph Miller, who convinced him that his Lafayette bar story was a gold mine. His new "literary agents," Bello said, instructed him to create a fictional account of the murders, and they supposedly offered Truman Capote $100,000 to write a book that would be advertised as the true account. The book would be called *The Lafayette Bar Massacre*, and the outline had already been sent to Viking Press and MGM Studios. It was this fictional account, Bello testified, that made up his *in the bar* version — which exonerated Carter and Artis as the gunmen. Miller and Ziem "were telling me we might make a couple hundred thousand dollars each," Bello testified, emphasizing "each."

Beldock and Steel tried to slash Bello's credibility, repeatedly invoking the witness's previous statements that contradicted his current testimony. Beldock combed through Bello's Essex County grand jury testimony and, point by point, asked Bello if he remembered making such a statement.

"If it's on" the transcript, Bello replied, "I said it."

"Well, is that true or false, sir?"

"False . . ."

"You correct me," Beldock said, "if there are any true answers as I read along. You stop me."

Line after line, Bello confirmed he had lied. Finally, an exasperated Beldock exclaimed, "You were willing to swear falsely that you saw Carter and Artis outside . . . the bar?"

"That's true," Bello said.

"Have you no shame at all?" Beldock asked.

"No comment," Bello said, then turned to the judge. "Excuse me, Your Honor. Can I go to the men's room, please?" Judge Leopizzi called for a recess.

Bello's flip-flops resembled testimony in another highly publicized case, the Kavanaugh-DeFranco murders. In 1966 Passaic County prosecutors linked the killings of Kavanaugh, a young suburban housewife, and DeFranco, a small-time Paterson hood; the special grand jury convened for their murders also indicted Carter and Artis. In each case, prosecutors relied on a felon to implicate the defendants — a tactic that typically raises a red flag in a courtroom. Witnesses under the thumb of the state have a clear incentive to testify for prosecutors in exchange for leniency.

In the killing of Johnny "the Walk" DeFranco, the prosecutors built their case around the testimony of Edward Lenney, another hood serving time in Rahway State Prison for armed robbery. In a statement to prosecutors, he implicated three people, including a police officer and a newspaper publisher, in the murder. Lenney then recanted his statement to a special prosecutor, acknowledging that he had been in Baltimore on the night of the murder. The special prosecutor asked the Passaic County Prosecutor's Office to dismiss the charges. But after a visit from a county investigator, Lenney retracted his recantation. The case went to trial, and his sentence was ultimately cut in half.

The statements of both Bello and Lenney — accusation, recantation, retraction — served the prosecutors' purposes, but the outcomes differed. Lenney's testimony proved worthless in trial court: all the defendants in the Kavanaugh-DeFranco case were acquitted in 1970.

After six days of grilling, Bello stepped down from the stand. His testimony had been contradictory, confused, and comical; his credibility lay in ruins. Yet he served a vital purpose for the prosecution. Humphreys wanted to convince the jurors that the trial was about money, not murder. A panoply of mercenaries — screenwriters, literary agents, folksingers, advertising men, and journalists — were seeking to profit from the Lafayette bar killings and impose their own view of justice on the law-abiding citizens of Passaic County. Carter's fancy clothes gave the impression that he too was cashing in. Fred Hogan, Selwyn Raab, and Hal Levinson all faced questions on the stand about their involvement with Bello, and Humphreys ridiculed the three men as "perverters of justice in this case, trying to sell a phony story." Prosecutors introduced letters written by the pseudo-agent Miller to MGM Studios and Viking Press, attempting to sell the publication and film rights to Bello's Lafayette Bar Massacre. A theatrical agent named Jerry Leopaldi testified about would-be movie and book deals.

On one level Humphreys was right. Many people were using Carter's story for personal gain. But Carter saw the argument as another tactic to poison the jurors' attitude against him and to divert attention from the issue at hand — evidence of guilt or innocence. The prosecutors spent days trying to show that Bello only recanted his testimony for a financial payoff. If true, it simply showed what a malleable and unreliable witness he was to begin with. But it reinforced the specter of "Madison Avenue hucksters," as Humphreys called them after the trial, swirling about Passaic County. The "us against them" atmosphere was buttressed by the presence of Beldock and Steel — two headstrong Manhattan Jews who swooped into working-class New Jersey and accused law enforcement officials of racism in an effort to acquit two black defendants. These differences in style and culture surfaced openly on occasion. In one exchange, Judge Leopizzi snapped at Steel for using the word "linchpin."

"I don't know what you mean by 'linchpin,'" he said. "Maybe that is something you ought to define for me. Does that mean you are going to lynch somebody?"

"No, no," Steel said. "The connection, the linchpin."

"Oh, linchpin. The connection, the link, the link. I never heard of linchpin. I get frightened when you use that word."

"You see," Steel said, "New York, linchpin. New Jersey, link."

"Lack of communication here," the judge concluded.

Outside the courthouse, the mood was far more relaxed than it had been at the first trial, which had occurred on the eve of New Jersey's worst race riots in history. While FBI reports showed the agency feared that a guilty verdict at the first trial would set off riots, there were no such reports about the second trial. By 1976, racial passions had subsided in Paterson; ironically, race took center stage in the trial itself.

Racial revenge was always the suspected motive for the Lafayette bar murders. Even before Carter and Artis were arrested, the authorities believed the shooting was in retaliation for the murder earlier that night of a black man by his former white business partner. Both shootings occurred in Paterson bars with shotguns. But in the first trial, the assistant prosecutor did not introduce the race motive, or any motive, either because the judge prohibited him or because the prosecutor concluded his supporting evidence was weak. Humphreys, however, believed he could not win the case without asserting a motive. At the first trial, the prosecutor had Bello and Arthur Dexter Bradley identifying Carter and Artis; now he only had Bello, more damaged than ever.* Humphreys needed Judge Leopizzi's approval to introduce the race motive because prosecutors are not allowed to make potentially prejudicial statements without showing that they have hard evidence to support such an allegation. Beldock and Steel knew that if Leopizzi allowed the racial revenge motive, the dynamic of the trial would change. They would not only have to prove their clients were not killers, they would also have to prove Carter and Artis were not racists.

Carter viewed the proposed race motive not as a lawyer but as a black man. In his view, whites were conditioned to believe the worst about blacks: blacks are lazy, they live in ghettos, they cannot keep a job, they cannot raise their children. Tell a white juror tha a black man is racist — particularly a black man like Carter, with spiffy clothes and a sneer — and that juror is going to welcome the news. *Put racial revenge in front of this jury,* Carter thought, *and the trial is over.*

Assistant Prosecutor Ronald Marmo was a lean, tenacious lawyer who handled some of the most important cross-examinations for the state. On December 1, in the judge's book-lined chambers, he argued that he be allowed to introduce in evidence, through police testimony, that a crowd of angry blacks had been seen outside the Waltz Inn after the shooting of Roy Holloway. This testimony would be the first step in proving a racial revenge killing.

Beldock and Steel were outraged, believing the testimony would create a specter of black mob vigilantism that was not connected to their clients.

"What they are seeking to do," Steel protested, "is to elicit testimony [about] an angry crowd of blacks that did not include Mr. Carter or Mr. Artis. From that, it's almost like the all-blacks-look-alike thing . . . It is about as racist an approach to a case as I have heard in my life."

"You know that doesn't impress me," Judge Leopizzi said. "As a matter of fact, I have an uncanny ability to turn my ears deaf when you start to talk nonsense."

Steel tried to gather himself. "All I'm suggesting, Judge, is without evidence of Carter and Artis being at the Waltz Inn scene, unless the

---

* Bradley stuck to his recantation. According to Carter's lawyers, Bradley told them he made a deal with the prosecutors that he would not testify for the defense in exchange for leniency over pending criminal charges.

Court is going to rule that there is some mythical connection between all blacks —"

"In Paterson, let's say," Beldock interjected.

"What do you mean, 'mythical'?" Leopizzi said. "I am going to rule that there is a mythical connection? I don't even understand what in the hell you are talking about."

The following morning, with the jurors not yet in the courtroom, Leopizzi ruled that he would permit the black mob scene, although he would defer final judgment on allowing the racial revenge motive. Sparks flew immediately.

"You are turning this trial into a racial nightmare!" Steel screamed. "That is what you are doing and you should know it."

"You know," Leopizzi shot back, "I'm not going to even respond to that idiotic accusation because that's all it is."

"It's the truth!" Steel bellowed.

"I can say this to you, Mr. Steel. You should learn to keep your mouth shut at the proper times and choose your words and you should think before you speak." Leopizzi cited Steel for contempt of court.

The motive debate raged on. Beldock and Steel argued that the state had no evidence showing that either Carter or Artis was angry on the night of the murders, that they urged anyone to retaliate for the Holloway murder, or that anyone urged them to retaliate. In fact, the whole revenge theory, they argued, was absurd on its face. Conforti killed Holloway over a business dispute, not a racial dispute. If Carter and Artis wanted to avenge that murder, they would have exacted retribution against Conforti, or at least Conforti's family or friends. But there was no direct link between Conforti and the four victims of the Lafayette bar.

In fact, there was at least one link. Both Conforti and the Lafayette bar victims were white, and Humphreys argued that it was Carter's hostility toward white people *generally* that motivated his alleged actions.* But Carter's behavior, even in the courtroom, belied the charge. He had lived most of his life in racially mixed neighborhoods. He had white friends, white boxing managers, trainers, and promoters, even white lawyers. How could Humphreys prove that he hated whites?

---

* The prosecutors applied the race motive to both defendants, but Carter was the focus of debate because he was viewed as the leader.

Humphreys believed the answer lay in *The Sixteenth Round.* He wanted to introduce the 1974 autobiography because, in his view, it not only proved that Carter was hostile to whites, it even showed him confessing to the Lafayette bar crimes. The confession emerged in his condemnation of New Jersey's juvenile prison system.

> I wanted to see [it] demolished from stem to stern, and I wanted to see it happen out of pure hatred and vengeance, as atonement for the crimes committed against me, and others just like me who have never had the nerve to voice their legitimate grievances as members of the human race. I wanted to be the Administrator of Justice, the Revealer of Truth, the Inflictor of all Retribution. I gloried in these thoughts.

Judge Leopizzi ruled that Humphreys could not introduce any part of the book into the trial. The judge said that the volume, among other things, could have been written in a sensational style to win support for Carter when he was in prison, and passages could easily be taken out of context. Carter, in fact, did see himself as a protector of other people. But Humphreys was so certain of his guilt that he could read a piece of the defendant's florid prose and find bloody fingerprints — a confession, no less — between the lines. Artis, unpublished, had left no such trail.

Even without introducing *The Sixteenth Round,* Leopizzi allowed prosecutors to assert a racial revenge motive, saying the state's supporting evidence "has a tendency to explain the conduct which would ordinarily and otherwise probably be unexplainable."

Outside the courtroom, efforts to bulk up the prosecutors' case took a macabre twist. The murder weapons — a 12-gauge shotgun and .32-caliber handgun — had never been found, despite the police's searching the streets and sewers of Paterson and dragging the Passaic River. But the prosecutors and their staff of investigators had developed a new theory about the weapons. It centered on Holloway's stepson, Eddie Rawls. Prosecutors argued in court that Rawls put up his friends, Carter and Artis, to commit the murders.* Then, after the shootings, according to the prosecutors, Carter and Artis drove to Rawls's house in Paterson, dropped off the weapons and their "bloody clothes," then

---

* Rawls himself was a leading suspect after the shootings but was never charged with the crime.

left. Now the prosecutors suspected that Rawls had found an exquisite hiding place for the weapons: inside the buried casket of his slain stepfather.

The theory made perfect sense — *if* the prosecutors were right about the gunmen and their motive. By stashing the weapons in the casket, the killers would be uniting a murdered man with the guns used to avenge his own demise. And if the prosecutors found the guns in the casket, the discovery would tie the Holloway murder directly to the Lafayette bar shootings, buttress the racial motive, and bring the trial to a dramatic dénouement.

Holloway was buried at nearby Fair Lawn Memorial Cemetery; its legend is "A Garden of Eternal Peace." In the very week that defense attorneys were railing against the racial revenge proposition, investigators hired a metals detector expert who scanned Holloway's graveside and concluded that there was something foreign in the coffin. Their expectations raised, investigators hired a second expert from Oregon; he concluded that a metal object, possibly a gun, was buried there. Prosecutors thought they had finally found the weapons — if no longer smoking, at least well preserved — and they received permission to exhume Holloway. On a raw, cold Sunday, cemetery workers used hoes to dig up the gravesite. A small crowd of onlookers, including the Bergen County medical examiner, a minister, the cemetery's undertaker, and Assistant Prosecutor John Goceljak, watched the proceedings. Soon a worker's hoe struck the coffin. The lid was lifted.

Only the deteriorated remains of Roy Holloway lay inside.

The guns were never found, and Holloway was returned to his "Garden of Eternal Peace."

Carter knew the trial was going badly. Patricia Graham Valentine, the reedy former apartment dweller above the Lafayette bar who testified in the first trial that she had seen the white getaway car, returned now as a well-groomed Florida beautician and mother. This time she had new and even more damaging testimony against Carter. She testified that hours after the killings, she was in the Paterson police station, and officers showed her a cartridge and a shotgun shell that they said they had just found in Carter's car. If jurors believed Valentine, her testimony undermined Carter's long-held contention that the bullets had been planted. Her memory about the getaway car had also sharpened over the years. Testimony from the first trial was read back to her, in which she said the getaway car had "the same kind of [butterfly] tail-lights" as Carter's vehicle, but she specifically said she could not identify Carter's white Dodge as the escape car. Now, ten and a half years later, Valentine was certain that Carter's car was the getaway vehicle.

Carter was also badly hurt by testimony of a number of his alibi witnesses from the first trial. A woman Carter had dated, her mother, a former male friend, and a sparring partner all took the stand and said that before the first trial, Carter or his lawyer had instructed them to lie, to say that they had been with Carter at various locations around the time of the murders. Beldock tried to blunt this testimony by showing that the witnesses had a motive for turning on Carter. The younger woman, Cathy McGuire, was now engaged to a Paterson police detective, and the former friend, Welton Deary, had actually joined the force. The sparring partner, "Wild Bill" Hardney, did not actually testify in the first trial; he had fled from New Jersey as he was being sought on charges of nonsupport for his paternity of an illegitimate child. Now, under cross-examination, Hardney described the heavy-handed tactics of New Jersey law enforcement officials. Working with Washington, D.C., cops, they rousted him out of his home one night at 1 A.M. and threatened to arrest him if he didn't change his original story. After Hardney confessed that his first story was concocted, a phalanx of three New Jersey law enforcement officials and fifteen D.C. cops arrested him at three o'clock one morning and took him into custody as a material witness, holding him in a New Jersey motel for three weeks.

Carter still had five alibi witnesses who testified at the second trial, but the former alibi witnesses, whatever their motives, had done their damage. For the first time, *black* witnesses were turning against Carter. Ironically, the state supreme court had previously ruled that alibi wasn't properly at issue because the defendants were admittedly within minutes of the murder scene at all times, and the moment of the killings could not be firmly established. But this nonissue had turned into a black-against-black spectacle. There was also testimony about Carter's alleged "search for guns" on the night of the murders. Specifically, he had inquired about his own stolen guns, including a shotgun, after he bumped into the man he suspected of stealing the guns, his former sparring partner Neil Morrison. Carter, Morrison, and two others drove to the apartment of a friend, Annabelle Chandler, now deceased, who had information about the theft. Witnesses confirmed that Carter left Chandler's without any guns, but the prosecutors told the jury that Carter's inquiry constituted a "search for guns." Beldock insisted that no witness said anything about a search, and no witness, save Bello, claimed to have seen Carter with a gun on the night in question. In the first trial, the judge precluded prosecutors from making the gun search argument because of its prejudicial nature, but no restriction was imposed in the second trial. The nexus of guns, inflamed racial passions in Paterson, and Rubin Carter had been raised in the jurors' minds.

As the trial dragged into its fifth week, with mind-numbing chronologies and detailed descriptions of car movements along Paterson's streets, fatigue set in. Jurors rocked back and forth in their chairs. The lawyers looked haggard. Reporters thumbed through books and magazines, passing time by casting characters in a Carter-Artis film. (Isaac Hays as Carter, Bill Cosby as Artis.) There was only one important witness left: Rubin Carter.

Artis had testified, and everyone assumed that Carter would too. For years he had been publicly proclaiming his innocence and demanding his day in court. It had finally come. Beldock and Steel both thought he had to take the stand to show jurors he was not a racist killer. But as the trial neared its conclusion, Carter believed it was heading the same way as the trial nine years earlier, and he was already thinking about his appeal. Leopizzi had indicated that prosecutors could introduce *The Sixteenth Round* into the trial if Carter took the stand. The book had numerous references to Carter's belief that America was a racist society. If allowed into the trial, it would be used to support the racial revenge theory. If not allowed, it would strengthen his appeal that the prosecution had no basis for the motive. Carter also feared that taking the stand could allow the prosecutors to introduce the Carolyn Kelley incident in an effort to rebut his position that he was nonviolent. Despite the absence of corroborating evidence, Kelley's testimony could devastate not only his defense but also his appeal. Finally, Carter knew through his law studies in prison that appellate judges are less likely to overturn jury verdicts if the jurors had seen the defendant testify and concluded he was lying on the stand.

When Carter told Beldock and Steel he was not planning to testify, they were furious. They had mapped their entire defense with the understanding that he would take the stand, and they knew the jurors would be more likely to assume guilt if he failed to refute the many charges against him. But Carter never took orders from anyone, including his lawyers, and he thought he had no chance before this jury anyway.

"If I take the stand, the jury will simply see a black man dueling a white man, and they'll believe the white man," he told his lawyers in a meeting late one night.

"If they believe that," Steel said, "they'll believe it ten times stronger if you don't take the stand."

Carter did not testify.

After six weeks and seventy-three witnesses, summations were made on December 20. Beldock and Steel went first, each speaking for two hours, occasionally overlapping in their comments. Like the defense lawyers in the first trial, they ridiculed Bello and reminded jurors that the initial physical descriptions of the assailants by three different witnesses did not match their clients. But now they had to address the racial revenge theory. Steel, the more passionate speaker, concluded:

> When that type of theory is included in a case like this, the case becomes a larger case, a case which claws at our guts and makes us come to grips with what type of people we want to be. That's where we end up in this case, what we all believe about our fellow Americans whose skin color may be different and what we will speculate about them. That's where we are in this case. Will you speculate that Rubin Carter is a racist because the state wants you to? Will you speculate that John Artis is a racist because the state wants you to?
>
> Ladies and gentlemen, you are the citizens of this country. You are its conscience. The Constitution of this country is a broad document. The Declaration of Independence of this country is a broad document. Both of those documents have meaning and meaning alone when individuals, citizens — you — say, "yes," those documents will live. The concepts of freedom, equality in those documents will breathe. Our history is not two hundred years old. It is now in this courtroom, and you stand between us and our own worst instincts.

Humphreys, in his summation, barely raised his voice and occasionally smiled; he returned to his theme that sticky-fingered profiteers were trying to line their own pockets at the expense of justice in Passaic

County. He ticked off the names: "Levinson, Hogan, Raab, Solomon, Don King, George Lois — all of these people trying to perpetrate a fraud, trying to produce this great police conspiracy. Well, they didn't get away with it and I don't think they will get away with it."

Humphreys constructed a metaphor — "six strands of evidence" that made a "rope strong enough to bring two killers to justice." The strands were Valentine's identification of Carter's car, Bello's identification of the defendants, the apprehension of the defendants on the night of the murders, the false alibi witnesses, the bullet and shell found in Carter's car, and the motive. On the last point, Humphreys said:

It's a very sensitive issue. None of us like to admit that things like race prejudice and anger and hate for people because of the different color of their skin exists in this world. We teach our children the contrary. We support civil rights. We support courses in our schools. We bear in mind the words of Reverend King, in which he had a dream of a day where people would judge his children by the quality of their character, not by the color of their skin. But, ladies and gentlemen, we don't live in that world yet and we certainly didn't live in that world in 1966. It was a world and it is a world filled with people who hate . . . We know that no group, no class, is immune from hate, and we know that revenge is one of the most powerful motives that any human being can have. We look around the globe and see it everywhere. We see Greeks and Turks and —

Your Honor, Steel interrupted, I object to Greeks and Turks and things outside this courtroom.

No, counsel is making a point, Leopizzi said.

Humphreys returned to his summation:

We see hate and anger and revenge there and we see people of Ireland fighting because of religion and we know that in 1966 there were many blacks with legitimate grievances, and some blacks and whites did not act as responsible law-abiding citizens . . . Should we say, well, these motives are too repulsive, too ugly, we don't want to deal with them? We have to deal with them . . . As much as you may want to look away, as much as you may want to say it couldn't have happened for that reason, it did happen for that reason. What other reason could it have happened for?

To convict or acquit, jurors had to return a unanimous decision. Beldock, believing a hung jury was his best hope, crossed his fingers for lengthy deliberations. Instead, the jury reached its decision on its first day — a total of nine hours, less time for lunch and dinner. In a replay of the first trial, the jury's foreman, Helen LaRocco, read the verdict in a whisper. Both Carter and Artis were found guilty on three charges of first-degree murder. The hushed courtroom erupted into shrieks as friends and family of the defendants sobbed uncontrollably. As jurors were polled, the black male juror sat with tears in his eyes, barely able to speak. After the jury left the courtroom lined with uniformed attendants, Beldock placed his arm around his expressionless client, and Carter found his cousin in the gallery. "Keep your head high," Ed Carter told Rubin. "Look beautiful, man, they can't take that away from you." Artis stood up and, clutching a red Christmas stocking someone had given him, winked at a supporter.

The night was cold, and in the glare of television lights outside the courtroom Humphreys and DeSimone walked out together. Carter had been released from prison on the first day of spring. Now he was convicted on the first day of winter. The circle was closed, the stars were in order. "In my judgment, the American jury system is the greatest instrument of justice in human creation," Humphreys declared. "The contest between the American jury system and Madison Avenue is no contest." DeSimone saw the victory in less grandiose terms. For him, the man accused of masterminding the framing of Carter, it was about personal vindication. "After twenty-seven months of being castigated and maligned in the media," he said, referring to the time since the recantations had been disclosed, "it's indeed a relief to find the jury system absolved me." Nearby, Beldock shook his head, his face red and eyes misted. "The good burghers of Passaic County can rest well in their belief that they have put their boogieman behind bars," he said. "This is a wrongful conviction and we will be back."

For Carter, the trial culminated nine months of freedom that had been almost as difficult as nine months of imprisonment. He felt buffeted from all sides — by white elites looking for a new black hero, by Tee looking for a husband, by Carolyn Kelley looking for revenge, and by Passaic County looking for a racist killer. Between the Kelley hearing and the murder trial, he had spent almost two months in court listening to accusations that he was a *batterer,* a *murderer,* a *racist.* He had never faced those kinds of attack in prison. His reconviction, oddly, brought him a sense of relief. Freedom had certainly brought no relief. At a press conference the day after the trial, Carter and Artis sat before a battery of microphones in the recreation room of the Passaic County Jail. Denim pants and shirt, issued by the jail, had replaced Carter's expensive suit. Also gone was the stridency in his voice. He kept his hands folded before him; he occasionally leaned back on the couch. He was calm. "I have not lost hope," he said. "But hope is all we have. We don't have our freedom anymore."

Artis's life was about to take a different twist. While the jurors were deliberating, he met an attractive woman who had been attending the trial as a curiosity. Dolly Williams was a social worker for the State of New Jersey, and she and Artis struck up a conversation in the courthouse. When Artis was sent back to prison, they corresponded and talked on the phone. Williams visited Artis in prison. They fell in love and were married in a prison ceremony in 1980. Dolly Williams, as it happened, was white. It was a fitting closure to a trial that began on the narrow evidence of guilt or innocence and then took on entirely new dimensions. While the jurors were concluding that Artis had killed three people because of his hatred for white people, he met a white woman who would become his wife.

Carter and Artis received the same sentences they'd gotten after their first trial. In the days following the verdict, Carter was held in the Passaic County Jail. Six days after the verdict, Tee gave birth to their son, Raheem Rubin Carter. Tee, recovering from a cesarean section, could not visit her husband. Days passed without Rubin's seeing his son. Finally his friend Thom Kidrin brought the bundled baby to the jail. Before they reached the visiting cubicle, a guard had Kidrin remove the newborn's diaper to check for contraband. Kidrin and the child also had to pass through a metal detector. When they finally reached the darkened cubicle, Carter, wearing a bright orange jumpsuit and oversize prison shoes, was in handcuffs and leg shackles. He embraced his friend. "Thank you, my brother." Kidrin handed the baby to Carter, and there was a moment of renewed energy, even glimmering hope amid the sliding gray bars and watchful guards. The top of Raheem's ears already had the same pinned-back contour as his father's, a genetic quirk safely transferred to the next generation. "Look at you, you beautiful thing," Carter said. "My baby, my son. I'm your dad and I love you."

Prison had already taken his daughter's childhood from him, and now Carter would miss Raheem's. He was just grateful that his son was too young to see him handcuffed and imprisoned. What could be worse than standing in shackles and having your son taken away from you by jailers, evoking nightmarish images of plantation atrocities in antebellum America. Kidrin and Carter, sitting together on a steel bench, talked about the heady plans they'd had during those brief months of freedom — speaking tours, maybe public office, a possible movie, more writing.

"Rubin, everything we've been working for for the past nine months is gone," Kidrin said. "Everything is changed."

Carter looked Kidrin in the eye. "Thom, you're wrong," he said. "Everything has just gone back to the way it was."

9

SEARCH FOR THE
MIRACULOUS

RUBIN CARTER, AT THIRTY-NINE, was back in Trenton State Prison. During his nine months of freedom, the State of New Jersey had not given away his prison identification number: he was still #45472. Since his 1967 conviction, he had spent 3,482 days in prison, although Judge Leopizzi, mindful of details, credited Carter with 3,496 days. The extra fourteen days stemmed from a two-week delay in sentencing after the second trial. Time served, however, meant little to Carter. In fact, his lot was far worse now than after his first conviction. He was not only a triple murderer but a racist triple murderer. He beat women — at least, that was how he was seen after Carolyn Kelley's charges. He had alienated his white supporters from New York, such as George Lois and Richard Solomon, who had done so much to publicize his cause but ultimately felt slighted by his embrace of Kelley and his black allies. But he had also antagonized his black supporters with the Kelley fiasco. His reconviction seemed like an anticlimax, the final turn in a downward spiral.

Thom Kidrin, who had attended the trial each day, tried calling Carter's celebrity supporters to once again ask for their help. "The same system you were protesting six months to a year ago has done it again," Kidrin insisted. Harry Belafonte and Muhammed Ali pledged their continued support, but most of Carter's marquee allies turned their backs on him. Kidrin, sensitive to Carter's shattered condition, shielded him from many of these rejections. He still hoped that Bob

Dylan would continue to help. But several months after the reconviction, Kidrin tracked down Dylan in his dressing room before he was to appear on *Saturday Night Live* and gave him a letter from Carter, asking if the singer would visit him.

Dylan, however, had moved on from the social themes of the Rolling Thunder Revue. Now, dressed in white patent leather boots and sunglasses with "BD" set in rhinestone, he read the letter, looked up at Kidrin, and motioned toward a television set showing roller skaters. "Do you like roller-skating?" Dylan asked. "Look at the cool stuff they do."

Kidrin was taken aback by the inane comment. He tried to bring Dylan back to the matter at hand: "Do you want to write something back to Rubin? I'll be down there next week."

Dylan remained opaque. "Tell Rubin I'll be down there in the springtime of my life," he said. He then began reciting a passage from the Bible.

If outsiders did not want to see Carter, Carter was equally reluctant to let them see him. Innocent or not, he always felt humiliated behind bars. But now he also felt as if he had let everyone down — his friends, family, supporters, and lawyers. He blamed himself for the stupidity of his affair with Carolyn Kelley, and he blamed himself for the courtroom loss. He continued talking to his lawyers, who were appealing the verdict, but he shut everyone else out, including his wife, Tee, who had visited him in prison regularly for nine years.

Tee was furious. She relied on welfare checks to support herself and their daughter, and now with a new baby to feed, she didn't understand why Rubin did not seek some kind of plea bargain that would return him home. Nevertheless, she still remained loyal to him and took pride that her family, while separated, remained united. But the Passaic County prosecutors made such loyalty untenable. After the second conviction, they wanted to charge Fred Hogan, the investigator in the state's Public Defender's Office, with bribery for Alfred Bello's recantation. Their theory was that Hogan used the $10,000 advance for *The Sixteenth Round* to make the alleged bribe. Hogan, however, testified that he gave the money, as Carter instructed, to Tee. Now Carter, some months after the second conviction, received a subpoena to appear before a grand jury in Princeton. When he arrived in chains and shackles, Tee was standing outside the courtroom.

"What are you doing here?" Rubin asked.

"I've got a subpoena," she said. "It has something to do with Fred Hogan and the money."

Rubin learned his wife was being squeezed. If she testified truthfully that Hogan gave her the book money, she would have to return her public assistance. If she testified that Hogan had not given her the book money, she would buttress the state's case that Hogan had kept the book money and possibly used it for a bribe. Ultimately, neither Rubin nor Tee answered questions from the grand jury. When the judge threatened Rubin with contempt for refusing to answer, he calmly responded, "You're right, Your Honor. I do hold this court in contempt." No indictment was ever issued against Hogan, but the incident persuaded Carter that he should divorce Tee, that their marriage gave the authorities an avenue through which they could attack either him or his friends. Ending the marriage, for Carter, severed one more tie to the outside world.

Trenton State had changed a bit since 1967. Prisoners were now allowed to wear their own clothes, to sport beards, even to wear rings, and Carter still had his. But he had not changed his attitude about prison itself. If anything, he was even more defiant. He made this clear from the very start of his second term by refusing to cooperate with the prison system's classification process. All incoming prisoners had to be classified at the Receiving Center, now at the Bordentown Reformatory. There, a panel of prison guards, social workers, and psychologists assigned convicts to one of the state prisons. Carter, however, sat in a holding cell and refused to appear before the panel. "I don't have time," he told a corrections officer.

His recalcitrance continued after he was sent to Trenton State. There, a guard told him to report to the tailor's shop for work. Carter, sitting alone in his cell, simply replied: "I don't have time." He continued to refuse to eat prison food, relying primarily on Kidrin to bring him canned goods and other items once a month. ("That beef jerky you brought me last week was the best food I've had since I've been in this place," he wrote to Kidrin.) Carter's anger came to a head five months after he reached Trenton, when the prison insisted that he work in the laundry room. He refused and was given a disciplinary charge issued in the name of the state Attorney General William Hyland. Furious, on June 11, 1977, Carter fired off a four-page, single-space typewritten letter to the attorney general, citing the case law that excused him from having to work in prison jobs. He also wrote:

> It is common knowledge within this institution, and any other institution that I have been in since being accused of this crime, that I have no time for anything except fighting for my freedom! ... The question is simply this: Do I now forsake eleven years of almost inhumane struggling and at this time passively accept a job in the laundry of this institution which would benefit only in the perpetuation of a morally bankrupted system? That is the question!

The attorney general never answered.

Carter's continued obstinacy earned him numerous trips to the prison "hole" and generated a raft of disciplinary charges. According to the prison records, corrections officer Marrero wrote on May 18, 1978: "Inmate refuses to participate in any aspect of the institution. Inmate has requested permanent idle status." Now Carter even refused to carry his prison identification card, which referred to each prisoner by his number. This annoyed a guard named Roy Earp, who approached him one afternoon in the prison yard.

"Where's your ID card?" Earp demanded.

"My name is Rubin Carter. I don't need an ID card."

Earp filed a disciplinary charge against Carter, lest other prisoners begin an ID uprising.

Carter often broke rules as a way to assert his own identity. He refused to post his name and ID number, as the rules required, on his cell door, on 2 Wing. Instead he put up a sign: "If your name is: Lola Falana, or Jayne Kennedy, or Sara Dash, you can wake me up. But if it's Not: Then hit the road Jack — and don't cha come back no more, no more no more no more! Hit the road, Jack!" Carter also made it clear, again, that he would not tolerate any guard's touching him under any circumstance. When a rookie guard conducted his first "prison count" in Carter's wing and found him sleeping, the guard reached into the cell and tapped his ankle. Carter shot out of bed.

"In here, motherfucker, if you want to keep breathing, you keep your hands to yourself." As the guard left the tier, amid jeers from other prisoners, he yelled back at Carter, "At least I'm not a murderer!" Later Carter wrote in his prison journal: "I will simply say this: if you ever put your hands on me in anger — then 365 days after you have struck me, you would have been dead for one solid year!"

Any hopes for a quick, successful appeal were soon dashed. The second trial's transcript was so voluminous that it took almost two years for Passaic County to give Carter's lawyers a copy. Separately, his attorneys believed that new evidence indicating juror misconduct would be grounds for a new trial. An alternate juror, John Adamo, testified that a juror had made open jokes using the Italian word *melanzana*. The word literally means "eggplant" but is also a derogatory reference to black people, the equivalent of "nigger." Adamo testified to hearing other racist remarks from both jurors and guards. A hearing was held in March of 1979 before the trial judge, Bruno Leopizzi, to determine if a new trial should be granted, but Leopizzi, doubting Adamo's testimony, ruled that there had been no juror misconduct.

In the first year of his second term, Carter showed familiar patterns of behavior. He pushed his lawyers hard, threatening to fire them, and was once again frustrated by their lack of progress. In a letter written on April 2, 1979, he chastised Myron Beldock for his failure to respond to his messages and warned him that the Passaic County prosecutors were outflanking him on his appeals. "I know you to be a better lawyer than the lawyering that is presently being lawyered, and I can't understand what's holding you back."

He wrote to Kidrin, asking him to buy a stylish blue-tinted monocle with a twenty-four-inch thin silver chair. He even drew a diagram to make absolutely clear what he wanted. He wrote to a friend in London about making his case a worldwide cause and to a theatrical producer who had once expressed an interest in his life. His rage against his enemies also had not abated. In his prison journal, he wrote: "DeSimone is so nasty; that when he was a kid his mother had to tie a pork chop around his neck so that his dog would play with him." He also wrote of Don King, who had mistreated one of Carter's friends: "We come here not to bury Don King but to praise him — although the vote was close."

Carter's anger and sarcasm masked deeper personal changes. Even the most strong-willed prisoners are inevitably worn down by sustained captivity, and the effects surface in different ways. As one long-term prisoner recalled in *With Liberty for Some:* "Visiting the zoo as a child,

I'd been struck by the way a lion — pacing then as I was pacing now — would progressively shorten the distance covered each time, anticipating the presence of the bars before he reached them, anticipating the need to turn and turning a step sooner . . . until finally he was no longer pacing but turning on himself, revolving on his own axis." He now found himself behaving the same way as the animal in the cage.

Carter knew the signs of becoming "institutionalized," the point at which convicts can no longer function outside the prison. Those inmates did not keep their cell clean or have their clothes laundered. They stopped taking showers. They no longer read newspapers or books. Their friends and family stopped visiting or putting money in their prison account. They could not buy toothpaste, mouthwash, or cigarettes. They prowled for cigarette butts in the prison yard, where they'd scavenge for shreds of tobacco to roll into secondhand smokes. Broke, desperate, and abandoned, they were permanent wards of the state. When such a prisoner was released, he was usually back within a year or so — just long enough, it seemed, to accumulate some spine-tingling stories that could be used to regale other inmates on his return.

Carter could feel himself slowly falling into this spiral. After his first conviction, he was energized by his efforts to free himself: studying the law, writing his autobiography, marshaling support for his cause. It was a dizzying, breathless experience . . . and it failed. Now, he increasingly felt exhaustion and despair. He had no money for his lawyers, for his family, or even for cigarettes. A two-pack-a-day man, Carter quit cold turkey so he too would not have to scrape tobacco out of discarded butts. His weight dropped to 139 pounds.

Carter's fears surfaced in a conversation with one of his New Jersey lawyers, Louis Raveson. The attorney was involved in inmate rights' issues and had ample exposure to a prison's corrosive environment. His wife was also a lawyer, and on one prison visit, a guard yelled out to her: "The kike is here to see the spic!"

Carter was typically upbeat when he saw one of his lawyers, grateful that someone on the outside was there to help him. But during one visit with Raveson, he was oddly downcast, and the lawyer tried to find out why.

"Inmates have to basically repress who they are," Carter told him.

"They have to take so much crap from authorities, it is so destructive, it becomes irreparable."

Carter described the process by which other long-term prisoners become institutionalized and why leaving the pen carries so much risk: "For all these years, they have so much anger that they have to swallow that the first person who looks at them the wrong way, they lose it. There comes a point where the prison should never set you free."

Raveson realized Carter was not talking about other prisoners but about himself. It was a sobering moment for a lawyer who was trying to win his client's freedom. But the admission revealed a great deal. To Carter, the prison was hell — but at least it was his hell. He knew when the lights came on, when the bells rang, when the cell doors opened. Outside the prison, everything was random and moved too fast. Freedom had become an abstraction. He still craved liberty — but he craved it as proof that he had cleared his name. When he won his first boxing match in South Africa many years earlier, the fans roared, "*KAH-ter! KAH-ter!*" He always cherished that moment, and he would not give up until his name was again hailed in triumph.

Carter befriended an inmate named Lester Riley, known as Moko. Convicted of rape, Moko had a blend of African and Indian features and spoke with a slight stutter. He retained, somehow, a sunny disposition in prison and was able to make Carter smile by telling him stories and jokes, and he occasionally joined Carter on walks around the prison yard.

On one sweltering day in June 1978, the two men were walking laps around the shadeless yard amid a noisy swirl of activity. While guards stood sentinel in their towers, inmates clanked weight machines, hit speed bags, and pounded handballs. The hot sun baked the loose red dirt, and waves of heat rose from the patches of pavement. Carter was sweating. He told Moko he needed to stop, and he crouched down for a breather. When he looked up, he found himself staring directly at the cement and brick fortress wall on the other side of the yard. As prisoners moved about and the sun beamed down and beads of sweat rolled off Carter's bright dome, he continued looking at this wall with razor-wire ribbon wrapped around the top. Suddenly, he saw a pinprick of light in the wall. It was a powerful, blinding spotlight, and it was growing bigger. He continued to stare as the crimson dust thickened and the heat rose from the ground, and he saw the light burn a hole through the wall. Now he could see the other side of the barricade. He noticed cars driving down the street, children walking to school. An odd calm came over his damp body. Carter was riveted. Freedom was within his grasp! He reached out, and just as quickly as the hole had appeared, it vanished. He looked around to see if anyone else had seen what he saw. Apparently not. He was confused, but he now had a new thought: perhaps the prison walls were not real. Perhaps he could walk right through that wall. All of a sudden, he had a new mission. As he later wrote:

> I resolved myself to find that "hole" in the wall again — only this time I was going to walk right through it! I had no doubt about that whatsoever. Even if the "hole" should sear the flesh from my bones as I passed through it, or if it should deposit me somewhere in the middle of infinity, or even if it meant my death, it had to be better than what was happening to me now. What did I have to lose but the nauseating stench of captured souls rotting away in pain, confusion and misery all around me?

Carter returned to his cell and wept. He looked at a handful of law books on his bookshelf, including his battered *Black's Dictionary,* and began carrying them out of his cell. This stunned the other inmates, who knew he had spent years studying those books.

"What are you doing, Mr. Carter?" an inmate asked him.

"Take them," Carter said, handing the books over. "I don't need them anymore. They didn't do me any good. I know that's not the way for me out of here now."

Besides Carter's lawyers, Thom Kidrin was about the only other person who visited Carter regularly in the immediate years after the second conviction. As a kid in the early sixties, Kidrin had watched Carter box on black-and-white television on the Friday-night fights. An intense, spiritual sort, he also grew up listening to Bob Dylan's music, and, inspired by the themes of racial justice and civil rights, he wrote his own song about Martin Luther King, Jr. In the early seventies, Kidrin was working for a film production studio in Manhattan when he joined Carter's defense committee, and few worked as hard as he. He always believed Carter's struggle was a historic event and that he could play a supporting role in this drama. He drove to Muhammad Ali's training camp in Deerlake, Pennsylvania, and, hoping to secure the heavyweight's support, sang a song he had written about Carter.

1. As a boy, Rubin loved the Army paratroopers' snappy uniform, but he enlisted in 1954, at age seventeen, because he needed to avoid the authorities after escaping from a boy's prison. *(Courtesy of Rubin Carter)*

2. Carter's wife, Tee, shown here with Rubin in the early sixties, had radiant beauty, but she concealed her scarred left hand from her husband for many months. *(Courtesy of Tee Carter)*

3. In 1966, the Lafayette Grill was a redoubt for white working-class patrons in a neighborhood facing an influx of black residents. *(Courtesy of the Paterson Museum)*

4. Carter and John Artis *(left)* leave the Passaic County Court after receiving their sentences on June 29, 1967. Fears that black residents would riot after the verdicts were issued proved unfounded.

(AP/ Wide World Photos)

5. Carter's refusal to wear prison garb led him to dress in clothes used in other parts of the pen. Here, in 1972 at Rahway State prison, he is wearing a barber's smock.

(UPI/Corbis-Bettmann)

6. In November 1974, Carter posed in the former Death House at Trenton State Prison, which had been turned into the Visiting Center. This was the site of Carter's first visit with Lesra and of many future visits with Lisa.

(AP/Wide World Photos)

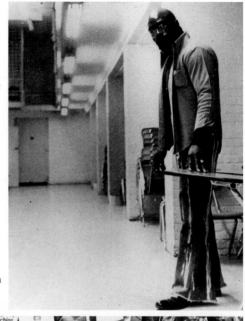

7. Muhammad Ali led a demonstration in Trenton on October 17, 1975, but Governor Byrne was more impressed with celebrities such as Ellen Burstyn *(to Ali's left)* than with appeals for Carter.

(AP/Wide World Photos)

8. Bob Dylan's arrival at a minimum-security facility in December 1975 created confusion when his handlers couldn't find any prison cells, but a steel grille was adapted so that Carter could be photographed behind "bars." *(Ken Regan)*

9. The commune, which prized secrecy, is shown here in the early eighties in a rare photo. *Top row, left to right:* Gus, Mary, and Terry. *Middle row:* Kathy, Martin, Lisa, and Lesra. *Bottom row:* Eitel, Sam, and Eric. *(Courtesy of Gus Sinclair)*

10. Carter was the first boxer in history to win an honorary championship belt, which he received in Las Vegas on December 16, 1993. *(Perry Catena)*

11. On the night of the shootings, a witness said the two gunmen were the same height. Thirty-three years later, at the University of Maryland Law School in Baltimore, Artis and Carter are still not close in height but remain linked in history forever. *(James S. Hirsch)*

In the summer of 1976, during the Democratic National Convention at Madison Square Garden, Kidrin somehow got into a press conference with Jimmy Carter and asked the nominee if he supported Rubin Carter and his struggle for social justice. Jimmy Carter said he didn't know much about the case but that Kidrin should give the information to one of his aides. After the second conviction, Kidrin rode on Amtrak from Manhattan to Trenton and, weighed down by large sacks of canned food, he walked for fifteen minutes along the train track to the prison, sometimes in rain or snow. During one visit, he showed Carter his vacation pictures from Jamaica and insisted that someday they too would smoke cigars on a beach dock, their feet dangling in the ocean.

Carter told Kidrin about his hole-in-the-wall experience. He explained how he had discarded his law books and that he was now looking for a new kind of reading. He had reached his lowest point ever, and he was searching for something that would help him make sense out of his life, a road map out of the wilderness. His depression and anger were debilitating, and he knew that if he was going to survive, in prison or outside, something would have to change. That put Carter on the right foot. He was always at his best when he had a goal, then pursued it with single-minded intensity. As a boxer, he trained his body. As a prisoner, he trained his mind to study law. Now, as an inmate again, he wanted to train his spirit. He wasn't sure where that would lead him, but he wanted Kidrin to bring him books about psychology, religion, philosophy, history — anything that might shed light on his interior being.

Kidrin was up to the task. He had long been fascinated by spirituality and metaphysics, and he believed that Carter needed to extricate himself from the science of the legal world. Carter wanted new books? Kidrin would find them. His friends, aware that he was now playing librarian, gave him texts about boxing or detective stories.

"This is horseshit," Kidrin told them. "I'm looking for books that will bend his mind in a different way."

It was the beginning of Carter's numinous retreat. His goal was to disappear inside the prison, to embark on a silent, anonymous journey. He would stay awake for two days straight, lay four or five books across his cot, and, with his one good eye, study them in the prison's gray light, his lips moving as he read. He shut out the rattling echoes around him and tried to tease meaning from the layered and sometimes abstruse

lessons of his literary guides. Many books came his way by happen-
stance; but if he liked a book, he would ask to read others by the same
author. This gave his reading some direction; otherwise it was a random
exploration of his inner self.

One of the first books he liked was *Man's Search for Meaning* by
Viktor Frankl, the Viennese psychiatrist's personal account of his survival at Auschwitz. Carter was struck by the parallels between the concentration camp and prison: each institution literally sought to strip
away the individual identities of its inmates. Prisoners in both places
were forced to give up their clothes, their documents, and their belongings, and they were identified only by a series of numerals. Both institutions operated through the mass movements of crowded men,
prompted by daily whistles or bells and commanded by surly captors.
Prison labor, regular beatings, and rote schedules shaped each place.
New Jersey prisoners, of course, were convicted in courtrooms before
judges and jurors; but in Carter's mind, the state had illegally incarcerated him in the same fashion that the Nazis had held Frankl. Their
respective crimes were their race and their religion.

Yet Frankl's slim volume, written in clean, powerful prose, raised
the possibility not only of survival in such extreme conditions, but
salvation. The path lay through "the intensification of the inner life,
[which] helped the prisoner find refuge from the emptiness, desolation
and spiritual poverty of his existence . . . For the first time in my life,
I was able to understand the meaning of the words, 'The angels are
lost in the perpetual contemplation of an infinite glory.'" For Frankl,
the infinite glory was contemplation of his wife's image, loving and
beautiful. Working in a trench one day, enveloped by gray snow in
the pale light of dawn, he experienced a surge of rejuvenation. He
wrote:

> In the last violent protest against the hopelessness of imminent death, I
> sensed my spirit piercing through the enveloping gloom. I felt it transcend
> that hopeless meaningless world, and from somewhere I heard a victorious
> "Yes" in answer to my question of the existence of an ultimate purpose.
> At that moment a light was lit in a distant farmhouse, which stood on the
> horizon as if painted there, in the midst of the miserable grey of a dawning
> morning in Bavaria . . . For hours I stood hacking at the icy ground. The
> guard passed by, insulting me, and once again I communed with my
> beloved. More and more I felt that she was present, that she was with me;

I had the feeling that I was able to touch her, able to stretch out my hand and grasp hers. The feeling was very strong; she was there. Then, at that very moment, a bird flew down silently and perched just in front of me, on the heap of soil which I had dug up from the ditch, and looked steadily at me.

Frankl wrote that concentration camp prisoners may be hemmed in physically, but not spiritually. They can choose whether to submit to their captors or to retain their dignity, and their objective is to be worthy of their suffering. Suffering, in fact, provides an opportunity to add deeper meaning to life, and man must accept his suffering as his single and unique task: "An exceptionally difficult external situation ... gives man the opportunity to grow spiritually beyond oneself ... One could make a victory of those experiences turning life into an inner triumph, or one could ignore the challenge and simply vegetate, as did the majority of prisoners."

Carter's spirits rose at Frankl's words, which he read over and over. He had always seen prison as a scourge on his spirit, not as an opportunity for growth. Frankl confirmed that true freedom could be realized not by digging through a prison barrier but by excavating one's inner life. He distilled other important thoughts for Carter, for example, quoting Nietzsche: "He who has a why to live for can bear almost any how." Carter had his why to live for. If he died in prison, he would have died a racist triple murderer. Just as Jews had to survive concentration camps so that they would not be forgotten by history, Carter had to survive prison so he would not be condemned by history. He had to live to protect his innocence, to clear his name, and he could bear almost any how — any punishment or pain — to realize that goal.

Carter also read *Siddhartha*, the most famous novel by the German Hermann Hesse. The story, written in 1922, tells of one man's search for self-knowledge. Siddhartha leaves his family for a contemplative life, then, restless, pursues more hedonistic pleasures. He attains wealth as a merchant, finds a lover, and fathers a child. But bored and sickened by his lust and greed, he continues his journey and finally arrives at a river. There, the sound and sweep of the water seem to symbolize the unity of all people and all existence. It signals the beginning of his new life — the beginning of suffering, peace, and finally wisdom, the moment from which "Siddhartha ceased to fight against his destiny."

It was this journey, this restless search for meaning, that resonated with Carter. As Hesse wrote:

> [Siddhartha] had been full of arrogance; he had always been the cleverest, the most eager — always a step ahead of the others, always the learned and intellectual one, always the priest or the sage. His self had crawled into this priesthood, into this arrogance . . . Now he understood it and realized that the inward voice had been right, that no teacher could have brought him salvation. That was why he had to go into the world, to lose himself in power, women and money; that was why he had to be a merchant, a dice player, a drinker and a man of property . . . That was why he had to undergo these horrible years, suffer nausea, learn the lesson of the madness of an empty, futile life till the end, till he reached bitter despair, so that Siddhartha the pleasure-monger and Siddhartha the man of property could die.

Carter knew that he too had been arrogant and had pursued self-indulgent pleasures, and now he was suffering for his vanity and excesses. He did not know whether he, like Siddhartha, would reach some flash of self-discovery, but he felt he was making progress. He read books by J. Krishnamurti, the Indian guru born in 1895, who wrote about truth and freedom and urged followers to find their original mind, which alone is free, and books by Immanuel Velikovsky, a controversial Russian astronomer who posited theories about world history. Carter read *The Autobiography of Malcolm X*, then instructed Kidrin to bring him the same books that Malcolm X read when he was in prison that were cited in the autobiography: Will Durant's *Story of Civilization*, H. G. Wells's *Outline of History*, W. E. B. Du Bois's *Souls of Black Folk*, Carter G. Woodson's *Negro History*, and J. A. Rogers's three volumes of *Sex and Race*.

Over the months and years, Carter read about Plato and Aristotle and Martin Luther King, Jr., and Gandhi and Jesus. He passed time by "tabernacling" with these men, rocking gently in his cell, eyes closed, talking to them about what he was learning. (He had never been deeply religious, and that didn't change in prison. As he wrote in a journal, "I've got no problems with God, and He's got none with me.") He felt he could reach beyond the prison walls and see political heroes like Nelson Mandela on the rock in South Africa or martyrs like George Jackson, the revolutionary prisoner who wrote *Soledad Brother*. He began reconsidering the precepts that had always governed his life. As he wrote in one of his journals: "A real revelation is not 'an eye for an eye' or 'do as others do, but just do it first,' but a revelation is to change worse to better; hate to love; war to peace; it means turning things around; a total change from the opposite of what it is now."

As Thom Kidrin made his monthly treks to the prison, he noticed subtle changes in Carter. His rapid-fire strident speech soaked with profanities was giving way to a more measured tone. He paused between sentences. He was philosophical. The tone of his letters also changed from that of impassioned victim to giddy graduate student. He wrote to Kidrin: "We seek the heights of <u>Truth</u> and <u>Knowledge</u> in all things around us, when it is really within ourselves . . . [The universe] is <u>not</u> an imperfect sphere on the road to perfection. It is perfect now. We are perfect now!"

Carter was even reappraising the prosecutors and judges who had put him away. "Maybe they aren't evil," Carter told Kidrin. "Maybe they're doing what they're supposed to be doing so I can meet my own destiny, so I can become what I'm supposed to become." Like metal tempered by fire, Carter thought he might emerge stronger, more durable. As Frankl quoted Nietzsche, "That which does not kill me, makes me stronger," and Rubin Carter felt he was getting stronger.

He reached a point in his studies where he believed he could read the first couple of pages in a book and determine whether the author had anything of value to say. One day he opened an obscure paperback by a writer whose name he could not pronounce. He read the first page and, like a prospector panning for gold, realized he had found something of amazing value:

> I had come to the conclusion a long time ago that there was no escape from the labyrinth of contradictions in which we live except by an entirely new road, unlike anything hitherto known or used by us. But where this new or forgotten road began I was unable to say. I already knew then as an undoubted fact that beyond this thin film of false reality there existed another reality from which, for some reason, something separated us. The "miraculous" was a penetration into this unknown reality.

The book, a favorite of Kidrin's, was Piotr Demianovich Ouspensky's *In Search of the Miraculous,* and it began Carter's immersion into a densely written, complex universe of ideas. Ouspensky, born in Moscow in 1878, was a noted mathematician and journalist when he became a pupil of the Russian mystic G. I. Gurdjieff in St. Petersburg in 1915. Gurdjieff, who was believed to have been born in the 1870s, promoted occult notions of the universe, which he claimed had been taught to him by wise men in Central Asia. Ouspensky took Gurdjieff's recondite teachings and made them somewhat more intelligible in such books as *A New Model of the Universe, The Fourth Way,* and *In Search of the Miraculous.* These works lay out elaborate theories and formulas explaining the mathematical structure of the universe, planetary influences, and the evolution of human development. Over the years, critics have derided these works as murky, New Age hokum, citing some of Gurdjieff's more ridiculous claims, such as, "All evil deeds, all crimes, all self-sacrificing actions, all heroic exploits, as well as the actions of all ordinary life, are controlled by the moon." But devotees believe that Gurdjieff and Ouspensky had powerful insights into the human condition. To Rubin Carter, who viewed his own life as a "thin film of false reality," these Russian gurus spoke the truth.

Theirs was a bleak view of human nature. They believed that people think they are "awake" as moral beings, but in fact they are "asleep," oblivious of their own unconsciousness and unaware of the evil acts they commit. It is useless to blame them for their misdeeds because they are not even aware of what they are doing. The problem is not that the world is evil — if that were so, what value has life? — but that people do not realize that they are unconscious and that they are only a shell of what they could be. In *The Fourth Way,* Ouspensky described a man who attaches two horses to an airplane and uses it as a carriage. Then he learns how to use the engine and turns the plane into a motor car. But the plane never takes flight. "That is what we are doing with ourselves," Ouspensky explained. "We use ourselves as a carriage when we could fly."

One key to self-knowledge, Ouspensky wrote, was understanding the harmful effects of "personality," or acquired behavior, on one's "essence," or innate character. A strong personality "means a strong influence of what is not your own, of what you have acquired — other people's words, other people's views and theories. They can form such a thick crust round the essence that nothing can penetrate it to reach you, to reach what you are."

Carter pondered his own "personality" for a long time, his persona as the flamboyant, swaggering boxer who intimidated others in and out of the ring. But he was even more intrigued by Ouspensky's conclusion that every man lives in a prison — of his own ignorance and illusions — and that he cannot escape this prison by himself. Ouspensky wrote: "If he decides to run away, he must be one of a number of people who wish to run away, for they have to dig a tunnel, for one man cannot do it alone; and they must have help from those who have run away before them."

This idea bothered Carter, the chary loner who had sealed himself off from most of the outside world. He figured he had two prisons to escape — a literal one and a metaphysical one — but he had no one to help him. Ouspensky, in *A New Model of the Universe,* introduced another notion that weighed heavily upon Carter. Self-knowledge and freedom were possible, Ouspensky wrote, but only for "an inner circle of humanity."

> Humanity is regarded as two concentric circles. All humanity which we know and to which we belong forms the outer circle. All the history of humanity that we know is the history of the outer circle. But within this circle there is another, of which men of the outer circle know nothing, and the existence of which they only sometimes dimly suspect . . . The inner . . . circle forms, as it were, a life within a life, a mystery, a secret in the life of humanity. . . . the members of the inner circle are civilised men living in a country of barbarians among savages.

On one level, Ouspensky helped Carter to understand his adversaries. They were not wicked, they were simply unconscious. Society had conditioned them and most everyone else to commit or tolerate injustice. The truth was evident to the "inner circle of humanity," but who exactly were its members and how could they help him?

Carter took these and other questions to some new inmates. When his friend Moko was released in 1979, he introduced Carter to two prison newcomers, Ulysses "Sam" Leslie, a lanky, light-skinned African American who had been convicted of homicide, and Robert Sigler, known as "Zig," a heavyset dark-skinned son of a coal miner, who had been convicted of armed robbery. Carter began tutoring Sam and Zig, walking around the prison yard with the two younger inmates, giving them some of his books and engaging them in long discussions. He also typed dozens of letters and sent them through the prison equivalent of office mail. He urged them to "die to the world," to surrender all that was false about themselves. As he wrote to Leslie on August 28, 1981:

We covered [ourselves] up with coldness, with intellectualism, with words, with excuses, with games, until we finally began to believe for ourselves that we could not feel or love! So now when we want to _feel_ and _love_, we have to dig ourselves out from under all the shit that we have piled up on ourselves throughout our lives, and in many cases in order to do it — it takes a great deal of TNT to accomplish the job.

Carter still wrote tirades in his journals about racism in America and prison life, but he could now see his experiences as a painful but necessary crucible for his personal development. He wrote to Leslie on April 21, 1982:

Sometimes readiness and change come only because of all the _heartache_ and _pain_ and deep _frustration_ that has gone on before. That is to say, every sin, every disease, every disappointment, every failure, every bit of difficulty that has ever _touched_ our lives have all been a very _necessary_ part of our entire experience _without_ which we would not have been made _ready_ or _prepared_ to receive the unfoldment of a truly _spiritual_ message. And I say this _knowing_, just as you _know_, that some of us have been _down_ and are presently _still_ down, into the very _depths_ of _human existence_ ... And yet whatever the _degree of difficulty_ each one of us has had, then it was perhaps _that_ degree of difficulty that each one of us _needed!_

Carter now looked with contempt on the very activities that he had once cherished. People who went to athletic events, discos, "pornoshops or houses of prostitution" were part of the benighted masses. He quoted Ibsen's Dr. Stockmann, which he culled from Ouspensky's _New Model of the Universe._ Society was threatened not by subversive ideas or radical opinions but by consensus opinions, or what Ibsen called "ageing truths": "All the truths belonging to the majority are like ancient rancid bacon or like rotten green ham; and from them comes all the moral scurvy which is eating itself into the life of the people around us."

But Carter was still optimistic about man's ability to rise above the morass. "So, yes, things can be changed," he wrote on April 5, 1980, to Steve Slaby, a civil engineering professor at Princeton University who worked on Carter's New Jersey Defense Committee, "but they cannot be changed by ordinary means. They can only be changed by an understanding of who and what we are ... And therefore, the struggle must go on — but the battlefields need to be changed, because we are continuously seeking for happiness and joy _outside_ of ourselves, when in actual fact they can only be within, and then we will be able to find them in other places."

Several months later, Carter woke up one morning and looked at the mirror in his cell. He saw the bald head, the goatee, the glower, but the image didn't register. He looked at himself for a long time, but it was as if he were looking at a different person. Carter's head had been shaved since he enlisted in the Army. He had always liked his head burnished and bald. It was the Hurricane's signature, a symbol of renegade power, virility, and defiance. It was intimidating, and, Carter now concluded, it was all fake. Pretense. *Personality.* Carter looked into the mirror and knew that he was no longer that person. The fulgent black dome, the chin beard and fearsome stare, were part of his Eldorado-driving, horseback-riding, vodka-swilling, priapic persona. They were not his *essence.* A new Hurricane was slowly emerging. For the first time in twenty-five years, he put away his Magic Shave. Carter, at forty-three, feared his hair would come in gray, but it came in thick and black. "I fooled my hair to think it was young," he later joked. The Afro literally softened Carter's edges. He also clipped his whiskers and, for the first time in years, his face was clean shaven. As Ouspensky wrote in *The Fourth Way,* "If personality becomes more transparent, impressions and external influences will penetrate through it and reach essence, and then essence will begin to grow."

While Carter continued his self-exploration, the outside world occasionally penetrated in remarkable ways. In December 1980, a guard went to his cell and told Carter that his father was in the hospital in Glassboro, New Jersey, and he had a pass to see him. Carter had not seen or spoken to his father in four years and did not know he was ill, but he assumed his condition was serious. It cost his family $500 for two off-duty guards to drive Carter to the hospital in a state vehicle. Lloyd Carter, the hard-working church deacon and switch-wielding disciplinarian, had had a stormy relationship with his youngest son. Rubin's wayward behavior as a youth had earned him many beatings, but his father admired his son's headstrong spirit. Lloyd also never doubted Rubin's innocence. He knew that no child of his could walk into a bar and shoot a room full of strangers. He attended every day of both trials and was heartbroken by Rubin's convictions. In his final years, Lloyd mellowed quite a bit, spending more time with his wife,

Bertha, at a family farm in southern New Jersey. Lloyd's hair turned a distinguished, courtly gray, but he retained his steely frame and unflinching faith — in God and in Rubin. He talked incessantly about his son's freedom. It consumed his dreams and his passions. "I know someday Rubin will be free," he often said. "I don't know if I'll be around to see it, but I know he will be free."

When Rubin reached his father's hospital room, his worst fears were confirmed. His father, now in his late sixties, had colon cancer. He lay, emaciated, with clear tubes running through his nose and a urine bag on the side of the bed. Lloyd was conscious and twitching and seemed uncomfortable. He couldn't talk. As the prison guards stood outside the room, Rubin walked to his father's bed. He wanted to touch his forehead, to hold him. The warmth of his hand, the safety of his arms would heal him, Rubin thought, and his father would rise from the bed and walk away. But standing before his father in shackles and handcuffs, Rubin could not reach out.

"I'm here, Dad, and I love you," he whispered. "It's sad you have to see me still in chains, but that's the way it is, that's just the way it is." Lloyd looked at his son and nodded.

An hour later, Carter was taken back to prison. That night he had a bizarre dream in which a blue and white "dog-horse" appeared before him and asked where his father was. In the dream Carter replied, "Paterson." He then woke up, puzzled, because he had just seen his father in Glassboro. Carter rarely spoke to his mother from prison, but the following morning he called her at her home in Paterson. He needed to find out where his father was. Bertha said that Lloyd had died shortly after his visit the day before; Bragg Funeral Homes in Paterson had already retrieved the body. Lloyd Carter was indeed in Paterson when Rubin so informed the mysterious dog-horse.

Rubin, disinclined in general to attend burials, did not go to his father's funeral. Over the years, he often wondered if he made the right decision in seeing his father on his deathbed — if he subconsciously wanted his father to see him in restraints. Rubin always resented that his father had told the Paterson police that his nine-year-old son stole clothes from an outdoor market. That led to Rubin's first encounter with the law, and it seemed to set the tone for the rest of his life. His current imprisonment was the culmination of all his battles with the police, and he wondered if he stood before his dying father, his hands and legs cuffed and shackled, to settle past scores, to get even. The thought troubled Carter for many years.

In May 1981, Carter returned to the Passaic County Court for the first time since his sentencing. It was a kind of coming-out party for him, the first time that his lawyers or almost anyone else outside the prison had seen his new look. He received his first shock when he was placed in the holding cell with other prisoners in the jail. In the New Jersey prison system, Carter's bare-knuckle reputation was legendary, his bad-boy image from his days in Paterson still the stuff of tall tales. Inmates respected someone with a "rep," and in his presence they tended to suppress their own boasting about how "bad" they were, lest he challenge them. But now the other prisoners continued with their strutting and jive talk after a guard whispered excitedly that "Rubin 'Hurricane' Carter is coming today." It dawned on Carter that no one recognized him. Wearing a red-and-white-check wool shirt and blue jeans and a full head of neatly cropped hair, he looked like anyone else, and he was ignored. He couldn't remember the last time that had happened. He had disappeared without disappearing. This seemed proof that his studies were working. The guards and prisoners were searching for Hurricane Carter's personality, but that was gone. What they saw was his essence.

He walked quietly into the courtroom through a side door, flanked by two prison guards, and smiled to a group of supporters. Sitting at his defense table was a new lawyer, Leon Friedman. A law professor at Hofstra University, Friedman had spoken to Carter on the phone a number of times but had never met him. "Who is this guy?" Friedman asked Myron Beldock as their client walked toward the table. Carter sat next to Beldock.

"Damn, Rubin, is that you?" Beldock asked.

"Yeah, it's me."

During a break, Carter also saw his son, Raheem, now four years old, for the first time since he was a newborn. They smiled, embraced, and were talking when a corpulent police officer intervened. "Okay, that's it," he said, separating them. As Carter took his seat, he thought about both his father and son: Lloyd's final image of him was a man in shackles, and Raheem's only image was of him in custody. It gave the boy a grievous connection with his deceased grandfather.

Carter was in court for a remand hearing, ordered by the New Jersey Supreme Court. It asked the trial court to determine possible prosecutorial misconduct related to a polygraph exam given to Alfred Bello three months before the 1976 trial. At the time, the prosecutors were supposedly trying to ascertain which of Bello's many versions of the Lafayette bar shootings was accurate. The polygraph examiner, Leonard Harrelson, filed a report with Carter's lawyers indicating that Bello's 1967 version was truthful. Unlike his recanted accounts, the '67 version had Bello standing *on the street,* watching Carter and John Artis flee from the tavern with weapons. The prosecutors confronted Bello with the polygraph results, which caused Bello to return to his original — and incriminating — testimony.

After the trial, however, Beldock was troubled by the lie detector report. He generally did not trust polygraph tests, and he did not see how a polygrapher could possibly extricate the truth from a congenital liar like Bello. This polygraph report in particular nettled Beldock because it had more questions — thirty — than he had seen on most other tests, and he could not figure out how Bello's answers produced Harrelson's conclusion. Harrelson himself was a highly regarded, seasoned examiner who was chief of the Keeler Polygraph Institute in Chicago, but at least one error in the report suggested he had been careless. Harrelson concluded that Bello was telling the truth when he testified at the "1966" trial. The trial occurred in 1967.

After the second trial, Beldock called Harrelson and asked him a simple question: Which of Bello's versions did he find to be truthful? Initially Harrelson was fuzzy on the details, but he said that Bello's polygrams showed that his *in the bar* account was truthful — the version that exonerated Carter and Artis. That directly contradicted his written report, which said Bello's testimony at the first trial, the *on the street* account, was truthful. Beldock spoke with Harrelson on the phone several more times and flew to Chicago twice to interview him. It turned out that Harrelson had never read the transcripts from the first trial and had mistakenly assumed that the *in the bar* version was used in the first trial. Harrelson's blunder might never have become important except for one fact: Harrelson had told members of the prosecution team, including Vincent DeSimone and Burrell Humphreys, the accurate results of the polygraph test in telephone conversations, but prosecutors never disclosed this evidence to the defense. In Beldock's view, that represented withholding of evidence and was grounds for over-turning the conviction. Assistant Prosecutor Ronald Marmo had already said that prosecutors used the lie detector test to bring Bello back to his original testimony. If prosecutors knew the results were false, Beldock believed that represented prosecutorial misconduct. It was again up to the trial court judge — Bruno Leopizzi — to sort out this mess in the remand hearing and issue an opinion.

While these revelations would ultimately prove enormously signifi-cant to Carter's case, the defendant was much more focused on another, more personal sort of epiphany. From the moment he had been arrested, he always insisted that he be fully involved in the courtroom proceedings. At his trials and various hearings, he sat at the defense table, sizing up witnesses, concentrating on every word, scribbling notes on a legal pad, conferring with his lawyers on strategy, absorbing every-thing he could. Now here he was again, fifteen years later, still sitting in a courtroom with lawyers and witnesses and a judge and complete strangers who didn't know anything about him. Once again he saw Alfred Bello on the stand and Judge Leopizzi on the bench and Marmo at the counsel table for the state.* There was talk about Rubin Carter the killer, the murderer, the gunman. Carter had heard it all before, and he was sick of it. He wrote on his yellow pad, "All these people who are seeking to protect this thing . . . It is very painful for me to sit here — the only African in the room — and watch as this poisonous system poisons . . ." At the end of the first day, Carter concluded he had had enough. These people were not talking about him; they were talking about themselves or about some other people. This proceeding was no longer relevant to him, and he would not dignify it with his presence. He had more important work to do. "I'm not going to listen to this anymore," he told Beldock. "I'm going back to prison."

The hearing continued for fifteen days. Bello, conceding that he had a serious drinking problem, testified that he had virtually no memory of any of the events in question — the trial, the polygraph test, or the night of the murder. Harrelson confirmed that, after Bello's polygraph test, he notified the prosecutor's office that Bello's *in the bar* story — the version that exonerated Carter — was true and that his written

* Absent was DeSimone, who had died in 1979. Humphreys was now a Superior Court judge in Passaic County, but he testified at the remand hearing.

report was in error. Harrelson denied that he had colluded with the prosecutors to falsify the report. He also testified that he was convinced that Carter and Artis were the actual killers — a preposterous claim, given that the most he could do was evaluate the truthfulness of Bello's statements, and Bello had never accused the defendants of committing the murder, just being at the scene of the crime.

In the end, Leopizzi wrote an eighty-page opinion in favor of the prosecutors. It was all too familiar for Carter. Just as his first trial judge, Samuel Larner, ruled that no prosecutorial errors had tainted those proceedings, Judge Leopizzi was certain that no misdeeds by the state had occurred on his watch either. Carter realized that no trial judge would ever impugn his own courtroom, and that justice was possible only in the state supreme court or in federal court. But he had no time to lament his latest setback. In his ongoing search for the miraculous, he was about to stumble on the inner circle of humanity.

10

THE INNER CIRCLE OF HUMANITY

AS A STUDENT at the University of Toronto in the 1960s, Rory "Gus" Sinclair gave money to draft dodgers and marched on the American consulate in Toronto to protest the Vietnam War. He demonstrated against campus recruiters from Dow Chemical because the company made napalm. He studied Marx. After graduating, he hitchhiked to the Yukon and worked in an asbestos mine, then made one of those trips around the world that is only possible when you're young and fearless and broke. He scraped through China, India, and Europe, reading a dog-eared copy of an Abbie Hoffman book along the way. When he returned in 1969, he thought the time was right to create something that would bring meaning to his life. He wanted to start a commune.

Toronto nourished a vibrant counterculture centered on the small downtown neighborhood of Yorkville, which served as a magnet for student dropouts and American draft dodgers, miniskirted flower children and self-proclaimed visionaries. There were plenty of drugs and free love and music, and it was easy to believe that the world could be remade on a wave of spirituality and enlightened thinking. Sinclair tapped into this heady optimism, seeking friends and college acquaintances who might be interested in a communal social experiment. The house would run on good socialist principles. Money would be put into a pot, and no one would go hungry. A rundown row house was rented in downtown Toronto in the midst of porno shops and liquor stores. In the first year, like-minded radicals drifted in and out of the house, but a core group eventually formed. It was an unusual mix of rich kids and poor ones, straights and gays, Catholics and Protestants, the nephew of a Nazi officer and the son of Jews who survived Bergen-Belsen. They were energized by the protest and politics of the era: they opposed the Vietnam War and despised any form of imperialism or colonialism; they distrusted government, scoffed at religion, and demonized parents; they believed that poverty was immoral, racism was a scourge, and business was corrupt.

While the commune's antiestablishment views may have attracted its eight to ten members, the group was held together by a charismatic woman who became its leader.

Lisa Peters was petite, with a square face and long dark hair.* She was not especially pretty and was certainly not feminine. She smoked and cursed and spoke loudly. Her grammar was poor and she shunned makeup and was proud that she never wore a dress for a man. She hated to have her picture taken because she was self-conscious about her nose. She had few material possessions and little money. What she had, however, was unflinching self-confidence, a riotous laugh, barbed opinions, and fearlessness. "I'd go toe-to-toe with God," she would say.

Her dramatic life story enhanced her mystique. As she told other members of the commune, she grew up in the small rural town of Emsdale in northern Ontario, about 140 miles from Toronto. Her mother died during childbirth, and she had been raised by an abusive, alcoholic father. He was a boxer turned evangelist, and he blamed Lisa for his wife's death. They lived in poverty, their home heated by a woodstove. After Lisa refused confirmation in their church, she ran away from home when she was fourteen. She ended up on the streets of Toronto in the working-class Cabbagetown neighborhood, so named because Irish immigrants in the 1840s planted cabbages around their shacks. Lisa hung out with "rounders," neighborhood toughs who liked to hot-wire cars and commit petty crimes. At seventeen she got pregnant. Still carrying her baby, she married a man who was not the child's

---

* Lisa's maiden name was Peters. According to Sinclair, her married name was Hetherington, which was the name under which she filed her taxes. In the commune, she often used Swinton after she and Terry Swinton paired off as a couple.

father. One day she looked at herself in the mirror, realized she could not stand the tedium of married life, and bolted from the union. Her son, Martin, was subsequently born, and she raised him by herself. She made some money working as a maid and nanny, but Lisa — ill educated, dirt poor, alone — lived on the edge. She described eating ice cubes to feed herself so she'd have money to feed her son.

Her cohorts in the commune, well educated and cultivated, were captivated by this game survivor from the grotty seams of Toronto. Her childhood scars sometimes surfaced in poignant moments. She was, for example, dedicated to giving other members of the group the perfect Christmas gift. This passion, she explained, stemmed from an experience she had as a ten-year-old. She had asked her father for a pair of white ice skates for Christmas, envisioning a sleek pair of women's figure skates. When she opened the gift, she found instead an old pair of boy's hockey skates, covered with a heavy coat of white house paint. When she recounted this story years later, disappointment and pain still etched her face.

But it was Lisa's intensity that enabled her to touch other people's lives. When Gus Sinclair met her, he mentioned to her that his father drank, using the same line he gave everyone else: "He has a small drinking problem, but it doesn't affect me." His father, in fact, was an alcoholic, given to binge drinking of rum, and that was a source of insecurity and shame to the young man. Lisa looked at him hard, then gently said, "Oh yeah, tell me about it." Sinclair realized that somehow she knew the truth, that he had been lying to others and even to himself about his father. For the first time, he expressed his pained feelings; Lisa leaned forward, listening intently to every word.

She had a way of cutting to the quick. One of Martin's friends, Sean Cunningham, spent considerable time at the commune. Sean had received a Catholic education, and one day, when he was thirteen, he confided to Lisa that he disagreed with the church's position on abortion. Without skipping a beat, Lisa said, "Good. You tell me what you think about it." Her openness was exhilarating and she praised Sean's wit; the teenager was enthralled. Sean had grown up in a troubled home, and now he knew Lisa, who laughed uproariously, talked candidly about sex, and never appeared to be wrong. Lisa sat in the corner of an L-shaped sectional couch, watching television or leading discussions, and Sean cherished the moments when he could curl up next to her.

Everyone in the commune needed Lisa in some way. She met Eitel Renbaum while she was volunteering at a drug intervention center for Toronto youths. Renbaum was eighteen, a heavy user of speed, and given to surly outbursts to anyone who tried to straighten him out. But Lisa admired his headstrong attitude. When she chastised him for using speed, he ridiculed her for experimenting with pot. He resisted her help, screaming invectives and trying to scare her off as he had others. But Lisa persuaded him to stay at the apartment where she lived with her son and Terry Swinton. (The commune's members had not consolidated under one roof yet.) Renbaum could remain, however, only if he stayed off drugs. Lisa helped him through long nights of paranoid visions and delusions, and he appeared to be on the right track.

But Lisa also had a febrile temper, and when Renbaum had a relapse, she ripped him to shreds. "You dumb son of a bitch!" she screamed. "I said you could come into my house, but you couldn't hit up. Everyone else says, 'Poor guy.' But now you're out on your ass. Fuck off!" Lisa, however, did not abandon her project. She sent Renbaum to the row house where Sinclair and others were living, and Renbaum finally did kick his habit. He stayed in the commune for many years, and other members of the group credited Lisa with saving his life.

A year after the commune was established, the group became bored with Canada and decided it was time to bestow good deeds on other parts of the world. Sinclair had been to Malaysia before — and that seemed as good a spot as any. Through a contact in the embassy in Ottawa, they thought they could find jobs there in a school or a health clinic. So five members of the group plus a child — Lisa's son — sold their possessions, got their typhoid shots, and packed their bags. They had a stopover in London, where they slept in Hyde Park for an afternoon. They knocked around England for almost a week, crossed the English Channel, and made it to Brussels by bus. On their flight to Kuala Lumpur, they had to stop in New Delhi, where the city's raw poverty was clear even in the airport. Lisa, in tears at the sight of bedraggled women and homeless children, gave all the money in her pocket to a woman in the ladies' bathroom handing out paper towels. Communism, she concluded, was the only thing that could save India.

This scaled-down Canadian Peace Corps finally arrived in Kuala

Lumpur, but the teaching or health care jobs never materialized. They had no contacts and no way to support themselves. In desperation, they decided to do something contrary to everything they believed in: they opened a business, demonstrating the resourcefulness that would mark all their endeavors.

They needed something to sell, so they looked around their new city and realized that colorful "batiks," or fabrics dyed with removable wax, were made in Malaysia. The material was used for shirts, dresses, headpieces, and other apparel, and they were popular with Toronto's youth culture. Terry Swinton, the son of a successful businessman, wrote to his father to borrow some extra cash, and a new business – Five Believers' Batiks Ltd. — was born. (The name derives from an obscure Bob Dylan song, "Obviously, Five Believers.") The new entrepreneurs knew nothing about fashion, marketing, distribution, pricing, or exporting. Even mailing a letter back home was tricky. But they instructed the remaining three members of the commune in Toronto to rent an inexpensive storefront, while the Malaysian group set off to buy fabrics and find tailors. It was summer, and the goal was to have merchandise ready for sale by the Christmas season. The first tailor they hired, a Malay, could only make traditional Malay men's shirts. He delivered a dozen caftans to the Canadians, but they were all too big. The group hired a more flexible Chinese tailor instead. When the first shipment was finally sent to Canada, the Toronto partners discovered that the Malaysian group had not put labels in the garments identifying country of origin and providing washing instructions. So they spent the night in an airport warehouse, printing labels by hand and sewing them on each piece of clothing. The items made it to their store for Christmas, and decent sales financed a new shipment.

Over time, the commune rotated members to Malaysia so that no one would be stuck there for more than a few years at a time. The Toronto side of the business scoured fashion magazines for apparel ideas, then every few months sent over a new order that included photographs and drawings. The Malaysian side made a sample of each new style and sent it back to Toronto for approval. Toronto also replenished older stock that was selling well. The business gradually migrated to larger storefronts and eventually settled in a shop in Yorkville Village, where the sex accessory stores and coffeehouses were beginning to give way to fancy boutiques. The store featured resplendent displays of bright fabrics and clothing set off smartly by chocolate-brown carpeting, stucco walls, and antique dressers. Sometimes the company's ambitions outstripped its judgment. New stores in the United States — in South-ampton on Long Island and in Palm Beach, Florida — fared poorly and were closed. But Five Believers' Batiks tapped into new markets in Canada by selling its product wholesale to large retailers such as Hudson's Bay Company. Five Believers' best year, 1976, produced a profit of more than C$50,000.

This windfall played a vital role in the commune's history, for it was used as down payment on a twenty-seven-room English manor on Walmer Road in downtown Toronto. Designed and built at the turn of the century by Eden Smith, a well-known Toronto architect, the house was expensive — C$190,000 — but it gave the group its first true communal environment. The new occupants lovingly restored and modified the house and its grounds of more than an acre. They papered the gabled third-floor rooms in small Williamsburg prints; burned off the old exterior paint and applied purple-brown and smoky-rose colors with putty trim; installed a three-by-six-foot skylight in the television room; sanded and polyurethaned all the exposed wood floors; installed a butcher's block and ceramic tile counters in the kitchen and painted wildflowers on the cabinet doors; and made a gigantic copper hood for a restaurant-size griddle and stove. They restored the garden by digging up and carefully replacing hundreds of limestone rocks that had been part of the original garden; they planted dozens of rhododendrons, azaleas, and flowering shrubs, then resodded the whole area. On the far hill, they designed and built a Japanese teahouse, and they used free truckloads of cobblestones from Toronto's streets to make a spectacular patio and steps at the rear of the house.

The house became the self-contained world that the commune craved. Its members rarely went to movies or plays, and they avoided socializing with anyone outside their circle, coveting their secrecy. Most of the men and women paired off. Dating or sexual activity outside the house was forbidden. Sinclair never had a partner in the commune and was therefore celibate for eighteen years, until he left. Six-foot fences surrounded the house, and when a knock was heard at the door, someone peered out a second-story window and alerted the group to the visitor. Phone calls were screened. Showing up at the house with a friend was considered an unforgivable breach of privacy, equivalent to inviting a stranger into your bathroom when a family member was taking a bath. Communications with parents were cut off. Sam Chaiton once sent postcards to his parents in Canada, but he gave them to friends who were going to France. They were to mail the cards back to Canada to persuade Chaiton's parents that their son had moved to Europe.

The commune did not want anyone to know how many people lived in the house or what the relationship of each member was to the other. Lisa's son was trained to call everyone in the house "aunt" or "uncle" in the presence of outsiders. Members would come and go through a service entrance, not the front door. Mary Newberry worked in a convenience store for eight years without telling anyone where she lived or whom she lived with. Such information was never disclosed. Only one resident of the house was listed in the phone book.

Lisa's influence grew over time. The group had one checking account, and Lisa, needing to approve expenditures, effectively controlled the purse strings. She decided what they ate for dinner and what television shows they watched. (She liked game shows and talk shows.) She insisted that the house be spotless, instructing others to wrap a cloth around a kitchen knife to clean corners, a trick she learned working as a maid. Terry Swinton's sister, Kathy, copied the way Lisa smacked her gum. Lisa never drank alcohol or used drugs; thus, no one else drank alcohol or used drugs. She also determined who stayed and who left the commune. She summarily kicked out Bob Bartolomei when he was in Kuala Lumpur because he had personality clashes with other members of the group. She sent him C$500 and told him he could return to any city in North America except Toronto.

Her political views shaped conversations inside the house. Lisa loved to read or talk about conspiracy theories, such as a secret relationship between the Ford Motor Company and the Nazi war machine. A favorite book was *The Robber Barons: The Great American Capitalists,* by Matthew Josephson, describing the abusive tactics of America's early industrial titans. Her outrage was also triggered by the historical injustices against black people of any nationality, but particularly black Americans.

Before the commune was formed, Lisa had taken a trip to America's

South, meeting blacks in blues clubs in Mississippi, Alabama, and elsewhere. She identified with the struggles of African Americans, and she loved their music. Blues artists like Lightnin' Hopkins, Brownie McGhee, and Mississippi John Hurt were played repeatedly in the house. The commune read books by or about Frederick Douglass, Richard Wright, James Baldwin, and Malcolm X, among other black subjects. Lisa believed that black Americans bore the pernicious legacy of slavery and that they still suffered beneath the heel of a racist white majority. With access and opportunity, blacks would flourish, but they lacked adequate education, housing, and employment. Lisa admired black men who would not be intimidated. *All God's Dangers: The Life of Nate Shaw,* by Theodore Rosengarten, was the story of a poor black cotton farmer in Alabama, and provided a rambling first-person account of his life, giving it an authentic, bluesy tone.* The son of a slave, Shaw in 1932 faced down a crowd of white deputies who had come to confiscate a neighbor's livestock, but he paid a heavy price for his defiance. He was shot three times and was sent to prison for twelve years. As Shaw explained: *"The nigger was disrecognized; the white man in this country had everything fixed and mapped out. Didn't allow no niggers to stand arm and arm together. The rule worked just like it had always worked: they was against me definitely just like they was against those Scottsboro boys . . . The nigger's voice just wasn't substantious to stand up for hisself."* Nate Shaw had died by the time Lisa read *All God's Dangers.* But she soon found another book about racial injustice in which the victim was very much alive.

By 1979, the commune had shut down the batik business as the spandex craze cut into sales of funky cotton apparel. Searching for a fresh moneymaker, the group met an inventor who had patented a device that would save gas. The contraption was to induce turbulence in the gasoline entering the combustion chamber, which would somehow produce a cleaner, more efficient burn of the gas vapors. Several members in the commune began looking for factory space to mass-produce the gadget, but before any serious money was invested, they had the sense to test it at an Environmental Protection Agency lab in Brooklyn, New York.

* Shaw's real name was Ned Cobb.

The miracle device turned out to be a bust when EPA tests proved it did not save gas. But while visiting the lab, the Canadians met a black teenager from Bedford-Stuyvesant, one of Brooklyn's worst ghettos, who was working at the lab on an internship financed by the city. Lesra Martin was more interested in playing tag or shooting his water pistol at friends than doing EPA work, but he was intrigued by the group of white foreigners who were visiting the lab.

Lesra, who was fifteen years old but barely five feet tall, and a friend named William Fuller began following the group around the EPA facilities. Their English was poor, and the Canadians struggled to understand them. But they were charmed by the teens' good humor and high spirits. One day Lisa, Renbaum, and Swinton offered Lesra a ride home. The drive turned into a journey of despair. The Canadians saw entire streets of desolation, where mattresses, garbage cans, and broken bottles were strewn all over. When they reached Lesra's home, he mentioned that the boarded-up building next door housed drug addicts and winos.

When Lisa and the rest of the crew returned to Toronto, they could not stop thinking about Lesra and William. The commune had helped Canadians in need, but could it do the same for two black youths in Brooklyn? The group decided to invite Lesra and William to visit Toronto for a long weekend, coinciding with an annual Caribbean festival. The youngsters were dazzled by the well-appointed surroundings. After they returned home, the commune made its boldest move yet. It wanted, in effect, to adopt Lesra, to bring him to Toronto to save him from his environment. William's family was relatively stable and prosperous compared to Lesra's. His parents, Earl and Alma Martin, had eight children, but both adults had a drinking problem and were on welfare. The family lived on the fourth floor of a condemned building that still housed eight families. The Canadians, returning to Bedford-Stuyvesant, bought Lesra a new television set to show their generosity. They appealed to his parents that their son was better off in Toronto. He needed a structured home environment and focused instruction if he — like his biblical namesake, Lazarus — was going to rise above the ashes of his surroundings. The Martins agreed, so Lesra headed north.

Lesra's arrival transformed the commune. Suddenly, eight adults channeled their energy into repairing the youngster's varied maladies. They bought him his first pair of prescription glasses, literally bringing his life into focus. They cut back his consumption of sugar to relieve nagging headaches. Antibiotics solved a runny nose while an improved diet helped him grow. A broken front tooth was capped. They called him the "ghetto urchin."

Lesra's guardians wanted to expose him to the world beyond the ghetto. They encouraged him to walk barefoot on the grass of a wooded ravine, so he could feel the softness of his new home compared to the glass-strewn streets of Brooklyn. New clothing brought comfort, and accessories evoked richness. Lesra soon had a velour bathrobe, Italian shoes, a sheepskin coat, and a gold bracelet. He learned to drive on the commune's Mercedes-Benz.

Lisa lavished attention on Lesra. When she wasn't actually with him, she spoke incessantly of his education, his physique, his clothes, or his health. In the social hierarchy of the house, whoever sat next to Lisa on the couch was in special favor, and now Lesra had that spot. She would spontaneously hug him, smother him in playful kisses, snuggle with him before bedtime, drape an arm around him while he was reading, and lean against him on walks in the garden. Her physical affection for Lesra prompted speculation among other housemates of a sexual relationship between the two — a relationship that struck some as inappropriate, given Lisa's role as leader of the commune. In one of the few group pictures of the commune, Lesra and Lisa are sitting next to each other on the couch, holding hands.

While he was being assimilated into a white world, Lesra did not leave the ghetto behind. In fact, he was encouraged to play up his streetwise persona. He liked to hunch up his shoulders, pull his cap over his eyes, and stick his hands in his pockets — antics that were playfully mimicked by others in the commune. When Lesra saw a Cadillac go by, he would say, "There go pimp." When his guardians saw a Cadillac, they would echo, "There go pimp." The Canadians wanted him to understand and celebrate black culture. They gave him a statue of an African drummer, observed a "soulful Christmas" by eating chitterlings, beans, and greens, and played Christmas carols by Ray Charles. Lesra was encouraged to dance and rap in front of the group. In a Superman rap, he chanted:

> Me and Supe Had a Fight
> Hit 'em in the head with a kryptonite.

Hit 'em so hard I bust his brain
And now I'm bustin' out Lois Lane.

While Lesra basked in all the attention, he was in Toronto primarily to get an education. Originally, he was going to be enrolled in a public school, but after he took a placement exam, the extent of his academic neglect became fully known. Lesra was supposed to enter the eleventh grade, but in fact he was illiterate. He didn't know the name of his country. He had never written a school paper and never read a newspaper. He could not even read street signs. He was no more adept in math, geography, or history. He also had no inkling of how far behind he was, for he performed at the same level as the other students in his Brooklyn class.

As a result, his new guardians would now have to be his teachers. They had already had plenty of practice. Lisa's son, Martin, was about the same age as Lesra; he had dyslexia, and for years the commune had educated him at home. Lesra now made it a class of two. Chaiton and Sinclair handled most of the teaching, but Lisa oversaw the curriculum. Their new student studied seven days a week. They started with the basics — grammar, arithmetic, diction — but in time Lesra would write papers, take tests, and do research projects. History lessons came with an Afro-centric bias. While black men and women built great African civilizations, he was taught, whites in this century were responsible for slaughtering millions in two world wars. Books by black authors or on black themes were also required reading.

The goal was to help Lesra gain admission to the University of Toronto. That seemed impossible at the outset, but the commune believed it was exceptional. Its members thrived on establishing lofty objectives, then rallying to achieve them, and Lesra was the perfect recipient of their largesse. They did not pity him for his deprivation but revered him for his sacrifices. He symbolized all that was wrong with America — a rich but complacent country whose institutional racism stifled the development of a whole class of noble citizens. "He was American racism invited to your dinner table each night, and that made him a god in his own way," Sean Cunningham said.

In the summer of 1980, about a year after Lesra had moved to the commune, several members and Lesra went to a warehouse book sale held by the Metropolitan Toronto Public Libraries. Paperbacks went for a quarter, and a crush of people scrambled for the bargains. Lesra and his guardians returned home with three cartons of books, including one by a writer they had never heard of, Rubin "Hurricane" Carter. Lisa was a boxing fan, and *The Sixteenth Round* piqued her interest. Carter seemed to be part of a disturbing trend of strong American black heroes, such as Malcolm X, who served time in prison.

If Lesra's life story struck a nerve with Lisa, Carter's tale hit her like a seismic jolt. She admired tough men, survivors like herself, and Carter was the quintessential survivor. His book supported themes long embraced by Lisa: racist public officials, courtroom conspiracies, and the indomitable will of black men. His profanity, his rage, and his righteousness all galvanized a woman whose moral indignation was easily triggered. Lisa made everyone else in the house read the book, and all agreed that Carter was an amazing man who had been grievously wronged. For Lesra, *The Sixteenth Round* represented a breakthrough. He had become despondent over his difficulties in reading, but he was able to read this book all the way through, paving the way for many more.

Published in 1974, *The Sixteenth Round* ended with Carter in prison, pleading for help. But there was no indication of what had become of him. Was he still in prison? Was he free? Lisa told Terry Swinton to call the New Jersey Department of Corrections, and an official broke the news: Rubin Carter was still in prison. Several members of the commune, including Lesra, went to the library and unearthed newspaper articles that made them familiar with Carter's life since the book was published. They learned about the recantations from key witnesses, about Carter's celebrity supporters, and about the second trial. They also learned that Carter was back in Trenton State Prison, estranged from his wife and two children, awaiting court appeals, and still protesting his innocence.

Lisa and the whole house were shocked and outraged, but they had no idea what they could do. Unlike Lesra, whom they could save by appealing to his parents, Rubin was inside a maximum-security prison with a triple-homicide verdict hanging around his neck. But Lisa saw an opportunity to reach out to their new hero and to further Lesra's education. Lesra had never written a letter, so he was instructed to write his first letter to Carter in prison. He too had been touched by

The Sixteenth Round. He had a brother who had served time, and many people in his neighborhood had been in prison, and he believed that he too could have met that fate had he not been pulled out of Bedford-Stuyvesant by his new family. Lesra's message, dated September 20, 1980, was carefully edited by members of the house. Lisa included a money order so Carter could buy stamps and respond. The envelope was mailed.

If the Canadians thought an American ghetto was equivalent to a prison, they would soon discover the real thing.

11

PARADISE FOUND

RUBIN CARTER typically ignored fan mail or letters with unknown addresses, but the white envelope with a strange Canadian postmark that was dropped in his cell in September of 1980 intrigued him. The blocky printed letters seemed to have been made by a child — fan letters typically came from adults who remembered Carter from his boxing days — and when he opened the envelope, Lesra Martin's note barely filled a page. But Carter was touched by its gentle tone: "The thought of writing you scared me, but not because of your reputation — I know you wouldn't hurt a flea (unless it bit you)."

Carter mulled over the letter for several weeks while Lesra and his guardians anxiously awaited a reply. Finally, they were rewarded. Carter thanked the youngster for his concern and inquired why he was in Canada and who exactly was caring for him. The response thrilled the commune. Lesra promptly wrote back, but this time Lisa and several others included their own notes as well. They plied Carter with questions: What was the status of his legal case? Who was handling the appeal? Was he still forswearing prison food? Was he writing another book? What did he think about the recent election of Ronald Reagan? Carter tried to answer the questions, but he wrote that he considered politics transitory, that most of his energies were now devoted to personal growth, and that he was "tabernacling" with the likes of Buddha, Socrates, Jesus, and Krishnamurti.

As Christmas approached, the Canadians mailed Carter a package of gifts, including a velour jogging suit in dark earth tones, a hat, socks, and a hand-drawn card of Carter in a jogging suit with a caption that read: "Keep On Keepin' On." Other letters kept him up to date on happenings around the house and on a home renovation business now bringing money into the commune. Lesra, encouraged by Lisa, asked Carter if he could visit the prison over Christmas, when he would be visiting his family in Brooklyn. Lisa believed the trip would be part of Lesra's continuing education, and Lesra, although nervous at the prospect, believed that he and Carter, as blacks, had a special bond that the Canadians could not share.

Carter was wary of any visit or, indeed, of any interaction with this group. He didn't know who these people were or what they wanted from him. Just as he felt he didn't have time for prison activities, he believed he didn't have time for friendships or pen pals. In return letters, he thanked the Canadians for the gifts but was vague about Lesra's offer to visit him. "All power to him if he can make it to the prison," he wrote, "and I wish not to disappoint him, but I may not be able to see him for reasons I can't talk about." He did not tell Lesra that he had not had any visitors in four years, save his lawyers, Kidrin, and one or two other friends, and he did not reveal that contact visits took place in the Death House.

Still, Lesra was determined to see Carter. He had never been on a train before. But on the last Sunday of 1980, his father dropped him off at Penn Station in Manhattan, and he rode Amtrak to Trenton. Several women on the train seemed like old friends, and they did share a common bond. Trenton State had contact visits on Sundays, and these women knew one another from their weekly trips. A nervous black woman noticed Lesra sitting by himself holding a package — Christmas cards from the Canadians. The woman saw the fear in the young man's eyes.

"How long has your father been in jail?" she asked.

Lesra was pleased at the thought of Rubin Carter as his father. "Awhile," he said. He noticed that the woman was also carrying a package, and he could smell the sweet potato pie inside, a treat for her son.

Once in Trenton, the woman invited Lesra to share a taxi with her and several others. Going in one cab, Lesra realized, was not simply a way for the women to split the fare; rather, their fears of the looming stone walls were more easily subdued by traveling as a group.

Entering the prison, Lesra saw a mail counter in a waiting room, where he tried to leave his package; the woman on the train had told him he could not take his bundle into the Visiting Center. But a prison mail clerk rejected the item, saying that all such parcels, excluding food, had to be delivered to the prison by the postal service. Crestfallen, Lesra stood at the counter for a long moment, then heard a familiar voice behind him.

"Don't let that stuff get to you," said the woman from the train. "It's more important that you see your father."

When a guard finally yelled out Carter's number, indicating he was in the VC, Lesra initially felt relief, but it quickly gave way to fear as he saw the taut expressions of those who were about to enter the holding bay. By the time he passed through the bay, trapped momentarily by the closed doors, he realized that prison was about control and humiliation — even for visitors. He felt safe once he and Carter, the last two standing without partners, met and hugged, and he knew Carter's presence in the VC was special. "Good gracious, Mr. Carter," someone said, "we haven't seen you here in a long time."

Carter immediately liked Lesra, a good-looking youngster, well mannered and brave. By now he had received many cards and several gifts from Toronto, but he had doubts about the living arrangements, particularly for Lesra. He asked him what books he was reading, what subjects he was learning, and how he liked the other members of the house.

Carter was privately suspicious of communes — he remembered the macabre end of Jim Jones and his followers — and he didn't see how a bunch of Canadians could teach Lesra about his roots, about black history and African culture. Carter believed that black Americans who never learned about their background were often shills for white authority. He placed the heavyweight champion Floyd Patterson, who had been embraced by mainstream America for his temperate social views and gentlemanly behavior, in that category. Only later did Carter realize that Lesra was in one of the most African-centered homes imaginable, where blacks were not only respected but idolized.

Lesra told Carter that the Canadians were more like a family than a commune, that he was reading Frederick Douglass, was learning about the contributions of black men in history, and he was working hard. Carter explained that he usually refused contact visits because he found the body searches humiliating, and Lesra felt responsible for subjecting him to such treatment for this visit. Returning to the holding bay, he felt anger more than fear, thinking about the body search Carter had to suffer before he could return to his cell. Carter himself, lying on his cot with the Polaroid photo of himself and Lesra, was pleased that he had seen his visitor.

When Lesra returned to Toronto, he told everyone about the woman on the train, the terror of the prison, the Polaroid photo — and the extraordinary man that was Rubin Carter. There was a sense of high excitement in the house, and all conversation revolved around what could be done for Carter. Everyone participated, but it was Lisa who made Carter her project. This was not Nate Shaw, the wrongfully convicted but now deceased cotton farmer in *All God's Dangers*, and this was not Lesra, whose prisons of poverty and illiteracy could be overcome with money, hard work, and education. Carter was locked away in a real prison right now, and he needed help. In the early months of 1981, Lisa told the other members of the commune, "I think we can get him out on a technicality." It was unclear if Lisa, schooled in conspiracy theories but not the law, knew what that actually meant. But it was obvious that Carter's freedom was foremost in her mind. Rubin Carter, she would say, "is my life's work."

Three weeks after Lesra's visit, Carter wrote a lengthy letter to the commune *(Dear Fightin' Canadians)*. He thanked them for the sweatsuit, socks, and hat *(The colors were my colors!)*, praised Lesra *(In my opinion, he is a very handsome little rascal)*, and explained why he was loath to visit people in the Death House *(where lost souls . . . are still flittering hopelessly about the place trying to find their way home)*. For Carter, writing a letter was easy; he had written hundreds. Talking on the telephone was different. Carter rarely called anyone on the inmate phone because he did not want to depend on the prison for anything. He also believed that the conversations were taped. But his "work," or reading, had forced him to question his old assumptions, to find new avenues for personal growth. Using the phone, he decided, would test his progress.

When the first call came, Gus Sinclair picked it up. "Will you take a collect call," the operator asked, "from Rubin 'Hurricane' Carter?"

"I'd be happy to take a call from Rubin 'Hurricane'—"

Lisa bounded off the sofa and grabbed the phone. Carter again thanked her for the letters and Christmas gifts and inquired about Lesra. He spoke a bit about the prison. It was small talk. But it was also a watershed. Rubin Carter had reached outside the prison walls to share a few moments with someone.

The phone calls continued, but for Lisa they were not enough. She needed to see Carter herself. In late February, Lesra, Lisa, Terry Swinton, and Sam Chaiton flew to Philadelphia, rented a car, and drove to Trenton State Prison. They parked across the street from the hulking penitentiary, and as they walked outside the prison wall, beneath the guard towers, Lisa bent over and retched. The foursome went through the same check-in process that Lesra had encountered two months earlier: the registering, the hand stamping, the frisking, the scanning by metal detectors. They thought it fitting that they visited Carter in the Death House where Richard Bruno Hauptmann had been executed forty-five years earlier for murdering the Lindbergh baby. Hauptmann, in their view, had also been wrongfully convicted.

Inside the visiting cell, Carter sat with his back to the wall. The Canadians were surprised at how emaciated he looked. He had lost twenty pounds since his days as a prizefighter, when his body had little fat to spare. He told the group that he heated canned soup in his cell with an electric coil or munched on nuts or the odd egg or onion or slice of bacon that an inmate would bring from the kitchen. But immersed in his studies, he told them, he would sometimes go two or three days without eating. He described the loss of his right eye and the absence of medical treatment in general. He was wearing a long-sleeve black shirt and sharply creased blue jeans, but the shirt cuffs were frayed, and his leather boots, while polished, were worn. Lisa asked if they could send him food and inquired about other needs, such as clothing.

While Carter greeted Lesra warmly at their first meeting, he was cooler to the Canadians. He privately considered their communal living arrangement odd and thought they were hippies. They weren't a family, they weren't a business, and they weren't a cult. It wasn't clear what they were, he thought, but why would anyone choose to live in a house with a bunch of other adults unless they were in prison? Carter also had painful memories of the many celebrity supporters who had pledged their help in the seventies, only to abandon him. Would these foreigners do the same?

The end of the visit brought a pleasant surprise. As his four guests prepared to leave, Lisa kissed Rubin, her lips soft against his face. He had not felt that in years.

The encounter sealed the Canadians' commitment to Carter. They joked that his ego was probably large enough for him to believe that most people on the planet discussed him at least once a day. But even Carter at his most egotistical could not contemplate how his case, his history, his family, his friends, his daily mood swings, monopolized the thoughts of this group. "He was a mythological creature to us," Mary Newberry recalled. "He was not real to us in a way. He was someone we were working for." Added Sean Cunningham: "He was bigger than life, a force that took over the house. He was wrongfully convicted. He was a celebrity. He was untouchable, and he was a beautiful, gentle man."

But Carter also took pride in his self-imposed deprivation. Everything inside his cell was hard or damaged or both: the walls, the floor, the bed, the toilet. He did not have a television or a radio or rugs or throw pillows or pornographic materials or any of the other paraphernalia that most inmates used to make their imprisonment more bearable. The absence of these items denied the warden the opportunity to take anything away; and in Carter's own mind, his asceticism made imprisonment more tolerable, not less. As he wrote in a journal: "Our frustration is greater when we have much and want more, than when we have nothing and want some. We are less dissatisfied when we lack many things than when we seem to lack but one thing."

Lisa, however, challenged him on these bedrock principles. In telephone conversations and in future contact visits, she told Carter that he was simply locking himself deeper into prison and negating his own humanity. She chastised him for being too serious and studious while denying himself laughter, comfort, and pleasure. He had to open his heart as well as his mind. His fears, she said, were controlling his life.

But fear, Carter said, was how one survived in prison. As he wrote to her:

> This place is built for destruction. It is designed to destroy any and everything that comes into contact with it, for it is unnatural, it is anti-human, and it must destroy! It has no other choice. So being frightened is not being afraid; it is being smart! . . . Being frightened means not helping your keepers keep you kept, and handling this place and its people as one would

handle a poisonous rattlesnake: always being completely respectful of its nature and what it is designed to do, and making damn sure that you always stay away from the business end of it!

Despite these fears, Lisa and her housemates were determined to subdue the rattler and bring joy into Carter's life. On one level, their beneficence was humanitarian. They saw a man starving, so they began sending monthly food packages via UPS. There was an elaborate roast, capped with a spiked crown and wreathed in red roses. There were deliveries of salmon, tuna, chocolate cakes with thick icing, sponge cakes, pastries, fruits, and nuts. These provisions roused Carter's long-dormant olfactory senses and satisfied a long-forgotten hunger. The moist meats and feathery cakes also had a powerful tactile dimension. Just holding a piece of roast or a slice of sponge cake, for Carter, was a balm on callous fingers.

The Canadians also hoped to prepare him for life outside prison by bringing radiant images of their own world into his cell. They began sending him photographs, rolls at a time, of their home and their city. They photographed their neatly trimmed lawn at dusk to capture the dramatic shadows cast by giant oak trees. They shot red Japanese maples, pink flowering honeysuckles and French hybrid lilacs in full bloom, low stone walls draped with perennials, and a pagoda over-looking a rock garden. They photographed the shoreline of Lake Ontario and the Royal Bank Building, its faceted mirror glass dusted with gold. Sunsets, snowfalls, and thunderstorms were all captured on film. Even a playful raccoon in the backyard merited several profiles. Carter noticed that the Canadians themselves were never in the pictures; that was not their style. In all, the commune sent close to five hundred pictures — what Carter described as a bit of "paradise in prison."

If the snapshots created a visual escape, other gifts appealed to different senses. Following Lisa's instructions, Mary Newberry made Carter a brown velvet robe with a boxer's hood. It was lined with chocolate-brown silk and edged in gold thread, every row of stitches straight, all seams properly hidden. With it was a pair of fluffy sheepskin slippers. Carter loved the robe. It caressed his back, and he proudly strolled through his wing to display it. The strolls, however, did not comply with prison regulations. In one instance, corrections officer F. Melicharek filed the following disciplinary charge: "While this officer was working on 2L on the above indicated time and date, I noticed inmate

Carter, #45472, stepping out of his cell wearing only a bathrobe 10 minutes after the mess movement had been called out. I questioned inmate Carter where he was going and he walked past me without responding. I ordered Carter twice to stop and reply and both times he did not comply with my order. I informed Carter that he had a charge."

The prison survived Carter's runway modeling, and he did not lose his robe.

The Canadians lived frugally and rarely bought designer clothes or fancy home accessories. The clothing they got for Lesra, while well made, was often secondhand. But they believed Carter deserved the best. As his forty-fourth birthday approached, the Canadians examined fabrics, colors, and styles to ensure that everything he had was first class, that his new shirts and socks and slacks would all fit. They wrapped their gifts in fancy paper with garish ribbons and bows.

Carter increasingly warmed up to his benefactors. As he wrote to them:

> You literally overwhelm a man! Letters and goodies are coming so fast, in so many different directions, penetrating, perforating, softening up this old toughened hide, until it's hard to know which direction is up, or which letter I'm answering. (Smile) Talk, without a directed purpose, has never come easy to me — that is, just talking to be talking and I do very little of it here. But now I know that more is needed, because it's necessary. It's to be loose. To be fluid. Not to be rigid. But it also embarrasses me. It makes me blush (Smile). Can you believe that. The Hurricane is really warm and cuddly and nothing but a gentle breeze.

But he did not want to give in completely to a life of comfort. This tension came to a head over Lisa's efforts to send him a television. By now, TVs were common in prison cells, but Carter didn't want one. It would be too easy for the warden to take it away. Lisa, in phone calls and letters, urged him to reconsider. She had given Lesra a new television in Bedford-Stuyvesant, and she thought Carter should have one too. A TV would not compromise his principles, she said. So what if the warden took it away? Even if Carter watched it for only one day, that was one day more of pleasure than he would otherwise have. By denying himself, he was effectively giving the warden more power than he already had.

Carter, conceding that he loved luxury, explained his ambivalence in one of his letters:

> Luxury is one thing and stupidity is another. To own a twelve thousand-dollar automobile while still living in a ten-dollar-a-week room . . . that's stupid. Because it cannot last long. And to have such luxury in a place that is daily seeking to destroy you, by your own efforts, is the same kind of stupidity . . .
>
> I know that I can have whatever I want in this place: it's just that there is nothing in this place that I want. I could own this mammy-jammy lock, stock and barrel! I could very easily have the Warden's job (in function, if not in title) if I will only sell myself and my ability and my self-respect and become a "good ole boy." And why not? All they want me to do is run their prison, create phony programs, keep order among the prisoners, and make the administration look good so they can say: "I've got Rubin Hurricane Carter working for me." And somebody else will say: "Oh, yeah, I thought he was a tough guy, what's he like?" And the Warden will answer with a satisfied smirk on his face, "He's a good ole boy, keeps those niggers right in line for me."
>
> So you see, as far as this prison is concerned I have nothing to do with it, and it has nothing to do with me! I only collect my mail here . . . So, yes, thank you: I would like very much to take you up on your most generous offer, for it has been a long time since I've watched any television, and perhaps now I might be able to handle it (Smile). Think so?
>
> You people are a bad influence on me! You're letting me get loose. (Good!)

The Canadians sent Carter a thirteen-inch color television, the largest the prison would allow. Carter told Lisa to send it to another inmate, Mr. Mobutu, a seventy-nine-year-old who locked on the same tier as Carter. No one in the mailroom would tamper with his stuff, Carter said. The television arrived in good shape.

"Rubin, Rubin, look at this, someone sent me a new TV," Mobutu told Carter.

"Yeah, I know," Carter said.

Unknown to Lisa, Mobutu took the shiny new TV to his own cell while Carter quietly carried Mobutu's old black-and-white set back to his own unit.

In letters to his fellow inmate Sam Leslie, Carter described Lisa and the commune as "the family," and he chastised Leslie for not also accepting "the family's" offer of support. "You were afraid of what someone else would see in you, weren't you? . . . You were scared of being opened up. And yet <u>that's</u> your salvation; to open up; to not be so serious about things which are not serious, and to be more humorous."

To Carter, accepting the commune as part of his life was a step on his own journey of self-discovery. He felt proud that he was willing to trust people again. Moreover, the Canadians seemed to prove that his readings were leading him in the right direction. They appeared to have walked right out of Ouspensky's "inner circle of humanity," a group whose detachment from society had placed it on a higher plane than everyone else. Each member of the commune was like a piece of a puzzle: separate, they were nothing; together, they were invincible. The commune's secrecy echoed the very words that Ouspensky used to describe "conscious" beings: "The inner . . . circle forms, as it were, a life within a life, a mystery, a secret in the life of humanity."

While everyone else slept, the Canadians saw the truth. They saw that the State of New Jersey had framed an innocent man. They saw racism and prejudice. And when they saw people in need, like himself and Lesra, they were willing to help. Ouspensky wrote that for a man to escape from prison — the prison of unconsciousness — he "must have help from the outside [and] he must work to dig his tunnel." Carter realized that the Canadians, by embracing him, by softening his environment, could help him escape his prison of bitterness and isolation. In due course they would help him escape his prison of brick and steel.

While everyone in the commune helped Carter, most of its members were peripheral figures in his life. He continued to talk to Lesra about his schoolwork, but he communicated principally with Lisa, and their relationship dominated their lives. Despite their disparate backgrounds, Rubin and Lisa saw themselves in each other. They were both estranged from their homes and families. They both lived in close-knit, rigid subcultures that distrusted outsiders. They were leaders within their own groups, and they were tough, stubborn, and fearless. They shared beliefs about the ubiquity of racism, the corruption of the American legal system, and the injurious effects of large institutions on human nature. They believed that people are inherently good but have been conditioned to act otherwise. Rubin and Lisa had little doubt that they were among the chosen few who understood these truths.

During the first two years, their relationship evolved over the telephone. At one point, a speakerphone was set up in the commune so that everyone could listen to Rubin, but Lisa mothballed the device. She wanted to talk to him exclusively and privately. She was possessive — "like a woman who had a baby and didn't want to cut the umbilical cord," according to Sam Leslie, who also communicated with her from prison. She believed that she could best empathize with Carter, hear his concerns, break down his shell. She tucked herself away in the commune's library and carried on conversations that would last up to eight hours as her housemates kept her stocked in cigarettes, coffee, and sandwiches. Kathy Swinton shooed away eavesdroppers.

The conversations were in part an extension of the gifts, an effort to expose Rubin to a world beyond the prison. Rubin, on the phone, held the photographs that had been sent to him. As Lisa described what the others were doing in different parts of the house or on the grounds, he would sift through the pictures and find the corresponding image so he could feel as if he were there. "You are here with us, and we are there with you," Lisa told him.

At the same time, Rubin brought Lisa into the penitentiary, describing to her the minutiae of imprisonment. The riot of noises that echoed through the tiers — cell doors slamming open and shut, the squeals of ancient radiators and water pipes, the rattling pushcarts carrying laundry, the constant movement of men, the ritual counts of prisoners — all could be heard through the telephone receiver in Toronto, and all provided a backdrop for Carter's recreation of prison life. This new guy was mopping the floor, that graybeard was taking a shower, these guards were coming on duty.

The telephone enabled the pair not only to enter each other's lives but to travel together on fairy tale adventures. They went to Paris, to Pakistan, to Africa, and described the people they saw, the music they heard. As Rubin later recalled, the idea was "to create so much fire within yourself, such tension, a crystallization takes place within your being. Personalities become scorched, and you merge into one. We were traveling by the inner body."

As these conversations deepened, it became clear in Toronto that Lisa was falling in love with Rubin. This surprised Sinclair and Newberry at first. For years, Lisa had been Terry Swinton's partner and lover. Swinton was like a father to Lisa's son, and she and Martin used Swinton's last name. But in the loose and rather peculiar dynamic of the commune, Lisa had actually changed partners, to Sam Chaiton, before her long-distance love interest in Carter. Regardless, there was no doubt where Lisa's passions now lay. Her endless phone calls merged with more frequent trips to Trenton, and a rhythm of travel developed. According to Sinclair, when Lisa returned from a prison trip, she would find herself exhausted but content. The following week she would be more energetic and antsy, and by the third week she would be in a state of nervous excitement. During that period she would say such things as, "he needs me down there," "he doesn't have the benefit of constant contact," "he needs extra guidance to get over" a particular problem.

"Nearly every four weeks," Sinclair later wrote in his own journal, "no matter what was going on at home, no matter the weather or what our financial situation might have been, Lisa left for Trenton, usually with Sam and sometimes with Terry, for a four-day visit."

The emerging romance showed itself in other ways. Lisa had always taken pride that she never dressed up for any man and that she never wore makeup. But she changed for Rubin. He told Lisa that he liked feminine women who dressed sharply. When he said that he wanted to see her wearing a chiffon dress so he could feel the softness of the fabric, she obliged. She bought other dresses and skirts and also wore makeup on her prison sojourns. Most surprising of all, perhaps, were the portrait photographs.

Lisa, self-conscious about her nose, avoided pictures of herself. But she had numerous pictures of Rubin in prison, most of which had been taken by other inmates, and she wanted Rubin to have a nice photograph of her. The picture was taken in the commune's home. The day before the shoot, Lisa went to a beauty shop, where her straight hair was given soft waves and ringlets. The next day, there was a buzz of anticipation at the house. Everyone was involved. Lisa spent several hours on her makeup, and she put on an off-white double-knit blouse with puffy sleeves that came to a tight wrist. Eitel Renbaum took the picture. Sitting in a hoop-backed Windsor chair in the living room, Lisa held a rose and smiled winsomely at the camera. She was also photographed outside under a tree. Renbaum shot an entire roll. After the pictures were developed, everyone in the house studied the results to determine which portrait was best. They then wrote lighthearted essays explaining why they chose a particular shot. Lisa sent the four top-rated pictures to Carter with all the essays.

Carter continued this selection game in prison, passing around the pictures to Robert Sigler and Leslie, who appreciated the gesture. "At first sight, all the pictures were equally beautiful," Leslie wrote to Carter. "In fact, looking at Lisa I said to myself, damn! She does not look white or black. She is just a beautiful woman." Rubin agreed. He gazed at all four for many hours and kept them safe in a folder in his cell. He later asked an inmate who was a skilled artist to draw Lisa's portrait in chalky pastels, and he gave it to Lisa.

Indeed, his feelings for Lisa grew in response to the attention she gave him. Conversations unfolded over the telephone and in visits while they sat together in former Death Row cells on the weekend or with a bullet-proof glass between them on weekdays. He began speaking candidly about his troubled relationship with his father and the hurt he still felt from the time his father struck him as a young boy after he bought ice cream from a white man. He shared intimacies that he had never disclosed before. He talked about his "sportin' life," or his years as a boxer, when he womanized, drank, and ran people out of bars like a bully.

Lisa even infiltrated his dreams. In one, a government bureaucrat was interrogating him, asking for his "registration number." Even in his dream Rubin wouldn't cooperate, but he suddenly told the bureaucrat: "You should ask her, she'll know what my number is." The person to ask was Lisa. In letters to Sam Leslie, Rubin described her as "my girl." In September 1981, Lisa visited the prison for two weeks. Afterward, Rubin fired off a letter to Leslie that explored a whole new subject. "Love is the key," he wrote.

[But] self-love for our purposes is completely and utterly <u>useless</u>, and there is no sense in even wasting time on it ... We are seeking Heaven; seeking pure bliss, and therefore <u>Conscious Love</u> is our ship! It is our salvation! It is <u>Love</u> that is Whole; a love that cannot change to <u>hate</u> ... Love for one's fellow-creatures; love for the birds and flowers and all the wise and won-drous workings of Nature ... The mind is for thinking what is true, and the heart for perceiving what is good. But the heart can learn only from another heart what the printed word cannot teach! So I am teaching you how to <u>love</u> first yourself, and then to love <u>everything</u> else!

Said Leslie: Lisa "was the only one who really touched Rubin. If you were a cold person, she could get it out from you. If you had a secret, you could share it with her. She could emotionalize you. She had entered into a world where he had entered. It was spiritual."

But Rubin felt Lisa's withering rebukes as well as her tenderness. In his letters to Leslie, he called her either "Sharp Tongue" or "Ms. S. Heart" (for Sweetheart). She wanted to put his past behavior in the worst possible light. She was trying to do what the New Jersey prison system could not do: to break Carter down, to get him to admit — not murder — but past misdeeds. Naturally, he resisted with all his force and refused to express contrition for his mistakes.

"You're a vicious motherfucker!" she yelled during one visit. "You're a liar, you're a drunk, and you steal. You're no good, and you run with whores. Rubin, you ain't shit!"

"I'm a player!" Carter retorted.

"You're a whoremonger!"

"Hey, I'm cool. I'm trying to get what I can get."

When Carter returned to his cell, he was fuming. "Who does she think she is," he told Leslie. "I don't want to see her nowhere, no more."

One telephone conversation ended with Lisa in tears and Carter, handing the phone to Leslie, saying, "I don't want to talk to that bitch."

Leslie recalled: "Here were two people struggling. Both wanted to love, but they wanted to love on their own terms."

Lisa's tenacity jarred Carter because no woman had ever stood up to him before. His relations with women had always been patriarchal, if not sexist. He used to tell his girlfriends or his wife to get his shoes, cook his dinner, iron his clothes. Lisa, of course, brooked none of that. In her house she gave the orders, and her minions followed. She expected Rubin to be equally attentive. When he sent her a mere unadorned note for her birthday, she was furious. "Seared me almost to death," Rubin wrote of her tongue-lashing. But he realized it was not the gift itself that angered Lisa but the spirit in which it was given. He had made no effort to make it special.

For all of the changes in Carter's life, he still dealt with the prison in his old, unyielding fashion, and the prison, like the "rattlesnake" he compared it to, sometimes bit back, as it did in December 1981.

Prison counts, in which inmates "count off" from their cells, were a timeless ritual at Trenton. They occurred every few hours and ensured that no inmate was missing. Typically inmates could count off from anywhere in their cell, but on the evening of December 5, 1981, a special "head count" was demanded. That meant inmates, when counting off, had to stand up and put their hands on their cell bars. Trenton was "declared in an emergency situation due to the possibility of an escape," according to prison records. "The institution was in an extremely stressful state." Carter, however, was not particularly stressed. He was sitting on his bed quietly reading and writing. He had not been subject to a "head count" in years, and he ignored the order. A guard named Phillips stood outside his cell.

"Stand up and count, Carter!"

Carter continued his reading.

"Stand up and put your hands on the bars!"

Still no response.

"Are you not going to stand up?"

Carter didn't even look at him.

According to the disciplinary report, "Inmate would not respond to any questions asked of him — also threw his copy of charges out of the cell. [He] would not answer when asked if he understood his rights." Carter was charged with "conduct which disrupts or interferes with the orderly running of the institution." He was shackled and taken down the tier to sounds of whispers from other prisoners: "They're taking Rubin out, they're taking Rubin out." He was put in a van with two other inmates who had also refused the head count, and the three were driven to the Vroom Readjustment Unit, behind the Trenton Psychiatric Hospital, where Carter had been in 1974. Then, a federal judge ruled that the New Jersey Department of Corrections had violated his due process rights and ordered him released after ninety-two days. His civil suit against the state was still pending.

Now Carter was back in the VRU. He was strip-searched three times before entering a dark row of cells, the Vroom's "hole." When he reached his cell, he was staggered by a horrific stench.

"Clean out that fucking cell before I go in there," Carter told one of the guards.

"That's not your cell," the guard said. "That's the guy next to you. He hasn't showered in months."

Carter was in the "hole" for fifteen days, where he watched (as he later wrote) "people being knocked in the head with sticks, their heads bursting open before my very eyes, their blood gushing out everywhere; guards in flak jackets, helmets, and shields, twenty and thirty of them, coming in droves, rushing in on some poor soul and then beating him down to the ground and into submission." Carter, by now, was so familiar with the brutal violence that he viewed it like "a horror movie that I just happened to stumble on to but not become part of."

He pled not guilty to the three charges that had sent him to the Vroom building: disruptive conduct, refusing to obey a charge, and group demonstration. His defense was that he never participated in prison activities and the administration knew that. Carter was found guilty on the disruptive conduct charge; the other two were dismissed. The penalty was to be in the Vroom building for one year and, for good measure, the loss of 365 days in "commutation time."

Prisoners typically *reduced* their sentences through commutation time. A ten-year sentence could be cut to nine years, or eligibility for parole could be moved up by a year. Parole was a moot issue for Carter. His refusal to apologize for his putative crime or submit to any form of prison rehabilitation negated any appeal to the parole board. With his latest infraction, Carter now owed the State of New Jersey three lives, two consecutive and one concurrent, *plus* one year. This was an unusual achievement. The longer Carter stayed in prison, the more time he owed the state.

After he was removed from the "hole," he was put into the building's general population. Vroom's accommodations were actually newer and bigger than his five-by-seven-foot cell in Trenton. His new cell had a stainless steel sink and a modern toilet. But the late-night beatings of inmates continued here as well. A prisoner who had killed a guard received nightly batterings. He managed to pry a brick loose from the cell wall, and Carter heard him using it to defend himself. The brick, however, did little damage to the guards' riot gear.

Carter himself was never attacked, but the isolation was difficult. The guards ignored all the inmates, who seemed too shell-shocked to talk. But unlike the first time Carter was in the Vroom building, now he knew a guard, who gave him access to a telephone. Each day Carter spoke to the commune, mostly to Lisa, giving her a detailed tour of this obscure nook of the New Jersey prison system. He joked that his banishment to the Vroom was a blessing because now he didn't have to send her a Christmas gift — better a lashing from guards than from her. In January of 1982, the Canadians racked up a long-distance bill of C$4,238.39.

By the middle of January, Carter's sentence was reduced on appeal. He was removed from the Vroom building, returned to Trenton State Prison, and placed in the isolated Management Control Unit for another seven weeks. His loss of commutation time was also cut: he now owed New Jersey an extra 180 days — or, by Carter's math, infinity plus six months. The MCU was known for years as Administrative Segregation; the prisoners called it "lockdown," and it was its own special hell. The rest of the prison ran like a timepiece. Mess at seven, count, out to work, back to cell, count, mess, count, back to work, and so on. The dimming of the lights, the serving of meals, the changing of guards — all were routine and predictable. But change the routine, and prisoners become addled. That happened inside "lockdown." Guards fed inmates at erratic times. Lights flickered on and off inexplicably. Some days prisoners got to leave their cells, go into the yard, and take showers; other days they didn't.

Carter remained in "lockdown" for at least four weeks. When his time was up, guards returned his books, papers, and clothes from the Vroom building. Carter loaded it all on a dolly and pushed it to his new cell. Haggard and hungry, he was breathless by the time he got there. Then he got angry.

"I'm not going in there," Carter told the guard accompanying him. "It's a pigsty." Pigeon excrement lay on the floor, the toilet was corroded, and there was no mattress. The guard ordered him into the cell, but Carter spun around and pushed the dolly back where he'd been. The prison was soon buzzing over his impudence. As a matter of principle, Carter had returned to a unit ordinary inmates would do anything to leave. This was, for Carter, not just another example of flouting the authorities. It also reflected his changing self-image. He had been wearing newer clothes, eating better food, and he didn't want to have to tell Lisa, Lesra, or the other Canadians that the Hurricane lived in a cell that reeked. As he returned to "lockdown," a guard asked, "Where you going? What's wrong?"

"If you seen that cell," Carter responded, "you wouldn't be asking me that question. My name is Rubin, not Fido."

Several days later Carter was assigned to another cell. He once again loaded the dolly with his possessions and pushed it through the prison hub, passing through various metal detectors along the way. When he reached his wing, a roar of applause went up from the other inmates; Carter smiled in satisfaction.

On a Sunday afternoon in early 1982, Carter walked into the prison yard, beaming, after a contact visit with Lisa. For many months they had comforted each other, yelled at each other, changed each other. She had become more feminine. He had become less bull-headed. As he walked in the yard, Leslie realized something had happened.

"I finally found my soulmate," Carter told him. "I hugged her and I had a beautiful time."

He described how he had finally learned how to talk to Lisa. "I was always talking to her like she was down when she was really up, and she kept telling me, 'You can't talk to me like that.' I understand what she means, that the man ain't got power over the woman, and the woman ain't got power over the man. It's just oneness."

In blending his book studies with his new social awareness, he described his experience as "the ecstasy of consciousness." In a letter to Leslie, he recognized his shallow treatment of women in the past and explained that mending those errors was possible through selfrecognition.

> I have always prided myself on being a womanizer . . . I have been under the same illusion that all of us are under. I am a sex machine . . . And that is where my manhood is . . . And then I find out I've never had a woman before in my life, never been satisfied, and all I've been doing is "jerking off" for 44 years. I know nothing about my body because I've never felt it before. Would you believe that I, the world traveller, the connoisseur of womanly flesh, have never really made love to a woman before? . . .
>
> So you see why it takes a very courageous heart to look at oneself without being afraid . . . The beautiful thing is that we can be <u>different</u>; we can <u>change</u>. We can be more powerful, and more intelligent, and more trustworthy, and more respectful than anything we have ever known before or could have imagined.

By 1982 Carter could take some solace in at least one development. John Artis had been paroled from prison on December 22, 1981. Carter always felt responsible for Artis's imprisonment. He knew that the authorities wanted him and that Artis was a regrettable but necessary expedient to realize that goal.

Indeed, from the beginning, investigators assumed that Carter was the ringleader, that he had somehow compelled Artis to walk into a bar and shoot a room full of strangers. There was, however, no evidence — certainly none introduced into the record — to suggest that Carter had such influence over Artis. What's more, the prosecutors' view that Artis was simply a misguided soul, the lesser of two evils on a warm night in New Jersey, was contradicted by the very evidence of the crime. According to the prosecutors: Carter carried the shotgun; Artis wielded the handgun. Carter killed the bartender, James Oliver, with one shot in the back, then wounded Hazel Tanis with a shot in the arm. Artis murdered Fred Nauyoks with a shot to the brain, blinded William Marins with a shot to the eye, then pumped four bullets into the body of Hazel Tanis. By the prosecutors' own measure, John Artis was more destructive and sadistic than Rubin Carter, yet Artis was viewed benignly. By the second trial, the Passaic County Prosecutor's Office had privately decided that if Carter and Artis had demanded separate trials and if Carter were reconvicted, it would drop the charges against Artis. But Artis's lawyer, Lewis Steel, decided that the two men should be tried jointly so that the two defense attorneys, badly outmanned by the prosecutors, could pool their resources and split the courtroom responsibilities in one trial. The decision, however, sealed the younger man's doom.

After the second conviction, Artis was sent back to the minimum-security Leesburg Prison Farm, but his years of imprisonment were taking a terrible toll. He'd begun to feel pain in his feet and hands. His skin felt clammy, and he had a diminished sense of heat and cold. He was diagnosed with Buerger's disease, a chronic inflammatory ailment that chiefly affects the arteries and veins of the extremities. Doctors told Artis that the prison's chill, the hard steel against his feet and hands, contributed to the disease, as had the many cigarettes he smoked while incarcerated. Artis had four toes on his right foot amputated while still in prison. In later years, two fingers were amputated from the second joint.

By the time Artis was freed on parole, he had spent fifteen years in prison for the Lafayette bar murders, the minimum sentence from his first conviction. At a news conference, he reiterated the position from which he had never wavered. He and Rubin were innocent of all charges. Asked if prison had rehabilitated him, Artis responded, "From what?" He was thirty-five years old.

Carter's spiritual growth and blossoming love for Lisa seemed to dovetail nicely with his legal progress. His case was once again under review by the New Jersey Supreme Court, and he was optimistic that he would again prevail. New Jersey's highest court had overturned the first convictions in 1976 because prosecutors had withheld from the defense the promises of leniency given to the state's two star witnesses, Alfred Bello and Arthur Dexter Bradley. Then, four years later, the high court once again granted a petition for certification from Carter and Artis and listened to their lawyers' oral arguments. This time the court sent the case back to the trial judge, Bruno Leopizzi, to make factual findings on whether evidence had been improperly withheld in connection with Bello's polygraph exam and whether a new trial was warranted. Leopizzi ruled against the defense. But the New Jersey Supreme Court again held oral arguments on March 9, 1982.

Carter and his lawyers had reason to hope. New Jersey had a three-tier judicial system: trial courts, the Appellate Division, and the state supreme court. If Carter believed that the trial and appellate courts were infested by politics and corruption, no such claim could be made of the state's highest court. It had a progressive tradition, long deciding on behalf of victims, tenants, and consumers. William Brennan, the U.S. Supreme Court's liberal avatar for thirty-four years, had served on the New Jersey Supreme Court in the fifties, and in the early eighties it was admired by the left. The prominent Harvard Law School professor Laurence Tribe told the *Bergen Record* in 1984: "It might be the best Supreme Court in the country — state or federal."

Leading the court was Chief Justice Robert Wilentz, a former state assemblyman known for his devotion to civil rights and individual liberties. He once blocked a bill in the state assembly that would have made it a crime to refuse to stand during the national anthem. As chief justice, a job he assumed in 1979, Wilentz wrote a controversial opinion known as Mount Laurel II, which prohibited communities from using zoning laws to exclude low- and moderate-income housing. His supporters said the decision allowed all residents, including blacks, to live where they wanted. His critics said the decision was legislation by judicial fiat.

It was clear, in Carter's case, that the chief justice supported the defense. During the first set of oral arguments in 1980, he accused Passaic County prosecutors of assuming that all blacks think and act alike. According to an account in the *Trenton Times,* Wilentz scolded the Passaic County assistant prosecutor John Goceljak, saying he found "invidious and intolerable" that the prosecutors thought it fair to assume that Carter and Artis would have been angry enough to kill simply because they were black. The oral arguments in 1982 seemed to have gone equally well, with Wilentz asking one of the prosecutors at the end of his statement: "Is that it?"

The chief justice, of course, had only one of seven votes, but his court was known for delivering unanimous decisions. As Wilentz himself told the *Record,* "We take seriously the proposition that there is value in a unanimous opinion, and there is value in not dissenting unless a justice feels very strongly about it. There's a desire on the part of the justices to understand the point of view of the majority and see if the minority can, in good conscience, join the majority or concur in a separate opinion."

After oral arguments, Carter's principal lawyer, Myron Beldock, thought that four of the seven justices — Wilentz and Mark Sullivan, Robert Clifford, and Morris Pashman — favored the defense. Beldock believed that the prosecutors' concealment and misuse of Bello's polygraph exam would be seen as a violation of *Brady v. Maryland,* which requires the prosecution to disclose evidence favorable to the accused.

By now Carter's soulmate was Lisa, his de facto son was Lesra, and his new family was the commune, and he would join the Canadians if he was released. They followed the court proceedings from afar, regularly evaluating Carter's chances for success by consulting his astrology chart. They had an almost fanatical attraction to astrology: they used the stars to invest in the stock market, in commodity futures, and in gold; most of the investments lost money. Sam Chaiton was the group's chief astrologer, and as the spring and summer months wore on, he evaluated how the stars were aligned for Carter. At the same time, Lisa urged her mates to keep the house spotless so it would be perfect on his release.

But freedom never came. On August 17, 1982, the state supreme court affirmed the conviction by a 4–3 vote. Justice Pashman — who had once been mayor of Passaic and the assignment judge of Passaic County — ruled against Carter. (Wilentz sided with the minority.) His lawyers suspected that Pashman had somehow been swayed by local political considerations. In the majority's opinion, Justice Sidney Schreiber addressed the tangled history of Bello's lie detector exam, two months before the second trial. The examiner, Leonard Harrelson, told the prosecution that Bello was telling the truth when he said he was *in the bar* at the time of the murders. This account effectively exonerated Carter and Artis as the gunmen. Unfortunately, Harrelson's written report of the exam stated the exact opposite. The written report said Bello was telling the truth when he gave his 1967 testimony, in which — unknown to Harrelson — Bello was *on the street.* Harrelson's erroneous report was then used by prosecutors to induce Bello to retract his recantation and to return to his original incriminating testimony.

Schreiber said that the prosecutors did in fact err in not disclosing to the defense the true results of Bello's polygraph. But he concluded that even if the undisclosed information had been turned over, it would not have changed the trial's outcome. Schreiber based this conclusion in large part on Harrelson's testimony from a fact-finding hearing the previous year. He wrote: "The Harrelson test results, if laid before the jury, would have established that an eminent polygrapher entertained 'no doubt at all' that Bello was truthful when he identified the defendants as the murderers." Regrettably, the eminent polygrapher had botched this one as well. Bello had never identified the defendants, in any testimony, as "murderers." Thus, the circle was complete. The prosecutors were allowed to conceal favorable polygraph information for the defense based on the false testimony of the polygrapher himself.

This convoluted logic prompted one of the most caustic dissents that observers of the New Jersey court had ever read. Written by Justice Clifford, it began:

A more egregious Brady violation than the one presented in this case is difficult to imagine. One need not go so far as to impugn the motives of the prosecution in order to reach that conclusion, for it can just as easily be attributed to an appalling lack of basic communicative skills on the part of the principal polygraphist and various members of the prosecution team. But whether the circumstances originate in unworthy motives, colossal bungling, or plain dullness of comprehension, the fact remains that the misunderstandings thus created have proven to be costly indeed: the State withheld from the defendants material evidence favorable to them in connection with the Harrelson polygraph and, unknown to defendants and their counsel, compounded the error by using the mistaken and erroneous polygraph report to get the prime witness against defendants to change his story again and go back to his original testimony given at the first trial. That all adds up to deprivation of due process and requires a reversal of defendants' convictions.

Clifford wrote that had the truth been known — that Bello's testimony stemmed from the misuse of key evidence by prosecutors — the testimony would have been rendered all but meaningless.

Never before could defendants argue so persuasively that Bello was in all respects a complete, unvarnished liar, utterly incapable of speaking the truth. When, as here, a key witness's reliability might well have been determinative of guilt or innocence, nondisclosure of evidence affecting credibility falls within the general rule that suppression of material evidence justifies a new trial irrespective of the good faith or bad faith of the prosecution.

One of Carter's lawyers, Harold Cassidy of Red Bank, New Jersey, came to the prison with a copy of the opinion. He had been helping out on the case since 1977, two years after he graduated from law school. Like others working on the case, he believed that Carter was part of black Americans' historic struggle for equality and justice in a system all too willing to compromise their rights if they stirred up too much controversy. Cassidy believed Carter's only crime was his blackness, and his imprisonment sullied the entire New Jersey legal system. He had also been certain that the state supreme court was going to overturn the convictions. But now he and Carter sat, clouds of cigarette smoke about them, in a small private room in Trenton State in a kind of funereal numbness. There was no explanation for the loss. Cassidy tried to assure Carter that his lawyers would not abandon him.

"This is just one more step along the line," Cassidy said. "You're obviously right. You're obviously innocent. We just have to go the next step." Carter, devastated, said little.

When he called the commune that night, he tried to read Clifford's dissent to them, but he spoke in an unusual monotone and kept stumbling over words. He had always ignored the prison noise but was now easily distracted. "Turn that tap off, brother," he said softly, as the mere sound of a faucet ruined his concentration. Lisa and her housemates were equally dismayed and incredulous. Nevertheless, Carter did not lose his grace. The following week he sent notes to the three dissenting judges.

"The ancient philosopher Diogenes spent his whole life searching for one honest man," Carter wrote. "I have found three. Thank you."

12

POWERFUL APPEALS

THE NEW JERSEY SUPREME COURT'S DECISION put Rubin Carter's name, briefly, back in the news. Since the second conviction, he had, for the most part, stopped giving interviews or making public statements. His supporters in the press, the advertising world, Hollywood, and the black community had long moved on to more promising issues. The state supreme court's contentious decision didn't reenergize the publicity machine that once supported Carter, but it did signal that the convictions of Carter and John Artis were not as clean as most observers assumed. The court's blistering dissent made it clear that there was at least a possibility that overzealous if not dishonest prosecutors had victimized the defendants.

The dissenting opinion, if adopted by a federal judge, could pave the way for a successful appeal. Unfortunately, Carter's battles in state court had effectively made such an appeal more difficult. To overturn the convictions, a federal judge would have to repudiate a jury verdict; a trial judge's rulings against the defense in two different hearings after the trial; the state Appellate Division, which affirmed the convictions; and now the well-respected state supreme court.

The prospect was daunting. What's more, Carter's lawyers were wearing down. Myron Beldock and others in his firm had been defending Carter for eight years and had nothing to show for it: little in legal fees, less in public acclaim, no courtroom victories. The same was true for Lewis Steel, whose client, John Artis, was on parole. But Artis also wanted the convictions overturned and his name cleared of any wrongdoing. Leon Friedman, who joined the team after the second conviction, now had a taste of defeat, and a clutch of New Jersey lawyers who were involved were also demoralized. The attorneys for Carter and Artis still believed in their clients' innocence, but after years of frustration, how much more could they give?

A blast of new energy was about to arrive.

By the time Carter returned to Trenton State from the Vroom building in 1982, the criminal proceedings against him had covered sixteen years, and he became increasingly despondent that the sheer size of the record had become too large for any appellate judge to comprehend. Testimony from many witnesses had evolved over the years — almost always to Carter's detriment — and he doubted that any judge would evaluate the original testimony, starting from the night of the murders. When he expressed these fears to Lisa Peters, she encouraged him to talk more openly about the case. Just as she craved every detail of his prison life, she wanted to know everything about the Lafayette bar murders and their aftermath. As she probed for more information, it was soon apparent that even Carter could not remember every detail. The only way Lisa — and, by extension, the entire commune — could understand the case would be by reading the actual court documents. For years Rubin had been dragging around a dozen or so boxes with thousands of pages of trial transcripts, court opinions, briefs, motions, exhibits, and newspaper articles. He believed this record would ultimately vindicate him, and he guarded it with his life. Now Lisa wanted pieces of it. Initially, her requests were small.

"Do you have a copy of that testimony?" Lisa asked.

"I've got it," Rubin said.

"Could you send it out to us?"

Carter refused to send any document through the mail but agreed to let Lisa or other commune members pick up documents at the prison. Giving them up, Carter knew, represented an important personal step. He viewed all of his dealings with the commune in the context of his ongoing studies. By now, he viewed the Canadians as part of "the inner circle of humanity," but he did not fully trust them. Surrendering his court documents — first piecemeal, then in large chunks — was a milestone in his willingness to rely on others. The transfer took months because the prison imposed weight limits on packages leaving the institution. Carter itemized each document that left his cell, and when the Canadians returned to Toronto, he called to confirm that the papers arrived safely. Finally, he and Lisa were literally on the same page.

As the commune delved into the case, its members also began to study Paterson and the taint of corruption that hung over the city. They read about the parallels between the Kavanaugh-DeFranco murders and the Lafayette bar shootings in a city reeling from Mafia infiltration, economic blight, racketeering, and vice. No wonder Carter got caught in Paterson's maw. What outspoken black man wouldn't?

The commune thrived on its us-against-them attitude, where enemies were clearly identified. This attitude, as former members describe it, often spilled over into ugly smugness. The house criticized other ethnic groups, nationalities, religions, and cultures. The French were arrogant; the Scottish, dour; the Irish, wild; Poles, stupid; Italians, violent; Americans, racist and jingoistic. The commune, despite its early acceptance of homosexuality, also ridiculed gays. Only heterosexuality was permitted in the house; homosexuality was a condition to be cured. Jews too were mocked: they refused to assimilate, they controlled all the media, and they had no respect for anyone but themselves. To remain in the commune, members who were gay or Jewish were forced to ignore or repudiate their identities.

Carter, in later years, complained to the Canadians about their haughty derision of others. But for now their felt superiority and their adversarial attitudes made them perfect allies in Carter's fight for freedom. He had few resources, but now he had new troops with money, intelligence, and passion. The enemy didn't have a chance. As Gus Sinclair put it, "The State of New Jersey was an ant to be stepped on."

The first contribution to Carter's case occurred after his loss in the state supreme court. As Rubin again bemoaned the complexity of his case, Lisa had an idea. The commune, working with Carter, should create a massive chart tracking the evolution of witnesses' testimony, a chart that could be used in building a federal appeal. Carter thought the idea was crazy. The record was splayed across thousands of pages of documents, and no one could possibly sift through all of it. But Lisa and her crew could. Over a six-week period, they reconstructed the case on a nine-by-three-foot chart. They placed key witnesses' names down the left side of the chart. Across the top, they identified fourteen separate occasions on which witnesses testified — to police, grand juries, special hearings, two trials, and, finally, at Alfred Bello's polygraph hearing in 1981. Every day, Carter searched through his own remaining records and read information over the telephone, which was taped by a member of the commune. The tapes were transcribed, and slowly the chart took form. Testimony was summarized, typed up, and pasted inside one of the boxes. Bello was the only witness to fill each of the fourteen horizontal boxes, with a different account each time.

The chart indicated that some witnesses became more hostile to Carter as the state's key witness — Bello — became less believable. Thus, Patricia Graham Valentine, according to the chart, originally told police in June of 1966 that Carter's car was "similar" to the getaway car. At the first trial the following year, she said Carter's car had "the same kind of taillights" as the getaway car, but she was not "specifically identifying it" as such. At the second trial, in 1976, Valentine testified that Carter's car was the "same" vehicle as the getaway car. She also testified at the second trial, for the first time, that she was in the police garage when Carter's car was searched and the police showed her the cartridge and the shotgun shell they allegedly found in Carter's car. In addition, the chart showed that the initial descriptions of the gunmen from two of the victims, William Marins and Hazel Tanis, as well as a description to police by Bello, were all contrary to the physical appearance of Carter and Artis. Vincent DeSimone, the chief investigator, also appeared to have cleared the two men of suspicion before the June 29, 1966, grand jury, when he said: "The physical description of the two holdup men is not even close" to that of Carter and Artis.

Lisa hoped the chart would be used as an exhibit in Carter's federal appeal. That never happened. But the chart buoyed him at a time when he was despairing from the loss in the state supreme court. It showed no new information, but it confirmed and bolstered, in a clean and graphic presentation, his belief that the witness statements against him had become progressively more damaging. More important, the chart proved that the commune was willing to fight for his freedom, to sacrifice all it had to destroy the enemy. His lawyers, he believed, needed more manpower, and now they would get it.

Carter's rejuvenation was obvious to his visitors. Harold Cassidy, the lawyer who delivered the news about the state supreme court decision, happened to return to the prison not long after Carter received the Canadians' chart. Cassidy was stunned. He had left Carter in a state of silent gloom. Now Rubin had a bounce in his step and could barely contain his enthusiasm for the next legal round. He took Cassidy into a room where the chart hung on a wall. Step by step, he pointed to the manifold inconsistencies in statements detail by detail and expressed utter confidence that any judge familiar with this record would see the injustice of his conviction. Bello, Bradley, Valentine, DeSimone — the whole sorry lot could not stand up to chronological scrutiny. Carter was ecstatic, and Cassidy, mesmerized, realized he was seeing Carter at his competitive best: the boxer who had been pummeled to the canvas was now back on his feet, dancing, jabbing, looking for an opening.

Carter typed up examples of what he considered prosecutorial misconduct dating from the first trial. The list included falsifying evidence, witness tampering, suppressing exculpatory evidence, and unlawfully appealing to racial prejudice. He sent the five-page list to Beldock with the note, "The Hurricane is on the move again."

The Canadians sent Beldock a second copy of the chart in October of 1982. At first he thought Carter alone had created it — he later learned about the Canadians — and thought it was an amazing distillation of a complex case. It had little bearing on the rest of the criminal proceedings, but it energized his flagging spirits. Many years after the case was over, the chart could still be found in his office.

Carter's upbeat spirits surfaced in a matter completely unrelated to his case. His interest in boxing had waned over the years; he had ugly memories of its financial corruption and the exploitation of young fighters. But he had a soft spot for the boxers themselves. Despite the game's brutality, he believed that boxers were the sweetest men he had ever met, a class of noble warriors who respected one another outside the ring and embraced one another after the final bell of a match.

So he was understandably concerned after the light heavyweight championship bout on November 13, 1982, between Ray "Boom Boom" Mancini and Duk Koo-Kim. Mancini battered Duk, knocking him out in the fourteenth round and sending him into a coma. As the South Korean struggled to survive, Carter watched replays of the fight on the black-and-white TV in his cell. He noticed how Duk, after the final blow, crashed toward the canvas, his head snapping on the lowest rope of the ring. One of Carter's sparring partners had once suffered whiplash by hitting his head on the lowest rope, and Carter had suspected that the velocity of a boxer's fall, combined with the tension of that bottom rope, created a mortal threat to prizefighters. Now, after watching replays of Duk's fall, Carter thought such tragedies could be averted, not by adopting other safety measures, such as mandatory standing eight counts or fewer rounds, but by simply loosening the turnbuckle and lowering the bottom rope.

Carter began writing letters about this to newspapers, a neurologist, boxing officials, fight fans, and various power brokers. He contacted the Washington lawyer Edward Bennett Williams, who in the early sixties had offered Carter a contract to play football for the Washington Redskins. (Carter declined, saying the sport was too dangerous.) Carter became obsessed with this lower rope — not only because he believed his idea could spare human tragedy but also because he saw it as a metaphor for society's misperceptions of truth. The rope was designed to protect boxers, to cushion their falls, but it could also savage them — the opposite of its intended purpose. In an impassioned letter he wrote to Angelo Dundee, the one-time boxing trainer for Muhammad Ali, Carter spelled out his idea:

> Given, even hypothetically, that this suggestion <u>could</u> be a viable solution, then the following question begs to be asked and answered: Throughout the long history of boxing, why, then, has this proposal never been put forward? Because it's <u>too</u> simple? Well, we have <u>all</u>, from time to time, been <u>prisoners</u> of one kind or another; we have all, at times, been prisoners to our <u>own</u> assumptions. Because we <u>assume</u> a thing is so, it must be so. And the assumption has always been that the <u>ropes</u> provide a safety factor and serve as a <u>margin of protection</u> for the boxer. But there may be a <u>tragic irony</u> here in that what is <u>perceived</u> primarily as a "protective device," <u>may</u> in reality be <u>itself</u> the cause of serious injury.

Duk Koo-Kim died on the day Carter wrote that letter, four days after his bout. His death was indeed attributed not to the force of the blows but to the position of the lower rope and the hardness of the canvas. The tragedy led to the development of a softer canvas; Carter's rope suggestion, however, was never adopted.

By Christmas of 1982, the Canadians had shown their commitment to Carter, and he was grateful that he now had a team of new recruits who would help him and his lawyers prepare for the next round of appeals. But his push-and-pull relationship with Lisa had reached a breaking point. As the two became more intertwined emotionally, confrontations became more frequent. He continued to share private thoughts with her, but he chafed at Lisa's penchant for passing those intimacies along to other members of the house or even coopting his experiences as her own. Once Carter told her about an unsettling episode just after he had completed an intense three-day period of study in his cell without food or sleep. He then took a walk around the prison yard and had a dreamlike sensation that he was falling into a hole.

"It felt as if I was underground and everybody was above me," he told her. "I was walking underground, and I began questioning myself, 'What the hell are you doing? Is this shit real?'" He told Lisa he began doubting the merit of his studies, and that frightened him. "What am I looking for?" he asked. He explained that he returned to his cell, closed his eyes, went into a deep sleep. When he awoke, he still felt those doubts, but he returned to his studies, and slowly, those fears, those uncertainties, began to fade. "I knew I was still on the right track," he told Lisa.

A few days later, Carter heard from one of the other Canadians that Lisa had had the most remarkable experience. She felt as if she had fallen into a hole! Carter simmered. She was getting too close to him now. He also felt that Lisa twisted some of his stories, particularly those about his days as a Paterson renegade, to make him look like more of a threat or a bully than he ever had been. Her confrontational style wore thin, and their arguments became more intense.

At the same time, they talked more seriously about their life together after Carter was freed — of which, despite his many setbacks, they were still confident. Rubin had never been physically attracted to white women, and he did not envision that changing with Lisa. But over time, his attitude did change as the intensity of the relationship increased. He had expressed his love for her and could foresee himself as her husband, lover, and partner. He wanted to be with her — but the commune was another matter. Each member excelled in something — cooking, gardening, writing, carpentry — and together they were a perfect whole. Carter believed they were a special class of individuals who saw truth, corrected wrongs, and transcended the unconscious world. But he also realized that they had developed "a learned helplessness," a dependence on Lisa to survive. That may have been fine for the others, but Carter was a solitary spirit who could never conform to a group or attach his star to another person. That conviction crystallized during a telephone conversation in which Lisa and Rubin, expressing their love for each other, began discussing marriage and a family. Lisa said that having children was not an option for them because mixed-race children were social outcasts. She also stated that she did not use birth control because she smoked. She suggested that Rubin get a vasectomy.

"Hell no, I'm not getting a vasectomy!" Carter fumed. "You can't ask a black man to do that!" He equated vasectomies with punishments meted out against slaves, who were cut for attempted escapes, insubordination, or other infractions. He also did not survive all these years in prison to be greeted, on his release, by an unpleasant and unnecessary surgical procedure. Lisa assured Rubin that other men in the commune had submitted to the operation, a fact later confirmed by those men.

Carter had had enough. He felt suffocated by all the attention, and he was afraid. Lisa and her mates were simply getting too close. As he later recalled, "When I was in prison, I could handle them on the phone for eight or nine hours a day, but now the talk of my living with them had occurred, and I began to say, 'Wait a minute.' It seemed like I was losing some of me."

He phoned Lisa and told her not to come for Christmas. Everyone in the commune had been trying to spruce up a 1970 Mercedes-Benz by scraping off the rust and preparing it for a new coat of paint; the car would be used to drive Lisa in style to Trenton, and she had her heart set on the trip. But now Carter, on the phone, was cold, unemotional, and abrupt. "I'm not calling anymore," he said, without giving a reason. "Good . . . bye . . . Lisa." Click.

This was not the first time Carter had been ruthless in severing ties with his supporters. Richard Solomon and George Lois had met the same fate. In Carter's mind, he did not have the luxury of treating his admirers with the respect they deserved. His only goal was to clear the murder tag from his name, and if you couldn't help him, you were gone. Despite the commune's unparalleled demonstration of support, he concluded that its infiltration of his life — and Lisa's unpleasant demand — diverted his concentration from his case.

Now they were gone. But unlike his summary dismissals of other supporters, he could not brush off his loss. This time he got sick. He had plenty of food in his cell, but he couldn't eat. He only drank coffee and smoked some borrowed cigarettes. He looked haggard and exhausted and did not go out in the yard for several days. Sam Leslie worried about his health.

Lisa took the breakup even worse. Her housemates knew that Carter could be stubborn, gruff, and wary, but she had assured everyone that the Rubin she was drawing out — cooperative, forthcoming, and tender — was the real Rubin. Now she was hurt, betrayed, and angry. While she tried to appear calm, she tore up his photographs and said it was his own stupidity and fear that caused him to turn his back on her. He would regret his mistake, she said, but she too was paying a price. She became listless, querulous, and morose. She began to experience severe back pain, the result, evidently, of a deteriorating disc in her spine, but the others assumed it was worsened by her depression. Sometimes she had to be carried up to her bed in the evening. She had difficulty sleeping, and she spent her days in front of the television, eyes glazed. She made intermittent forays into the daily life of the commune. Sometimes she gave advice on teaching for Lesra, sometimes she organized work details, and sometimes she sorted out the menu for the day. Mainly, she mourned the loss of her soulmate.

Carter did not have time to remain lethargic. He was thinking about the Caruso file.

At the 1981 remand hearing on Bello's polygraph test, an important new character joined the familiar cast. In the summer of 1977, Richard Caruso had worked as an investigator on the Carter-Artis Task Force in the Passaic County Prosecutor's Office. He quit his job right before the trial began to join the Essex County Prosecutor's Office in Newark. After the trial, Carter's lawyers learned that Caruso might be willing to discuss how the investigation had been conducted — specifically, what the prosecutors knew about Bello's polygraph. Harold Cassidy called Caruso and asked if he could stop by to talk.

During the meeting, Caruso was clearly distressed about the Carter-Artis investigation. On the one hand, he was reluctant to betray his former employer by talking to a member of Carter's team. He was about thirty years old and studying to be a lawyer, and turning his back on his former employer could jeopardize his career. On the other hand, the clean-cut investigator believed that the justice system should be just, and he was bothered that justice was not evident in the Carter case. He began talking, in generalities, in several conversations with

Cassidy over the following few months. Caruso believed there were two investigations of the murders. One, the public investigation, was simply a charade; the other was a clandestine inquiry, directed by Vincent DeSimone, that withheld evidence and manipulated witnesses. Caruso told Cassidy that he believed Patricia Graham Valentine's description of the getaway car, focusing on the butterfly taillights, was suggested to her by a Paterson police officer on the night of the murders. He said investigators had been under instructions not to take notes, and that his own efforts to interview witnesses had been thwarted by those running the task force.

These were tantalizing disclosures, but the details were often vague, and the most damaging information, such as that surrounding Valentine, was hearsay. Caruso hadn't been at the scene of the crime; he was just passing along information he had heard from others. Cassidy, for his part, was interested in what the prosecutor's office knew about the Bello polygraph and whether it had failed to disclose the true results of the exam. Judicial appeals are not about guilt or innocence but about whether defendants were deprived of their constitutional right to a fair trial. In Cassidy's view, the mishandling of Bello's polygraph represented the strongest ground on which Carter and Artis could claim they received an unfair trial.

Caruso did have some firsthand information about the polygraph. He said he had heard in the office that Bello initially had "flunked" the lie detector test. Thereafter he heard that the results were inconclusive and finally that Bello had "passed" the test. That sequence echoed what the defense lawyers had already learned in their interviews with Leonard Harrelson, the polygraph examiner; namely, that Harrelson had told the prosecution that Bello was telling the truth when he said he was *in the bar* (which exonerated Carter), but then indicated the exact opposite in the written report. Caruso's description — that Bello "flunked" and then "passed" the test — undermined the pretense that the prosecutor's office was impartial in its search for the truth.

Cassidy noticed something else in his first meeting with Caruso — a thick folder of notes Caruso had brought with him. He had ignored the prohibition against taking notes, and now he held them close to his vest, like a poker player hiding a straight flush. But he was not ready to show his hand.

Beldock and Steel knew that the notes, if detailed and thorough, would be their first glimpse behind enemy lines, substantiating defense claims of prosecutorial misconduct and withholding exculpatory evidence. Beldock drove out to Lakewood, New Jersey, to meet with Caruso. Caruso brought his file but was still reluctant to turn it over. He told Beldock that he was studying for the New Jersey bar exam and didn't want to do anything that would hurt his career.

"I won't do anything that will harm you, but it's important that I know this stuff," Beldock pleaded.

The meeting lasted about an hour, and in the end Caruso did turn over the file. It was at least a hundred pages, with scribbled and typewritten notes. Beldock read through it quickly and became convinced that the "Caruso file," as it came to be known, was the most damaging proof yet that Carter and Artis had been railroaded. He took no notes, he took nothing out of the file, and he gave it back to Caruso to keep. Beldock didn't want to raise any suspicions that he had tampered with evidence.

Beldock wanted to introduce the file as part of his questioning of Caruso at the 1981 remand hearing. There Caruso repeated what he had previously told Beldock and Cassidy: that he had heard Bello had initially flunked the polygraph only to pass it later. Richard Thayer, a former prosecutor in the government corruption unit of the prosecutor's office, also testified that he had heard similar comments.* Judge Bruno Leopizzi ruled against the defense, and he also blocked the defense's efforts to open the Caruso file. He ruled that it did not relate specifically to the lie detector issue. At the insistence of the defense, he sealed and impounded Caruso's notes, but then denied a subsequent application to have the file unsealed, inspected, and copied. The defense appealed that decision to the state supreme court, but the court, in affirming the convictions, did not address the Caruso matter.

After the court's decision for the prosecution in August of 1982, the defense was faced with a strategic dilemma. Should it take the appeal to federal court in a habeas corpus petition, or should it seek a state order to open the Caruso file and hope its contents outlined prosecutorial misconduct, which could then be used to overturn the conviction. The defense could not do both simultaneously, because a habeas

---

* Thayer quit his job in part because he was disillusioned with the office's handling of the case.

corpus petition can only be reviewed if all state remedies have been exhausted.

Leon Friedman had joined the defense team in 1978 specifically for his expertise in federal appeals. A balding, professorial man who evoked gentle authority, he relished good publicity. In later years, he hid a porno magazine in his law office that had a favorable article about the legal work on Carter's case. Friedman was also cut from the same liberal cloth as Beldock and Steel. He was driven by ideals of racial justice, and he had battle scars from the civil rights movement. Friedman had been a lawyer for the American Civil Liberties Union and had represented civil rights activists in the South during the sixties. He wrote a book called *Southern Justice* and was a co-author of a definitive five-volume history of justices on the U.S. Supreme Court. He recognized the historical importance of the Carter case — the nexus of race, law, and celebrity — and he happily joined the team when Beldock asked him. Lew Steel, on meeting Friedman, said, "Well, you have a great reputation. Let's see how good you are."

After losing in the state supreme court, Friedman argued that they should "go federal." He felt the prosecutors' misconduct was so clear-cut, especially regarding the Bello polygraph and the motive of racial revenge, they could win on the existing record. Pursuing the Caruso matter through state court, he feared, would be taking another swim through the swamp: an ugly, protracted journey that would once again end in defeat. But both Beldock and Steel, who knew the facts of the case better, did not want to give up the Caruso file. If they lost the federal appeal, they would have no more remedies in state court, and the case would be over. They believed the Caruso information would offer conclusive evidence of official misconduct. How could they leave that on the table? The decision was made, with Carter's consent, to try to open the file and use it for further state appeals. They would take one more swim through the swamp.

The many years Carter had spent immersed in his case had made him something of a jailhouse lawyer. When Sam Leslie wanted to appeal his murder conviction, he asked Carter for help. Carter knew the format that an appeal had to take: a procedural history of the case, a statement of facts, and then the legal arguments, citing precedents. He wanted to appeal Leslie's conviction on the grounds of "ineffective assistance of counsel" — fancy talk for "he had a rotten lawyer" — and he planned to file a motion for either a new trial or at least an evidentiary hearing. The latter could be used to place in the record evidence that his lawyer had not used in the trial. Carter typed up the brief but, like any writer, knew he needed another set of eyes to check the spelling, the grammar, and the logic. He needed someone who would not charge a fee, would be sympathetic to the case, and would be totally committed to helping them.

He called Lisa.

Carter considered Terry Swinton a brilliant thinker and a literary "nitpicker." Sam Chaiton had been an English major and was a fluid writer. They had done the most research into Carter's case, and with lines of communication once again open with Lisa, they were willing to edit Sam Leslie's brief. By the time everyone finished, Leslie was able to file a sixty-five-page brief in a state court in Monmouth County.*
Initially, Rubin told Lisa that his call was "strictly business." But clearly it was more than that. They had met on a higher spiritual plane while discussing human nature and the universe. But what Rubin really missed were Lisa's vivid accounts of the changing seasons, the sublunary evidence of life at the commune: the pageant of flowers blooming in the garden, the freshly cut grass along the lower meadow, the first snow dusting the branches of an oak tree. All along, Lisa wanted Rubin to crave physical freedom, not just spiritual freedom, and she had succeeded. Instead of fearing the outside world, he now ached for it. But he remained behind bars, where he — in his own words — had been "subdued, canned, and warehoused." Since cutting off ties with Lisa, he felt all his conversations had been at a "lower level," and he had to reconnect with his source of energy and love.

"I got to get out of here," Rubin told Lisa on the phone. "You made it so I can't stay here any longer."

In the latter months of 1983, Carter showed his love in a memorable way. When he entered prison in 1967, he refused to give the authorities his ring, which had a gold band and diamond. He also refused to

---

* In time, the Canadians hired a private investigator, Herbert Bell, to find new defense witnesses for Leslie, obtain affidavits, and submit exculpatory evidence into the record. A supplementary brief was filed on Leslie's behalf. A new trial was ordered and he was eventually freed.

surrender his watch or shave his goatee. He had shaved it when he let his hair grow and had stopped wearing his watch. But he continued to wear the ring as a symbol of his independence. Lisa questioned his fixation on the jewelry, stressing that he should not be identified with his own physical possessions. This "state of identification" was contrary to his own goals of finding a higher plane of consciousness. If he wore the ring to snub the prison, wasn't that allowing the prison to dictate his behavior?

Carter realized that, in one stroke, he could sever his ties with this problematic symbol and powerfully reconnect with Lisa. He took off the ring, put it in a heart-shape cloth with white trim, and sent it to her for Christmas. Arriving a year after Rubin had stopped talking to Lisa, the ring was a glorious emblem of his love. From the beginning of their relationship, Lisa had been seeking that type of expression of commitment. He had always withheld it until now. She had a jeweler cut the diamond as well as the band in two; she wore her half and sent the other half to Rubin, who tucked it away.

There was no more discussion of biracial children, vasectomies, or other sensitive topics. With the love between Rubin and Lisa firmly reestablished, only one thing mattered: his freedom. And just as he had made a commitment to Lisa, she was now ready to make an equally dramatic commitment to him. She decided to move to Trenton with several members of the commune. "We are in for the duration," she told him. "We will be with you, and we will be free." Carter was stunned but grateful.

The commune's belief that it could help free Carter was buttressed by another remarkable achievement. Lesra, illiterate three years earlier, had been accepted by the University of Toronto. Now twenty years old, he had undergone two years of home schooling and one year of public schooling in Toronto. He had also begun to date a young woman named Paulene McLean. Born in Jamaica, she had been a nurse in England, had only recently moved to Toronto, and was trying to find her way. Her romance with Lesra blossomed, and she ended up joining the commune. She was, in a sense, a double bonus, adding to the mix another black face as well as her nursing skills.

Carter had always played an active role in Lesra's education. While the young man's guardians taught him the basics, Carter pushed him to strive for perfection. Once, Lesra mailed him an assignment for which he received a grade of 98. Carter sent it back, asking, "What happened to the other two points?" He instructed Lesra to read great black authors, such as Richard Wright and W. E. B. Du Bois, emphasizing the richness of the black heritage. He also told him to read books that had influenced his own thinking, including Plato and Ouspensky (the latter proved to be a bit too dense).

Despite his progress, Lesra faced a considerable obstacle before he could qualify for admission to the University of Toronto. Incoming students had to be proficient in a second language, and Lesra knew only English. But Sinclair, who had worked in a registrar's office at the university in the late sixties and still knew a few officials, asked that the school accept Lesra's fluency in *black English* as his foreign language. It was a bizarre appeal, but it worked. The commune always seemed to find a way.

When Lesra received his letter of acceptance, he achieved what he thought had been an impossible dream. He was so excited, he could barely get the words out when he spoke to Carter on the phone. Said Rubin: "I expected nothing less from you." If the commune could get a once illiterate ghetto kid into college, why couldn't it get an innocent man out of prison?

By the end of 1983, Lisa, Terry Swinton, and Sam Chaiton had moved into a low-rise apartment building in Ewing Township, about a twenty-minute drive north of the Trenton prison. To finance two domiciles, the commune had to sell their cherished English manor in Toronto. While the group had purchased the house in 1976 for its generous size and spacious grounds, the city's booming real estate market had turned it into a brilliant investment as well. According to Sinclair, the house they bought for C$190,000 was sold seven years later for C$540,000. In addition, the commune wanted to sell off the property's back two lots separately, generating storms of protest from neighbors and various local officials who wanted to protect a deep ravine. The commune members themselves had once seen property development as a poisonous outgrowth of free enterprise, but a potential windfall of real estate profits had softened their hostility toward capitalism. They severed the lots, sold them off, and pocketed another C$300,000.

The Canadians now had money to direct toward Carter's freedom.

The commune members who remained in Toronto, including Sinclair, had to find new but inexpensive digs. One day they were living in a 6,000-square-foot home; the next day they moved into a 2,000-square-foot house in another part of downtown Toronto. They had to renovate the place, and they felt cramped and abandoned, sleeping in rooms with peeling plaster and sawdust everywhere. But the complaints were few. A little discomfort was a small price to pay for helping Rubin Carter. Besides, it could have been worse. They could have been living in New Jersey.

By the time the Canadians had settled in Trenton, Carter was frustrated with the progress of his case and with his lawyers. In pursuing the Caruso file in state court, the defense finally got access to his notes in December 1982. Beldock and Steel believed they did indeed offer fresh evidence of prosecutorial misconduct.

According to the notes, as later summarized in a brief to the U.S. District Court of Newark:

• Patricia Graham Valentine, at the scene of the crime, identified the taillights of the getaway car as being "long and narrow — rectangular," and it was Officer Greenough who told Valentine that the car had "butterfly" or "triangular" taillights. Valentine's car description, of course, had been critical testimony at both trials.

• Valentine did not cry when Carter's car was brought to the scene after the shooting, directly contradicting trial testimony and casting doubt on the allegation that Carter's car and the getaway car were the same.

• Before the second trial, Valentine conferred with Vincent DeSimone in Florida, where she was living, and in Paterson, contradicting trial testimony.

• Sometime after the first trial, Valentine — who always denied receiving any reward — was able to purchase a home, although she was understood to have had no assets previously.

• Caruso had spoken to a witness who placed the skid marks made by the getaway car farther up the street and out of sight from Valentine's window.

• The victim William Marins, who failed to identify Carter in the hospital emergency room, was in fact familiar with Carter's face and appearance before the shooting, making his omission all the more significant.

• Avery Cockersham, who lived next to the Lafayette bar, had told police in 1966 that he had seen the gunmen making their getaway and that they were not Carter and Artis. Cockersham had died by the time the defense learned about him from Caruso's notes.

• Contrary to prosecutors' representations, Vincent DeSimone was actively involved in the reinvestigation of the murders in 1976, attending meetings, preparing witnesses, and controlling the flow of information to investigators. Caruso had been told there was a special file containing evidence and information referred to as the "Chief's file." The owner of the Lafayette bar at the time of the shooting told Caruso, "Vince told me not to say certain things."

It took a year to sort through the information and file a motion seeking a new trial or dismissing the conviction. Once again, Judge Leopizzi would be ruling on the matter, and once again the case was bogged down in state court.

As Carter chafed at the delays, he did get one piece of good news in 1983. Nine years earlier, he and four other inmates had filed a civil suit against the New Jersey prison authorities regarding their illegal transfer from Trenton State; Carter and one other inmate had been sent to the Vroom Readjustment Unit. With the exception of Carter, all the transferred inmates settled their civil suits in exchange for placement in a minimum-security prison or some other benefit. Carter didn't settle, and now he won.

U.S. District Judge Dickinson Debevoise, agreeing with Carter that his rights had been violated, wrote that the prisoner was motivated by the belief that if "inmates treated each other with kindness and concern regardless of race or creed and took responsibility for their own lives, the atmosphere of the prison would be transformed . . . I have no doubt of Mr. Carter's sincerity and dedication to [the] peaceful resolution of prison problems." The judge determined that Carter's unconstitutional confinement in the VRU entitled him to compensatory damages of $30 a day, or — at ninety-two days of confinement — a total of $2,760. It was a relatively modest sum, but after years of legal setbacks, Carter felt good that he finally had won something. The victory also marked the second consecutive time that a federal judge saw a legal dispute his way, not the State of New Jersey's way. Carter knew that the federal courts had long been more sympathetic to civil rights issues and to blacks in general, and he began to feel that only in a federal court did he stand a chance for justice.

With Lisa, Swinton, and Chaiton now in Trenton, Carter had more contact visits than ever before. He found his own way of repelling the invasive body searches. On one occasion, when a guard ordered him, "Spread your cheeks," Carter passed some gas in the guard's face. The next time he appeared, the guard said, "Go ahead, Rube."

In conversations, Lisa tried to get Carter to talk about his case, not in tirades but through reasoned analysis. To this end, she did not accept his position that he was blameless for his imprisonment. His threatening comments in the *Saturday Evening Post* and his denunciation of the police invited suspicion and made him a target.

"You are the master of your own fate," she said.

Carter still saw himself as a victim, but he came to recognize how his words had stirred up fear and hostility against him and contributed to his plight. That recognition enabled him to talk about the case objectively and to give the Canadians guidance. Carter was desperate to find evidence to prove his innocence, and there was nothing his soldiers wouldn't do. Carter wanted to review the original police reports, so he sent Swinton and Chaiton to Beldock's office. They spent an entire afternoon photocopying reports, exhibits, photographs, and other material that had been turned over in discovery before both trials. Swinton and Chaiton, trying to confirm the time of the Lafayette bar murders, tracked down the telephone operator who took the emergency call to the Paterson police reporting the crime. They suspected that her initials on a telephone company document attesting to the time of the call had been forged by DeSimone. The operator herself, who was in her seventies, wouldn't talk to the Canadians, but Carter hatched a scheme to get her initials. He hired a private investigator, who delivered flowers to the woman. To receive them, she simply had to initial the receipt, which she did happily. The Canadians took her initials and the original document to a handwriting examiner, who, using spectrograms and enlarged photographs, concluded that the initials on the original document were forged.

Meanwhile, Carter's cousin Ed told him about a surprising encounter he had had with a cabby. The driver, a white man, knew his passenger was related to Rubin. He told Ed Carter that he knew Rubin was innocent because he had seen him at the Nite Spot when the murders occurred, but he would not testify for fear of police reprisals. But the prospect of an alibi witness, a *white* alibi witness, was too much for Rubin Carter to let go. One afternoon in the spring Ed Carter staked out the cab company, watched for the driver to come on duty, then got in his cab. They drove to East Eighteenth and Governor Streets, where the Nite Spot had been. There, Beldock also jumped in the cab. They pleaded with the driver to come forward. He confirmed his original story but still refused to testify.

The investigation continued in the junkyards of Canada, where Sinclair and Lesra searched for 1966 models of a Dodge Monaco and Dodge Polara. Valentine told the 1966 grand jury that the getaway car was a Dodge Monaco; Carter's white rental car was a Polara. Valentine described the getaway car as having taillights that "lit up like butterflies," wide on the outside, then tapered toward the center. That description, as was brought out at the second trial, fit the taillights of a Dodge Monaco, not the Polara. Unfortunately, there were no photographs of the Polara with the taillights turned on. Chaiton and Swinton called junkyards in New Jersey but couldn't find the models they wanted. So Sinclair, in Toronto, began calling junkyards around Canada. He found the cars in two different places — one near Kingston, 160 miles east of Toronto, and one at Archie's Wrecking, about 200 miles away in northern Ontario. Sinclair and Lesra drove out to the junkyards and photographed both cars. The pictures showed that the Monaco, but *not* the Polara, had triangular taillights that extended across the back as described by Valentine.

Months passed, and the sleuthing, the stakeouts, and the search for witnesses continued. Ultimately, most of the evidence accumulated was not used in court, but for Carter the process was still valuable. For years he had lived in a kind of timeless prison void, immersed in his books, his writing, and his legal studies. He had, more recently, spent hours in conversation with Lisa, creating their own private world of fantasy trips and philosophical connections. But now he was on the phone coordinating his troops, assembling information, barking strategy. It felt good.

On May 6, 1984, Carter's cell door on the fourth tier mysteriously slid open, and Sam Leslie entered. "Hey, man, I want to see you about something," he said. Leslie locked on the first floor, called the flats, and the two men walked to his cell. When they arrived, Carter stopped in his tracks. A group of inmates were jammed in and around the cell.

"Surprise!"

It was Carter's forty-seventh birthday. Lisa had put money in Leslie's account to buy ice cream at the commissary. She also sent in a huge blue and white birthday cake, shaped like a boxer's glove, with pineapple on top. The cake was so big, it had to be cut in four pieces to pass through the prison mailroom. There was soda as well. "Man, we got you!" Leslie cried.

Carter was speechless. Even before prison, he never cared much for celebrating birthdays or holidays of any kind. Inside prison, such occasions were depressing reminders that another year of misery had passed. Lisa decided that this year would be different. During her many visits to the prison, she'd gotten to know other inmates as well as Rubin, including Leslie, and she enlisted their help. Even the guards were in on the plan, opening Carter's cell and allowing the party to take place. Rubin called Lisa and thanked her profusely, then carefully described the proceedings: the cake was cut up, a slice was placed on each paper plate, a scoop of vanilla ice cream was dropped on the side of the plate and softly merged into the icing, and the plates were taken to each cell on the tier. Even the guards got plates. Lisa hung on every word, and Rubin had to admit it was a right fine birthday.

The party was a small but meaningful step in Carter's reintegration into the prison and, indirectly, the outside world. But Lisa wanted Rubin to do something far more dramatic.

"It's time for you to move out of Trenton," she told him one day.

"Move where?" Carter asked.

"Back to Rahway State Prison."

"Say what?" Carter asked incredulously. "I know Trenton better, and the last time I was in Rahway, they sent me to the Vroom."

But Lisa insisted. She emphasized the practical advantages of the move. It was closer to his New York lawyers, and the environment was also less restrictive. Inmates and their visitors could sit outdoors, drink coffee together, and more easily relax. Telephone privileges were also greater. Moreover, Lisa believed the move would be part of Carter's "deinstitutionalization." She was certain that Rubin would be released — she regularly checked the astrology charts to predict just when —

but she worried, not without reason, that freedom would be a difficult adjustment. Trenton State Prison had put him in a bleak but predictable groove. A new environment would force him to break that pattern.

Carter adamantly resisted the idea. He knew every creaking pipe in Trenton State — he had spent seventeen years of his life there, dating back to the late fifties — and it was, well, home. But as he and Lisa continued the debate, tensions were rising in the prison. A new guard was harassing Carter for his lengthy use of the telephone, claiming he was taking more time than the rules permitted. Then, one night when the lights failed to go off at the usual time, Carter suspected something was amiss. The following day, he heard through the prison grapevine that fifteen young prisoners had been shipped to Trenton for refusing to eat their liver dinner at the Southern State Correctional Facility in Cumberland County. When they arrived, Carter was told, they were beaten, kicked, and brutalized. Carter sent word that the new prisoners should describe what happened in signed statements. He sent their statements, which described an orgy of violence against them, to the New Jersey chapter of the American Civil Liberties Union. Several guards were ultimately suspended — but Carter had seen enough. He applied for a transfer to Rahway.

As he was waiting for a response, Lisa came for a contact visit. The Death House had been retired as the Visiting Center; now an open room served instead. During a contact visit, prison rules allowed for touching — a kiss, a handshake, or a hug — when a visitor arrived and departed. Otherwise, no contact was allowed; even touching the other person's chair was prohibited. On this day, Rubin and Lisa sat in folding metal chairs, and Rubin had his arm around the back of hers. When a new guard walked by, he told Carter to get the arm down. Carter ignored him. When the guard came by again, he yelled, "Get your arm down," then pushed it down himself.

Carter flew to his feet and cocked his left fist. "He touched me, dammit! He touched me!" Since Carter's first day in prison, his rule was ironclad and well known: no prison employee touched him, ever. Anyone broke that rule, he'd fight to the death. The visiting hall hushed. Suddenly Lisa leaned over and whispered, "Read my lips, Rubin. If you hit him, I'll knock you out."

"Say what?"

"I said if you hit him, I'll knock you out."

Carter remained in his crouch, his meaty fist prepared for launch. The rest of the room, prisoners and guards alike, stood frozen. But before anyone could make a move, before any shackles could be pulled or riot bells sounded or blood drawn, Rubin "Hurricane" Carter broke into a smile. Then he started laughing, deep howls that stunned the room. He wept with laughter and could hardly speak. He had indeed met his match in this fearless slip of a woman from the North. Carter sat back down, his arms nowhere near Lisa's chair.

Carter's transfer to Rahway was granted; he moved on June 29, 1984. While he was keeping a low profile in prison, he was still probably New Jersey's most celebrated convict, and his transfer generated a spate of news articles. A spokesman for the state's Department of Corrections was quoted saying that Carter was older now and no longer in need of a maximum-security environment. It had been ten years since he had left Rahway, and many of the same sergeants, lieutenants, and captains, as well as prisoners, were still there. Initially, no one recognized Carter with his full head of hair, but the Hurricane was soon connected with his former associates. Like the prisoners at Trenton, the inmates at Rahway treated him with considerable respect, the byproduct of both his reputation and, by now, his age. Carter feared that a young punk might try to make his name by challenging him, but it never happened. He was still, to most inmates, Mr. Carter. When he was waiting for his permanent cell assignment in a wing called the ghetto, the head of the "Lifers' Club" sent a runner, a prison messenger, to give Carter a package of soap, toothpaste, deodorant, and cigarettes to tide him over until his personal belongings arrived. After three days in the ghetto, Carter was assigned to a cell on a kind of honor tier. It was relatively quiet, with about twenty men. Unlike Trenton, where he had to descend four flights of stairs to reach the phone, this tier had its own two phones.

Moving also to Rahway were Lisa, Swinton, and Chaiton. Even if they were still in New Jersey, they were glad at least to be heading a few miles north. In Rahway they were physically closer to Carter than they had been in Trenton. They rented a high-rise apartment close enough to the prison so that they could see its rotunda, and Carter continued to merge his own life into theirs.

At designated times in the evening, he went to the prison's top-floor

Drill Hall and looked out the window and over the prison wall. In the distance he could see candles flickering on the balcony of the Canadians' apartment. In the quiet of the evening, Carter simply stood, arms folded, and watched the candlelight greeting. The Canadians also used more advanced communications technology, installing a three-way calling system on their phone so they could easily connect Carter with his lawyers. Sometimes, Carter would listen in as Swinton or Chaiton used the phone for such tasks as calling a nearby library to research his case. The phone also became a kind of kitchen accessory. Lisa would stand near the stove and offer Carter elaborate descriptions of the food being prepared. There were breakfasts of bacon and eggs, pancakes and maple syrup; lunches of fish and chips; elegant dinners of beef Wellington and crab with béchamel sauce; desserts of angel food cake, chocolate mousse pie, and homemade chocolate eclairs. Lisa stuck the phone next to the frying bacon, and Carter, listening, savored every sizzle. The Canadians were allowed to send two twenty-five-pound bags of food per month to Carter. Lisa described the laying out of dinners in plastic containers, sitting on beds of lettuce garnished with parsley and cherry tomatoes and baby carrots.

After a care package was prepared and described on the phone, Carter would look out the window of his wing. His tier was high enough so that he could glimpse part of the half-circle driveway leading to the prison as well as a pond and the mailroom. The Canadians parked their car so Carter could see them leave the vehicle with the carton of food and head toward the mailroom. It was not exactly room service, but by prison standards it was pretty close.

In Trenton, Carter had received pleasing essentials. But now, with a new wave of gifts, his cell took on the trappings of a princely pad. He could run his toes through a plush Persian area rug; gaze at Impressionist paintings by Gauguin, Monet, and Cézanne, or Rubens's *Head of a Negro;* clutch thick navy blue Fieldcrest towels monogrammed "RHC"; or wrap himself in a brown satin sheet and rest his head on a brown satin pillowcase. These accessories brought color, texture, and spirit into the gray cubicle. The Canadians also sent a triple-decker black stereo system and a cache of tape cassettes: Otis Redding, Wilson Pickett, Merle Haggard, Sam and Dave, James Brown, Aretha Franklin, Johnny Paycheck, Johnny Cash, Buffy Sainte-Marie, Bob Dylan, Elmore James, Gil Scott Heron, the Staple Singers, Percy Sledge, Memphis

Minnie, Sweet Honey in the Rock, Lightnin' Hopkins, Willie Dixon, and the Rolling Stones.

Carter was mellowing, dismantling his defenses. He even involved himself in the prison laundry. Seven years earlier, he had sent the state's attorney general a petulant four-page letter outlining why he refused to work in the laundry room. He would not produce any goods or services for the State of New Jersey, and he would not help the prison run its operations. But now a laundry crisis was brewing on 6 Wing. Inmates were sending their dirty clothes to the laundry, but items were missing when they returned. Accusations of theft were made, and tempers were rising. Some inmates were reluctant to send out the clothes they bought for themselves. Most of the clothes were issued by the prison; an inmate typically received two pairs of striped pants, several shirts, three or four pairs of underwear, and socks — hardly an extravagant wardrobe. But clothes were among the few things that prisoners could call their own, so losing even a sock was significant.

In the middle of a heated discussion about the disappearing apparel, Carter stepped in. "I'll take this chore," he said. Heads turned in disbelief. Carter would be the laundry runner for 6 Wing. Each Wednesday, he would roll a pushcart through the tiers, stuff in all the dirty clothes, and take them to the laundry, where other inmates did the washing and pressing. Carter rationalized his willingness to take this job by saying it benefited the prisoners, not the prison. But it still marked, for him, an unprecedented integration into prison life. He tackled the job as he did every other important project — with relentless intensity and do-or-die focus. This was not about laundry. This was about order. This was about respect. This was about doing things the right way.

Carter vowed that every piece of clothing he received in 6 Wing would be returned. He went to each cell and, using a black Magic Marker, identified each garment. A shirt in Cell 30 on the fifth tier, for example, was marked "5–30." Each laundry day, Carter got at least 170 pairs of pants, 200 shirts, and small mountains of underwear and socks. He recorded every item of clothing on a piece of paper. When he went to the laundry, he informed the man in charge that he wanted the exact same number of items returned and he wanted the pants perfectly pressed, seam to seam. When Carter picked up the clean clothes, he counted everything before he left, and if anything was missing, he demanded that it be replaced on the spot. The clothes washed and fully accounted for, Carter wheeled his pushcart back through the prison. When the inmates were in the yard or at their prison jobs, he stacked each man's clothes in his empty cell. The laundry had never run so well.

Carter continued to recount his daily experiences to Lisa, either on the phone or during visits, and these experiences became part of the symbolism of Carter's personal growth. There was, for example, an old onion that Carter first received from the Canadians in Trenton and had brought with him to Rahway. When he unpacked the onion, he discovered that it had grown green shoots. How could an onion grow anything in a prison cell? Terry Swinton, the gardener in the commune, explained to Carter that an onion is a bulb, and if properly tended and cared for, it would grow long stems and blossom with flowers. So Carter scooped some soil from the prison yard into a plastic bag, brought it to his cell, and planted the onion bulb. He watered it daily and gave Lisa updates each morning. If an onion can grow flowers in prison, then why couldn't Carter blossom as well?

This sense of transformation was captured in a Native American folk tale that the Canadians gave Carter. Jumping Mouse was unhappy simply being a mouse. He wanted more. So he went on a search for the Sacred Mountains, but his journey was filled with peril. He was, after all, only a mouse, and he was easy prey for eagles. But Jumping Mouse had a generous heart and was willing to help others. On his journey, he gave up an eye to save a dying buffalo, and the buffalo, in turn, gave him protection for part of the journey. Then Jumping Mouse met a gray wolf who had lost his memory, so Jumping Mouse gave up his other eye to restore the wolf's ability to recall. The wolf took Jumping Mouse to the Sacred Mountains, but, now blind, the mouse concluded his journey was fruitless. He couldn't see and would be eaten by an eagle. Jumping Mouse fell asleep. But when he awoke, miraculously, he could see, and he looked upon the Sacred Mountains. Then he was told by a frog to leap in the air. He did — and he went higher and higher, soaring into the sky. "You have a New Name," called the frog. "You are Eagle."

Lisa and her housemates, who were captivated by Indian folklore in general, loved Jumping Mouse as a parable for Carter. Just as the mouse had to rid himself of his mouse ways, Rubin had to rid himself of his angry ways, his harsh ways, his secluded ways. Then, he too could soar like an eagle. But it was not enough for Carter to simply read "Jumping Mouse." He called together other inmates and read the story aloud to them, complete with the imitations and mannerisms of mice, buffalo, frogs, and other animals. Carter taped these storybook hours on his new stereo and gave the tapes to the Canadians, who then listened to them, enraptured.

Carter had indeed come a long way from his morose and monastic ways of yore. He now ate well, he lived in relative comfort, he worked in the prison, and he was avoiding confrontations with the authorities. Yet this made his incarceration all the more intolerable. He was living a better life, both materially and spiritually, and that made him all the more desperate to start his life anew. He was innocent of the crimes for which he was serving, but he could no longer suffer and sacrifice for the sins of others. They were either going to let him go or he was going to leave on his own. Regardless, he had to leave.

Unfortunately, Carter's legal battles were mired in the New Jersey court system. Beldock and Steel continued their efforts to bring the Caruso matter forward. Once again, they found themselves before Judge Bruno Leopizzi. In oral arguments on November 18, 1983, and January 20, 1984, they contended that the Caruso file showed that the prosecution had withheld and suppressed material evidence during the 1976 trial and the 1981 polygraph fact-finding hearing. But Leopizzi was now more frustrated with these lawyers than ever before. Their refusal to let the case die seemed to infuriate him, for he believed they were mocking the system with their endless appeals. At the second hearing, in January, he stormed off the bench at one point, yelling, "I am sick and tired of your nonsense. That's it." Leopizzi ruled against Carter and Artis, finding lack of due diligence on the defense's part. He also ruled that the prosecutor's office did not have knowledge of Caruso's notes and that their content was immaterial.

Beldock and Steel appealed Leopizzi's decision to the state Appellate Division on February 29, 1984. With that appeal still pending, they tried to have it heard directly by the state supreme court, but the request was denied by the court on September 6.

On the evening of November 14, a strategy meeting was held at

Rahway State Prison with Carter, Beldock, Steel, and Friedman in a private room. Friedman was struck at how Carter walked around the prison as if he owned it. The question at hand was the same question they had had for two years: Do they continue to pursue the Caruso matter in state court or do they go federal with a habeas corpus petition? Beldock, of all the lawyers, had been most directly involved in the accumulation of new evidence and flushing out the Caruso file. He talked about the alibi cabdriver and the new photographs of the Dodge models' taillights. No one disputed that both were powerful evidence of Carter's innocence, but the lawyers were still deeply divided about what course to take. Beldock and Steel did not want to foreclose any opportunity to overturn the conviction, and filing a habeas corpus petition would probably force them to bury their "unexhausted claims" in state court: namely, the Caruso file and the evidence derived from it. They were inclined to continue the pursuit in state court. Friedman, however, believed the federal claims were strong enough on their own. "We can win on the issues we've already exhausted in state court," he kept saying. But the risk was clear: if Carter lost in federal court, there was no second chance.

Despite his able counsel, Carter always kept his own, and he would make the final decision. He concluded that he had to get out of prison now; he had squandered enough years of his life in the quagmire of the New Jersey court system. Besides, there were no guarantees that the Caruso material would produce a favorable result in state court.

As the meeting dragged on, tempers flared, particularly between Carter and Steel, who had locked horns before on strategy.

"We can't go back!" Carter said. "The problem we've always faced is that the state wants to keep a stranglehold on this thing and never let it go. No, we have to move ahead, and without further delay. Look, I'll be frank with you. This place is intolerable. I won't stay here, now that's that!"

"But if you lose, you could rot in jail," Steel said.

"Lou, don't ever question my commitment to my freedom."

Carter turned to Friedman. "Leon, how do we short-circuit the system?"

Friedman laid out the strategy. They would submit a petition now that still included claims in the state court. If a federal judge refused to review the petition because of those claims, Friedman could always withdraw them at that time.

"Leon, you're a genius!" Carter said.

But it would take more than genius for Rubin Carter to win his freedom. It would also take luck.

13

FINAL JUDGMENT

FOR ALL OF Leon Friedman's confidence, the chances that Carter would succeed in federal court were slim. In filing the appeal, Carter and his lawyers placed their hopes on one of the law's most cherished concepts — the writ of habeas corpus. But the unique circumstances of Carter's case made such a grant extremely unlikely.

The "great writ," as it is known, dates back to the Magna Carta as a means of challenging arbitrary imprisonment. Habeas corpus is Latin for "release the body." In the United States, the writ enables a federal court to overturn a criminal conviction by a state court on constitutional grounds — literally, to "release the body" of an unjustly convicted person. So sacred is this concept that in 1868, the U.S. Supreme Court called the great writ the "best and only sufficient defense of personal freedom."

But the great writ is often seen, particularly in conservative circles, as hubris writ large. According to this view, habeas corpus benefits criminals by allowing their convictions to come under attack in federal court after all appeals in state court have been exhausted. Habeas corpus appeals, critics say, aggravate the relationship between the state and federal judiciary by permitting a federal judge to swoop in, declare a constitutional violation, and overturn a state conviction.

Such protests have always been a bit exaggerated. In reality, federal judges are reluctant to issue the writ. In 1985, the year Carter's petition was filed, about 8,000 were filed by state prisoners, and only 3 percent, or 240 cases, were successful. The reluctance is understandable. Many petitions are simply last-gasp efforts by convicts whose appeals have no merit. Moreover, federal judges properly show deference to jury verdicts. Jurors, unlike a federal judge, were at the trial, they saw and heard the witnesses, and they evaluated the credibility of the evidence. Their verdicts represented the will of the community. Federal judges who would promiscuously overturn those verdicts would undermine faith in the jury system.

Thus, Carter's petition was a statistical long shot, but it was problematic for other reasons as well. The case had already been thoroughly scrubbed by New Jersey courts. In its nineteen years, it had produced forty volumes of testimony from the first trial, fifty volumes from the second trial, twenty volumes from supplementary hearings, hundreds of exhibits, and four fully reported state supreme court opinions. No federal judge could pity Carter for not having had his day in court.

The sheer scope and complexity of this record presented significant obstacles for Carter. Somehow, he and his lawyers had to explain to a federal judge what the case was about, what constitutional violations had occurred, what the legal test was for judging the errors, and why the errors were sufficient to require that the convictions be overturned.

At the same time, a federal judge reviewing a habeas corpus petition is supposed to evaluate only the law, not the facts of the case. In theory, innocence or guilt is irrelevant in deciding whether to issue the writ. The determination is made strictly on whether unconstitutional means were used to convict. But the facts of the case do matter, because judges — already reluctant to overrule a jury's decision — are even more skittish about throwing out a verdict if they believe the defendant is guilty. Carter knew that to win a federal appeal, he would have to convince a judge not only that he had been wrongfully convicted but also that he was innocent. He would therefore need a judge who was willing to read, analyze, and untangle the epic proceedings of the case, which by now had all of the enigmatic characters, convoluted plot twists, and grand contradictions of a Russian novel.

He also needed a judge with courage. Unlike a multimember appellate court, the judge sitting in the U.S. District Court in New Jersey would be acting by himself. There would be no unanimous verdict or split decision, no majority opinion and no dissent. There would simply be one person, one decision. The safe route, the easy route, the *expected* route, would be for a judge to affirm the convictions, to rubber stamp the status quo. This was not 1976, when Carter was the darling of the left and when Hollywood trendsetters hailed his liberation after the first conviction was thrown out. This time he had no constituency for his freedom save family and friends.

Regardless of what the record said, no matter how much new exculpatory evidence was unearthed, Rubin Carter was still a convicted racist triple murderer who, the last time he was on the streets, was accused by one of his most loyal female supporters of assault. At the height of President Reagan's popularity and in the midst of rollbacks in civil rights and affirmative action programs, any judge who let Carter go free would do so with little public support. In the closely knit world of the New Jersey legal establishment, a federal judge who granted Carter the great writ would have to repudiate his peers in state court — supreme court justices, appellate judges, trial judges, prosecutors, and investigators. The federal judge would almost certainly face vilification for freeing a man twice convicted as a cold-blooded killer. And if Carter, once released, committed a heinous crime, the judge who freed him would be held responsible. Would any judge in New Jersey take such a chance? Would any judge even give Carter's case the time it would take to make a fair determination? Finding such a judge could be Carter's last hope for freedom.

Once Carter decided on November 14, 1984, to take his case to federal court, the petition took two months to complete. Petitions are simply complaints delivered to a court. Typically three or four pages long, they give an overview of the case and the grounds on which the appeal is being made. The court then determines whether the petition meets the criteria for further consideration. If it does, the petitioner files a formal motion and the state responds.

But given the tortuous history of Carter's case, his lawyers, Beldock and Friedman, and the defendant himself felt a much longer petition was necessary. In fifty-seven pages, it identified twelve separate grounds for habeas corpus relief.* The twelfth ground was the Caruso issue, which was still alive in New Jersey. Carter's lawyers were going to argue that it was technically exhausted because of unreasonable delays by state courts and was therefore admissible in federal court.

The petition was filed on February 13. The case would be assigned

* John Artis filed a separate petition that incorporated all of the grounds in Carter's petition and added three more that applied to him alone.

to one of six judges in the Newark division of the U.S. District Court, where it was filed. Cases were assigned on a rotating basis, known as "going on the wheel." When a new case came in, a court clerk would assign it to the next judge "on the wheel." Carter hoped that Judge Clarkson Fisher, who had released him from the Vroom building in 1974, would draw his case. He believed that Fisher had treated him fairly before and would do so again. Instead, the wheel turned up a man Carter had never heard of. In fact, none of Carter's lawyers knew much about Judge H. Lee Sarokin.

Sarokin was born in Perth Amboy, New Jersey, in 1928, the son of a newspaperman with a gritty, alliterative byline: Sam O. Sarokin. Initially a reporter for the *New York World-Telegram,* Sam Sarokin later bought a collection of New Jersey suburban weeklies and wrote editorials for them. He was a gifted wordsmith; friends kept his letters, filled with lapidary phrases and felicitous allusions, for decades. Lee Sarokin embraced his father's love of writing, and a poem he wrote in high school showed an early sensitivity toward racial discrimination. Called "Sight," it described a blind ten-year-old boy whose parents prevented him from playing with his "little colored chum." ("He was blind in his eyes, but not as blind as many men who see.")

Sarokin's greatest passion, however, was his drums, and he played in a college jazz band called the Dartmouth Sextet. One summer the band hopped aboard an ocean liner for Europe, earning free passage by playing every night. In Europe they made their way to postwar Paris on bikes and knocked around jazz clubs, looking for work and scraping by on the fumes of ambition. One night, at a club called Vieux Columbia, the brilliant black American saxophonist James Moody invited Sarokin and his group onstage to play. Moody, impressed, asked the sextet back, then back again. Moody was only a few years older than the white musicians from Dartmouth, and they began to hang out together. One night in Moody's apartment, Sarokin asked his new friend why he lived in Paris. It bothered him that so talented a musician was not performing back home. Moody, who grew up in Georgia, shrugged and said, "I'm much more comfortable in Paris than in the United States."

Barred from sleeping in the nicer motels, prevented from eating in decent restaurants, Moody described discrimination in ways that Sarokin had never contemplated. The conversation stuck with the student.

He was dismayed that this enormously talented musician had sought exile in Europe because he was not treated properly in the United States, and he thought that someday he would like to do something about it.

But back home, Sarokin largely sat out the civil rights movement. After graduating from Harvard Law School in 1953, he spent twenty-five years as a civil litigator, often representing individuals in product defect or negligence cases. He married, divorced, remarried, had three children, and was a well-respected if relatively unknown lawyer in Newark, then the center of New Jersey's legal community. He thought that being a judge would be interesting — advocacy work, he felt, never quite suited his mild temperament — but he did not seek a judicial appointment. If he had not been an ardent basketball fan, he probably never would have made it to the bench.

In the early seventies, he was asked as a favor to do a real estate closing for the New York Knick star Bill Bradley. Sarokin didn't do much real estate work, but in his younger days he had a pretty good jump shot, and he admired Bradley, who had graduated from Princeton. Sarokin was happy to take on this assignment, and he and Bradley became fast friends. Sarokin once challenged him to a game of one-on-one on a municipal court along the Jersey shore. Using the car headlights for illumination, they battled until midnight before their cheering wives. Bradley, by now retired from the NBA, won, but Sarokin, more than six inches shorter, gave him a respectable game.

In 1978 Bradley, a Democrat, ran for the U.S. Senate and selected Sarokin to be his finance chairman. Most lawyers have to contribute to or participate in many campaigns to secure the right political connections, but Sarokin's first real campaign paid an immediate dividend. One year after Bradley's landslide victory, President Carter named Sarokin to the federal district court in New Jersey. He did not take the job for the money — at $54,900 a year, he took a 75 percent pay cut.* He became a judge because he knew he had something to say.

Judge Sarokin would become a clarion voice for the little guy, defending the rights of the least powerful and protected in America against the forces of big government and big business. He took up the

* According to Sarokin, federal judges used to say they were the lowest paid people in the courtroom — excluding, one assumes, prisoners.

cudgel on behalf of the black firefighter facing layoffs, the long-term cigarette smoker dying of cancer, the disabled senior citizen fighting to maintain his social security benefits, and the mentally retarded child in need of an education. His anger was easily triggered, his sensitivities clear. Sarokin once fined an attorney from Jersey City $1,000 because the lawyer, in his closing argument, referred to a forty-two-year-old black plaintiff as "boy." At a sentencing workshop at the Federal Correctional Institute in Butner, North Carolina, Sarokin met a young black man with no prior record who told him he was in prison for altering two $2 bills to $20 bills. He was sentenced to twenty years, ten years for each bill. Sarokin investigated the man's story, discovered it was true, and — outraged — contacted the American Civil Liberties Union. The young man was eventually released on a pardon signed by President Reagan.

Sarokin's record did not suggest a predisposition for issuing writs of habeas corpus. At the time of Carter's petition, he had only issued one or two writs in his six years on the bench. Sarokin told his clerks that virtually every habeas petition that came into his office lacked merit. Many were made by prisoners who didn't follow the procedural rules. But a judge, Sarokin said, must resist the urge to disregard the petitions because one in a hundred may have legitimate claims.

In his chambers, Sarokin was old-fashioned and low-key. He asked his clerks, usually trained at Harvard and Yale, to run out at lunchtime for his tuna sandwich and milk. But he made no effort to conceal his political leanings. The most prominent object hanging on the walls of his office was a framed photograph and letter from Senator Ted Kennedy, congratulating him on his appointment.

Sarokin proudly defended his judicial activism. He believed that judges had a responsibility to speak out on important social issues, to stimulate debate. His job was not simply to interpret the law but to influence public opinion, and he tried to do this by mixing wit, sarcasm, and ire in his rulings. While most judges rely on dry, cautious prose, Sarokin vented his emotions freely. His supporters praised his opinions as courageous and discerning; detractors said they were sanctimonious and preachy. But all agreed that his impassioned rulings set him far apart from his buttoned-down peers.

For example, in *Hildebrand v. the United States,* the Internal Revenue Service sought to impose personal liability on the volunteer trustees of a nonprofit organization that failed to pay withholding taxes. The organization had been established to assist the needy after the Newark riots. Sarokin ordered the IRS commissioner to appear before him in person, and, ruling that the agency could not hold the trustees of the charity liable, Sarokin wrote:

> This matter portrays the government at its rigid and Orwellian bureaucratic worst. The plaintiffs in this action were engaged in selfless, dedicated charitable activity ... The compassionate federal government, and particularly the well-known, warmhearted Internal Revenue Service, has chosen to reward them with personal liability for nonpayment of withholding taxes ... Is it more important that withholding taxes be forwarded to the Treasury to be devoured by the giant bureaucratic monster or be utilized to provide food, shelter and care for the downtrodden?

In another case, he reprimanded the Small Business Administration for trying to collect a $300,000 loan from a destitute and mentally disturbed widow. He wrote, "Better to have no government at all than a government devoid of compassion and basic human decency." And in yet another case he wrote, "This court has already concluded that the Department of Health and Human Services has no heart, but it appears now as if its brain is going as well." In lambasting the sluggish movement of New Jersey lawmakers, Sarokin wrote, "While the Neros of Trenton fiddle, Newark burns." Perhaps Sarokin's most amusing opinion arose from a copyright dispute concerning Care Bears. In a three-page decision in verse, Sarokin ordered the defendants to stop manufacturing look-alike bears and said in part:

> Children should be able to buy the bears they know.
> Toys like these should bring happiness and laughter.
> To find they own a different bear could be an awful blow.
> Instead, the kids and "Care Bears" should live happily ever after.

But during his early years on the court, Sarokin drew the greatest attention for his opinions concerning race, specifically affirmative action disputes. He did not ask for these cases but got them because the other judges in the district give up part of their calendar when a new judge is appointed, disposing of cases they don't want. In not-so-refined court parlance, this is known as "releasing the dogs." When Sarokin arrived, the other judges were pleased to unload on him a kennelful of controversial cases about race.

This opportunity dovetailed with Sarokin's own interests. His unabashedly liberal views ran against America's conservative tide, and he relished saying so. "There is a distant and echoing bugle now heard in the land sounding the call for retreat from the battle against discrimination," Sarokin wrote in 1981 in *The United States v. New Jersey.* "If we are to preserve our democracy, these are not times to retreat, but to advance the cause of civil rights." He presided over a 1980 consent decree calling for an affirmative action program for minority firefighters in twelve New Jersey cities. When one of the cities, facing a fiscal crisis, threatened to lay off firefighters, a dispute arose over which group — whites, who had more seniority, or blacks, who were hired after a court-ordered decree in recognition of past discrimination — should suffer the brunt of the layoffs. The case was before Sarokin but the same issue was soon to be heard by the U.S. Supreme Court. He could have deferred making a ruling; instead, when asked by reporters in an off-the-record meeting, he said: "I know my decision is going to be reversed, but I have something important to say." He ruled that the black firefighters should keep their jobs, but that the federal government should provide some financial compensation to the laid-off whites. Affirmative action plans, he wrote:

> arose out of the recognition that this nation had oppressed its minority citizens, either purposefully or through the operation of more subtle social and economic forces. These plans seek more than to remove the nation's heel from the back of minorities, but to reach down and to lift up those persons who have been deprived and discriminated against for centuries. The plans recognize the insufficiency of merely removing existing barriers. Affirmative action is necessary in order that historical imbalances and inequities not be prolonged well into the future.

The ruling was hailed by liberal constitutional scholars like Laurence Tribe of Harvard. But the U.S. Supreme Court overturned Sarokin, as he expected, ruling that seniority rights and the practice of "last hired, first fired" should remain undisturbed. William Bradford Reynolds, who was in charge of the Justice Department's Civil Rights Division under President Reagan, called Sarokin's ruling "the most bizarre reading of the Constitution" he had ever seen, a derogation that Sarokin took as a compliment given its source.

Of this there was no doubt: Rubin Carter could not have personally chosen a judge more ideally suited to hear his case than H. Lee Sarokin. Numerous court observers doubt that any of the other five judges in the District Court's Newark division would have considered Carter's petition seriously. Louis Raveson, a Rutgers law professor who was also part of Carter's defense team, said that Carter could not have found a more sympathetic judge in the entire country. Leon Friedman believed that regardless of which judge Carter drew, they had a better chance in federal court than in state court — but Friedman also knew they were quite lucky to draw Sarokin.

To Carter himself, it was confirmation that he was one step closer on his search for the miraculous.

On February 20, Sarokin issued an order to the state to file a response to Carter's petition by March 31. The deadline passed, and the Prosecutor's Office did not respond. Carter wanted his lawyers to file a Motion for Default Judgment in the district court. Friedman resisted, saying Sarokin would never rule in their favor on such a motion.

"It's a waste of time," he said. "Why go through with it?"

"I want to make them follow the rules," Carter said, a telling comment for a man in prison.

The motion was filed.

To keep the pressure on, Terry Swinton, Sam Chaiton, and Ed Graves, a junior lawyer in Beldock's law firm, assumed the task of filing all the relevant state court briefs, appendices, and opinions. The undertaking took a solid week of collating and photocopying. In April Swinton delivered the thirty-five-pound box of documents directly to Sarokin's chambers at the federal district court in Newark.

The Motion for Default Judgment flushed the prosecutors out of the brush. They filed a response, arguing that the inclusion of the Caruso issue meant that Carter had not exhausted his state remedies. On those grounds they wanted the district court to disallow the petition and prevent the substance of the case to ever be debated. The wheels of justice had once again slogged to a halt.

Carter simmered at the delays. He called his lawyers at least once a day, asking for updates, barking at them, pushing them, demanding that they somehow "short-circuit the system." If anyone knew how to, it was Friedman. He was the high priest of constitutional law, a professor who lectured about habeas corpus to federal judges at conferences, who had studied every habeas corpus writ ever issued, and who at times displayed a dazzling if off-beat intelligence. One morning, he and several others on Carter's team were in a restaurant in Newark waiting to go to court; Friedman was intently reading court documents he was about to present. The restaurant was bustling, the eggs were frying, and an all-news station blared on the radio. Still, Friedman read his documents and discussed the case's finer points. About forty-five minutes later, while he was buttering a piece of toast, he looked up from his papers and said, "That's the third time that story has come on the radio since we've been here."

Friedman had an idea for "short-circuiting" the system, but it was risky. He suggested they file a Motion for Summary Judgment. Doing so meant there would be no hearings and no witnesses. They would simply file briefs and make oral arguments. The prosecutors would be expected to do the same. The judge would rule on the record, making, as it were, a "summary judgment." Friedman believed that the existing record showed sufficient prosecutorial misconduct to carry the day and that Sarokin would not need to investigate further to find in Carter's favor. Win or lose, it would be fast, efficient, and — for Carter — final.

The idea appealed to Carter's pugilistic instincts. As a boxer, he always went for the knockout punch, quick and decisive. He hated going the distance, where his fate lay in the arbitrary hands of judges. Ironically, that was exactly what he chose by filing a summary judgment motion. But he wanted to be the aggressor, to stay on the offensive, and to keep the prosecutors on their heels. A Motion for Summary Judgment would force the showdown he craved.

But there was still the problem of the Caruso issue. In a proposal laid out by Friedman, Carter could file a "mixed petition," which would have both exhausted and unexhausted claims, then he and his lawyers could write a separate brief arguing that the Caruso matter was technically exhausted. That argument, however, had little chance of winning. More likely, they would have to delete Caruso, which meant they would lose the evidence forever. Beldock and Steel, as before, disagreed with this all-or-nothing strategy. They did not want to lose what they considered to be the clearest evidence of prosecutorial misconduct.

Carter knew the facts of his case better than anyone, and (not lacking modesty) he believed he knew the law better than his own lawyers. He instructed them to file the "mixed petition" and, if necessary, to expunge the Caruso material. He then secretly ensured that his lawyers could not do otherwise. He wrote a letter to Sarokin, saying that if his lawyers were asked to remove the Caruso material from the petition and they failed to do so, then he, the judge, must remove his lawyers as his counsel. Carter gave the letter to Terry Swinton, who would be in the courthouse when the lawyers presented their oral arguments to Sarokin. Carter had fired a previous attorney, and he was prepared to do so again. The letter was never used, but it showed how Carter trusted no one, not even the lawyers who had served him loyally for so many years and who had no intentions of defying his wishes. The letter also underscored the urgency of his situation. Procedural delays were less important to his lawyers because time was not their enemy. But time was Carter's enemy. He felt he had no more time to give the State of New Jersey.

Carter continued his daily conversations with Lisa, either on the phone or in person. She delivered his marching orders to Terry Swinton and Sam Chaiton as they helped the lawyers and quietly conducted their own investigation into the case, and she relayed all the information back to Carter. The pair still butted heads occasionally, but this time Carter did not let the tension escalate. He couldn't afford to. He knew that as long as Lisa was committed to him, the entire commune would follow.

Swinton and Chaiton were his principal foot soldiers. Swinton and his sister, Kathy, were two of the original commune members and the only siblings in the group. Their father was an Austrian who had fled the Third Reich, moved to Canada, and become a successful business-man. Terry, born in 1946 in Montreal, took a different path in life. A barrel-chested student activist, he once told a reporter that he was expected to "wind up doing corporate law, living in the right part of town." But he was more philosopher than capitalist — like Carter, a fan of Krishnamurti. His specialty was gardening, and his soothing presence served him well in his occasional role as the public face of the commune, dealing with reporters, real estate agents, and other outsiders. He was also Lisa's partner for many years and her son's de facto father.

In contrast, Chaiton was more dramatic and reactive, and the pair sometimes played "good cop, bad cop" while helping Carter. Chaiton would badger the lawyers for something, then Swinton would ask for it sweetly. Four years younger than Swinton, Chaiton was born in

Toronto, the son of Jewish survivors of the Nazi concentration camp at Bergen-Belsen. He had been a student at the Toronto Dance Theatre before joining the commune around 1973. Balding and with a prominent Adam's apple, he was smart and calculating, a good writer and an excellent instructor, who served as the principal teacher for Lisa's son and then Lesra. He was also the commune's astrologer and was the closest to Lisa.

Swinton and Chaiton fancied themselves a shadow law firm, calling themselves Carter and Partners. They were, initially, paralegals, couriers, and prison valets, delivering drafts of briefs among three Manhattan law offices and Rahway State Prison. (The lawyers rarely saw or spoke with Lisa and did not understand the dynamics of the group.) Swinton and Chaiton camped out in an office across the hall from Beldock's. For weeks they photocopied records, organized exhibits, and proofread. As the motion slowly took shape, they retrieved from a file room a complete set of transcripts, stacked the documents in a cart, and hauled them into Graves's office. There they checked a blizzard of citations that had to be used to support every statement in the motion. It is the least glamorous and most tedious part of practicing the law. But the Canadians would have done anything to help Carter, and their attention to detail impressed the veteran lawyers.

Steel referred to the Canadians, affectionately, as "this thing," an alien presence that had mysteriously landed in their midst. He once told Swinton or Chaiton vaguely about some witness testifying in a long-forgotten hearing. "Do you know what I mean?" Steel asked. Twenty minutes later, the Canadians returned with the transcript open to the correct page and asked, "Is this what you mean?"

The Canadians were not only true believers but irrepressible noodges. They saw themselves as Carter's surrogates, and they would not let his lawyers relax. The first time Swinton met Leon Friedman, he stopped by the lawyer's office to pick up a section of one of the briefs that was due shortly. Friedman came out to meet him.

"I'm Terry Swinton," he said. "I'm working with Myron Beldock's office on Rubin Carter's appeal, and I understand that you have a section that's ready and that it's supposed to go over there."

"It's not ready yet," Friedman told him.

"That's okay," Swinton said. "I'll wait."

Friedman, aghast, went up to his office and finished the section.

The Canadians' passion to help Carter had an endearing purity — they had, after all, no apparent motive except righting a wrong — but their obsession with him could be trying. Lou Raveson, the Rutgers professor, said the Canadians were like insufferable clients who would not stop calling their lawyer and demanding more of him — but whose persistence, in the final analysis, was justified. Friedman said, "In some ways, they were difficult people because of their monomaniacalness. You sit around with them and you want to talk about baseball or the latest movie; but, no, they just want to talk about Rubin."

Nonetheless, the Canadians gradually moved from gofers to fully trusted partners of the defense team. After the State of New Jersey filed answering papers to one of Carter's briefs, Swinton and Chaiton photocopied every case that the prosecutor's office cited. Shortly thereafter, Swinton grabbed Friedman.

"Leon, I know you are the world's greatest expert on habeas corpus, but I was reading one of the cases that the prosecutors cited in their behalf, and I thought this might be helpful." He then quoted some passages that Friedman knew very well, and Friedman explained why those passages were not helpful. But Swinton then cited another passage, and Friedman came up short.

"That statement is in that case?" he asked.

"Here it is," Swinton said, showing him the goods.

It was a detail that Friedman had overlooked, and he immediately put it in the brief he was preparing.

Emboldened, the Canadians soon began rewriting passages without consulting anyone. When Friedman discovered an unfamiliar statement in one brief, he called Graves. "Who put this in?" he demanded.

"The Canadians put it in," Graves said.

"Are you sure it's right?" Friedman asked.

"Leon, if the Canadians say it's right, it's right."

On another occasion, Friedman walked into his office and found Swinton typing away at his computer, reworking a brief. Friedman, who considered himself an accomplished writer and the man in charge of the appeal, was outraged.

"What the hell are you doing?" he fumed.

"I thought it sounded better this way," Swinton said.

Friedman read it and had to agree.

The night before Carter's lawyers were to appear before Sarokin,

Swinton and Chaiton sat with them around the office, reviewing the prosecutors' positions and preparing rebuttals. Chaiton spoke up: "Leon, I don't know if you are interested, but I came up with a new way of meeting the argument about materiality," that being the key issue in the Bello polygraph claim.

"Sam," Friedman replied, "I am interested in anything you have to say."

A division of labor was established for the motion and supporting briefs. The lawyers handled the legal analyses, and Carter and the Canadians wrote the facts. That included the ballistics evidence, the identification of Carter's car, the evolving statements of key witnesses, the movements by the defendants on the night of the murders. Kathy Swinton, who had come to New Jersey to lend a hand, typed these sections out, and the Canadians delivered them at night to Beldock's office in Manhattan. They first gave the passages to Ed Graves, who edited their work. Then a legal assistant, Amanda George, typed the information into a word processor, weaving it into the draft under review by all the lawyers. They often worked until five or six in the morning, consulting transcripts, checking citations, and proofreading.

To Beldock, creating the Motion for Summary Judgment and its supporting briefs — the writing, the editing, the legal papers whipping back and forth across the Hudson River each night — was the greatest example of teamwork he had ever experienced, filled with wonderfully creative touches. In one brief Beldock, who played the drums, slipped in the phrase "ground beat" as a subliminal reference to Sarokin's musical passion. But the process of preparing the documents was often contentious. Carter, inspired by Lisa, pushed for more strident and accusatory language while the lawyers stressed the importance of standard legal prose.

"There is a traditional style of legal writing, an objective statement of facts, but Rubin didn't accept that," Ed Graves recalled. "He would edit word by word, sentence by sentence, and he wanted to advocate in every sentence of every filing."

From the day Carter was initially convicted in 1967, he had accused New Jersey prosecutors and investigators of committing a crime against him, and that sentiment clearly emerged in the "Joint Memorandum

Regarding Exhaustion of State Remedies," which described in detail
the contents of the Caruso file. The introduction read in part:

> There is one overriding reason why this case has been such a protracted
> and exhausting ordeal: namely, petitioners [Carter and Artis] have never
> enjoyed a full, fair and unforced disclosure of the facts to which they have
> been constitutionally entitled. For the prosecution to now claim a lack of
> exhaustion is insufferably galling. It is akin to plucking a man's eyes out
> and condemning him because he cannot see. The petitioner has always
> sought swift and effective administration of justice. It has consistently been
> the misconduct of the State, under the color of law, which has frustrated
> and prolonged its realization.

Habeas corpus motions typically run thirty pages. Carter and Artis, in
consolidating their petitions, requested permission to file an extra-long
Motion for Summary Judgment. It filled two hundred and fifty-three
pages, excluding tables and appendices. Neatly bound, it was almost
two inches thick, with seventy-one separate references in the Table of
Cases. The original twelve grounds for overturning the conviction were
consolidated into seven.

Sarokin had played tennis a few times with the former prosecutor
Burrell Ives Humphreys, but he had not followed Carter's case and was
apparently unfamiliar with its history. When Sarokin's children learned
that this new case had been assigned to him, they gave him a copy of
Bob Dylan's "Hurricane." He declined to listen to it.

Though Sarokin had Carter's motion, the Passaic County Prosecutor's Office did not file a responding brief on the grounds that there
were still unexhausted claims — the Caruso issue — in state court.
Regardless, Sarokin scheduled a hearing for oral arguments.

It was held on Friday, July 26, 1985, at the U.S. Courthouse and Post
Office in downtown Newark. Built in 1936, the neoclassical structure
had a pale limestone exterior. The U.S. District Court, including Sarokin's office, occupied the third floor. The wide hallways, ornate mold-
ings, Greek statues, and marble pillars breathed quiet elegance. Chaiton
and Swinton arrived at 9 A.M., a full hour before the hearing was to
begin. They were to call their housemates at their apartment in Rahway
as soon as the hearing ended, so they searched the floor for pay phones
and found four: near the elevators, outside the bathroom in the jurors'
lounge, outside the press room, and between the clerk's office and
Sarokin's chambers. They sat in the first row of spectator seats behind

the waist-high wooden partition, armed with briefcase, briefs, and note-pad. Carter's cousin Ed Carter and two other friends were also in attendance.

About an hour later, Friedman, Beldock, Steel, and Graves entered the paneled courtroom and sat behind the counsel table next to the empty jurors' box. Representing the state was First Assistant Passaic County Prosecutor John Goceljak, whose involvement in the case dated back eleven years. The former prosecutor, Humphreys, was now safely ensconced as a superior court judge in Hudson County.

Sarokin took the bench in his full-length black robe. He was balding and soft-spoken, with dark-framed glasses and a long, angular face.

"Who wishes to be heard first?" Sarokin asked.

Friedman stood up. The first order of business was the Caruso brief. It was filed with the Motion for Summary Judgment and included detailed descriptions of alleged prosecutorial misconduct. But now Friedman was going to preempt any challenges by the prosecutor and delete the Caruso brief himself.

"Now, on the issue of exhaustion," Friedman said, "we are today — and I told Mr. Goceljak this yesterday — we are amending our petition, formally amending our petition to delete the one unexhausted claim, the Caruso file . . . The respondent says one of them is unexhausted, and for that reason he has a defense to the whole thing. We are deleting it."

"You do that formally?" Sarokin asked.

"We are formally doing that," Friedman said. The discarded brief had still served a purpose: Sarokin had read it; and while it would now be expunged from the record, Carter's camp assumed the information would cause him to doubt the state's case further.

Friedman explained that John Artis was taking a "different procedural stance" — his lawyer, Lew Steel, continued to pursue the Caruso matter in state court. For Carter, Friedman said the exhaustion issue was over, "and we are now prepared to argue the merits." Goceljak, denied any more opportunity to stall, agreed to debate the merits of the case.

Friedman, wearing a navy suit, his face tanned, looked comfortable before the judge. As a professor at Hofstra and a regular lecturer at judicial conferences, he was practiced in streamlining complex legal issues. He told Sarokin that the state used a theory of racial revenge to explain the Lafayette bar murders. The prosecutors, Friedman said, "argued to the jury in very forceful terms that the reason these three people were killed in the Lafayette bar was not for robbery, but only because they were white. Now, if the prosecutor had stood up before the jury and said something like this, 'Ladies and gentlemen of the jury, blacks are a tribal people, and like tribes they seek revenge on anyone that attacks them, and not only are they tribal, they are murderous, because if any one of them are attacked by an outsider, they will seek revenge on an outsider' . . . If the prosecutor had said it outright, there would be no issue. I mean, we would all agree you just can't say all blacks are murderous and these people killed these white people because they are black. Now what the prosecutor tried to say is that there is a predicate for it . . . [But] what is there in this case that would justify the prosecutor's effort to make this into a racial war murder? Was there any evidence that the underlying killing — did Conforti [a white man] kill Holloway [a black man] because of race? Any evidence of that? None whatsoever. Was there any evidence that the defendants knew the victim? Did they know Holloway? No evidence at all. The testimony was that they didn't know the victim; they knew his stepson. Was there any evidence at all that Carter and Artis had hostility toward whites? . . . No evidence was introduced to demonstrate that the petitioners had had hostile attitudes toward whites."

Point by point, Friedman shot down the "predicates" that prosecutors had used to convince the trial judge to allow the racial revenge theory. At its core, Friedman said, the prosecutors' argument was: "'Ladies and gentlemen of the jury, these defendants killed those victims because the defendants are black and the victims were white.'" Friedman said that as a purely legal issue, the state cannot appeal to race on that basis. "As we say in the brief, it is this whole appeal to blacks as the bogeymen who are going to come in and rape the white women and kill them. And that is exactly what it was."

Friedman then turned to the issue of the Bello polygraph, describing how the wrong results had been given to the defense and used to reshape Bello's trial testimony. The polygraph affair was a serpentine trail to follow, but Sarokin asked the kind of precise, technical questions that could only be asked if he had carefully read the motion. Friedman wrapped up after close to an hour and a half. Beldock, who had not intended to speak, stood up and added a few points that arose from

Sarokin's questions. Then Steel took the floor and assailed the state for relying on "group guilt" to convict Carter and Artis. "Both Mr. Beldock and I told [Judge Leopizzi], 'When this race issue comes in, what are we to do?' Can't win. Because it overwhelms the process . . . It pollutes the process. It destroys the process."

After a short recess Goceljak stood up, and it fell to the mild-mannered prosecutor to defend a case that he had not tried. Ronald Marmo, the intense chief assistant prosecutor who had tried the case with Humphreys, was apparently on vacation; he certainly would have been more adamant, if not persuasive, than the balding, plumpish Goceljak. Beginning in a defensive, almost apologetic vain, Goceljak said "that the two defendants, just the two defendants took it upon themselves to do their own brand of justice. Unfortunately, it happened to be in the context of racial revenge."

Sarokin, who had already thought about what questions he would ask, cut to the heart of the race motive: "What evidence was there to support that argument?"

Goceljak said that after Frank Conforti, a white man, killed the black bartender, Holloway, Conforti was arrested, and there was testimony that "some of the neighborhood people who were primarily blacks had gathered in front of the tavern. They didn't know what had precipitated the killing of Holloway; all they knew is he was dead. And there was testimony that certain of these individuals made some angry remarks to the police officers who escorted Conforti out." Goceljak said that Carter and Artis were friends of Holloway's stepson, Eddie Rawls, and later that night Rawls went to the police station and "caused a furor over the arrest of Conforti."

Sarokin interjected: "How was any of that attributable or even admissible against the defendants in this case?"

Goceljak began to ramble. He said Carter saw Rawls and expressed his condolences, then Carter went on "what we call a search for guns" (disputed vigorously by the defense at the trial and in its federal briefs). Goceljak said there was talk in Paterson about a "shaking" in the community, which "applies to some type of unrest or whatever." He said there was evidence that the slain bartender at the Lafayette bar was a bigot. "Now, when you put all of that together," he said, "it indicates for their own purposes Carter and Artis decided they were going to revenge — avenge — the killing of their friend's stepfather.

So our contention is that this is not so much a racial revenge theory as it is — I'd like to denominate it a revenge theory that has racial overtones."

Sarokin shifted in his chair. In his mind, the incidents did not explain why Carter and Artis specifically wanted to avenge the Holloway murder. He repeated his previous question: "How is the gathering of a group of blacks [relevant] to these defendants?"

Goceljak said that Carter had testified before a grand jury that he heard a "shaking" was going to occur. "Now it can be inferentially drawn that he might have heard about this group in front of the tavern where Holloway was shot. The point is, he was aware that there was a feeling — there was an uneasy feeling among the black community because Holloway had been shot."

"Let's assume that's true. Does that go to his motivation?"

"Well —"

Sarokin, his voice rising, cut him off. "Suppose he saw a gathering, throwing stones, screaming, yelling — is that attributable to him?"

"It's attributable to him," Goceljak replied, "if there's evidence to show that he acted upon it. Now, the professor mentioned that we were not able to per se attribute hostility to Carter. Well, I think the answer is to that, actions speak louder than words. If the jury were to find that Carter in fact was the individual, one of the individuals who did the killings, they could attribute to him the motive in that he had trained it upon himself to do this."

Sarokin was flabbergasted. "But isn't the order wrong there?" he boomed. The motive, he said, is supposed to explain the crime, not vice versa. Goceljak, abandoning his argument, said the prosecutor felt he had to introduce evidence of motive in the second trial because the absence of a motive in the first trial "did present a problem."

Sarokin gave him one last opportunity to salvage his case. "Was there any testimony by virtue of anything either Mr. Carter or Mr. Artis said that would support this motive?"

Goceljak: "That they themselves said — other than Carter's testifying that he knew there was going to be a shaking? That he had — he knew that it was the stepfather of his friend, and then his own action — I don't think there's anything else specifically where they had made comments."

Beldock, Steel, and Friedman sat in quiet jubilation. For nine years

Carter's lawyers had argued that the racial revenge motive was an insidious appeal to racism unsupported by evidence, and for nine years the argument had fallen on the deaf ears of New Jersey judges. Finally, they had found a judge who would not countenance the prosecutors' tribal inferences, twisted logic, and retrograde attitudes. As Goceljak said, jurors could attribute motive to Carter because *he had trained it upon himself to do this,* like a savage responding to jungle impulses.

Sarokin also grilled the hapless prosecutor about the Bello polygraph, and by the end of the hearing there was little doubt where his sympathies lay. After agreeing with Goceljak on the date on which his office had to file its responding brief — August 31 — the judge threw an added bonbon to Carter's lawyers: "If the respondent's brief is as good as the petitioners' brief, further oral argument may not be necessary."

"I'll try not to make it as long, Judge," the prosecutor said dryly.

As Sarokin was about to step off the bench, Ed Carter could not contain his joy. "Have a nice vacation, Judge!" He then leaned forward and whispered to Swinton and Chaiton, "Damn! I hope nothin' happens to him over the summer!"

14

THE EAGLE RISES

IN HIS RAHWAY CELL, Rubin Carter took out the yellow notepad that he used to track the progress of his case. He had just gotten off the phone with his elated lawyers, who called him from outside the courtroom. Carter had already read some of Sarokin's opinions, and his lawyers confirmed his belief that the judge would view his case as another example of overbearing agents of the state trampling the rights of a citizen. Carter wrote on his notepad: "Orals Federal Court. For all intents and purposes, it appears that we may have won our arguments. Wow!! The judge gave the state 35 days to answer."

Carter realized that Lisa had urged him to transfer to Rahway to prepare him for his next transfer — to Toronto. For now, he had suspended his qualms about her communal way of life and looked forward to living in a safe, comfortable home, far beyond the reach of anyone in New Jersey. Meanwhile, the Canadians continued to help him transform his cell. When his onion bulb eventually withered away, he told Terry Swinton of the setback. "Can you get me some flowers?" he asked.

That was no small request. The prison, oddly, prohibited inmates from having flowers in their cells, but breaking the rules made the Canadians' next caper — plant smuggling — all the more alluring. As part of a food package, they brought in a green bulb with a papery skin that looked like an onion. They told a puzzled guard in the mailroom, who inspected it, that it was a Jamaican root vegetable called an *obeah*. You boil it and eat it. The guard accepted the story, unaware that *obeah* is Jamaican for "voodoo." Carter now had his prized contraband, an amaryllis bulb. He quietly scooped dirt from the prison yard, packed it in plastic food containers, and planted the bulb, half in, half out. But there were problems.

"Do you have light in the cell?" Swinton asked.

"I have one light," Carter said.

Swinton explained that to blossom, the bulb needed sunlight; otherwise it would die. He had an idea. "If you get a bank of lights, they will act like the sun."

Carter knew that an inmate can get anything he wanted in prison: drugs, weapons, alcohol, women — you name it, it's available. Now, he had to get ... the sun. He asked one of the inmates, a skilled carpenter, to build a light fixture that held a half-dozen light bulbs above the shelf where the amaryllis was planted. Basking in the light of this bright jury-rigged orb, the bulb fired out a tall green stem that gave way to five huge purple blossoms. Guards, instead of confiscating it, complimented Carter on its vibrant color; one guard, needing to buy flowers for his wife, asked Carter the name of his bloom. The Canadians next brought in daffodils and other perennials. Carter kept some and gave away the rest to other prisoners, prompting discussions of soil texture and watering schedules on 6 Wing.

As yet another manifestation of the outside world appeared in his cell, Carter began to feel that he could influence the outside world itself. When he realized that a man in an adjacent cell was dying from lymph cancer, he feared that the authorities would let him waste away. So he called the Canadians and told them to call the New Jersey Department of Corrections. "Don't identify yourself," Carter said, "but tell the department that a man is dying of lymph cancer in Rahway State Prison, in 6 Wing Left, cell 36. If he is not taken to a hospital, tell them you will personally call every newspaper around and tell them how you let people die in your prisons." The prisoner was soon taken to an outside hospital, where he received chemotherapy.

Back in the courthouse, Sarokin was preparing his decision. He knew his ruling, however it turned out, would be appealed by the losing side and an appellate court would carefully scrutinize his opinion, and he needed extra manpower to help him with the unusual length and complexity of the case. Law clerks are generally responsible for checking the accuracy of the briefs, including the factual record and the legal citations. Under the direction of a judge, the clerks also draft the body of the opinion. But Sarokin's two clerks could not tackle the Carter case in addition to their existing responsibilities. The appendix to Carter's Motion for Summary Judgment was more than twenty thousand pages, including transcripts from trials and hearings, motions, briefs, police records, newspaper articles, and court exhibits. So Sarokin got permission to hire a clerk specifically for this case, and he approached Bruce Rosen. A bearded reporter with dark lank hair, Rosen had written numerous (and essentially flattering) stories about Sarokin for the *Bergen Record*. He was also an aspiring lawyer and took classes at Seton Hall Law School. In August, after the oral arguments, Sarokin invited Rosen into his chambers and told him he had the Carter case before him.

"I think this is very important," the judge said. "I think a grave injustice has been done. But I can't tell you what I'm going to do until you agree to work for me."

Bruce Rosen knew exactly what Sarokin was going to do. Accepting the offer would force him to take a 50 percent pay cut from his $35,000-a-year reporter's salary, would divert him from his law studies, and would eat into his time with his wife and two young children. But Rosen was a huge Bob Dylan fan. He'd covered Dylan's concert at the Clinton Correction Institution for Women, and he was familiar with Carter's case. He knew this job would not be a conventional clerkship. It would be part of history. He accepted Sarokin's offer.

While Carter's lawyers had other clients to serve — clients who, not incidentally, generated revenue — Carter and the Canadians were preparing for the next battle. While waiting for the prosecutors to file their responding brief, they began working on the petitioners' reply. Once the prosecutors filed, Carter would only get one week to submit his response. So he and the Canadians reviewed the prosecutors' main state briefs, anticipating a recapitulation of the same arguments. They began writing their rebuttals in advance, specifically on the factual portions of the case.

The prosecutors filed their papers, "Respondents' Brief in Opposition to Petitioners' Motion for Summary Judgment and Habeas Corpus Relief," on August 30. It was one hundred and fifty-seven pages long. Once again working all-night sessions, Carter and his team effectively used the prosecutors' brief to their own advantage. They wrote in their reply brief that the state's case, *by its own words,* was so riddled with contradictions and inconsistencies that no reasonable person could conclude that the defendants were guilty. From the case it presented in 1976, the state would have the court believe that the police had on the night of the crime the following evidence: Valentine's identification of Carter's car at the scene of the crime; Bello's accurate description of two men who resembled Carter and Artis; Bello's identification of Carter's car as the getaway car at the scene of the crime and at police headquarters; an officer finding a .32-caliber bullet and a 12-gauge shotgun shell in Carter's car; Carter and Artis failing lie detector tests; Carter and Artis giving conflicting statements. According to Carter's reply brief:

> If all the above is true, as [the prosecutors] maintain, how is it even conceivable that Carter and Artis were released by the police that day, not charged with anything or even held as suspects in the face of this mountain of incriminating evidence? How also with all this "evidence" could Lieutenant DeSimone go on to effectively exonerate the petitioners before the grand jury twelve days later? (Including, of course, telling the grand jury that Carter and Artis passed their lie detector tests.) Obviously, the answer is that the above evidence did not exist.

At the end of the brief, Beldock included an unusual but fitting footnote: "Counsel acknowledge the substantial assistance of petitioner Carter in the preparation of the factual discussions in the brief." He also wanted to mention Swinton and Chaiton, but, in keeping with their private ways, the Canadians politely declined.

With all the briefs finally in hand, Sarokin turned to Bruce Rosen on his first day of work. "This is what we're going to do," he said, pointing to the defendant's Motion for Summary Judgment on his desk. "There are seven reasons why the defense thinks it should get relief." He ticked off each of the seven on the open pages before him. "I want you to research point one and point two, and I don't want you to research the others," he continued, striking off the unavailing points with his pen. Points one and two were the state's racial revenge theory and the state's failure to disclose the results of the Bello lie detector test. "I've read the briefs," Sarokin said, "and this is how I think it should come out. Show me whether I'm right or wrong."

Rosen squirreled himself away in the tiny office used by Sarokin's clerks, reviewing the briefs, checking their accuracy against a twenty-thousand-page record, reconciling factual disputes, and beginning to hammer out his boss's opinion. For the *Brady* violation on the Bello polygraph, Rosen, as instructed by Sarokin, basically adopted the dissent in the 1982 New Jersey Supreme Court ruling. But finding in favor of the defense on racial revenge took more work because no judge had ever found a constitutional violation on those grounds. To support Sarokin's position, Rosen drew on previous court rulings to establish the proper use of motive and race in a criminal proceeding and to determine whether an improper use of either violated Carter's right to a fair trial. Rosen ultimately quoted from or cited more than eighteen cases, creating the standards by which Carter's own case could be tested.

The weeks dragged on for Carter. Confident but tense, he began preparing himself to leave prison. It was autumn, so the Canadians bought him a sheepskin jacket (similar to the one they bought for Lesra), an olive sweater, a button-down cotton shirt, pleated wool slacks, and brown leather boots. He wanted to leave in style, casual but polished, a clear sign that he had not been defeated by the prison.

There was one hitch. When the Canadians checked the clothing at the Rahway mailroom, a guard pulled out a ruler and measured the boots from the heel to the top of the ankle. The boots, alas, were too high by a quarter of an inch. But Chaiton and Swinton were not going to let a witless shoe rule interfere with Carter's sartorial desires. On Chaiton's next contact visit with Carter, he entered the visiting room wearing the brown leather boots. The two men sat across from each other, and at one point during the conversation Carter removed his battered black shoes; Chaiton did the same with the boots. When it was time to wrap up, Carter walked out of the visiting room wearing a fine pair of brown leather boots; Chaiton left in a pair of old black shoes.

As fall moved toward winter, the silence from the courthouse made Carter nervous. What was taking so long? Was there a joker in the deck? His confidence began to falter. Three years earlier, he had been certain that the New Jersey Supreme Court would rule in his favor. Maybe Sarokin would disappoint him as well. Clumps of hair began falling out of his head. He slept fitfully. He couldn't eat. The hypnotic rhythms of the prison — *count up, count up, all wings count up, yard in, yard out* – began to make him dizzy.

Finally, on November 6, Bruce Rosen called Beldock's office to report that Judge Sarokin's decision would be released the following morning. He also called the prosecutor's office — but was met with silence. Rosen figured that the prosecutors knew the news would be bad. Court watchers familiar with Sarokin's record began flinging rumors around. "They're letting the Hurricane go! They're letting the Hurricane go!"

Back in Rahway, Carter was told that the next day was decision day, and his spirits soared. He promptly began clearing out his cell and distributing his belongings to other prisoners. He gave away his Ouspensky books, his plants, his Impressionist paintings, his musical tapes, his Persian rug, his typewriter, his monogrammed towels, and his brown velvet robe — all the civilizing influences brought by Lisa and her cohorts. He even gave away his electric coil, which had cooked his meals for almost two decades. When a prisoner emptied his cell, it meant one of three things: he was crazy, he was going to commit suicide, or he was going home. Rubin Carter was going home. Swinton stopped by at night and picked up his court papers, his other writings, and a few personal belongings. By the time Carter returned to his cell, he had nothing. His living space, oddly, had returned to the hard, ascetic cell that he had survived in for so many years. It now felt . . . empty.

Lying on his cot, Carter decided that staying in the cell was no longer an option. In reality, he might very well have to stay. Even if his conviction was overturned, he would still stand indicted for murder, and he could be held in prison without bail. But in Carter's mind he was walking out the next day. He was either walking out under the authority of Judge Sarokin or he was walking out on his own. And if they killed him as he walked out of prison, that was fine by him also. Either way, he would no longer be held captive by the State of New Jersey. Either way, Rubin Carter, #45472, was going home.

The next morning, a Thursday, Ed Graves and Lewis Steel drove to the federal courthouse in Newark. Kathy and Terry Swinton had arrived at nine-thirty and were waiting by the phone. Absent was Sam Chaiton, who was house hunting up in Toronto so that the commune, now including Carter, could immediately move into a large, comfortable dwelling. There was a delay at the courthouse because the opinions were late coming back from the printer. It was now almost eleven. Finally, Graves and Steel were called into Sarokin's chambers. Terry

Swinton called Lisa, who was already on the line with Carter. A three-way hookup was established. Lesra, Gus Sinclair, and the others were back in Toronto, waiting.

Rosen met the lawyers outside Sarokin's office in a vestibule.

"Congratulations," Rosen said, handing Graves the opinion.

Graves thrust the opinion over his head, raced out into the hall, and screamed, "We did it! We won! We won!" Terry Swinton blurted the same words over the phone, and Carter, stunned, raised his eyes and shouted: "We won! We won!" In minutes, word had swept through the prison, then radios were carrying the news. Carter tried to get Swinton to read him the opinion, but inmates flocked around him, patting him on the back. "Rube, you've won!" "Rube, you're on the radio!" From a Rahway apartment to Manhattan law offices to a home in Toronto to the prison itself, there were hugs and tears and gratitude and astonishment. The journey had been a success, and it was miraculous.

The opinion itself was long, seventy pages. Sarokin found that the state had violated the constitutional rights of Carter and Artis on two separate grounds: that the state violated the requirements of *Brady v. Maryland* by failing to disclose the results of the lie detector test given to the state's only eyewitness, Alfred Bello; and the state, in claiming the killings were motivated by racial revenge, violated the Equal Protection and Due Process rights of petitioners by improperly appealing to racial prejudice. Both violations, Sarokin concluded, were vital in helping the state convict the defendants, and therefore the violations met the legal standard for overturning the convictions. In short, the state had cheated.

Even by Sarokin's own standards, it was an audacious opinion. He could have overturned the convictions exclusively on the *Brady* violation, citing the arid details of the prosecutors' failure to disclose crucial evidence. The dissenting justices in the state supreme court decision in '82 had already laid out the legal reasoning behind the *Brady* violation. Had Sarokin simply adopted that reasoning and stopped there, he would have, in effect, sided with the minority opinion, but the foundation for such an opinion would already have been laid. That was not the case with the racial revenge issue. He had to support his decision with his own legal reasoning, citing appropriate precedents, applying them to

Carter's case, and drawing conclusions that no judge had ever reached before.

While Rosen drafted a dispassionate narrative of the case, Sarokin supplied the thunderbolts, writing his own introduction and conclusion, inserting a few choice passages and deleting others. True to form, he used the opinion to speak out on the insidious role of racism in America and the need to protect individuals against the unlimited power of the state. His aim was not simply to overturn a wrongful conviction. It was to shame the prosecutors, judge, and investigators who were responsible for it. "The court has determined that the writ must issue," Sarokin wrote in the introduction.

> The extensive record clearly demonstrates that petitioners' convictions were predicated upon an appeal to racism rather than reason, and concealment rather than disclosure. The jury was permitted to draw inferences of guilt based solely upon the race of the petitioners, but yet was denied information which may have supported their claims of innocence. To permit convictions to stand which have as their foundation appeals to racial prejudice and the withholding of evidence critical to the defense, is to commit a violation of the Constitution as heinous as the crimes for which these petitioners were tried and convicted.

Sarokin belittled the prosecutors at almost every turn. He concluded that the evidence used to support the revenge theory did not implicate the defendants and should never have been allowed in the trial. The core of the state's argument, he wrote, was the following:

> A white man killed a black man. Petitioners were friends of the stepson of the victim and expressed their condolences. They heard there might be a "shaking." Ergo — they set out to murder four strangers solely because they were white as an act of revenge, and notwithstanding that one of the alleged murderers was well known in the community and easily recognizable.
>
> Underlying the prosecutor's theory and summation is the insidious and repugnant argument that this heinous crime is to be understood and explained solely because the petitioners are black and the victims are white. Without that unacceptable assumption, the prosecution's theory of racial revenge becomes a thin thread of largely irrelevant evidence and impermissible inferences.
>
> . . . Obviously, the death of the stepfather of the petitioners' friend, standing alone, would never explain why petitioners would shoot four innocent persons who were strangers to them. Notwithstanding the lack of evidence

that petitioners had a background of racial animosity against whites or had any such feelings after the specific death involved, the prosecutor was permitted to render the illogical logical, by relying upon petitioners' blackness and the victims' whiteness. Thus the jury was able to draw inferences based solely on the race of the petitioners and the victims. An appeal to racial prejudice and bias must be deplored in any jury trial and certainly where charges of murder are involved. For the state to contend that an accused has the motive to commit murder solely because of his membership in a racial group is an argument which should never be permitted to sway a jury or provide the basis of a conviction.

Sarokin did not rule on the defendants' guilt or innocence, but he did attack the state's evidence. While the prosecutor told the jury that there were "six strands of rope" to convict the defendants, Sarokin said that each strand was "frayed." He then wrote in detail why the evidence was weak. The strategy by Carter and his lawyers paid off. By submitting lengthy briefs, detailing the flawed investigation over hundreds of pages and including the Caruso material in a supporting brief, they had created an unshakable doubt in Sarokin's mind about the guilt of Carter and Artis. In one section, Sarokin wrote almost verbatim from Carter's reply brief about the improbability of the police releasing Carter and Artis after the murders if indeed the police had — as the state alleged — so much evidence against them.

There was one other important decision to address: appropriate relief. Sarokin and Rosen had numerous discussions about what language they might use to dissuade the state from trying the defendants a third time. Sarokin used several rhetorical tactics, emphasizing practical problems, disparaging (again) the state's case, and pleading for compassion.

The killings that led to the petitioners' indictment and conviction occurred nearly 20 years ago, and to retry such conflicting events, further aggravated by dim memories, does not appear to serve the interests of justice. Moreover, to again use Bello as such a key witness, after his unbelievable series of recantations and recantations of his recantations, his complete and utter malleability at the hands of all parties, and his own sordid criminal history, would probably place his competency as a witness beyond the outer limits of due process. Yet, even though a new trial may very well be a practical impossibility, this is a decision that in the interests of comity should be made by the state ... Therefore, the court will grant the writ as to both petitioners, mindful that the state can seek a retrial, but hopeful that constitutional considerations, as well as justice and compassion, will prevail.

The opinion was shot through with irony: the very arguments that the prosecutors had used to convict Carter and Artis were now being directed back at them. Prosecutors had gone to endless lengths trying to prove that Bello had been manipulated by outside mercenaries — literary agents, screenwriters, and journalists — to recant his initial testimony. Now Sarokin concluded that in fact it was the prosecutors who, using the false results of the polygraph, had manipulated Bello into providing damning testimony against the defendants.

Similarly, Prosecutor Humphreys, in his summation, said that racism was an undeniable reality of America, using that theme to ascribe motive for the murders. "None of us like to admit that things like race prejudice exist," Humphreys said. ". . . As much as you may want to look away, as much as you may want to say [the murders] couldn't have happened for that reason, it did happen for that reason."

Now Sarokin, in his conclusion, turned that argument on Humphreys: "It would be naïve not to recognize that some prejudice, bias and fear lurks in all of us. But to permit a conviction to be urged based upon such factors or to permit a conviction to stand having utilized such factors diminishes our fundamental constitutional rights."

He added:

> Furthermore, the prosecution has resources unavailable to the average criminal defendant. Therefore, it is imperative that information which is essential to the defense in the hands of the prosecution be made available to the accused. If trials are indeed searches for the truth rather than efforts to conceal it, full and fair disclosure is necessary to protect and preserve the rights of the accused against the awesome power of the state.

It would be some time before Carter and his lawyers could read and analyze the opinion. The immediate issue, on its release, was how much longer Carter would have to stay in prison. From the courthouse telephone, Ed Graves read to Carter that Sarokin recommended that the state not retry the case. But Carter had been down that road before. He assured Graves that his adversaries were not about to quit and urged him to immediately file a motion demanding his release, to stay on the attack, and not to let his enemies regroup. But Graves, after consulting with the other lawyers, told Carter that the prosecutors had until the following week to respond to any motion regarding his discharge. Besides, Graves said, they should give prosecutors the time as a matter of "professional courtesy."

Carter was livid: "Did you say courtesy? Was what they did to me courteous? I got no reason to be courteous, Ed. You tell those bastard prosecutors that they've got until this afternoon to read the goddamn thing and be in court."

Graves called the prosecutor's office and spoke to Goceljak, telling him that at two that afternoon they were going to make a motion to have Carter released immediately. Goceljak said they hadn't read the decision yet. Fine, Graves said, we'll give you twenty-four hours. Goceljak agreed to be in court the next day — unaware that he could have taken a whole week. Carter, at last, had his opponent on the ropes, and he was not about to let up.

Back at the prison, the inmates continued to rattle cups, holler, and give Carter hugs, handshakes, and high-fives. So did several of the guards. Television helicopters swooped above, getting aerial shots for the evening news. Newspaper, television, and radio reporters arrived, desperate for the first interview. But Carter was keeping a low profile, declining all interviews.

Not everyone at Rahway was thrilled. In Carter's epic battle of wills with prison authorities, there was still time for one more skirmish. The prison had private rooms where inmates could meet with their lawyers. Over the years, at Rahway and Trenton, Carter had always met his lawyers in these rooms. The night Sarokin decreed that his conviction was illegal, his lawyer Harold Cassidy arrived at the prison to go over the next day's procedures. A guard walked Carter out of his wing and through the prison hub. Three years earlier, it had been Cassidy who went to Trenton State Prison and told Carter of his crushing loss in the state supreme court. Tonight's rendezvous would be emotional and triumphant — but then Carter realized the guard was taking him toward the area for "window visits," where inmates sit behind bulletproof glass. The authorities were going to treat him, a wrongfully convicted man, like a dangerous prisoner, like scum. Carter had won, but the prison took one last opportunity to make him submit to its rules, to try to humiliate him.

Carter stopped just as he reached the window visiting area. He looked up at the guard. "You can kiss my ass," he said. He turned and walked back toward his cell. Even in victory — *especially* in victory — Carter would not succumb to his captors. Soon, a guard told Cassidy: "Rubin Carter refuses to see all visitors." Cassidy got back in his car and drove away, unaware of what had actually happened.

The next day, Friday, November 8, was sunny and beautiful. Carter was escorted by a motorcade of federal marshals to the federal court-house in Newark. The building was surrounded by reporters, television crews, and curiosity-seekers, all jostling for position. Police officers tried to maintain order. With the front of the courthouse jammed, the marshals took Carter through the back. Even there reporters were congealed around the sidewalk, door, and stairwell.

Carter was not a free man yet. He wore handcuffs, a restraining belt around his waist, and chains that ran from the handcuffs to the belt to shackles around his legs. But Carter had worn these bindings so often, he moved naturally, as if he wasn't a prisoner at all. As he waded through the crowd, he kept hearing shouts: "Where's Rubin?" "Where's the Hurricane?" No one recognized him. *No one.* Onlookers who were searching for a bald head, a goatee, and a solid slag of muscle did not recognize this man, now forty-eight, physically trim, with a full Afro, mustache, and eyeglasses. Four years earlier, at the polygraph hearing in Paterson, he had had the same experience. To Carter, his anonymity was magic, proof that his years of study and self-reflection had indeed transformed him. He smiled.

Carter was released from his handcuffs and shackles before he reached the packed third-floor courtroom. He walked in and made his way to his lawyers' table. Dave Anderson, in a column in the *New York Times* the following day, said that Carter "appeared to have walked out of a men's shop window instead of his Rahway prison cell." He was greeted with hugs by Beldock. Also at the table were Lewis Steel and Ed Graves, as well as his New Jersey legal team, Harold Cassidy, Lou Raveson, Jeff Fogel, and Ron Busch. To Carter's regret, Leon Friedman had not been able to get away from a conference he was chairing. Carter looked in the gallery and saw Terry and Kathy Swinton, who nodded at him, a signal that their plans were set. He also saw Ed Carter, John Artis and his wife, Dolly, and *New York Times* reporters Selwyn Raab and Dave Anderson.

Goceljak and Ronald Marmo represented the Passaic County Prosecutor's Office.

"All rise!"

Judge Sarokin took his place on the bench, Rosen standing at the side. Carter peered at Sarokin and thought his features — the receding hairline, the penetrating eyes, the winglike expanse of his robe, the glasses — made him look like an eagle. Carter always had confidence in his instincts about other people, his ability to quickly judge character and motivations. He looked at Sarokin for a long time and was convinced — absolutely convinced — that the judge could see the truth and would do the right thing.

The issue was straightforward: whether Carter would be set free or kept in prison. Steel, however, spoke first on the last remaining issue for his client, Artis. On October 29, the New Jersey Supreme Court denied certification on the Caruso file. For all the excitement about it, the former investigator's notes turned out to have little value as an issue for appeal. But this time the rejection by the state's highest court was a blessing. Steel told Sarokin that his client's claims were officially exhausted in state court, thereby removing any uncertainty that Artis was also entitled to the writ.

Sarokin asked the prosecutors if they had any objections. They had none.

He signed an order that officially granted the writ of habeas corpus to Artis.

Beldock spoke next.

"I wish to apply, in accordance with the Order to Show Cause, that Your Honor release Mr. Carter, to enlarge his release and that you do so unconditionally . . . We do not have funds. I trust Your Honor will not require there be any bail in the sense of security posted."

"Why don't I hear from the prosecution as to what, if anything, they suggest that I do, and then we will decide what we are going to do," Sarokin replied.

As Carter had predicted, the prosecutors were not about to give in. Goceljak told Sarokin that they intended to file a notice of appeal that afternoon with the U.S. Third Circuit Court of Appeals, and that appeal gave them the right to ask Sarokin to keep Carter in prison. Goceljak explained that Carter was a "threat to the community. Chief Assistant Prosecutor Marmo is prepared to discuss that aspect of our application. I am representing to this court that we — "

"A risk to the community," Sarokin interrupted, "that has arisen subsequent to these charges?"

Carter's supporters, who had come to celebrate his liberation, gasped as they realized the prosecutors were going to try to keep him in prison. Marmo stood up. While Carter and his lawyers viewed Goceljak as a functionary, Marmo had a bit more at stake, for he had tried the case with Humphreys. It was, surely, the most widely publicized case of Marmo's career, as he helped the prosecutor's office overcome the incursion of the "Madison Avenue hucksters." Now his convictions lay in tatters, the taint of racism hung over his head, and he stood face to face with Sarokin. He had molten to dissuade the judge from releasing Carter.

"We suggest to you, sir, that if you look at the defendant Carter's background, every aspect of his background, Your Honor, suggests a man who is a risk to the community, a man who is dangerous, who is violent and who is a legitimate threat to the community."

Suddenly, the decorous legalese was thrown out the window, and Marmo revealed how Carter was viewed inside the prosecutor's office: "If you look at his juvenile record, if you look at his adult criminal record, if you look, sir, at his military record, if you look at his psychiatric record, I suggest to you, you will find the most frightening statements you have ever read in a psychiatric report. They were to me, and I have been a prosecutor eighteen years, and I am accustomed to reading what psychiatrists say about people."

Marmo came with the psychiatric reports in hand — the very reports that the prosecution team read before deciding to retry Carter in '76, the reports that confirmed to them that this man should never walk the streets. "What is startling here," Marmo said, "is the fact that the authorities in prison predicted that the offense we contend the defendant committed would in fact occur. They said, Your Honor, 'He continues to be assaultive, aggressive, hostile, negativistic, sadistic, he thinks he is superior, he has grandiose paranoid delusions, this individual is as dangerous to society now, as the day he was incarcerated.'"

Marmo neglected to mention when the report had been written. Sarokin would not be fooled.

"What is the date of that?" the judge asked.

"Nineteen fifty-nine, and these same findings are adopted and continued by psychiatrists into the 1970s." Marmo began reciting from another psychiatric report, but Sarokin cut him off.

"Again, I would appreciate it if you would give me the dates."

Marmo acknowledged that this report too was from 1959, but he was undeterred by the dust of twenty-six years.

"I am interested in evaluations that were made since his last incarceration," Sarokin said.

Marmo had not spent all of his aging bullets. "I am going to get to that, Judge. This is by Dr. Farrell: 'He is an emotionally unstable, aggressive individual, embittered, hostile. When the time arrives that Rubin's ring aspirations do not exist, he will become more aggressive . . .' Another doctor, Dr. Carlin, says, 'This man appears to be extremely dangerous.' These were examinations and diagnoses and impressions that were made in '59 and '60, before [the Lafayette bar murders] occurred. When he returned to the [prison] and was examined by psychiatrists again in the 1970s, the psychological and psychiatric examinations of 1959 and the 1960s seem to sum this man up very well . . ."

Sarokin again asked the date of one of the examinations.

"This is 1970," Marmo said.

"You mean there hasn't been one in fifteen years?"

In fact, Carter had refused to see any more prison psychiatrists after 1970, holding them, like the other prison officials, in contempt. The psychiatrists were paid in part to determine whether an inmate had been rehabilitated, but Carter, insisting on his innocence, refused to cooperate. He was proudly unrepentant of a crime he did not commit — an attitude that ended the possibility of a productive relationship with a prison shrink.

"Have there been any instances of violence," Sarokin asked, "in the last ten years?"

"Judge, he wasn't out of prison for one month when he assaulted a woman, punched her, kicked her, and stomped her," Marmo said, referring to Carolyn Kelley's allegations. He continued that Carter "had all kinds of disciplinary violations well into the eighties . . . What I am suggesting to Your Honor is that there isn't a place in Rubin Carter's past where you can't look, whether it is a juvenile record, his school record, there are notations there that he was terrorizing other children in school when he was just a youngster. This is important and revealing information . . ."

Teenage "terrorizing" did not interest Sarokin. Just as he repeatedly asked Goceljak in July if he had any testimony to support the racial revenge theory, Sarokin kept asking Marmo the date of the most recent psychiatric report. The prosecutor finally conceded that he had nothing more recent than 1970.

"All right. Anything further?" Sarokin asked.

Marmo launched one final attack, pleading for more time to present documentation of Carter's violent past, repeating the Kelley charges and alleging that Carter had proven since "he has been twelve years old that he is a dangerous, violent person and the things that professional people said about him in the sixties and seventies have proven true."

It was a shrill, exhaustive attack. But it gave the full courtroom a vivid view of exactly what kind of man the prosecutors thought Carter was. It helped explain why they had pursued him with every resource they could muster, why they were not about to give up, and — perhaps — why they had withheld or misrepresented evidence in two separate trials and appealed to racism in one trial. What are constitutional violations when the alternative is letting a monster roam free?

Beldock, speaking next, sought to dispel Marmo's portrait of Carter as a beast. He disputed his characterization of the Kelley incident and said that Carter, before his '66 arrest, was a well-respected member of the community who owned a home in a racially mixed neighborhood where he lived with his wife and daughter.

Sarokin said, "Do you know, Mr. Beldock, and this may be against your client's interest, but I will pose the question to you nevertheless, do you know of any instances in the past ten years of any acts of violence by Mr. Carter?"

"I do not, Your Honor. The only incident that has been reported, of course, is the incident that he spoke about" — the Kelley matter — "and that we had a hearing about . . . I know Mr. Carter, because I have had him in my house. He has been with my children. I have been with his children. All these things that we are hearing here are the spooks, literally, the spooks of the prejudice of Paterson. I am sorry to put it that way, but there are, as Your Honor pointed out in the opinion, two complete and divergent views of this case, and the view that Mr. Marmo is pressing before you is a view that he will never relinquish, no matter what the facts are and no matter how many years of good life by Mr. Carter, he will continue to believe that and press it before a court. It is not fair. It is twenty years. Mr. Carter should be released immediately."

Sarokin adjourned for a recess. Carter was taken out of the courtroom to wait in a holding cell down the hall. At first he was outraged by the attack, but the anger dissipated. Marmo was simply talking about a different person. He was not that man. Carter's lawyers and supporters feared that Sarokin would take the safe route, keeping Carter in prison. He had already overturned the conviction. How much farther on a limb could he be expected to go? Carter, however, was confident, even serene. "Don't worry, don't worry," he told Beldock. "We're free, we're free." Carter knew: the eagle would soar.

Sarokin and Rosen walked back to Sarokin's chambers. "So, what do you think?" the judge asked his clerk.

Never having had someone's fate in his hands before, Rosen tried to give a balanced review. He recapitulated all the arguments on the state's side — Carter's criminal record, withering evaluations by psychiatrists, the Kelley incident. He then restated the defense position — Carter was a respected citizen of Paterson, the psychiatric reports were old, his conviction was improper. To Rosen, it was an excruciating choice.

Sarokin pondered his options, then shrugged.

"I'm gonna let him go."

The judge sat at his desk and wrote out his decision. As usual, he thought carefully about the words he used. Forty minutes passed, and restless fears began to sweep through Carter's supporters in the courtroom.

Finally, Sarokin emerged.

"Ladies and gentlemen, I am about to render my opinion in this matter, and I would very much appreciate it if everybody would remain silent until I conclude it. It is very brief.

"I have reviewed the materials submitted by the state, and nothing in the proffer submitted by the state relates to any current evidence that Mr. Carter poses a risk to society. I am reluctant to deny the state a full opportunity to be heard, and that hearing can take place in the future if the state persists in its request for continued incarceration.

"In the interim, I cannot, in the face of the conclusions reached in my opinion and the injustices found, permit Mr. Carter to spend another day or even an hour in prison, particularly considering that he has spent almost twenty years in confinement, based in part upon a conviction which I have found to be constitutionally faulty. To deny relief sought would be inconsistent with my own ruling and render compassion meaningless. If my ruling is correct, Mr. Carter's past imprisonment may have been a travesty. To continue it would even be a greater one. If I am incorrect, either an Appellate Court or a trial court, should another jury convict, would require Mr. Carter to return to prison. There is no evidence before me now which would permit me to conclude that society will be harmed by his immediate release. In the face of these two alternatives, human decency mandates his immediate release. The historical purpose of a writ of habeas corpus is served by Mr. Carter's release. It is disserved by its denial.

"Therefore, petitioner shall be enlarged and released forthwith on his own recognizance without surety; the only condition being that he shall keep the state apprised of his residence."

Before Sarokin finished, Ed Carter's twenty-eight-year-old daughter, Charmaine, began clapping, then leaped up and yelled, "Yeah!" The decorum of the proceedings was shattered. High-pitched shouts of joy rose from the crowd. Carter's supporters stood, whistled, clapped, and hugged. Sarokin quickly rapped his gavel, then finished his statement above the swelling din.

"An order will be entered to this effect and I am confident that Mr. Carter will not disappoint this court or all those persons who believe in him. Court is recessed."

The scene was the opposite of the courtroom upheavals following Carter's two convictions. Instead of peals of agony and sobs of despair, the room rocked with triumphant howls, victorious embraces, and tears of happiness. Now it was the prosecutors who sat stunned and defeated as Carter rose, the conquering hero. He had been, for almost two decades, a stolid courtroom figure, and he next did something that many people had never seen him do before. He smiled. Yes! Rubin Carter smiled and waved and pumped his fist. He embraced Beldock and whispered, "Thank you, brother. We did it."

Sarokin quietly left the courtroom and returned to his office. In later years, he described Carter's briefs as among the finest legal papers he had ever read. Asked about his decision to release Carter, he said, "If he's an evil man, then I'm no judge of character."

The marshals led Carter through the courthouse throng to a sealed-off area where he would officially sign out. He was met by a private investigator, Mims Hackett, who had previously helped on the case and had watched the court proceedings. Beside him was a friend, an African, wearing a blue ski jacket. Carter discreetly handed his sheepskin coat and sunglasses to the African, who gave up his blue jacket in return. The marshals escorted "Mr. Carter" downstairs, notwithstanding the fact that he was now thirty years younger and had no mustache. The real Rubin Carter blended in as one of the escorts.

Outside, on the sunny courthouse steps, Beldock, Steel, and Artis were answering questions from a swarm of reporters. Beldock looked up in the sky, exhaled, and said, "New Jersey has never looked so beautiful." The case, he said, "should never have happened. It's a case of passion and prejudice that was wrong from the beginning. And the judge's decision said it loud and clear."

Meantime, reporters looking for Carter finally spotted a parked limousine and headed its way. When they saw the black man in the sheepskin coat, they thought they found their prey. Several reporters ran right past Carter as the African slipped inside the limo and sped off, leaving reporters briefly chasing behind on foot. Carter quietly entered a nondescript car, slid into the back seat behind Hackett and Ed Carter, and sped off. At one corner, as arranged, they met Terry and Kathy Swinton in their rental car. Carter thanked his cousin and Hackett, switched cars and drove off with his Canadian family. They had won the battle, but the war was not over.

15

VINDICATION

RUBIN CARTER THOUGHT he could fly. Standing on the balcony of the Canadians' apartment in Rahway, he looked into the distance and saw row after row of other residential balconies, their waist-high metal railings adorned with hanging plants. He thought he could leap off the edge and float above the rooftops to another balcony, rest a spell in a padded chair, then soar once again to another balcony on another street, in another town, in another galaxy. No metal rails could contain him anymore. Carter could see something else from the balcony. He saw the yellowish dome of the prison where he had awakened that morning. There was nothing imaginary about that. He felt an unspeakable sadness for the anonymous men who lived there, hidden from the world beyond. He felt a chill and went inside.

On his first night of freedom, Carter and the Canadians hugged and laughed and cried. Their victory had been forged through cooperation, sacrifice, love — and secrecy. The Canadians had worked on the case for three years without anyone knowing, save Carter's lawyers, and their silence gave the triumph an added mystique, as if an invisible force had broken down the prison walls. The celebration reflected the commune's idiosyncrasies. There were no celebratory toasts because there was no liquor, Lisa having banned alcohol long ago. Carter's prodigious thirst for booze had not been satisfied since he had been free nine years earlier, but he did not resent his temperance. He saw it, at least for this night, as part of his own transformation. Ordinary people drink to celebrate, but he was not among ordinary people. To be sober was to be awake, to be conscious — as he was. The celebration did not include music. The Canadians simply didn't need it. Their voices were music, conversation their song. It was Carter's first time outside the prison with the commune, and it was unlike any experience he had ever had. The festivities culminated with a big dinner of turkey, mashed potatoes, dressing, carrots, and chocolate cake.

But at dinner Carter discovered that even though he was out of prison, he had not escaped its long shadow. His eyes began secreting a thick fluid, sealing them shut. He tried washing away the sticky substance, but it continued to flow. His right eye had been lost since his first year in prison, but now the left eye was closed. Rubin Carter, on his first night of freedom, was blind.

The buildup of stress had apparently caused these secretions, and it took days for the problem to ease. In addition to being sightless, Carter was also stuck in America. Contrary to his expectations of going to Toronto — the commune had already found a seven-bedroom mansion there, including a pool — he was ordered to stay in the United States pending a possible appeal or the dismissal of the original indictment against him. After his left eye sealed, Carter's lawyers returned to Sarokin's court and asked that the "order of release" be modified so that Carter could seek medical treatment in Canada. Sarokin denied the request, noting that Carter could surely find a good doctor "in these vast United States." Fortunately, Paulene McLean, Lesra's girlfriend and a nurse, was in Rahway at the time and tended to Carter until his left eye opened and his vision returned.

Carter's relationship with Lisa also entered a new phase. In prison he had had conflicting feelings for her. Some days he saw her as his lifetime partner; at other times he assumed their differences — she ran a commune, he was a loner — made any such union impractical. After he won his freedom and moved in with the group, his feelings came into sharper focus. He decided he would not become Lisa's lover. He knew that her partners had to undergo vasectomies, and that he too would have to, in his words, "come under compliance." That had broken them up once before and was still unacceptable to Carter.

In addition, he had never been sexually attracted to white women before Lisa. While that had changed in prison, he resumed his original romantic preferences in freedom. Finally, his last prison relationship, with Carolyn Kelley, had led to disaster after he was released, and until he had won complete vindication — namely, when the charges against him were dropped — he wanted to avoid any missteps. If a romance with Lisa ended badly, he feared he would be abandoned by the entire group or even, as with Kelley, face public attacks by erstwhile allies. Carter believed his let's-be-friends approach with Lisa was his best guarantee that the Canadians would remain his energetic supporters. In matters of the heart, it was another cold calculation, but Carter knew the commune had the time, money, and intelligence to help him battle future appeals.

According to Carter, Lisa was unhappy that the relationship did not reach its logical conclusion, but the disappointment did not cause a split between them. Rubin continued to live with the commune, and Lisa apparently hoped that over time he would reconsider his platonic ground rules.

Until the prosecutors made their next move, Carter intended to lie low. He had learned his lesson from the last time his conviction had been overturned. Then he had basked in his martyrdom, holding press conferences, giving speeches, and condemning the authorities at every turn. His scorn may have won applause and fueled speculation that he would run for public office, but it deepened the enmity between him and the prosecutor's office, which repaid him with a second conviction. Now he was determined not to antagonize his zealous adversaries further.

Weeks passed, and Carter's hopes began to rise that the prosecutors would let this case die. But the confrontation had now become a blood feud — as Bruce Rosen, Sarokin's clerk, was about to learn. After Sarokin released Carter, Rosen was at law school and saw the Passaic County prosecutor, Joseph Falcone, in the hall. Falcone had been first assistant prosecutor during the second trial, and he now ran the office. He walked up to Rosen, stood nose to nose with him, and, according to Rosen, began yelling, "You helped a murderer go free! You helped a murderer go free!"

The week before Christmas 1985, Carter received notice that the prosecutor's office had submitted a motion and supporting briefs to the Third Circuit Court of Appeals requesting that he either be reincarcerated or undergo a psychiatric examination. The submission was more than three hundred pages. The Memorandum in Support of Motion, signed by John Goceljak and Ronald Marmo, rehashed

Marmo's contentions that Carter was a "substantial threat to the community." It even noted that, as a child, Rubin's school records showed he was "very wild" and had a "bullying attitude." Carter was now forty-eight years old.

Panic swept Carter's camp. If Marmo succeeded, Carter would be tossed back in prison pending the outcome of the state's appeal. And unless they moved quickly, he would be spending another Christmas behind bars. The prosecutor's motion revealed once again the visceral hatred that Marmo and the others in his office had for Carter. That his conviction was unlawful — that he did not, in the eyes of the law, commit murder — was immaterial to their argument. They wrote: "The appellants are concerned that Rubin Carter's liberty, in all likelihood, will cause great harm to the community . . . There is very good cause for this Court to believe that Rubin Carter will act out violence while outside the environment of a correctional institution."

Myron Beldock requested and received a ten-day extension from the Third Circuit Court. Then Carter, the Canadians, and the lawyers mounted a vigorous counterattack. In addition to disputing the "facts" of his record and of the Lafayette bar murders as laid out by the prosecution, the defense had to rehabilitate Carter from character attacks. Carter included a letter from the former New Jersey governor William T. Cahill, a Republican, who commended him for helping to bring about a "peaceful settlement" to the Thanksgiving prison riot at Rahway in 1971. Included in the reply brief were previously written comments about Carter's prison record from federal district judges Clarkson Fisher and Dickinson Debevoise. Both men had praised his record when they ruled in his favor over his illegal transfer to the Vroom Readjustment Unit. Carter's brief even included a comment from Frank X. Graves, Paterson's law-and-order mayor, who had contributed to the pressure-cooker environment surrounding the murders. Graves had left office in 1966, but by 1985 he was once again mayor of Paterson as well as a New Jersey state senator. The day Sarokin released Carter, Graves was quoted in a newspaper, saying of him: "I don't consider him any threat. He came out once before [in 1976] and he lived in peace in the community."

On January 17, 1986, a three-member panel of the Third Circuit Court released its decision, summarizing the prosecutors' argument in this fashion: "Documents submitted in support of the State's application are intended to show that Carter is a dangerous sociopath and a human 'time bomb.'"

Ticking or otherwise, the court ruled unanimously against the prosecution. The Third Circuit could only order Carter's reincarceration or a psychiatric exam if it had reason to believe that Carter would not appear in subsequent court proceedings. The state, the court said, "concedes Carter is not concerned with flight."

In other words, prosecutors believed that Carter would commit dreadful violence, but at least he'd show up in court to defend himself.

Carter had won another round in federal court, but the assault on his name reminded him of the danger he was in nevertheless. How much provocation would the police need to throw him back in jail on a trumped-up charge? The decision was made: Carter and the Canadians would go underground — but in high style. They sublet an apartment in the swank Delmonico building, above Regine's disco, on Park Avenue and Fifty-ninth Street in Manhattan. The owners of the building were technically not allowed to sublet, but everyone did, the doorman being rewarded handsomely for turning a blind eye.

The apartment had only four rooms, including a tiny four-by-four-foot kitchen with an eighteen-inch-long counter. But the monthly rent, according to Carter, was a staggering $8,000, more than twice the rent for the commune's mansion in Toronto. Living at the Delmonico, surrounded by elegant sidewalk awnings and double-parked limousines, served a purpose. With one black man living with a white woman and several white men, they believed they needed the accouterments of wealth to inoculate them from harassment.

The apartment was conveniently located between Beldock's Midtown office and Leon Friedman's place on the Upper East Side, and it was only two blocks from Central Park. One day Carter and Terry Swinton were walking through the park and came across a groundhog whom park vendors called Fifth Avenue Phil or Broadway Ed. Swinton, who had diabetes, carried chocolate to treat any episodes of low blood sugar, and Carter borrowed a piece and offered it to the groundhog. To the surprise of onlookers, the animal took the chocolate right out of his hand. Carter began feeding Phil — or Ed — on a regular basis, petting him and chatting with children, assuring them that the critter meant no harm. Parents sometimes took pictures of their children, the groundhog, and the strange black man whose name no one knew.

During this period, Carter did not contact his two children, his mother, his siblings, or his former wife, who still lived in their Paterson home, an oil painting of Rubin on the wall. His family had always stood by him and defended him, but his feelings of shame and mortification caused him to break away from them. Prison had estranged him physically and emotionally. Now the conviction had been overturned, but the wounds were too deep to repair. He had only seen his son, Raheem, now nine, twice in the boy's life. He had not seen his daughter, Theodora, in nine years. Carter could reach out to a groundhog, but he could not reconnect with his own children. Lisa and the Canadians had brought him out of his shell, but he would retain a wall of detachment from outsiders. In freedom as in prison, seclusion provided sanctuary.

Freedom did allow Carter to reconnect with one of his passions — horses. He had begun riding as a child, and he admired mares that were ornery but in full stride blended power, speed, and grace. When he was arrested, he owned such a mare, named Bitch, who was so surly that only Rubin could ride her. After he went to prison, she was abandoned and eventually put to sleep. Now free, Carter was eager to get back on a horse. One Sunday he and Swinton drove out to the stables at Van Cortlandt Park in the Bronx, where there were hundreds of acres of trails.

"We'd like to rent some animals with a little spirit in them," Carter told a heavyset woman who ran the stables.

"Hey, Joe!" she yelled. "We've got some John Waynes here. Get Mighty Mite and Apples."

Mighty Mite was a balky, dirt-encrusted quarterhorse who badly jounced Carter along the trails. Afterward, Carter brushed down the animal and walked him in the park, but the horse didn't eat grass. Carter ripped out a few blades and tried to feed the animal by hand. Several days later he returned and asked for Mighty Mite. After another rough ride he groomed the animal's reddish coat, combed out its neglected mane and tail, and tried to feed him, but now he brought sugar cubes. In time, Carter learned that Mighty Mite had been abused by his previous owners and that his penchant for hurling riders scared off most customers. The stable had considered destroying him. Carter continued to comb the horse, revealing a beautiful flaxen mane and golden tail; he smoothed out Mighty Mite's trot and trained him to obey commands and make jumps. The rides were exhilarating; moreover, he now felt responsible for the horse.

"It would be wrong for us to introduce a horse to kindness and sweetness and just leave it there," he told Lisa. "Once you do that, you're obligated."

She agreed. The Canadians bought Mighty Mite and Apples, the spotted appaloosa, for $1,200 apiece. The horses were rechristened with Native American names, Indians occupying a special place in the Canadians' pantheon of victims. Mighty Mite became Red Cloud, after the brave Sioux warrior (or Rubin), while Apples became Lakota, which means "the people" (or perhaps, in this context, the Canadians). For many years Carter meticulously cared for Red Cloud, seeing himself in a horse apparently headed for the glue factory but rescued by strangers.

In July, Bob Dylan came to New York for a concert at Madison Square Garden, and Carter and several of the Canadians went to hear him. While Dylan had avoided Carter's efforts to reach him after the second trial, Carter held no grudges. He knew that Dylan, more than anyone else, had made his case a national and international cause, and he wanted to thank him.

By now Dylan had had his own taste of courtroom battles related to Carter's case. In "Hurricane," Patricia Graham Valentine enters the barroom, cries out, calls the cops, and — after the suspects are identified by witnesses as "middleweights" — nods her head. Valentine was displeased by her role, so she sued Dylan, alleging that by nodding her head, Dylan implied that Valentine acquiesced in the lie of the other witnesses. A federal judge in the Southern District of Florida ruled against Valentine. So did the U.S. Court of Appeals for the Eleventh Circuit, noting that Valentine's "interpretation [of the song] does not construe the words as the common mind would understand them but is tortured and extreme." Carter, who believed that "tortured and extreme" summarized the case against him, had his own theory about Valentine's suit. He believed that the Passaic County authorities had put her up to it as retribution against Dylan. Dylan escaped any damage from the suit, but he had a new appreciation for Carter's endless legal woes.

During the concert, Dylan dedicated a song to Carter, and afterward

Carter went to his dressing room. Standing unnoticed in the doorway, he watched the singer sip Jack Daniel's and hold court for a group of admirers. Dylan suddenly turned, looked up, and met Carter's eyes. His enthusiasts in the room followed him, and Carter felt as if all the respect that had been flowing to Dylan had been redirected toward him. The two men embraced. Dylan asked Carter if he wanted to join him on his current tour, but Carter explained that he was still fighting the prosecutors, still defending himself on appeals. After about a half hour, Dylan asked him to stop by his hotel room the next day. He had something to show Rubin.

Dylan was staying in a plush hotel suite overlooking Central Park. When Carter arrived, he pulled out two pairs of boxing gloves that Carter had given him. Dylan wanted to shadowbox, so they put the gloves on and bobbed and weaved like two kids on a playground. When Carter unleashed a left-right combination, Dylan let out a scream — then realized the gloves never touched him. Both men laughed and touched gloves. "You're safe with me, brother," Carter told him.

After the prosecutors lost their bid to send Carter back to prison, they turned their attention to their principal appeal of Sarokin's decision. However, owing to a rather embarrassing oversight, they could no longer pursue Carter's co-defendant, John Artis. Sarokin had issued writs of habeas corpus for both Carter and Artis, who was under parole supervision. But in filing a notice of appeal to the Third Circuit, the prosecutors wrote only Carter's name on the notice. The result: even if the Third Circuit overturned Sarokin's decision, the ruling would apply only to Carter. The prosecutors' lapse was a fitting conclusion to Artis's involvement with the Lafayette bar murders. Rubin Carter was always the man the authorities wanted. Even those who believed he was guilty could not easily explain Artis's role. Why would a nineteen-year-old kid, with no police record and sterling character references, walk into a bar one night, shoot two men, then train his pistol on a middle-age waitress and pump four bullets into her midsection at point-blank range? No explanation, save the discredited racial revenge theory, was given to explain Artis's sudden descent into madness. Nevertheless, he spent fifteen years in confinement. He could have copped a plea and fingered Carter for the murders. He would have then been freed and hailed as a hero in some quarters for ensuring that Carter would be locked up for the rest of his life. But Artis refused, saying he would not falsely accuse any man to save his own hide. Instead, he survived as the forgotten man — forgotten by the public, by the media, and ultimately even by the prosecutors.

In late January 1986, Carter learned that Marmo's proposed appendix to his Third Circuit appeal included material that was "outside the record"; that is, information that had not been presented to Sarokin, which violated rules of federal procedure. Carter vehemently protested to his lawyers, demanding that a motion be filed to strike the offending submission. Initially, Friedman resisted Carter. He explained that given the expected size of the appendix, at least twenty thousand pages, the information Marmo wanted to include would not hurt them. Marmo, for example, wanted to add Carter's boxing record (to refute Sarokin's erroneous claim that his career was "peaking" when he was arrested), and he wanted to include an outline of the script for *The Lafayette Bar Massacre* (allegedly to show that Bello recanted his first testimony for commercial purposes). He also wanted to submit a picture of Carter's actual car to the Third Circuit, even though it had not been submitted to Sarokin.

Carter had bent the rules of federal procedure himself in the appendix he filed with Sarokin. He included the photographs of the Dodge Polara and Dodge Monaco, even though those pictures had never been submitted to a state court. The pictures showed that Valentine's taillight description did not match the Polara's. Carter literally sneaked the photographs into the appendix — Friedman would have objected had he known — but he rationalized that they truthfully showed the discrepancies between the two cars. The prosecutors, probably caught unaware, never objected.

Now Friedman argued with Carter, insisting that the few new documents in the prosecutors' appendix had nothing to do with the two matters on which Sarokin had overturned the conviction. Friedman also understood that his profession involved a continuous series of compromises: you give a little on one issue today, and opposing counsel will give a little on another tomorrow.

"This is petty stuff," Friedman told Carter. "If we try to keep this material out, the court might think we have something to hide."

"I don't care," Carter said. "If they're going to make us play by the rules, we're going to make them play by the rules."

Friedman realized that this was the difference between being a lawyer and being a boxer. Boxers don't compromise. They go for the knockout. Friedman filed a "notice of motion" to strike new material from the appendix.

The Third Circuit agreed, ordering in late March of 1986 that the appendix not include material that had not been before the district court. But by now the materials included in the appendices had been assembled, reproduced to form seven sets, collated, and bound into 89 volumes per set, amounting to 623 volumes. They were boxed and delivered by station wagon to the federal courthouse in Philadelphia. A local newspaper, presumably alerted by Marmo's office, sent a photographer to cover the grand event. It published a picture of men using dollies to cart away the towering boxes, as if an overwhelming paper trail — 140,000 pages! — was proof of overwhelming guilt.

But the 623 volumes violated the court order. As the prosecutor later said in court filings, he believed any disagreement over nonrecord items could "probably be rectified" with Carter. After all, Carter only disputed eighteen documents in an appendix of 20,000 pages. What's eighteen documents among old friends? If Carter refused to permit the improper material, then Marmo's office would have to retrieve all 140,000 pages, withdraw the nonrecord material, rebind the 623 volumes, and ship them back to Philadelphia — at the expense of Passaic County's taxpayers.

After two decades of being on the defensive in court, Carter finally had the upper hand. His nemesis was in a vise, and he was going to squeeze. "The idea," said a defense lawyer, Ed Graves, "was to wear them out and crush them to the earth."

The Third Circuit sent the matter back to Sarokin for him to determine what was or wasn't in the record. Just as Carter spent years going up and down the state ladder on appeals and hearings, constantly finding himself before a trial judge who had already ruled against him, now Marmo was in a similar position at the federal level. Sarokin, holding hearings in July and August, requested that opposing counsel sit down and determine for themselves the straightforward question of what was in the record. But the hostility on both sides was too great for any kind of agreement. It fell to Sarokin to make the decision — and he ruled against Marmo, finding that the state included fourteen items in its appeal papers that were not of record. The judge was particularly irked at Marmo's contention that he did not submit the entire record to Sarokin on the habeas petition because the state did not anticipate an unfavorable ruling. That position, Sarokin said, was "ludicrous."

It was increasingly clear that the prosecutors were adrift in the less familiar waters of federal court. In September they filed a motion with the Third Circuit to "supplement the record" of the appendix. That motion was denied, forcing them finally to retrieve their inadmissible documents. Then, in October, prosecutors filed a 191-page brief. The page limit was 50, and the clerk of court refused to accept it. The prosecutors appealed that decision to a circuit judge, who denied the appeal. *That* decision was appealed to the circuit court panel, which likewise denied it. In a last-gasp and highly unusual effort, prosecutors then appealed a procedural matter to the court en banc, meaning all nine judges. That appeal, in January 1987, was also denied.

Marmo's attitude toward Carter explained this mad but useless flurry of maneuvers. Carter "is a dangerous and violent assassin," Marmo told the *Chicago Tribune* in a story on February 8, 1987. "He always has been and always will be." The import was clear: murder was his crime, but barbarism is his *nature*. Of Sarokin, Marmo said: "Here comes one judge who says a lot of sensational things to get attention, who makes numerous errors and misstatements about the case and turns the case upside down. We cannot let it stand." The article also noted Marmo's singular fixation with the case. According to some, the article said, Marmo "is so obsessed with the case that he pursues it almost alone without the support of his office."

In their own way, the Canadians were as obsessed as Marmo. By the summer of 1986, Gus Sinclair was called down from Toronto to provide additional manpower. In the minds of Carter and the Canadians, they were engaged in the legal equivalent of guerrilla warfare, fighting a reckless and relentless enemy that needed to be confronted at every turn. That meant researching, writing, and delivering numerous briefs and motions in response to maneuvers by the prosecutors. Carter's lawyers continued to handle the legal issues, but they were happy to cede the grunt work to Carter and his friends, who kept digging for further evidence of Carter's innocence. At one point, Sinclair enlarged a map of downtown Paterson and brought together copies of all the police reports from the night of the murders. Using different color markers, he traced the movements of each police car on duty that night. He went over the reports again and identified where individual officers claimed to be at specific times. Multicolored lines careened around the city amid the fateful landmarks — the Nite Spot, St. Joseph's Hospital, police headquarters. By the end of the exercise, the Canadians concluded that the original police documents could not support the story that was later told to convict Carter. The map, of course, was not admissible on appeal — only material in the record could be submitted — but in theory Carter could use the map if the state tried him a third time. Every scrap of evidence that proved his innocence, regardless of its provenance or reliability, was to be harvested and preserved.

By October of '86, Carter and the Canadians wanted to be closer to their horses and craved more breathing room for themselves. So they moved forty-four miles north to Mount Kisco, although they told people they lived in the tonier town of Bedford. (Mount Kisco had seceded from Bedford in 1978.) This was horse country, where clock towers were wound by hand each week, shiny Bentleys slowly cruised along dirt roads, and waist-high stone walls circled eighteenth-century homes. For $3,000 a month, the group rented a quaint three-story home with a curving driveway, a crooked fence post, a ramshackle red barn, and a small pasture. They remodeled the barn for Red Cloud and Lakota, spruced up the house with plants and paintings, started a vegetable garden, and settled into their secluded world.

Anonymity remained a priority — with good reason. Carter had told the courts that he was living with a cousin, Harriet, in South Jersey, and that mail should be sent to him there. That summer Harriet called Rubin to report that several white men had showed up at her house. They claimed to be friends of Rubin's and asked to see him. When Harriet, suspicious, asked to see identification, the men acknowledged that they were investigators from the Passaic County Prosecutor's Office. They asked Harriet if Rubin lived there, and she confirmed that he did. When they returned several days later, they questioned an old man concerning Carter's whereabouts, and they followed, stopped, and questioned Harriet's fifteen-year-old son. What the investigators didn't appreciate was that they were in Carter country — an enclave where his grandfather once farmed and where dozens of Carters now lived. The investigators were repeatedly told that Rubin was indeed in their midst. When one investigator asked a woman if she was aware that

Carter was a triple murderer, she firmly reminded him that he had been cleared of that crime.

Even in Mount Kisco, Carter and the Canadians were not taking any chances. At the time, Carter had no checking account, driver's license, or credit card. But he was mingling with neighbors and supervising stable men, and he needed a name. Hurricane Carter was too recognizable, so finding a pseudonym — one that did not evoke locker rooms and boxing rings but a name with class and distinction — became a house project.

Rubin "Hurricane" Carter, ferocious boxer, insolent prisoner, and alleged assassin, was ultimately dubbed Robin Wellington.

He gradually became another cog in the communal wheel. He awoke between five and six in the morning and headed for the barn, where he fed and groomed the horses and raked out their stalls. He cut the grass, repaired the fence, and was generally responsible for outdoor maintenance. The slower pace of Mount Kisco, combined with the commune's easy camaraderie, suited him. Swinton tended the garden. Sinclair cooked the meals. Lisa read and watched television. Chaiton read the astrology charts and worked on the computer, often on Carter's case. Meals, always simply prepared, were an important part of the day. A typical dinner consisted of meatloaf or roast chicken, mashed potatoes, and homemade bread. Homemade was always important. Even the cat food was prepared at home (cheap liver with rice and vegetables). The group ate off their laps in the TV room, watching the news or a movie and talking about the day's events.

The relaxing atmosphere made the house an ideal spot for Carter's cousin, Ed, when he fell ill. Now in his fifties, he had been diagnosed with pancreatic cancer. Rubin invited him to stay with them for a few weeks, hoping he could repay his cousin's years of support with the fresh air of the countryside. His body frail but his spirit strong, Ed told stories about Adam Clayton Powell and Martin Luther King, Jr., and his wife and his children and his harrowing experiences on the front lines of the civil rights movement. The Canadians cooked him egg sandwiches and comforted him, and Rubin and Ed commiserated with each other over the years they had lost because of Rubin's imprisonment. One night, toward the end of his stay, Ed rocked in his chair and considered the peculiar group around him. "I've been here with white folks and with black folks, and I haven't heard a word of racism," he said. "I just feel like I've come up here and found a little piece of heaven." At the end of Ed Carter's stay, Rubin took him to Memorial Sloan-Kettering Cancer Center in Manhattan to see a specialist who was running an experimental program for terminally ill patients. But it was too late, and Ed died a couple of weeks later.

Meanwhile, Rubin and Lisa continued their uneasy dance. They still had long conversations and took walks together, but Carter recognized that the unique dynamic they had while he was behind bars — a blend of mutual belligerence, succor, and love — could not be easily replicated outside. Lisa's temper had served a purpose for Carter while he was incarcerated. It forced him to confront his past mistakes — his womanizing, his drinking, his penchant for fighting — and facilitated his own search for meaning in his life. Her outbursts had jolted him out of complacency. But now her ridicule was not redeemed by a higher purpose, it was simply petty. One morning Carter was about to leave the house with Sinclair for a day of riding; Red Cloud and Lakota were already saddled and waiting. As Carter reached the door, Lisa stopped him.

"Where are you going? Riding again? Jesus, you never think of me, do you?" Lisa, who had a bad back and couldn't ride, accused Carter of selfishness.

Carter knew that if he had a falling out with the empress, he could lose the support of the entire empire. He still needed the Canadians to help him in his legal battles. He also had no money and no place to go. So he went to the barn, unsaddled Red Cloud, and returned to the house, where he plunked himself in front of the television for the rest of the day, simmering in silence.

More serious problems had developed between Lesra Martin and the Canadians. Lesra was now a student at the University of Toronto, majoring in anthropology. He still lived with the commune but was spending less time at home. Over the years, the group had lavished gifts and clothing on him, tutored him, given him proper medical care, and ensured his successful escape from Brooklyn. He had grown from a scrawny, illiterate fifteen-year-old street kid to a physically fit, well-spoken young man. Living with the Canadians, however, was never easy. He and Lisa's son, Marty, were friendly rivals for the attention of Lisa. He faced the same restrictions, no matter how nonsensical, that everyone faced in the commune. Pizza, for whatever reason, was discouraged, so he, Marty, and their friend Sean Cunningham would sneak out of the house to get a few slices.

Lesra continued to look at Carter as a father figure, and the quest to free him gave Lesra and his guardians a common agenda. But Lesra was now a twenty-two-year-old college student, and he needed his independence. While Rubin, Lisa, and the others were living in Manhattan, they got word from Toronto that Lesra was spending less time at home and, when he was home, he was unpleasant and aloof. The break finally came when Lesra became involved with a woman at school. Serious dating outside the commune was not allowed, and Lesra was still partnered with Paulene, who had joined the commune because of him. According to Carter, Paulene called Lisa in Manhattan. Lisa told her to put Lesra on the phone and told him to pack his bags and leave. Several months later, Lesra called the house in Mount Kisco. He spoke to Sinclair for a while and then talked to Carter. "Lez, my brother! Talk to me!" Rubin boomed. There was a long silence. Lesra expressed remorse for his departure, but Carter could do nothing for him. He ended the conversation by telling Lesra to call him anytime he felt like talking. It was, however, several years before they reconnected.

On January 20, 1987, the prosecutors finally filed an appeal that complied with the rules of federal procedure and was accepted by the Third Circuit Court. In his opening, Marmo complained bitterly that the court had refused his noncompliant briefs, and those briefs would have shown that Sarokin's ruling presented "slanted and distorted views . . . Because of the exceptional circumstances of this case (twenty-year, eventful history, two lengthy trials, approximately twenty thousand pages of appendix, etc.) we cannot make this same case in a brief of fifty pages." To rehabilitate their case, to try to convince the three-judge panel that Carter was the murderer, Marmo reintroduced the trial cast of George Lois, Selwyn Raab, Harold Levinson, Fred Hogan, literary agents, publishing executives, and celebrities; he mentioned fundraising concerts for Carter at Madison Square Garden and the Astrodome, and he declaimed: "The strength and majesty of our judicial system is founded on the exposition of the truth through a process of submission of evidence and argument to a body of neutral citizens and not through a process of imagery conjured by Madison Avenue public relations and the collection of uninformed celebrities."

But Marmo was like a general fighting his last battle. The "Madison Avenue hucksters" — or, as Burrell Ives Humphreys called them in his summation, "perverters of justice" — may have resonated with the jurors in Passaic County but not with the Third Circuit Court of Appeals. Its responsibility was to evaluate Sarokin's decision to throw out the convictions on the *Brady* violation and on the appeal to racial prejudice.

If Marmo had been angry at Carter's previous tactics, the defendant's next trick infuriated him further.

Carter felt he needed more than fifty pages for his reply brief in order to refute point by point Marmo's assertions that the evidence pointed to his guilt *and* to prove that the prosecutors had violated his constitutional rights. While the rules limited the size of the brief, there were no limitations on the size of the type. So instead of using their lawyers' printer, Gus Sinclair found a small family print shop in Port Chester, New York, that used a thinner font, which shoehorned more letters on each line and more lines on each page. Carter also packed the brief with footnotes, printed in a smaller point size, thus squeezing in even more detail. Carter also used boldface type for the first time as well.

The same division of labor continued — the Canadians and Carter wrote the facts, the lawyers wrote the law — and the two sides continued to clash over the tone of the brief. In an early draft, a sentence in the Preliminary Statement referred to the prosecutors as "strident." Beldock objected that it was too, well, strident. It was certainly not standard usage for a legal brief. Lisa, however, was adamant that "strident" stay. So was Carter, who believed this was not a standard case and therefore deserved nonstandard language. Standard language had kept him in prison for nineteen years. "Strident" survived.

The Third Circuit brief — slim letters, long footnotes, brazen boldface — was bound in the mandatory red cover and dubbed the Red Zinger.

Marmo filed a reply to Carter's brief. In the Introduction, he wrote: "It should be noted that the brief which [Carter] had a year to prepare would, according to our calculations, amount to a hundred pages if it were typed employing the format, margins and size of type utilized in the brief of the [prosecutors]." Marmo had been outfoxed, and he knew it.

On August 21, 1987, the Third Circuit affirmed Sarokin's ruling in a unanimous 3–0 decision. Written by Judge Ruggero Aldisert, the opinion concluded that the prosecutors had indeed withheld critical evidence in failing to disclose the true results of Bello's polygraph, violating Carter's due process rights to a fair trial. The court, however, did not dissect the entire case, as Sarokin had, and apparently saw little reason to delve too deeply into the much-disputed twenty thousand pages of appendix. Instead, the court concluded that Bello, as the state's only eyewitness identifying the defendants at the scene of the crime, was obviously crucial to the state's case. The opinion quoted the New Jersey Supreme Court's dissent in '82, noting that if the defendants had known the true state of affairs, they could have argued persuasively "that Bello was in all respects a complete, unvarnished liar, utterly incapable of speaking the truth."

This decision was a major victory not only for Carter but also for Sarokin. Carter's adversaries would not be able to attribute the overturned convictions to a bleeding-heart liberal outlier, and Sarokin himself felt enormous relief that his legal reasoning had been supported. The prosecutors, of course, had lost another round in federal court, and by now their blatantly dishonest handling of Bello could not have been more thoroughly dissected. Since the polygraph fact-finding hearing in 1981, seven out of eleven reviewing judges at the state and federal level had concluded that the prosecutors withheld evidence, committed a *Brady* violation, and deprived Carter of a fair trial. For all the hard legal work by the Canadians and Carter, it was Myron Beldock who deserved the victory toast, for it was he who, after the trial, playing a hunch, called the polygraph examiner in Chicago and discovered that the defense had been misled by the prosecutors. This was a winning issue, Beldock had reasoned, *if the justice system works.* Ultimately, it did.

What was absent from the Third Circuit's opinion was also noteworthy. There was no ruling or even discussion of the racial revenge motive, even though Chief Judge John Gibbons asked Marmo about the motive during oral arguments. The court ruled that its *Brady* decision made it unnecessary for it to also rule on the racial revenge violation. Similarly, the dissenting judges in the state supreme court decision had been silent on the racial revenge question. The message: judges who could avoid the subject of race — but still rule in favor of Carter — did just that.

Carter did not learn about the court opinion from his lawyers. Rather, in the weeks leading up to the decision, the commune repeatedly called the court clerk to find out when the opinion would be released. When the date was announced, Swinton and Chaiton drove to Philadelphia to pick it up. While the outcome was a huge win, Carter and the Canadians didn't throw a party or celebrate in any traditional way. For one thing, they had few if any friends outside the group, besides the lawyers. Moreover, parties drew attention. They were déclassé and boisterous and showy, and merely suggesting one would have been in poor taste. As Carter recalled, "Our celebration would be someone saying, 'Let's go out to lunch,' or, 'Let's go out for coffee.' So we'd all get ready to go out, then get in two cars and go to a café somewhere. It was a quieter, gentler celebration, but far more intense."

Marmo continued his push through the courts. In November he filed a Petition for Certiorari, to have the appeal heard before the U.S. Supreme Court. The high court only accepts appeals that it believes involve important constitutional questions. According to Friedman, Marmo's petition cited seven or eight habeas corpus cases that the Supreme Court had ruled on in recent years and argued that Carter's case would represent another important component in this evolving area of the law. Friedman, however, stood that argument on its head, arguing that the Supreme Court in fact had ruled on about a dozen habeas cases in recent years and that Carter's case would be redundant. The brief, bound in an orange cover, was designated the Orange Squasher. Carter spent another Christmas with his fate still uncertain. Then, on January 11, 1988, the Supreme Court declined to hear the prosecution's appeal. There were no more appeals. Sarokin's decision would stand. "We whupped their constitutional asses," Carter said, "all the way to the Supreme Court."

The final victory was still not at hand. Carter and his lawyers were confident that Passaic County prosecutors would not retry him. How could they? In the years since the murders, their case had been shredded. Bello, at the '81 hearing, testified that he had no memory of what happened on the night of the crime. Sarokin had taken the racial revenge motive off the table. DeSimone was dead. The Caruso file gave the defense ammunition to undermine Patricia Graham Valentine's car testimony. The murder weapons had never been found. There were no eyewitnesses placing Carter and Artis at the scene of the crime.

Nonetheless, a battle raged inside the prosecutor's office over whether to try Carter and Artis a third time. By now John Goceljak was acting Passaic County prosecutor, and he sought out Donald Belsole, director of the division of criminal justice for the state Attorney General's Office, which had supervisory control over the county prosecutor's offices. Goceljak himself was on the fence about bringing Carter back to court, but he explained to Belsole that different factions in his office were fighting over the issue. He asked Belsole for advice, and Belsole understood that Goceljak would follow his recommendation.

The case fascinated Belsole. He had been a habitué of Greenwich Village in the sixties and a Bob Dylan devotee who initially learned about the case through "Hurricane." Belsole could still recite the lyrics by heart. He knew that Sarokin's opinion had soiled many reputations in the Passaic office and that the faction who wanted a retrial, which he assumed was led by Marmo, did not want to see Carter walk away in triumph.

But during this period Belsole met with Beldock and Friedman, who asked that Carter not be retried. According to Friedman, Belsole said that the prosecutors believed Carter was going to sue the state for civil damages, so if they had to go back to court, they may as well retry the case. Beldock and Friedman knew that Carter had no interest in filing a civil action. To do so, he would have to present himself as a victim, claiming injury from his imprisonment. To plead for compensation would give the State of New Jersey the opportunity to deny him something he wanted, and Carter would not put himself in that position. Furthermore, he never wanted to walk inside a New Jersey courtroom again.

As a result, Beldock and Friedman struck a compromise with Belsole. According to Friedman, Belsole said: "Do I have your word as lawyers that you are not planning to bring a civil rights action for damages against anyone in New Jersey associated with this case?"

"On our word as gentlemen and lawyers," Friedman said, "you have our representation that we're not going to sue."

Belsole categorically denies that any such deal was made. But he did recommend to Goceljak that Passaic County not take Carter back to court. His recommendation, he said, reflected what he thought was in the best interests of Paterson, the practical problems in retrying the case after so many years, the negative publicity that it would engender, and the fact that Carter and Artis had already spent, collectively, thirty-four years in prison. Justice, he decided, was best served by moving on.

On February 19, 1988, Goceljak filed a four-page application in the Passaic County Court in Paterson to dismiss all charges against Rubin Carter and John Artis. The application noted that the case had "received the attention of more courts and proceedings than probably any case in the history of this state and possibly any other state."

Eight days later, State Superior Court Judge Ralph Martin had fifty-two indictments to dismiss. The first one was No. 167-66, entitled "The State of New Jersey versus Rubin Carter and John Artis, defendants." In a near-empty courtroom, Martin intoned, "Motion by the prosecutor's office to dismiss the indictment is hereby granted. Next case." The final act in a twenty-two-year ordeal took two minutes.

"It's good to finally win one in the Passaic County Court," Lewis Steel told a reporter afterward.

This time Beldock threw a dinner party at his Greenwich Village apartment for everyone associated with the case. Toasts were made by several lawyers, by Sinclair, and finally by Carter, who stood up and quietly thanked everyone. He also acknowledged Lisa. When he finished, he sat down, leaned over, and touched her hand.

Beldock, in an interview years later, said that despite the insuperable odds and countless setbacks, they won through the sacrifices of so many and the teamwork of all involved. "The real story," he said in barely a whisper, "is the fact that good triumphs over evil, and how hard it is to get there." Tears began to well in his eyes, and for a moment he couldn't speak. "I'm also a sentimentalist," he said, almost in disgust. "Now you know that about me."

While the criminal justice system eventually corrected itself, Carter's case was a reminder of how costly such battles are. Beldock's firm alone put in more than an estimated eleven thousand hours of work and incurred $100,000 in expenses. The fees for all of Carter's lawyers would have totaled between $4 million and $5 million. The lawyers' pro bono contributions were immense, but as Beldock liked to say, "Money is not the only currency." The commune also racked up huge expenses, including their pricey sojourns in Manhattan and Mount Kisco. Lisa would tell Carter, "It took us more than a million dollars to get you out of prison." The commune's accountant, Michael Murnaghan, said it was more like $400,000. Regardless, Carter was lucky to have wealthy lawyers and supporters who could underwrite his fight for freedom; few prisoners have that luxury. But it was Carter's own belief in his cause, his refusal to surrender, and his personal charisma that motivated so many to give so much.

His ultimate legal triumph, however, was tempered by the personal price he paid. He lost nineteen years of his life to prison and almost three more years of unimpeded freedom. He lost an eye. He lost his boxing career, and he lost the prime earning years of his life. He lost his marriage, and he lost time with his children, family, and friends. But neither the State of New Jersey nor Passaic County offered any compensation or apology. Belsole, of the state Attorney General's Office, believed that amends or apologies would have mocked the criminal justice system. Carter's case — the convictions and their aftermath — was the result of an adversarial process. Everyone was doing his job, according to Belsole. The prosecutors believed Carter was guilty, and they did everything they could to convict him. Carter and his lawyers did everything they could to exonerate him. The battle continued for more than two decades. That is how the system works, and no one, particularly on the state level, owed Carter anything.

If anything, hostile feelings for Carter simply intensified with his vindication. When the charges were dropped, Adele, the daughter of the victim Fred Nauyoks, said: "It's just unbelievable. [Carter] is just a bad person. I just hope he doesn't hurt somebody else. It just seems that our courts and judges help the people who do the things, and the victims get the short end of the stick."

Law enforcement officials in Paterson have also not changed their views. Edwin Englehardt was the police commissioner when the murders occurred and was at the scene of the crime. Thirty-two years later, Englehardt, now the Passaic County sheriff, was asked by a reporter if Carter was owed an apology. "Apology for what?" Englehardt said. "He should have apologized to the State of New Jersey for all the free room and board he got [in prison]. I would have liked to have pulled the [execution] switch on him myself." The sheriff helpfully indicated that Carter's room and board came out to $77 a day. Carter, understandably, does not feel safe in Passaic County.

Englehardt also repeated a claim often heard among Carter's enemies: he was set free because of a "technicality." As Leon Friedman likes to respond: "It was a technicality — it's called the U.S. Constitution."

Over the years, various jurors from both trials have been interviewed, and none has ever publicly expressed doubt about Carter's guilt. Carl Matonak, a juror at the first trial, told a reporter thirty-one years later that he had not changed his mind. "In my opinion, this guy's lucky to be around, breathing air," he said. "Based upon everything that I know, this guy is guilty."

Carter's years of isolation had frozen his image in time. For many, he will always be seen as a brew of turbulent forces that stalked across TV screens in the early sixties, when Friday night fights were grand theater and Carter a mesmerizing villain. At the time, Carter's defiant words, hard face, and grim persona conjured up dark fears in white America. Carter burnished this militant image with angry prison interviews, shrill speeches, and *The Sixteenth Round*, which glorified bloody combat and dripped rage like sweat from a towel.

Carter had traveled from imprisonment to freedom, but few knew about his other journey. He had disappeared inside a medieval prison, had turned his cell into "an unnatural laboratory of the human spirit," and was shown the light of civilization by the "inner circle of humanity." As Carter said, "When you can't look out, you look in" — and he looked within himself for many years. Fighting for his innocence was easy. Fighting for his dignity against the strictures of prison was more difficult. But fighting for his heart's ease, for peace of mind, for some meaning to his life — that fight had been the hardest yet. He was forced to go the distance, and doing so brought him both victory and redemption.

After more than two years of seclusion and eleven years since he had held a press conference, Carter was prepared to face the public again. On a pleasant, sunny day — a rare February 29 — he held a midday press conference at the Plaza Hotel in Manhattan. It was his coming-out party, and it was held in inimitable style. His lawyers rented the pink Baroque Room, lit by crystal chandeliers, overlooking Central Park. Waiters dressed in formal attire served croissants, danish, coffee, and tea. At a small table by the door, several of the Canadians checked in reporters and handed out information about the case. Selwyn Raab of the *New York Times* tried to interview one of the Canadians, who declined to give his name, identifying himself only as a businessman. He told Raab that he and his "wife" and other Canadian friends became intrigued with Carter's plight, had sent him delicacies like chateaubriand in prison, and helped him financially. At the elevated front table sat a carefully selected white-and-black mix of Carter's lawyers and supporters. Dylan's "Hurricane" wafted through the room as about eighty people, half of them journalists, took their seats. Most of the reporters represented publications from New York and New Jersey; several TV cameras were also set up. Even Lisa, who typically shunned public events, attended. Carter rose from the front table to cheers from his supporters. As always, he had a great sense of theatrics, but this time he also had a surprise.

At the age of fifty, he looked remarkably fit. His well-groomed Afro and mustache had not a speck of gray. His face was smooth and seemingly without a mark, a boxing scar over his right eye blending indistinguishably into his ebony skin. He lacked the bulky musculature of his prizefighting days, but he also did not have an ounce of fat. He was dressed in a tan suede jacket, white shirt, dark tie, and navy trousers. For reporters who had not seen him since the seventies, it was as if Carter had been given a makeover ten years earlier, then preserved in formaldehyde. Carter remembered his press conference after his release from prison in 1976, when he claimed he had been "raped of his freedom for nine and a half years." He assumed that the reporters, particularly those from New Jersey, expected to hear the same denunciations today.

"Ladies and gentlemen of the press," he began in a carefully scripted and memorized speech.

"On June 16, 1966, twenty-two years ago, I left my home in Paterson, New Jersey, for a meeting with my business manager to discuss an upcoming prizefight. But little did I know that the events of that evening would sound the bell ending my career as a professional boxer and mark the beginning of quite a different kind of fight, a fight in which the prize was life itself — and freedom. Well, we have just won that fight. The sixteenth round is finally over. It is over! Yes!

"The State of New Jersey has just now seen fit to dismiss the charges and the indictment — the same indictment that they used twenty-two years ago to try to take my life by seeking the death penalty. But they failed to get the death penalty, I am delighted to report. Instead, they sentenced me to a life of living death — and there is no other way to describe the nature of prison. Prison destroys everything that is valuable in a human being. It destroys families — it destroyed mine. It destroys one's dignity and self-respect in too many ways to even mention here. It got to me, and I knew I was innocent. It gets to everybody.

"I have seen people die in prison — needlessly — from the lack of medical attention and sheer neglect. And in that regard, I have always considered myself as being lucky because all I suffered was the loss of one eye, while John Artis, a mere teenager I barely knew in 1966, and who would not have gone to prison had he not asked for a ride home that night, was not so fortunate. He contracted, in prison, an incurable circulatory disease. To date, he's had several fingers and toes amputated, and he can only expect more of the same in the future. Now, that's horrible. I mean, for what? For simply asking for a ride home? It's incredible.

"But you know I think what struck me most about being released from prison was that for twenty years, I was considered a danger to society. I was locked away in an iron cage for not one but three of my lifetimes. I was a prisoner, a number, a thing to be guarded with a maximum of security and a minimum of compassion. Not a person. Not a human being. But a body to be counted fifteen or twenty times a day. Even when I was brought to the federal district court to be released — and I think many of you were there to witness this — you saw me chained, you saw me shackled, and you saw me handcuffed. I had to be escorted by three carloads of heavily armed guards. Man! I frightened myself, I appeared to be so dangerous. But the very next moment, with the stroke of a judge's pen, I'm free. Completely and utterly free, with all of the rights and protections that everyone here takes for granted. Suddenly, I can walk out of the door — as if the last twenty years had never happened. As if society was telling me, 'Never mind.' One moment I'm a championship prizefighter. The next moment — and for twenty years thereafter — I'm reviled as a triple murderer. Then the next moment, I'm an innocent man who's been wrongfully imprisoned. Now, you try to make sense out of that, because I'll be damned if I can. It is just too much!"

Carter continued, at times evoking the ministerial cadences once used by his father in church. He inveighed against the death penalty, noting that he was not the first and would not be the last innocent person whom the state would try to execute. He reiterated the horrors of prison and disabused reporters of the illusion that convicts are coddled. "Where is the proof of this?" he asked. "Just go sixty miles south of here to a place called Trenton, New Jersey, and you will find a unit there called the Vroom Readjustment Unit, and I challenge any reporter to go into that building, to see the devastation, come back and report that to the people, and I guarantee you that the building will be torn down brick by brick before the sun goes down that day." Carter also complained about the "unchecked and unbalanced" power of the prosecutors and emphasized the importance of federal review of state court criminal proceedings. He then issued a proper thank you.

"The most powerful enemy of justice is inertia, maintaining the status quo, or, let's not ruffle any feathers. And that's why I want to acknowledge here today, and sing the praises of, Federal Court District Judge H. Lee Sarokin. His clarity, his wisdom, and depth of understanding [are] incomparable. For he alone had the courage to face squarely the issue that the state courts for nineteen years had sidestepped, and that is that the poison of racism had permeated the state's entire case. To not throw out these convictions, so wrote Judge Sarokin, would be to commit a crime as heinous as those for which we were unjustly convicted. Now, ain't that saying a mouthful?"

Carter geared up for his dramatic conclusion.

"The question invariably arises, it has before and it will again: 'Rubin, are you bitter?'

"After all that's been said and done — the fact that the most productive years of my life, between the ages of twenty-nine and fifty, have been stolen; the fact that I was deprived of seeing my children grow up — wouldn't you think I have the right to be bitter? Wouldn't anyone under those circumstances have a right to be bitter? In fact, it would be easy to be bitter. But it has never been my nature, or my lot, to do things the easy way. If I have learned nothing else in life, I've learned that bitterness only consumes the vessel that contains it. And for me to permit bitterness to control or infect my life in any way whatsoever, would be to allow those who imprisoned me to take even more than the twenty-two years they've already taken. Now, that would make me an accomplice to their crime — and if anyone believes that I'm going to fall for that . . . then they are green enough to stick in the ground and grow!

"Thank you."

Applause rang out for this eloquent, magnanimous, and indeed surprising speech. When all was quiet Carter said, "I'll be happy to answer your questions." But there was silence, as if reporters were shocked by what they had seen and heard. Finally Carter said, "No questions? Great." He took a step away from the microphone, feigning a quick exit. He chuckled. Then reporters laughed. A subtle prank from the Hurricane had loosened them up. About twenty minutes of questions followed.

"What are you going to do now?" one reporter asked.

"I'm going to cultivate my garden," he said.

"Are you ever going back to Paterson?"

Another easy question. "No," Carter said. "I will never step foot back in Paterson for any reason, at any time, forever."

The next day Carter, Terry Swinton, and Sam Chaiton piled into their old blue Mercedes and headed toward Canada. When they reached the border in Buffalo, they paid the toll and crossed the bridge but were approached by an official from Canadian Customs. Fearing that the authorities would stop him, Carter had dressed like a dapper college professor in a tweed sport coat with suede elbow patches and a matching wool turtleneck sweater. It was a cold evening, and snow dusted the ground. The customs official asked for Carter's residence and citizenship. Carter said he lived in New Jersey and was an American, explaining, hesitantly, that he was going on vacation.

The customs officer, suspicious, handed him a piece of yellow paper and directed him to the Manpower and Immigration office across the parking lot. Chaiton was nervous as they drove up to the building and stepped inside. In a quiet, fluorescent-lit room, Carter handed the piece of paper to a ruddy-faced official with gray hair.

"Why were you sent over here?" he asked.

"I don't know," Carter said.

"What's the purpose of your visit?"

"Visiting friends," Carter said. "And traveling."

Carter shifted his weight. He feared the next question.

"Have you ever been convicted of a crime?"

Carter hesitated. He didn't know how he could possibly explain the past twenty-two years to a Canadian bureaucrat.

"Yes," Carter said.

"You know, then, that you're not eligible to enter Canada."

"B-b-b-but . . ." Carter's stuttering suddenly reappeared with the fears that he would be turned back.

The officer, not missing a beat, continued his questioning: "How long were you in jail?"

"Twenty years," Carter said.

"What were you in for?"

"Triple homicide."

"So you did your time, you're out on parole, and barring any unforeseen circumstances, you're free?"

"No."

"Then how did you get free?"

"My conviction was overturned."

"Where?"

"I was exonerated by the federal district court in New Jersey, I was exonerated by the Third Circuit Court of Appeals in Pennsylvania, and I was exonerated by the U.S. Supreme Court."

The official looked at him for a long moment, then raised his eyebrows. "Hey, Joe!" he yelled across the room. "This is the guy I was telling you about, the guy on TV who spent twenty years in prison for something he didn't do." He reached across the desk and extended his hand. "Welcome to Canada, Mr. Carter."

16

TEARS OF RENEWAL

FOR NINETEEN YEARS, Rubin Carter fought prison's web of controls and regulations and resisted its communal dehumanization. His total opposition to the prison was a matter of principle — as an innocent man, he would not be treated as a convict — but his lonely rebellion also echoed his conduct as a free man. He never followed the crowd and he never joined groups. As a boy, he walked a different route to school from that of his brothers and sisters. As a boxer, he did the opposite of what his trainer told him. As a prisoner, he defied the administration at every turn.

And as a free man, he could no more live in a commune than an eagle could live in a birdcage.

By the time Carter gave his dramatic speech at the Plaza Hotel, he had lived with the Canadians for almost two and a half years. They had rescued him from the States, and he was grateful. But the attributes that made the Canadians perfect allies for the imprisoned Carter — their circle-the-wagons paranoia and lockstep lifestyle — made them insufferable for the liberated Carter. Within the commune, individual identities were suppressed. The Canadians lived together, traveled together, worked together, and bedded together — although their libidos, at this point, were languid. "It was the most sexless house I've ever been in," Carter later said.

The Canadians rejected the label of "commune," which they thought to be a sixties fad. They felt themselves to be sui generis. They could do anything — from importing batiks from Malaysia to freeing a convicted triple murderer from New Jersey — as long as they did it together.

Once in Canada, Carter and company retained their life of sub rosa splendor. They leased a nineteenth-century country home in the suburb of Woodbridge, about a thirty-minute drive northwest of Toronto. The house, set back from a graceful road that wended through thickly branched trees and velvet lawns, had previously been a home for unwed pregnant women. As the Canadians did with all their living quarters, they renovated or redecorated, making it uniquely their own. In this case, they adorned the house with Aubusson rugs, original lithographs, and prints of Old Masters. They also had a swimming pool with deck chairs and, in the driveway, the blue Mercedes and a Jeep Cherokee, the latter purchased specifically for Rubin.

It was evident to outsiders that Carter, a celebrity who enjoyed the limelight, was ill suited for this furtive, inscrutable clan. When a *Toronto Star* reporter, Susan Kastner, visited Carter in the summer of 1989, she was allowed to speak with only one person besides Rubin. The spokesman identified himself as "T," which was one more letter than the *New York Times* had been given the previous year. Kastner was told that seven people lived in the house, but there were no other signs of life besides Carter and T. The grounds were eerie, bereft.

Sitting by the pool, Carter wore a beautifully cut dove-gray linen shirt, his speech as fluid as a mountain stream. He smiled proudly, showing off his C$16,000 worth of dental work to repair his eroded enamel and a severe underbite, which had developed in prison. ("The only dental care they had in prison," Carter later said, "is, 'Yank it out!'")

Earlier that day, Carter's face had gone rigid at the sight of a front-page photograph in the *Toronto Star*. A convicted rapist who had escaped custody had been apprehended by police, and the black-and-white picture showed the rapist on the street surrounded by cops, his wrists handcuffed behind his back, his head snapped back, howling like a wolf. Mad Dog was his nickname, and Carter felt a pain deep inside. "Everybody assumes he's an animal who needs to be penned up," he told Kastner. "But he could have been just like me."

It was a jarring moment for the reporter, who realized how the serene setting belied Carter's years of trauma. At the same time, T (Terry Swinton) seemed to take undue pride in Carter. Kastner wrote that Swinton "shoots Carter a warm, proprietary glance. 'Doesn't he look great now, though? Young, healthy?'" To Kastner, the whole situation

— this black survivor of New Jersey's prisons turned fashion plate sitting with the mysterious T at a vacant country estate — was bizarre. She didn't say so in her column, but she sensed that nothing quite fit.

Indeed, Carter's life in Canada, from the outset, was anything but serene. The relationship between Lisa and Rubin never blossomed, and tensions between the two surfaced immediately. Lisa hassled Carter over what time he awoke (he was always a late sleeper) and whether he was sufficiently committed to the house. Carter bristled at being told what to do and where to go. When a visitor knocked, everyone in the house would hide and Swinton would answer the door. Carter refused to hide. He also complained to Lisa about her disparagement of former commune members, people of other nationalities and religions, and outsiders in general.

Nonetheless, Carter initially had good reasons for staying with the group. He had no money, no way of making a living, and no place to settle down. He wanted to live in Canada — he thought Canadians were more tolerant than Americans — but it would take time for him to qualify for landed immigrant status and for health and insurance benefits.

He also wanted to repay his debt to the Canadians. They had spent at least $400,000 on his freedom, and they had been supporting him in grand style since his release from prison. He was determined to leave the commune no worse off financially than when it met him. He could earn money by lecturing and by selling his story through a book, movie, or both. Paying off the debt would take years, but he would not be satisfied until he did.

Lisa also hoped that Carter's story would generate income for the house, but their deteriorating relationship soon overwhelmed all other concerns. His reluctance to conform continued to anger her. According to Gus Sinclair, one day Lisa propped a leg against a wall and held up her arms as if to protect herself from a falling pile of bricks. "That bastard is as tough as they come," she said, "and I feel like I have to stand like this to keep him from overwhelming me."

Less than five months after Carter had been in Canada, Lisa decided he had to leave. She threw his suitcases and his clothes in the hall, told him to get out, then retreated into her own bedroom until he was gone. Sinclair made reservations for Carter to fly to Philadelphia, gave him C$500, and helped him pack. Carter asked for several small favors.

Most important, he wanted what had been prepared so far of a screenplay of his life, written by Chaiton, Swinton, and Carter. Sinclair asked Chaiton for a copy, but he was told it was not Carter's for the taking.

"I'm sorry," Sinclair told Carter.

Carter was more relieved than angry. The house was claustrophobic. He didn't know what he would do, but maybe it was best for him to move on. "Let's get going," he said. He got into a car with Eitel Renbaum and headed for the airport.

The commune's autocratic environment took its toll on other members. Sean Cunningham, Marty's friend, slept at the commune four or five nights a week for seven years to escape difficulties in his own home. Like the others, he found a self-contained world that seemed to protect him from outside forces, but he severed ties with the house when he realized how damaging the experience was. The members of the group "had a twisted and infantile way of wanting to belong," he said. "The house took away our inner voice, our spirit. It took years to recuperate from that."

A month after Carter was shown the door, Gus Sinclair left, disillusioned by the experimental living arrangement he had helped create eighteen years earlier. What began with so much idealism and positive energy, he felt, had long ago devolved into a "quasi-tyranny" with petty infighting among members. The crusade to free Carter was the group's last great accomplishment, but now all he saw were crass efforts to cash in on the achievement through book and movie deals. The commune, according to Sinclair, had C$100,000 in the bank at the time, but he was given only C$1,500 as his parting share. He was dropped off at the local YMCA — but was told the YMCA had not had rooms for more than twenty-five years. Sinclair realized how long he had been isolated.

Rubin Carter, however, would not be gone long. He knocked around the United States, staying with friends and relatives in New Jersey, New York, and Virginia, borrowing money and trying to sell his own book or movie deal. He had working titles — *No Holds Barred and No Bars to Hold* and *The Hole in the Wall* – and several chapters written, but he found no buyers. While traveling between the two countries, he contracted tuberculosis, a disease that he picked up in prison but that did not manifest itself until now. Hospitalized in Canada, he called

Lisa, who invited him back to convalesce. The pair reconciled, and their relationship entered a new phase, becoming a partnership grounded in mutual self-interest.

In 1989 Rubin and Lisa were married, and she took his last name. The marriage, Carter said, did not reflect an amorous breakthrough between them. In fact, the longer he stayed in the commune, the less emotional intimacy existed between them, a development that Carter said satisfied both parties. The marriage addressed the practical considerations of Carter's gaining landed immigrant status, for the Canadian government was more likely to grant it to the spouse of a citizen. Carter felt his union with Lisa solidified his position in his adopted country. Whatever his motives, the marriage confirmed to outsiders that he had indeed found a home.

Lisa had a clear incentive to keep Rubin with the group. He was their product — or, as Carter described it, "a trophy horse to fill the coffers." Swinton and Chaiton were writing their own book about the Canadians' involvement with Carter, and it would look odd if the hero of the story were estranged from his saviors.

Carter and the Canadians presented a unified front for many years. They appeared together before journalists, at public ceremonies and conferences, and for publicity events surrounding the book eventually finished by Swinton and Chaiton, *Lazarus and the Hurricane.* Published in Canada in 1991, it described how a group of do-good but unidentified Canadians (their last names are never given) saved a grateful Lesra Martin and Rubin Carter from their respective plights of poverty and imprisonment. The movie rights were purchased, and proceeds from the book and film went to the house. Slowly, Carter was paying back his debt.

The commune's obsession with privacy meant that Carter still effectively lived underground. From Woodbridge, the group moved again to a six-bedroom, half-timbered house in King City, about twenty miles north of Toronto. They converted the structure into a European hunting lodge and built a two-stall barn for their horses. Carter had few contacts outside the house. External friendships were still forbidden, but one outsider managed to break through. Perry Catena was a financial planner in Toronto whose stout, muscular build evoked the stature of a middleweight. He heard Carter on the radio and was captivated by his story and his voice. He then read *The Sixteenth Round* and, spellbound, drove up to King City to find him. Catena knew there weren't many black men in the small town, so someone had to know his whereabouts. Catena went everywhere in King City — the bakery, grocery store, church, doughnut shop, fire hall, drugstore, real estate office, hockey arena, several restaurants, and an art museum. He even went door-to-door in residential neighborhoods. With the exception of a drugstore owner who had sold Carter cigarettes, *no one had ever seen the man.* Yes, Carter was free, but he was tucked so far away that he was virtually invisible.

A year later, Catena learned that his stealth hero had surfaced to give a speech at a Toronto high school. Through the school, Catena left a message with "Rubin's people." Three weeks later Terry Swinton called and, in an initial screening, spoke with Catena for an hour. Three months later he called again and arranged for Catena to visit Carter. Eventually Catena spent the day at the elusive King City house and was invited back, later becoming one of Carter's few good friends. Other admirers who lacked Catena's persistence never got close.

In the early nineties, Carter began to break out of his seclusion and become politically active, focusing on an issue close to his heart — wrongly convicted prisoners and Death Row inmates. Before his own arrest in 1966, Carter had never been political. He was rarely motivated by any cause beyond his own success. At the time, he also recognized that blacks were under siege, physically and legally, so he became outspoken in advocating that blacks use whatever means necessary to defend themselves, particularly against the police. His caustic remarks embellished his militant reputation; in prison, in the years leading up to his second conviction, his message had evolved into a racial indictment of the criminal justice system. Now in his fifties, Carter had lost none of his indignation over injustice, but he was no longer the firebrand. He was now willing to channel his passions through more constructive protest. His own experiences had taught him that the best way — indeed, the only way — to beat the system is to work within the system. Verbal grenades may get the headlines, but they don't overturn wrongful convictions or stop state-sponsored executions.

A Canadian carpenter named Guy Paul Morin drew Carter into his role as spokesman for the wrongly convicted. Morin had been charged with the 1984 rape and murder of a nine-year-old girl. Acquitted at his first trial, Morin was tried a second time in 1992 and convicted. The linchpin to his conviction was an alleged "jailhouse confession," in which two inmates testified that Morin had confessed to the crime when they were in jail together. The inmates had also made deals with prosecutors for leniency in their own cases. Carter knew about such deals. A defense committee was formed for Morin, and Carter was among those who spoke on his behalf. Eighteen months after Morin's second trial, his conviction was overturned thanks to new DNA evidence that exonerated him of the crime.

The defense committee formed on Morin's behalf decided to stay in business. It changed its name to the Association in Defence of the Wrongly Convicted (AIDWYC), and Rubin Carter was named its executive director. Carter gave the association an attractive, high-profile leader who was proof that unjust convictions do occur. The association, in turn, gave Carter a platform from which he could speak out on the criminal justice system, and it gave him a life outside the commune.

Carter's living arrangements, however, continued to concern his friends. They noticed that when he traveled by himself, the first thing he did when he got off the plane was call home. Then he would call again as soon as he reached the hotel and again when he reached his room. A dependence on the prison had been replaced by a dependence on the commune. Fred Hogan, the public investigator in New Jersey who was Carter's first ally to research the murders, noticed that when he talked to Carter on the phone, one or two of the Canadians were always on the other line. "Instead of hanging up, they would stay on the fucking phone," Hogan later complained. "It was a control thing."

Michael Blowen, a reporter for the *Boston Globe,* interviewed Carter in King City and remained friends with him. During his visit, Carter was wearing sunglasses to shield a troubled eye. When Blowen asked a question, Carter looked out of the side of his sunglasses at Chaiton or Swinton to make sure neither of them was going to answer. Later, when Carter gave a speech at Harvard University, Rubin, Lisa, Chaiton, and Swinton visited Blowen at his home. Any time a question was directed toward Carter, Lisa answered for him. Blowen also realized that the Canadians forbade anyone in their group to drink alcohol. "The drink of choice was basically tea, and when you went wild, you maybe had a cup of coffee," Blowen said. When he met Carter once at Boston's Logan International Airport — without the Canadians — Carter drank whiskey, laughed, and was more relaxed than Blowen had ever seen him.

But Carter's drinking was also a serious matter. His alcoholism had effectively been dormant for twenty years. In prison, he stopped consuming the "hooch," or wine, concocted by the inmates after the Rahway prison riot in 1971, when a massive drunk was considered the cause of the uprising. While Carter could not drink in front of the Canadians, he binged when he was beyond their view. On one occasion the commune's accountant, Michael Murnaghan, invited Carter on a fishing trip to Alaska. Over the objections of his housemates, Carter accepted. Murnaghan never saw Carter take a sip, but after several days he found an empty crock of vodka that Carter had consumed.

In 1992 Carter again complained to Lisa about his lack of freedom — every time he left the house, someone escorted him — and once again he was told to leave. This time Carter left in his own Jeep, crossed the U.S. border, and headed for New York City. But an eye problem again brought his travels to a halt. This time, a burning sensation in his long-gone right eye created the worst pain he had ever felt. He couldn't drive, so he called the commune and asked for help. Chaiton flew to a small town in upstate New York, found Carter in his Jeep on the side of the road, and drove him back to Toronto. Once in the hospital, Carter learned that his tuberculosis from several years before had reappeared in a different form. Apparently a TB "germ" had attached itself to the stitches that prison doctors had left inside the right eye. The vessels in the eye were so fine that antibiotics could not purge the "germ." Doctors told Carter that he would have to have the infected eye removed and replaced with a glass eye. The procedure relieved the pain but left Carter with another reminder of the long reach of prison. "I have two eyes," he said. "One sees out, the other sees in."

To see his own entrapment clearly, Carter needed the help of a former foe.

Wilbert "Skeeter" McClure, an Olympic gold medal champion in 1960, had two prizefights against Carter in 1966. A fluke event before their first match in Chicago cemented McClure's respect for his opponent. McClure weighed in at 160 pounds — a half pound more than middleweights were allowed. He had to lose it by the opening bell or forfeit the match. McClure went to the locker room to relieve himself. As he stood at the urinal, Carter strolled in and told him that he didn't care about that half pound and that he wouldn't want to win by forfeit anyway. McClure lost the weight; he also lost the bout in ten brutal rounds. He left the arena believing that he had been beaten by a relentless puncher and a class act. Their rematch two months later — the penultimate bout of Carter's career — ended in a draw.

McClure's path crossed Carter's again in 1993, at the thirtieth anniversary dinner of the World Boxing Council. The WBC wanted to honor Carter in some way and, initially, proposed giving Carter a plaque. No thanks, Carter said. He had enough plaques. He wanted something else. Denied the opportunity to fight again for the championship, he wanted an honorary championship belt. The WBC had never awarded one before but decided this was the time to break precedent.

On December 16, 1993, at the Sahara Hotel in Las Vegas, Carter received a green and gold honorary belt inscribed with the signatures of each member of the WBC. He invited several of his old boxing opponents as his guests, including Skeeter McClure. Carter was accompanied by Lisa, Swinton, and Chaiton. In Carter's moment of triumph, McClure noticed that something about his friend wasn't right. For several days, every time McClure saw Carter — in the hotel lobby, in a coffee shop, on the street — he was surrounded by these enigmatic Canadians. They always had smiles on their faces, but the smiles seemed contrived. His observations were grounded in years of professional training, for he was a psychotherapist in Boston and had studied group behavior. Dr. McClure had also noticed Lisa's control over Carter and the entire group, and he didn't like it.

The last straw was the night of the black-tie awards ceremony. Carter sat next to McClure at a round table, with the Canadians on either side of them. Carter was drinking vodka, but he kept pushing his glass in front of McClure to make it look as though it wasn't his drink. McClure realized what was going on.

"We got to talk," he whispered to Carter. "Alone."

"I don't know if I can get away," Carter said.

"How about up in my room?"

"No, they'll follow us."

"Then let's take a walk outside."

McClure stood up and told the Canadians that they were going for a walk.

"We'll come with you," one of them said.

"No, we're going alone."

"We'll follow along."

McClure, furious, shot them all a savage look and said that he and Rubin were leaving by themselves. They left the ballroom.

"What the shit is this?" McClure said, still fuming. "You traded one damn prison for another."

Carter explained his predicament. He didn't have any money of his own, or credit cards, or his social insurance and health care cards. He also described how much the Canadians had sacrificed on his behalf; they had sold their home to help him. He felt he could not leave until he had paid his debt.

"But when will the debt be paid?" McClure demanded. He said that Carter could move to Boston and stay at his apartment and use his car. But he needed to set a date, a reasonable date, when he would leave the commune. "Then you can be psychologically and emotionally free."

By the time Carter returned to Toronto, another restriction had been imposed in the house. Lisa had quit smoking and had made everyone else in the commune quit as well. Carter had smoked, with only a few breaks, since his first imprisonment. Plowing through two packs a day, he had no intention of quitting now. The commune's ban on alcohol had already denied him one of his other pleasures. Under this new edict, Carter had to sneak outside and light up behind the barn. He felt as if he were a child hiding from his mother and father.

The child finally lashed back. Carter went to Chicago in February 1994 to give a speech at a law conference. Chaiton accompanied him. The conference organizers invited them to dinner; toward the end, Carter excused himself to go to the bathroom. There, he had a quick smoke, then headed back out. When he opened the door, Chaiton was waiting for him.

"Were you smoking?" he demanded.

Carter glared. Chaiton then stepped close and began frisking him for a cigarette pack.

"Get your motherfucking hands off of me!" Carter yelled, swatting Chaiton away. "You never put your hands on me!"

Chaiton had violated the very rule that he knew all too well, the rule that Carter would have killed any prison guard over: no one touches him *in anger*. Chaiton had put himself squarely in the camp of Carter's former jailers or any other enemy. Carter returned to his hotel room without saying anything else. On their flight back to Toronto, they sat in different rows. When Chaiton tried to change seats with the passenger next to Carter, Rubin told the passenger not to move. At the airport, they were picked up by Kathy Swinton and Paulene McLean, and Chaiton described Carter's presentation on the way home. Carter said nothing. At the house, he went straight to his room and began packing his bags. Terry Swinton and Chaiton pleaded with him to stay. It was cold and snowy, and night was about to fall; but Carter finished his packing and headed for the front door.

"I love you," he said, "but I can't stay here anymore."

This time he was leaving on his own. He had less than C$100 in his pocket, but by now he had his own bank account and a credit card. He got into his red and black Jeep, pulled out of the King City driveway, and headed for Toronto. He never looked back. And he never gave up his cigarettes.

Since that day, Carter has never denigrated the Canadians. They may have been his new jailers, but he will always be grateful for their help, their charity. In prison he had no reason to begrudge their paternalism and their smugness. They brought him hope and love at a time when virtually everyone else had abandoned him. In the courtroom, they brought energy and savvy against implacable foes. Carter might have won his freedom without them, but his lawyers, already outgunned and exhausted, would have had to work that much harder to succeed. In Lisa, Carter met his equal — in his words: "tough on the outside, beautiful on the inside, and totally fearless." She did what the New Jersey prison system could not do: she broke him down and forced him to confront himself. Theirs was surely one of the more improbable prison love affairs, but it made Carter a gentler, better person.

To the Canadians, Carter ratified their worldview about corruption and racism in America, about the nobility of blacks, and about their own superiority. They picked up *The Sixteenth Round,* saw an injustice, and decided to fix it. With both Carter and Lesra Martin, they showed that they were uncommonly gifted at saving African Americans in trouble; but then they were incapable of friendship, of meeting these blacks as peers rather than victims. Their strict rules and desire for total control made any healthy relationship impossible. "The only thing that mattered," Carter said, "was to be dependent on that house, to learn to never be separated from the group. It's a process of learned helplessness, but I could not learn to be helpless."

By the time Carter left King City in February 1994, he had lived in Canada for six years, but he barely knew the roads because he rarely drove; Chaiton and Kathy Swinton were the commune's designated drivers. But Carter reached Toronto and managed to find the flat he was looking for. He knocked on the door, and Lesra Martin answered.

Martin had graduated with honors from the University of Toronto, diligently sending Carter his essays and report cards and once consulting him on a questionnaire about racism. Martin then earned a master's degree in anthropology from Dalhousie University in Halifax, Nova Scotia. Halifax had been a terminus on the Underground Railroad during the Civil War and still had a strong black community. Then he enrolled in law school at the University of Halifax but flushed out after one year. By now, both his parents had died. With no place to go, he returned to Toronto in 1993 and moved back into the house in King City.

He was delighted to reunite with Carter, calling him "Pops." When he first met Carter in prison, he was reeling with self-doubt and growing frustrations from trying to read. He thought he was stupid. But Carter had inspired him by example: his limited education did not deter him from speaking eloquently or writing passionately — and he didn't quit. Martin decided that neither would he. Now, back in the commune, they took long walks together, with Carter dispensing advice on everything from schooling to sex. But spending time alone together was difficult under the probing eyes and ears of the Canadians, and Martin had to get on with his life. He moved into a flat in downtown Toronto and returned to the university for doctorate work in sociology. One day when Carter drove into Toronto by himself for a haircut, he called Martin from the barber shop and asked to visit his apartment. He thought that someday he might need Martin's help.

When Carter showed up at his door on that snowy night, Martin, now thirty, was glad to let him in — even if he didn't have the space. The apartment had only one room, one bathroom, and no couch.

Martin slept on a mattress in a loft while Carter slept on the floor. They quickly found a three-story home to rent in a racially mixed neighborhood west of downtown Toronto. Now they would not only be father and son but also roommates and partners. At the time, Carter was leading the defense committee in the Guy Paul Morin case; without the commune's support, the committee agreed to pay Carter for six months or until he could find another source of income.

Carter went to work, writing, lecturing, and traveling — often taking Martin with him. Carter had always been poor with details, so Martin booked their flights, held their tickets, reserved hotel rooms, and drove their rental cars as well as editing and typing Carter's speeches. Carter was a stranger to technology, so Martin used the computer and bought a cell phone, a radio, a stereo, and other gadgets that helped make the house complete. They also double dated, dining out and going to movies and nightclubs.

Their camaraderie, however, belied a certain competitiveness. Martin had a master's degree and was working on his doctorate — he was far too qualified to be a glorified administrative assistant — while Carter's formal education had ended in eighth grade. Carter sensed that Martin did not like being in his shadow. When they quibbled over the wording in Carter's speeches, Martin would glare at his roommate and make it clear that he thought he was better qualified to make the final decision. The rivalry also surfaced in social settings. After Carter asked a woman to dance in a nightclub, Martin would approach the same woman and ask her to dance. "Whatever I was going after," Carter said, "he wanted to show that he could get it first. I would say, 'Why are you always competing with me?'"

The rivalry, however, did not interfere with their work, which ultimately took Carter someplace he thought he'd never return to — Death Row.

Rolando Cruz had been on Death Row at Illinois's Downstate Menard Correctional Center since 1985. A self-described smartass street punk — "I hated the cops and they hated me" — in the ghettos of Aurora, Illinois, Cruz had been convicted of raping and murdering a ten-year-old white girl in preppy Naperville. Like Carter, he always proclaimed his innocence, and, like Carter, his conviction was overturned, leading to a retrial that sent him back to prison. Cruz was also a prison rebel — but he was far more violent than Carter. He once pulled out the sink in his cell and used it as a weapon, he got into some thirty fights with guards over the years, and he spent much of his time in solitary confinement. But his case, enmeshed in state politics, racial tensions, and dubious evidence, was also a lightning rod for criticism and controversy. By the summer of 1994, Cruz's appeal of his second conviction had been before the Illinois Supreme Court for more than a year, and the long wait was tearing away at him. One of his lawyers, Lawrence Marshall, begged Carter and Martin to visit him.

Cruz typically turned away visitors, dismissing their show of empathy as sentimental pretense, and he wasn't particularly interested in meeting Carter. For his part, Carter had never been to a Death Row besides Trenton's, and he wasn't keen on entering any prison. But, convinced that Cruz was innocent, he agreed, and he, Martin, and Marshall visited Cruz in a special room for the institution's most dangerous prisoners. The tiny cell had a solid partition down the middle with a three-by-five-foot rectangle knocked out, iron bars in the open space. Cruz sat in a chair wearing handcuffs and leg shackles. Carter, on the other side of the bars, wore a gray blazer and black trousers.

Cruz knew of Carter's exploits in the boxing ring and in prison, and he wanted to impress him. He bragged about how tough he was on the street and in the pen, how he didn't take lip from anyone, particularly the wimpy-assed guards. Cruz told Carter that he didn't eat prison food or wear prison clothes, that he was a *political* prisoner, that he did not accept his prison number, and that it was not *his* cell but the *state's* cell.

Carter knew the rap. He could have been looking at himself: different shoulder, same chip.

"You can't bring that attitude out of there," Carter said. "You've got dedicated people out here working for you, and we're coming to get you. But you can't leave with that bullshit attitude. You owe it to those people working for you, and you owe it to me." Carter raised his voice. "When you walk out those doors, you have to walk out clean. You cannot walk out with those chains and shackles."

Carter was angry. He stood up and grabbed the steel bars with both hands. "You have got to get these walls out of you!" He began shaking the bars with all his strength. His face sweating, his hands moist, he shook the bars again and bellowed, "You have got to get these walls out of you! Out of you! Out of you!" The steel rods shook and the wood trim around them vibrated and the words echoed in the cement chamber. It was like a flashback to his own years of horror; he saw a shackled image of himself through the bars. Tears of anger and frustration welled in Carter's eye, tears for himself as much as for Cruz. The outburst had everyone else in the cramped room in tears as well. Carter, exhausted, sat down. At the end of the meeting, he and Cruz embraced outside the cell when they said good-bye. A photograph was taken, and Carter gave him his phone number.

"Call me next time you're tempted to beat the shit out of a guard," he said.

Several weeks later, the Illinois Supreme Court overturned Cruz's conviction, and a third trial was ordered.

Carter felt he was making a difference with his work, and he was pleased that Martin was beside him. He rarely saw his own children or, by now, grandchildren, and he had severed all ties with the commune. Lesra was his family, and he envisioned the two expanding their work to include advocacy for education, job training, and other social needs. But on their way home from the airport in Toronto after visiting Cruz, Carter learned that this family too would not stay together.

"Pops, I think I'm going back to law school," Lesra said.

Carter assumed he intended to go to the University of Toronto.

"I'm thinking about going back to Halifax."

"What?"

"I'm going to go back to Halifax."

"When did you decide that?"

"It's always been my dream."

Carter was shocked and felt betrayed. He thought Martin was committed to their work. Now, without any warning, his partner would be leaving in less than a week. Like any father, he thought he deserved more consideration, but Martin had other ideas than to follow in his father's footsteps. Like any son, he wanted to make his own way.

"If that's your dream," Carter said, "then go."

Over the next three years, the two men spoke on the phone cordially but infrequently. Then all ties were bitterly severed in a dispute over money. Some years earlier, Martin had bought the blue Mercedes from a member of the commune, then sold it to Carter. Carter paid the insurance premiums and taxes on the car, but the ownership papers had never been transferred into his name. In 1997 a neighbor of Carter's borrowed the Mercedes and totaled it. An insurance claim was to be sent to the owner of the car — Lesra Martin. Carter called Martin to say he would be receiving a check for $10,000 from the insurer. He could keep $3,000 for himself — Carter knew Martin was strapped for cash — and should send $7,000 to him. When Carter received his check, it was for $3,000. Carter, outraged, had no recourse. When Martin sent him a wedding invitation in 1998, Carter didn't attend.

Carter's involvement with Rolando Cruz did not end when he left the Illinois prison. Several months later Cruz, waiting in the DuPage County Jail for a new trial, was about to tear apart a guard. But, as instructed, he called Carter first.

Carter knew what he was going to say. In talking to Cruz's lawyer, he had learned that Cruz's father had died the previous year. He also learned that a baby Cruz had fathered right before his arrest had been put up for adoption, and that Cruz's mother, sister, and aunt had been hit by a car in Texas and severely injured. Carter used that information to dramatic effect. When he began to speak, Cruz was taken aback by the authority in Carter's voice.

"You know what your problem is," Carter said. "Your father died and you didn't cry. I was the same way. My father died and I didn't cry. You're from the street and you're a bad motherfucker. So was I! But you got to learn how to cry. Your baby was given away and you didn't cry. I lost my babies and I didn't cry! You need to turn on that faucet. Your baby sister almost died and you didn't cry. It's like a fountain. You got to open up the valves every now and again and let the water pour through. Otherwise all the pipes get rusted. You think you're a tough ass, but you've got to learn how to cry. You need to learn how to *live* before you're ready to come home. You're not ready to *live*, you need to learn how to cry. The only way you're going to be ready to *live* is if you let the water *baaare-ly* drip out. Eventually, you'll let the water *flooow* and then you'll be able to live again."

Rolando Cruz did not fight the guard. The following year, on November 3, 1995, he was acquitted in his third trial and freed after ten years of imprisonment. Carter was in the courtroom gallery. In his apartment near Chicago, Cruz keeps the photograph of Rubin and himself embracing in prison. Four years after winning his freedom, he has an unfulfilled dream: he wants to go to his mother's house, take a hot bath, pour a glass a milk, lay down next to her, and cry.

Rubin Carter had learned how to cry, to suffer, and to live again. But he still had one more prison to overcome — alcohol. His years in the commune kept his drinking under control, but once he was on his own, the demons returned, first gradually but then more destructively than ever. He roamed about Toronto at night, visiting four or five liquor stores to spread out his purchases and conceal the extent of his consumption. The clerks would hardly care, but Carter's pride prevented him from allowing anyone, even a sales clerk, to know the scope of his addiction. The alcohol took its toll. He missed business appointments, and his speech was slurred. Sober, Carter had testified persuasively before the U.S. Congress on the importance of habeas corpus and had spoken at Harvard and Yale law schools. When drinking, however, he was just another drunk. No one was calling to hear him speak, certainly no one who would pay. He was no longer receiving a salary from the AIDWYC, which was short on funds itself. He was spending up to C$650 a month on Russian vodka. He was alone, and he was broke. Then — yet again — he went blind.

In the summer of 1997, he began losing vision in his left eye. Carter visited eye specialist after eye specialist, but no one could determine the problem. He was caught in a terrible cycle. The darker his vision became, the more housebound he was. The more housebound he was, the more alcohol he drank. The more alcohol he drank, the darker his vision became. Finally Carter visited a specialist who diagnosed the problem as cataracts. An operation in January 1998 repaired the damage, and during his recuperation he stayed off the bottle. At one point he got the shakes, began hallucinating, and ended up back in the hospital. But he remained sober and thought he had conquered his temptations. Then, passing a liquor store one day, he bought one of those miniature vodka bottles served on an airplane. He couldn't resist, and now the little bottle was just jumping out of his pocket, begging to be drunk. He did just that and was quickly back for more.

Mood swings and lethargy defined Carter's downward spiral. In March he flew to Atlanta to give a speech at Emory University. Stephen Bright, the director of the Southern Center for Human Rights, met Carter at the airport at 11:30 A.M. and saw that he already had bloodshot eyes. At a noon speaking engagement, Carter rambled and made inappropriate remarks. At the end of the speech, Bright grabbed Carter's arm and whisked him away before any questions could be asked. The following night Carter gave another sloppy performance at another event. Bright had seen Carter drink excessively at an event in Washington a few years earlier; now his concern deepened.

Five months later, Bright came to Toronto to receive an award, and Carter sat with Bright's parents. Also at the table was Charles Ogletree, a professor at Harvard Law School and a friend of Carter's. Again, Rubin had too much to drink. Ogletree and Bright pulled Carter over to one side.

"You may not like what we have to say, but we're going to try to save your life," Ogletree told him. "You're letting these demons destroy you."

Carter was in denial. "I'm all right," he said. "Everything's okay, baby. I love you."

But this time Carter's friends would not turn their back. Both Bright and Ogletree knew that Carter was not simply another black man who had been unjustly convicted. His blend of courage and charisma could make him a role model for youngsters and a spokesman for social justice. Vodka was killing a national treasure, they felt, and they were going to do something about it.

The following day, a Sunday, Bright called Carter in the morning and said he wanted to come over to his house at one o'clock. Rubin knew why he was coming. There were few men whom Carter would listen to, but Stephen Bright, whose organization provides assistance to inmates on Death Row, was one of them. As Carter said, "You don't play with Stephen."

The two men sat on a marble bench in Carter's garden. Amid the pansies and petunias and rock paths, Bright got to the point.

"There is something I got to talk to you about."

"I know what it is," Carter said.

"This is a real problem and it's something you've got to deal with. It's apparent to me and it's apparent to a lot of people."

"I'm going to take care of it myself," Carter assured him.

Bright said no, that wasn't good enough. He said the time had come for Carter to check himself into a detox center. "I'm going to take you myself," he said.

"I don't have the time right now," Carter protested — invoking the same line he had often used to reject any suggestion that he participate in prison activities. But now Carter's time was running out, and Bright knew it.

"I'm not leaving here until you come with me," he said. "You can't put this off."

This time Carter assented. He packed his bag, and Bright drove him to the hospital that afternoon, where he stayed for several weeks. Carter hasn't had a drink since. Going cold turkey wasn't easy, but like other challenges in his life, once he marshaled all the force of his will, he succeeded. Nowadays, Carter's lifestyle bears little resemblance to that of yesteryear. When he travels, the former night owl stays out of bars and prefers coffee in his room. At home, he no longer keeps any guns; he thinks they're dangerous. He no longer follows boxing because he believes the sport is barbaric. Gardening is his greatest passion. Carter has sacrificed and suffered to reach this point, but, vindicated of all criminal allegations, liberated from the Canadians, free of booze, he has found his peace.

In prison he found a story in *A New Model of the Universe* that traced his own journey in life, and years later he would recount the story to friends:

The King of Arabistan had heard about the parting of the Red Sea and the miracle of the Exodus. He then learned that Moses himself was camping in his territory. So he summoned his best painter.

"I want you to go to Moses' camp and paint the exact portrait of this man," the king instructed.

The artist followed the instructions, went to Moses' camp, and returned to the king with the portrait. The king then gave the picture to his sage, who was wise in the science of physiognomy, and told him to describe Moses' personality based on the physical traits of his face. The sage did just that.

"King," the sage said on concluding his analysis, "the man in this portrait is a cruel man, he is a conceited man, he is greedy and haughty and filled with a desire for power."

"That can't be," the king said indignantly. "This is Moses, a man of God. Either my painter has made an error in his portrait, or my sage has made an error in his interpretation. Whoever is wrong will have his head lopped off."

So the king went into the territory himself and found Moses. He showed him the portrait. "My artist says he painted your exact portrait, but my sage says you are a cruel man, a conceited man, greedy and haughty and filled with a desire for power. I know that either my artist is wrong or my sage is wrong, and whoever made the mistake will have his head lopped off."

"Do not do that," Moses told the king. "Both men are right. Because in my life I have been all of those things — cruel, conceited, greedy, haughty, and desirous of power. I have been all of those things, and resisting them has been my greatest task in life until now they are my second nature."

The moral of the story was always understood. Rubin Carter was not a killer; but he too was all of those things, and resisting them has been his greatest task in life until now they are his second nature.

In January 1999, Carter gave a fund-raising speech for the Jewish Community Center in Vancouver. A boxing ring had been set up in the middle of a hotel ballroom. An auction raised money, and a fine dinner was served. Then it was Rubin's turn. After a film clip highlighting the intertwining stories of Lesra and Rubin, Carter took the podium. In formal attire, he delivered his motivational stump speech with a few well-timed anecdotes about Sonny Liston and Muhammad Ali and the powerful message of going the distance, never giving up, pursuing your dream. "If I can stand before you tonight," he said, "believe me, miracles can happen." He spoke for forty-five minutes without a hitch and was given a standing ovation.

Everyone thought the evening was over, but then the emcee proclaimed: "I'm pleased to announce that also joining us tonight is Lesra Martin!"

Martin was now a prosecutor in Kamloop, British Columbia, about three hours from Vancouver. He was no longer anyone's little boy. He was stocky, he wore an expensive suit, and he was a *prosecutor.* The audience gave Lesra a hero's welcome as he walked to the podium and embraced an emotional Carter. The two men hugged as the audience, unaware of their sudden and very public reconciliation, continued to cheer. Like a father who lost his wayward son, Rubin could not let go of the man who had now returned to his arms. The Lesra who had hurt him was not the real Lesra, that was simply a . . . *personality.* The youngster who had touched him in New Jersey's Death House had returned. Finally Lesra took the microphone as Rubin dabbed tears that fell from his one eye. Reading from prepared remarks, he directed his words toward Rubin.

"I want to take the opportunity to tell you how truly inspired you make me feel. You know, in your career as a prizefighter you simply refused to be knocked to the ground or knocked to the mat, and today you are still fighting. But today you fight for the liberty and freedoms that many of us have taken for granted. Your energy and your vitality are nothing short of a miracle. I applaud you for your tireless efforts on behalf of all those in our society who are most in need, who are most in danger of being stripped of life, liberty, and dignity. Those, as you know, are the wrongly accused and wrongly convicted . . .

"I will always be in your corner. You are beautiful, Rubin." Lesra looked up. "I can feel your head swelling already. If I don't stop, there won't be enough room for both of us." He paused, then spoke from the heart.

"Rubin, I miss you."

Carter, standing to his side, responded earnestly, "I miss you too."

Martin continued. "As you may have gathered, I don't know much about sports. But I do know about going the distance, and I'd like to say what it means to me . . . In the video you watched, mention was made of the book *Lazarus and the Hurricane*. But it has a passage that has special relevance to me. It refers to a struggle that young Lesra had in learning to read and write, a journey filled with fear, anger, and frustration. But the worst part was a voice in the background that said over and over again that you can't do it. And from time to time I still hear that voice. The difference today is, I am no longer afraid. Have you ever heard such a voice? I can tell you that coming to terms with it, understanding it, that is going the distance . . . We are who we are because of who we were. So I stand here tonight as a voice of all those young Lesras who can't. I stand as an example of what access and opportunity can truly mean.

"Thank you, Rubin, for showing me the way."

Carter swung by the microphone and, above the applause, said, "Those were the kindest words I've ever received from a prosecutor."

The evening was over. Carter and Martin stepped down and stood with their backs against a wall. A small gathering surrounded them.

The well-wishers, forming a semicircle, pushed forward and craned their necks to get a better view. Rubin and his friend were pinned in ... the white strangers kept looking at them ... there was noise and confusion and movement ...

The scene was a faint echo of an infamous scene so many years earlier, when Rubin and another friend were pinned against a wall by a semicircle of white strangers, trying to catch a better look at suspected killers outside the Lafayette bar. But now the white strangers came not for blood but for autographs. They stood close and shook Carter's hand, touched his sleeve, and thanked him for the inspiration of his life.

EPILOGUE

IN THE AFTERMATH of Rubin Carter's long struggle, the players in
the saga have moved on with their lives. So too has Carter, but his
scars appear at unexpected moments. This I learned the first night I
met him.

I initially called Carter in June of 1998. I told him that I didn't believe
the story of his life had been told yet and that I'd like to do it. After
many conversations, he agreed to cooperate. Four months later, we
met in New York and stayed at a hotel in the Gramercy Park area. It
was an old hotel, comfortable if not commodious. Carter's room had
two locks, a standard bolt and a hanging chain. The bolt worked fine,
but the chain was broken. Rubin went to the front desk and asked the
manager to fix it, but it couldn't be done that night. Rubin returned
to his room and bolt-locked the door. He then stacked two heavy
suitcases against it. Then he jammed his desk chair against the doorknob
to immobilize it further. He then opened the armoire so that a wood
panel hung between the door and his bed. If an intruder did break
through the bolt and the suitcases and the chair, he would not be able
to take a clear shot at Carter in bed.

The scars remain. But fortunately for Carter, so does his sense of
humor. As soon as I saw him, he made his feelings clear about his
accommodations, which I had arranged.

"Jim, this hotel is not my style," he said, waving his arm across the
cluttered room. "Look how small this is. My cell was bigger was than
this!"

I had told Rubin that I would only do this book if I could walk through any door in his life and write what I found, good or bad. He consented, and he authorized his family and friends to speak with me. As I interviewed them, I was reminded many times what is often forgotten in cases of unjust convictions: the price of imprisonment is not simply the years taken from the defendant but also the pain endured by those who love him.

In Paterson, I had scheduled an interview with his first wife, Tee. She lived in the same three-story home with white aluminum siding she had lived in with Rubin. When I arrived, only their son, Raheem, was home. Raheem, now twenty-one, let me in the living room, then closed the door behind me and locked it with a chain lock.

Tee never showed up. Instead she sent Theodora, their daughter, now thirty-four. She has children of her own, but Rubin rarely sees them or her. Theodora said she did not resent her father's absence. He had been gone for too many years for it to be any other way. "No matter what he does, I love him," she said. "Sometimes I'd like to be more in contact, but mentally we're together. We have a bond that cannot be broken." She also gave me a handwritten note from Tee. Dated November 8, 1998, it was titled *13 Years of Freedom:*

... Let's go back to the beginning.

My feelings about the whole mass of confusion. The situation didn't seem real. It was like a dream. Yet reality.

One day I was a complete family woman. I had a husband that was successful and a daughter.

Quicker than a blink of your eye my family structure disappeared. My husband was accused of something he could not and would not do.

The charge was Murder!

Not one nor two, but triple.

I cannot fathom anyone in their correct conscientiousness [who] would think My husband Rubin The Hurricane Carter could have committed this crime.

It has been a great ordeal for me and Our children.

Husbandless and fatherless and not understanding any of this.

Of course, we have encountered all types of people. There were some that would embrace and have sympathy.

Then there was some that would mock and ridicule. This is what me and my children had to endure.

Through it all Rubin and myself held it together. We were Unity. With his strength and my support combined. We still had a strong and firm foundation.

The Government tried everything with in their power to break this strong willed man, but could not.

The Government used trick tactics. They subpoena me to testify against "Fred Hogan."

As I sat in the Grand Jury Court Room stunned. I just sat there numb when the police brought my innocent husband out chained and shackled.

Then the prosecution asked me questions I had nothing to do with and had no understanding of.

I thought right then and there. This shit is deep and it's really happening. I also said God please help us . . .

After this intense questioning they did not achieve what their intent was.

I had nothing to say and Rubin did not cooperate with the judicial system.

The Government snatched away the sole means of support for me and the kids.

Once that started to happen We decided it would be best to get a divorce.

The Government finally succeeded in our separation physically, but never mentally.

I still love Rube and I know he still loves me as well.

At times I sit back and invision if this would not have taken place.

We would all be a normal family. A wife with a husband, a daughter, son and grandchildren.

Even though life may not be what you expect, however it is what it is.

Through it all we all still have Unity . . .

Mae T. Carter

A few months later I called Tee, and we have had several nice chats. She has graciously answered my questions and sent me photographs of Rubin and herself. Theodora told me that when Rubin calls, Tee still gets a twinkle in her eye. I mentioned that to Rubin, who slowly shook his head with a half smile, half grimace, on his face. It was a rare moment of Rubin showing pain and regret. "That's my Tee," he said quietly.

In a home several blocks away from Tee's, I interviewed Rubin's mother, Bertha; his four sisters, Lillian, Beverly, Rosalie, and Doris; and his remaining brother, Lloyd Jr. (Jimmy died a number of years ago.) They sat around a large dining room table with Bertha at the head. In her nineties, she looked radiant in a blue dress, her hands demurely folded in front of her. "I loved every one of my children," she said, "and I taught them to be truthful."

When her husband died in 1980, the newspaper ran a story that said the father of Rubin "Hurricane" Carter, a convicted triple murderer, had died. That story, shaming the family, prevented the Carters from properly grieving Lloyd's death, and it still pained Bertha. So too does the very suggestion that Rubin was ever capable of committing the Lafayette bar murders.

"If you told me that Rubin walked into that bar and beat them to death, I'd say, 'He did it,'" one of the sisters said. "But he was never raised to go anywhere to shoot them down like dogs. We were not raised like that."

Rubin's siblings used to visit him in Trenton State Prison until one day he refused to see them anymore. It was too humiliating. There were no photographs of Rubin in the house, where several of them live, and the family rarely sees him. In some ways, he is every bit as detached from his family today. But there is no anger, just relief and resignation.

"He's free, he's alive, and he knows that we're here, that the family loves him," Lillian said. "He just says he can't come down here."

Carter has also lost touch with the commune, which is back in the apparel business. It has a company called Big It Up International — "big it up" being a Jamaican phrase for "respect." It sells track suits, hip-hop bucket hats, knitted V-neck sweaters, and boxers that feature a condom-size pocket in the front. A *Toronto Sun* article about the company included an interview with only one employee — a young Jamaican credited as its founder. He described Big It Up as a "co-operation," not a "corporation."

Carter does keep in contact with H. Lee Sarokin. Each November 7, the anniversary of the decision to overturn the conviction, Carter calls the retired judge at his home in southern California and thanks him. Sarokin's ruling turned out to have repercussions in his own career. In 1994 he was nominated for a seat on the Third Circuit Court of Appeals in Philadelphia. In approval hearings by the U.S. Senate, Republicans assailed him as soft on crime. Even though Sarokin had freed only a few other prisoners besides Carter in his fifteen years on the bench, he was pegged as "Let 'em go, Lee." The Senate approved his nomination, but less than two years later, during the 1996 elections, the presidential candidate Bob Dole and other Republicans bashed Sarokin as an example of a Clinton judicial appointee more sympathetic to criminals than to victims. (Carter's name was apparently never mentioned.) Sarokin resigned in June of '96 to protest these efforts to "Willie Hortonize the federal judiciary."

Sarokin maintains that the Carter decision was one of his most important, given the scale of the injustice. He keeps an audiotape of Carter's Plaza Hotel speech, and when he's glum he listens to it. His spirits rise with Carter's words.

Carter's wrongful convictions did not impede the careers of those who put him in prison. Vincent Hull, the assistant prosecutor during the first trial, was later elevated to a Superior Court judgeship in Passaic County. The trial court judge, Samuel Larner, moved to a higher court, the Appellate Division. Burrell Ives Humphreys, the former civil rights leader who felt personally maligned by Sarokin's decision, was later named Superior Court assignment judge in neighboring Hudson County. Ron Marmo, who told others he considered quitting the law after the final disposition of the Carter case, was made a Superior Court judge in Passaic County. John Goceljak, the veteran prosecutor whose involvement in the case began in 1974, continued to work in the Passaic County Prosecutor's Office until he died in 1999. And Vincent DeSimone was formally promoted to chief of county detectives just days before Carter was sentenced for the second time in January of 1977. He died two years later.

In the meantime, Carter's lawyers soldier on. Lewis Steel and Leon Friedman continue to practice law in New York. So does Myron Beldock, who at seventy hasn't slowed down a bit. Even Raymond Brown, Carter's first lawyer who is now in his eighties, is still defending clients in New Jersey courtrooms.

The legacy of Carter's imprisonment was driven home to me during a conversation in which Rubin described to me what happens to longtime prisoners. He mentioned an inmate named Hooper Head Jones, a large, balding man about six foot two who stood with his knees close together and his legs angled outward. He worked in the prison sports department. "He was in prison when Bruno Hauptmann was there," Rubin said. "Hooper Head Jones's state number was 18998 and mine was 37850" — meaning that 18,851 prisoners had passed through Trenton State between Hooper Head and Rubin.

"Wait a second," I said. "I thought your prison number was 45472."

"That was my number the second time I was in prison. I'm talking about my number the first time I was in prison."

Rubin had just described Hooper Head Jones awkwardly puttering around the athletic field as if it had happened that morning — when it happened *forty years ago*! A good lesson: you can take the man out of the prison, but you can never take the prison out of the man.

While many of Carter's family and friends regret his quasi exile in Canada, he has, in fact, begun to open up and reach out to others. I saw this in my own dealings with him. When I first called him, I was unaware of his drinking. For many months he was often moody or aloof, and in retrospect I sense that this was related to his drinking or the stress of kicking the bottle. But by January an amazing thing happened. Rubin's spirits lifted. He was buoyant, even giddy.

"When people wake up in the morning, it's a miracle — they just don't know it's a miracle," he would tell me.

He was again able to fulfill his speaking engagements and play an active role as executive director for the Association in Defence of the Wrongly Convicted. He led a group of Canadians on a mission to Texas to fight for the release of a Canadian man who was scheduled to be executed. He granted live interviews on network television, and his name appeared on the front page of the *New York Times*. (The mission ultimately failed, however, and the Canadian was executed.) In Vancouver, he appeared on Vicki Gabereau's daytime talk show. Before going on, someone mentioned to Rubin that Gabereau had run for mayor of Toronto in the 1970s. When Rubin sat down across from her, almost before she could ask the first question, he told the host, "I just want you to know on behalf of all Torontonians, I apologize that more of us didn't vote for you for mayor." Gabereau cracked up, and the audience cheered.

Carter fulfilled a promise to his friend Thom Kidrin, now the president of a Boston company that develops Internet software for traditional audio CDs. In prison, Kidrin once showed Rubin photographs he had taken on vacation in Jamaica. Rubin pledged that when he was free, he would go with Kidrin to the beaches of Jamaica. He finally did just that in the early months of 1999, the two men renting a beach house, smoking cigars, and dangling their feet in the ocean that Rubin had once seen only in pictures.

Also in 1999, Rubin publicly thanked John Artis for the first time in a speech at the University of Maryland Law School in Baltimore. John and his wife, Dolly, drove in for the speech from Portsmouth, Virginia, where he counsels troubled youths and gives speeches, particularly to kids, about his own odyssey through the New Jersey criminal justice system. ("I tell them, 'If it can happen to me, it can happen to anybody.'") On this occasion, Rubin praised his co-defendant's courage for never accepting an offer of freedom in exchange for pinning the blame on him.

Rubin, in short, is having fun, and even his most painful experiences can be a source of bemusement. We were talking about his drinking on the phone one day, and I referred to Prosecutor Marmo's insistence that he was a danger to society.

"Marmo got it half right," I told Rubin. "You were a danger, but the only one you ever endangered was yourself."

Howls of laughter poured through the telephone receiver. "You're right!" Rubin yelled. "You're absolutely right!" He had faced down many enemies, from within and without, but having beaten them all, he could have the last laugh.

On another occasion Rubin visited Boston, where I live, and we went to a dinner party. The house was set back from the street, and when we left, we had to walk down a long gravel driveway to reach the main road. It was late at night and the area was poorly lit. Rubin, walking next to me, reached out and grabbed my elbow. We continued walking, and I realized Rubin couldn't see. This seemed so . . . unlikely. Everything about Rubin — his independent personality and strident spirit — seemed to preclude that he would ever reach out for a helping hand. He absorbed blows to his body and psyche that would have felled most men, and maybe he is invincible. But for a few moments he was vulnerable, old. We walked in silence. When we reached the road, he dropped my elbow and proudly strode to our waiting car.

SOURCES

This book is an authorized biography of Rubin "Hurricane" Carter. He cooperated fully with the effort, but the interpretations and conclusions are my own. Over the course of a year, I interviewed Carter for hundreds of hours, either in person or on the phone, and he shared with me his many letters and personal journals from prison. He also encouraged his family, friends, and lawyers to cooperate with my requests for interviews, records, letters, or other helpful material.

I visited the three prisons that incarcerated Carter and further interviewed guards, administrators, and inmates who knew him. I also sought interviews with Carter's adversaries — the trial judges and principal prosecutors, or their representatives, and various investigators. Many of these individuals declined to speak with me, but several did grant me interviews, including John Goceljak, who died in August 1999. In all, I interviewed close to 120 people for this book.

I also read thousands of pages from Carter's voluminous court records, including transcripts from two trials, briefs submitted to federal court, and the reported decisions by the New Jersey Supreme Court and by two federal courts. In addition, I drew on Carter's military, police, and prison records, as well as his FBI records, obtained through the Freedom of Information Act.

In reconstructing scenes for this book, I relied on these records, personal interviews, televison broadcasts of press conferences, interviews, and boxing matches, and newspapers and magazines, including the *Trentonian,* the *Paterson Evening News,* the *Morning Call,* the *Newark Star-Ledger,* the *New York Times,* the *Bergen Record,* the *North Jersey Herald News,* the *Toronto Star, Newsweek,* and *Sports Illustrated.*

Both *The Sixteenth Round,* Carter's autobiography published in 1974, and *Lazarus and the Hurricane,* written in 1991 by members of the Canadian commune, were rich sources of material. I corroborated most of the dialogue that first appeared in both of these books, as I did with quotations or dialogue that appeared in news accounts.

Sean Cunningham, Mary Newberry, and Gus Sinclair, former commune members, as well as Carter himself were interviewed at length about the group. Lisa and her current housemates declined my request for an interview until after the movie about Carter was released, which was long past my deadline. Lesra Martin talked to me about his relationship with Carter but would not discuss his experiences in the commune.

While many books contributed to my research, several volumes deserve special mention. *On Paterson,* by Christopher Norwood, provided a vibrant history of the city and the social pressures affecting Paterson in the 1960s. *The Society of Captives,* by Gresham Sykes, carefully examined the sociology of Trenton State Prison in the late 1950s, and *With Liberty for Some,* by Scott Christianson, placed imprisonment in a broader context spanning five hundred years. Larry Sloman's *On the Road with Bob Dylan* documented the singer's Rolling Thunder Revue and his encounters with Carter. Other helpful books included Joyce Carol Oates's *On Boxing, The Autobiography of Malcolm X,* J. Palmer Murphy's *Paterson and Passaic County,* Joseph Thomas Moore's *Pride Against Prejudice: The Biography of Larry Doby,* David Remnick's *King of the World,* F. Lee Bailey's *The Defense Never Rests,* Taylor Branch's *Parting the Waters* and *Pillar of Fire,* Nelson Mandela's *Long Walk to Freedom,* Robert Shelton's *No Direction Home: The Life and Music of Bob Dylan,* Donald Woods's *Biko,* Hermann Mannheim's *Pioneers in Criminology,* and Hyemeyohsts Storm's *Seven Arrows* (which includes the "Jumping Mouse" fable).

Demographic data about blacks in Paterson in the 1960s were derived from a 1990 article in *The Statistical and Geographical Abstract of the Black Population in the United States,* and information about urban riots in 1967 came from the *Journal of Urban History,* November 1, 1998.

ACKNOWLEDGMENTS

Many people contributed to this book, but I owe special thanks to three individuals.

My agent, Todd Shuster, called me in June of 1998 to tell me that Rubin "Hurricane" Carter might be willing to work with an author on a book about his life. Todd knew of my interests in sports, race, and pop culture and recognized both the dramatic power and historic significance of Carter's life. Todd gave me exceptional guidance on both my proposal and my manuscript, pushed me to find new dimensions to the story, and encouraged my effort throughout.

I have worked with many fine editors in my career, but Eamon Dolan, executive editor at Houghton Mifflin Company, is by far the most gifted. He sharpened the themes of this book, helped me shape the overall narrative, and edited each line with rigor. He demanded excellence on every page, but he wrapped his demands in such gentleness — "more lyrical, please," he wrote in one of my margins — that not meeting them would have been unconscionable. Like Todd, Eamon believed that Carter's story was both a compelling personal tale and a glimpse into American life, and he insisted that this book be worthy of the man.

I also owe a special thanks to Connie Hubbell, radiant proof that loyal employer is not an oxymoron. This book could not have been written without her support.

While Carter's exploits in the boxing ring and courtroom supplied dramatic set pieces, the most important parts of his life occurred in the relative seclusion of prison and in the Canadian commune. Thus, I am grateful to those who helped lift the veil on these two very private worlds. Sam Leslie, a former inmate at Trenton State Prison, shared a trove of Carter's letters with me and provided valuable insights about his relationship with Lisa. Former commune members Gus Sinclair, Mary Newberry, and Sean Cunningham helped me understand the group's history, motivations, and idiosyncrasies; Gus especially shed considerable light on a living arrangement that defied easy explanation.

John Artis, true to form, unselfishly gave me many hours of his time, reconstructing numerous events in this book. John was patient, considerate, and never asked anything in return for his contribution.

Carter's many lawyers — Myron Beldock, Lewis Steel, Leon Friedman, Ed Graves, Raymond Brown, Arnold Stein, Louis Raveson, Jeff Fogel, and Harold Cassidy — all gave me guidance about the case and their client. I owe a special thanks to Myron, who trusted me with his trial transcripts, and Leon, who shared the federal briefs with me and was my most helpful source about the criminal proceedings. Judge H. Lee Sarokin also generously responded to my many questions, and his authorization of his former clerk, Bruce Rosen, to speak with me deepened my understanding of his decision.

Thom Kidrin probably has the keenest insights into Carter, and I'm grateful that he shared them with me. Others who enriched my understanding of Rubin include Dave Anderson, Martin Barnes, Michael Blowen, Stephen Bright, Perry Catena, Rolando Cruz, Tariq Darby, Robert Hatrack, Fred Hogan, Ernest Hutchinson, Susan Kastner, James Lieber, George Lois, Bobby Martin, Skeeter McClure, Michael Murnaghan, Charles Ogletree, Tommy Parks, Selwyn Raab, Steve Slaby, Richard Solomon, and Linda Yablonsky.

Paterson is fortunate to have Vincent Waraske as its city historian. His passion for the city emerged clearly in my many conversations with him, and I don't think I ever asked him a question that he could not answer. Giacomo De Stefano, curator of the Paterson Museum, and E. A. Smyke, Passaic County historian, also shared their news clippings, photographs, and insights with me.

Win Wahrer plays a unique role in Carter's life. She is the executive secretary of the Association in Defence of the Wrongly Convicted in Toronto, but she also takes care of all Carter's scheduling, travel plans, and correspondence. Her kindness and support made my task far more enjoyable.

I owe a special thanks to my friend Robert Kerr. Whenever a legal question arose, I winged him an e-mail, and Robert, an attorney, sent back a detailed response that would make any law professor proud. I am also grateful to my friends Richard Lorant and Hans Chen, who bailed me out whenever my computer misbehaved. My thanks as well to Luise Erdmann, who was a superb manuscript editor for *Hurricane*.

My parents, Ed and Gloria Hirsch, gave me the two things any writer needs — curiosity and indignation — and have always been my biggest fans. So too have my siblings, Irl Hirsch and Lynn Friedman, and their families.

I wrote *Hurricane* from a desk in my bedroom, which I turned into a repository of Rubin Carter court records, news clippings, and memorabilia.

My wife, Sheryl, to whom this book is dedicated, accepted this state of affairs with her usual good humor, grace, and understanding, and she encouraged me through the late nights and long weekends that this book required.

Last, I thank my daughter, Amanda. Born several weeks before I began this project, her sweetness and smiles could melt the heart of the most hardened criminal, jaded judge, or cynical scribe.

INDEX